AFRICAN HARVEST

*The captivating story of Michael Cassidy
and African Enterprise*

Other books by the author

My Rough Diamond
Festo Kivengere
Out of the Black Shadows

Edited

Twelve Modern Disciples
Bittersweet
Faith under Fire

A former Editor of the Church of England Newspaper, and Press Officer to the Diocese of Peterborough, Anne Coomes is author of two notable books on Africa, the biography of Festo Kivengere, and *Out of the Black Shadows*, the story of Stephen Lungu. She is a Reader in the Church of England and Editor of the popular church magazine resource, parishpump.co.uk. She lives in Cheshire, UK, "with her husband David and two rough collies".

AFRICAN HARVEST

The captivating story of
Michael Cassidy
and
African Enterprise

Anne Coomes

MONARCH
BOOKS
Mill Hill, London and Grand Rapids, Michigan

AFRICAN ENTERPRISE

First published in the UK in 2002 by Monarch Books,
Concorde House, Grenville Place, Mill Hill, London NW7 3SA.

Published in conjunction with African Enterprise

Distributed by:
UK: STL, PO Box 300, Kingstown Broadway,
Carlisle, Cumbria CA3 0QS;
USA: Kregel Publications, PO Box 2607,
Grand Rapids, Michigan 49501.

ISBN 1 85424 599 6

British Library Cataloguing Data
A catalogue record for this book is available
from the British Library.

Front cover: (girl) Panos Pictures

Book design and production for the publishers by
Gazelle Creative Productions Ltd,
Concorde House, Grenville Place, Mill Hill, London NW7 3SA.

Dedication

To Jean Wilson

dearly loved, magnificent "Queen Jean" of African Enterprise.

Without your vision, endless patience and sheer gritty determination, this book would never have been written.

"Out of the plains, the jungle and the veld of Africa are being carved... the cities of Africa, which will herald the new age, and decide the destiny of the continent."

John Tooke, Pietermaritzburg, 1977

"When Jesus saw the crowds, he had compassion on them, because they were harassed and helpless, like sheep without a shepherd. Then he said to his disciples, 'The harvest is plentiful but the workers are few. Ask the Lord of the harvest, therefore, to send out workers into his harvest field.'"

Matthew 9:36–38 (NIV)

"This is harvest time in Africa. Our pan-African AE teams must move quickly through the harvest, while it is yet day, and while the reaping opportunities are so gloriously numerous."

Michael Cassidy, Blantyre, 1983

"To evangelise the cities of Africa, through word and deed, in partnership with the church."

African Enterprise's mission statement

Contents

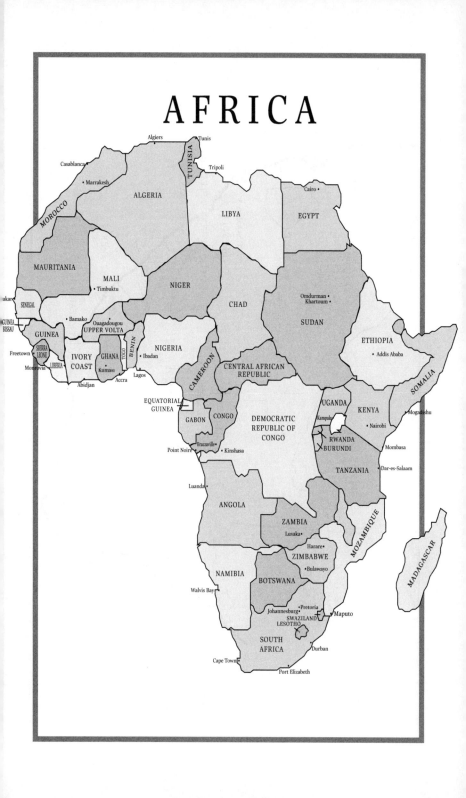

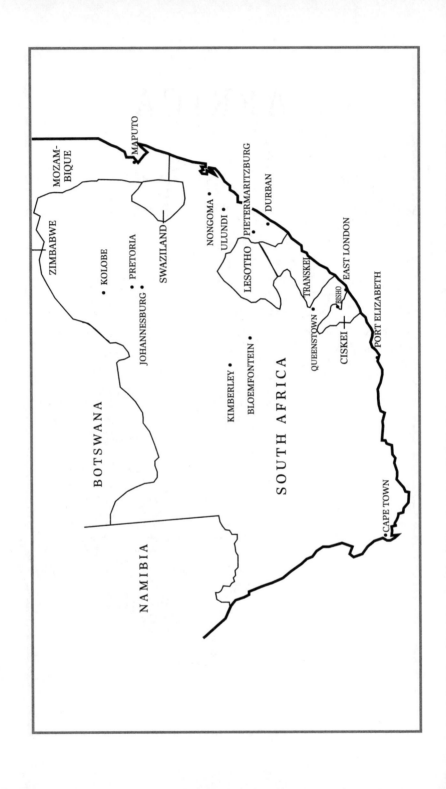

FOREWORD
by Dr Billy Graham

On this 40th anniversary of the beginning of the African Enterprise ministry, I am happy to write this foreword commending this story of Michael Cassidy and African Enterprise. I am thankful to God for Michael's life and ministry and for the work which God used him to raise up on the African continent. Michael and I have been friends for many years, as I was with the late Bishop Festo Kivengere who joined Michael in 1971 to share in this great evangelistic enterprise across the continent of Africa and around the world.

Michael tells me we first met briefly in a crowd in Cambridge when he was a young student there in the mid-1950s when I conducted a mission to that University. I am humbled and thankful to learn from Michael that he first came to faith through a young man converted in our Crusade in Harringay Arena in London in 1954. Then he also tells me that his call to evangelism took place in the basement of Madison Square Garden during our New York Crusade in 1957.

But we only got to know one another well when I came to South Africa at the invitation of Michael and African Enterprise to participate in the South African Congress on Mission and Evangelism in Durban in 1973. That for me was a memorable time as it was my first and only ever visit to South Africa. It was a privilege to be part of that landmark moment as the churches came together from across the spectrum to bring a fresh witness into apartheid South Africa and to seek to bring together both evangelicals and ecumenicals so that a more balanced gospel, with both the vertical and horizontal dimensions operating, could be brought to that struggling country.

In 1974, both Festo Kivengere and Michael participated (along with most of the AE team) in the Congress on World Evangelisation in Lausanne. But we experienced in 1976 in Nairobi what I consider to be probably the greatest ecumenical gathering of Christian leaders in the history of Africa. I was one of only two American speakers that had been invited to the Pan-

African Christian Leadership Assembly (PACLA) when 800 African leaders from some 49 out of 51 countries came together to examine the task of mission and evangelism across that great continent. I was privileged to speak both in the Congress itself and at the major public rally in Central Park, Nairobi, when the late and great Festo Kivengere interpreted for me into Swahili, as he had done on my very first visit to East Africa some years previously.

And so the contacts between African Enterprise and the Billy Graham Evangelistic Association have continued over the years in different crusades and conferences. It has been a privilege for our Association to encourage African Enterprise along the way as it has experimented with different types of evangelistic methodology.

So I commend this volume by Anne Coomes. It is a story which I think will inspire and encourage you too into the labours of mission and evangelism wherever you are.

BILLY GRAHAM
Montreat,
North Carolina
June 2002

Author's Acknowledgements

That this book is actually in your hands is as great a surprise to me as anyone.

Several years ago I got a phone call from Jean Wilson, International Treasurer of African Enterprise. She had just returned from an African Enterprise International Partnership Board meeting in Switzerland. The board had decided that it would be good to have the story of AE written down somewhere, and asked Jean to think of someone to do this for them.

Jean thought of me.

For one thing, I already knew African Enterprise. I had written a biography on the head of their East African team, Bishop Festo Kivengere, in the late 1980s. I had also ghosted the autobiography of the head of their Malawi team, Stephen Lungu, in the mid-1990s.

I jumped at the chance. Write the story of AE? The story of AE. Put like that, it slipped so easily off the tongue. No problem! Dedicated evangelists, a great cause, lots of action, lots of good stories – it would be a delight.

It was a nightmare.

I began by leaving the damp miseries of a Cheshire winter for the suffocating humid heat of a Pietermaritzburg summer. I settled into a chalet in the AE Centre and was shown up to the neat concrete building that serves as the AE archives. I walked in, and gasped. I was surrounded by literally hundreds of boxes on dozens of shelves. Paper. Paper everywhere. Nearly 40 years of minutes of dozens of different kinds of meetings, endless correspondence, articles, newsletters, in-house publications, you-name-it.

"Here you are, then," said the kindly Colleen Smith, Michael Cassidy's secretary, looking around at those towering boxes. "I'll leave you to it." She turned to go, and then paused to look in awe again at all those boxes. Solemnly, we surveyed them in silence. Then fervently and with a chuckle she exclaimed: "Rather you than me!" and hurried away.

At that instant a small lizard shot out from under some loose papers. He looked left, up at the boxes and right, up at the shelves. He looked at me in horror. He scurried out that door as fast as his little legs would take him.

Left quite alone, I stood there, coffee cup in hand. A little niggle began at the back of my mind: *What have I taken on?*

In the following five weeks, I found out. I lived in those archives. I got to know the lizards that came and went. I got to know the large green snake that lived in a patch of vegetation nearby. I climbed the shelves, hoping there were no poisonous spiders lurking anywhere. I opened boxes, dozens of boxes, and went through each of them. I found thousands and thousands of pieces of paper. Some of the papers I needed had copies attached; I took the copies. Other papers were file copies only. These I would need to photocopy.

But there was only one photocopier on site, and this was in constant use by the busy AE secretaries from 8 am every morning. What to do? I didn't fancy being alone in buildings after dark. So I began to creep up to the office block at 4.30 am each morning. It was just light, and very peaceful. A family of little monkeys breakfasted on the lawn, and looked astonished as I trudged by each day with my arms laden with papers. A serial dawn photo-copyist was something new in their experience (in mine, too).

At the end of five weeks I was very dusty, very dazed, and slightly frightened. I had amassed nearly 25 kg of paper and notes to take home with me. Then it was on to Nairobi, to spend time in the AE East African Centre, where again I was kindly let loose in the archives, and again mounted up the paperwork to take away. This was the rough material in which I would spend the next year foraging around. There were thousands of fragments of AE history to be extracted and organised into a coherent story. Quotes, dates, places, names, incidents, missions, initiatives, meetings, conferences, observations: each one had to be extracted, filed (so that hopefully I could find it again!), and finally slipped into the correct place in the emerging story.

Back in England, in the months that followed, what a story emerged: the story of literally hundreds of Christians in active ministry throughout Africa and the world over a 40-year time-span. I found it inspiring, heart-warming, dazzling, and supremely daunting to try and tell.

What was clear above all is that the work of African Enterprise is unique, and began very much in the biblical fashion, with God calling one man: Michael Cassidy. The story of his call, and how his background and talents so superbly fitted him for this enormously challenging role, has turned this story into half biography of Michael, half history of AE as an organisation. When there was too much history to chase and include on wider fronts of AE's work, and difficult content choices had to be made, I followed the thread of Michael's activities as this in a special way is his story.

In the years to come, there will be biographies of Michael to be written, and complete histories on African Enterprise as well. That even part of this vast story has now been told, however modestly, is due only to the tremendous support I have received throughout this project.

My thanks above all must go to Jean Wilson. She got me into this, and only her great patience and perseverance and kindness got me through it and out the other side. She is truly a friend to rely on when the way ahead seems impossible!

My thanks also to Michael Cassidy who has been astonishingly generous. He gave me total access to both AE's private archives and some of his own. He has given unstintingly of his time, both in private interviews (when his secretary was banging on the door, reminding him of other things he should be doing instead), and in sending me tapes in answer to dozens of questions that cropped up as the months went by. Michael also worked some kind of miracle that enabled him to give nearly four weeks in order to go over the book in its final stages. I am very grateful for this, for he gave a bright editorial polish to my final draft, smoothing the various still-rough edges, filling in the cracks, and adding extra little details here and there that give the book an added clarity and richness. Any mistakes that remain are entirely my own doing, and I take full responsibility for them.

My thanks to Olave Snelling, Michael's sister, who made so much time for me despite her busy broadcasting commitments in London. What started out as a business relationship has become a warm friendship, and to Olave I owe the wonderful detail in the early chapters on family background and early years. She entertained me for hours with story after story of their childhood in Maseru, and we even managed to tell Michael a thing or two about himself that he hadn't known!

My thanks to the many AE evangelists whom I met during my stay in Pietermaritzburg: Abiel Thipanyane, Dave Peters, Orpheus Hove, Stephen Lungu, Nii Amoo Darku, Antoine Rutayisire, Berhanu Deresse, Edward Muhima, Gershon Mwiti, and Emmanuel Kopwe. My chats with them convinced me that evangelists are very special people indeed, with the most extraordinary gift for bringing God into everyday conversations.

Evangelists seem to be God's lightning conductors for sending the good news of Heaven down to Earth. Wherever they go, the lightning of spiritual awakening strikes, people are spiritually galvanised, and many are earthed in a new faith in Christ. Many Christians lead devout lives without ever leading more than a few friends to Christ. An evangelist will tend to make converts wherever they go.

For example, one AE evangelist staying at the AE Centre had agreed to talk to me after he came back from the dry cleaners in town. But while waiting in the queue in the dry cleaners he had got talking to some Hindus about Christ (as one does!) So he arrived back at the AE Centre with them in tow, for further discussion. Two hours later, they had become Christians, and I made another effort to talk to the evangelist. We were just settling down to it when the Hindus-turned-Christians returned with some little idols they wanted help in destroying... Another evangelist took me to see a local alligator farm, and afterwards, in the restaurant over coffee, ended up praying with the waitress who was serving us...

I go to dry cleaners and restaurants all the time, and these things just don't happen to me! It was a revelation to see these men using their extraordinary spiritual gift quite matter-of-factly in their everyday lives. They certainly practise what they preach!

Next, my warmest thanks to John Tooke and David Richardson, both of whom have clocked up many years service with AE, and have enough exultant, moving and downright hilarious memories and stories between them to make this book twice the size it is already. They kindly made time out of very busy lives to read my manuscript, and make many valuable suggestions.

My thanks to Jamie Morrison, Michael's assistant, not only for his help with editing, but for his friendly perseverance in keeping the lines of communication constantly open between England and South Africa. Also to Colleen Smith, Michael's retired secretary, but very specially Brenda Harrison, Michael's new secretary who helped with most of the home-straight typing and retyping of edited chapters.

My thanks too to Ralph Jarvis, and other staff reporters over the years, for their descriptive and compelling reports of missions and other AE initiatives. It made past copies of *AE Update* a rich treasure trove of stories!

My thanks too to Sarah Willson and Gillie Goodwin for their extraordinary work on the Index. Their good humour and willingness to go the extra mile are astonishing.

My thanks to my publisher, Tony Collins, who has nerves of steel and the patience of Job. Tony began this project as a sane, cheerful man, and surprisingly, he still acts and looks the same.

My thanks, finally, to my family, with whom I look forward to getting reacquainted, now that this book is safely on your shelf.

Introduction

By the middle of last century, Africa was on the move and going places.

But where?

No one knew for certain. To paraphrase Charles Dickens:

It was the best of times, it was the worst of times. It was the age of high ideals; it was the age of unbridled corruption.

It was the spring of hope, it was the winter of despair. It was the season for education, wealth, and independence; it was the season for ignorance, poverty and oppression.

There were men with black skins on the thrones and in the presidential palaces of emerging nations; there were men with black skins who were not allowed on so much as the same buses as whites.

Everyone was in a headlong rush to glory; everyone was in a headlong rush in quite the opposite direction.

In short, it was Africa in the late 1950s.

Thirty new, free, independent African nations had been born out of old European colonies and protectorates. The vast continent was a seething cauldron of change. Old tribal ways of life were breaking down as millions of people left their rural homelands and flooded into the new, burgeoning cities.

Urban Africa was growing fast and chaotically. The battle was on for its soul. Everywhere ideologies and political self-interests clashed, while men with selfish ambitions vied for power.

Politically, Africa was a free-for-all. Tribes warred against one another, the communist Soviet bloc poured in propaganda and armaments, and the West urged development, pouring in billions of dollars in aid, and yet more armaments.

Religiously, Africa was a free-for-all. Traditional witchcraft and all manner of occult practices were endemic. On top of this, Islam was on the march, broadcasting its message with militant fervour, and gaining thousands of converts.

Christianity had been planted the previous century, and had taken root across the continent. But churches and mission stations were often isolated, poorly resourced, and separated by denominational divides imported from the West. Christians desperately needed encouragement, teaching and grounding in their faith, and unity, which in many cases simply did not exist.

On top of all that, South Africa's turbulent history had left her one of the most fractured societies in the world. White was uneasy with white: the Boer War had left a profound bitterness between the Afrikaner and British. So much so, that Christians from the Dutch Reformed churches had little or no contact with Christians from the English-speaking churches.

White was even more uneasy with black – this was the age of apartheid, when discrimination against black people was built into the laws of the country. And the vast majority of white Christians had little or nothing to do with black Christians.

Where in all this colourful, pulsating, energetic, unorganised chaos was an answer, a unifying factor that could provide the vast continent with a framework upon which to build its future, and to tackle its problems?

The answer, for Christians at least, had to be: *Christ*.

In 1957, God called one person. With him, our story begins, in the best tradition of a story straight from the Old Testament...

In the beginning... there was an obscure young man who was deeply sad because of the oppression and misery he saw in his land. He yearned for his people to be at peace, and wanted to help, but he didn't know what to do for them.

Like Moses fretting over the slavery of the Israelites, he came of a good family and education, and he knew political leaders. So like Moses, he thought at first that direct, compassionate political action from the top down must be the answer.

But then, like Samuel serving Eli in the temple, he unexpectedly encountered God. And when God called to him, he replied as also does Isaiah: "Here am I, Lord, send me."

Like Caleb and the spies sent out by Moses into Canaan, he and his friends began by spying out the land, and felt, despite the many enemies therein, "It is a good land that the Lord our God is giving us."

Like Joshua marching around Jericho, he and his young team marched in on a song and prayer to claim the land for their God. And imposing shut doors flew open before them.

Like Nehemiah rebuilding the breached wall of Jerusalem, he and his team had the same sense of urgency for the need to repair, to seek reconciliation, to strengthen and to fortify the church. And, like Nehemiah, he was given the wisdom in dealing with opposition from many quarters, and perseverance to go ahead with the task, and not be confused and distracted away from all he was sent to do.

Like Daniel, he and the team would soon find they were living in quite a lion's den...

But like Shadrach, Meshach and Abednego, although modern Nebuchadnezzars might throw them into the fiery furnace time and again, he and his team would never walk alone.

Just Another Day at the Office

5.00 am Maseru, Lesotho. Abiel Thipanyane rises, dresses quickly, and goes into the studio. His live radio programme is due to begin in less than half an hour. He places his notes in front of him, adjusts his headphones, and settles down comfortably. He is about to remind several hundred thousand black Africans that Jesus will be there for them as they rise to face another day.

6.00 am Lilongwe, Malawi. Stephen Lungu smothers a yawn and glances at his wife. "Would you like more tea?" she asks politely of their tearful guest. He has been sobbing for some time now, exhausted after a night's counselling. Six hours before he had been threatening to kill himself. Instead, Stephen had persuaded him to come and talk... and talk and talk. By dawn the man had found peace through a new faith in Christ. But all this talking was thirsty work...

7.00 am Cape Town, South Africa. David Peters hurries up the street – the pastors' prayer meeting will begin soon. Already, all 200 of them are crowded into the church. It bodes well for the forthcoming mission...

8.00 am Pietermaritzburg. Car after car trundles through the rush-hour streets, all heading for the unlikely road called Nonsuch... the staff at the African Enterprise Centre are beginning a day's work. Throughout the night dozens of e-mails have been coming in, like homing pigeons, from around the world, from Pasadena to Australia – invitations to new missions, tying up details on missions in progress, discussions over the financing of some new project. Sometimes the secretaries wish that the pace would slow down just a little...

9.00 am Zimbabwe. Orpheus Hove clears his throat and smiles cheerily at the 200 pastors gathered before him for a seminar on discipleship.

10.00 am Rwanda. Antoine Rutayisire grasps the wheel of his small truck tightly as it bounces over the dirt roads on its way to the Rwanda refugee camp. The boxes of literature and relief supplies shift about...

11.00 am Accra, Ghana. Nii Amoo Darku drives out to see how the street kids' project is progressing, with all those young girls learning to do hairdressing or sew.

Noon: Addis Ababa. Berhanu Deresse works in his study on the next training course he is preparing for the missions in Debrezeit and Nazaret.

1.00 pm Vancouver, Canada. David Richardson has a lunch-hour meeting for business people eager to hear more of the gospel and of the work of AE.

2.00 pm Kampala, Uganda. Edward Muhima visits State House to see President Museveni and Mrs Janet Museveni about the progress of the gospel campaign against Aids in Uganda.

3.00 pm Nairobi, Kenya. Stephen Mbogo answers a phone call about the Kenya team's upcoming mission in Thika.

3.30 pm Kinshasa, Congo. Nico Nteme sits down in a radio studio to broadcast a gospel message to the people of his city.

4.00 pm Dar es Salaam, Tanzania. Grace Kalambo calls her Board Chairman, Bishop Owdenberg Mdegella, to discuss problems in the upcoming mission to Zanzibar.

5.00 pm Monrovia, California. Malcolm Graham makes final checks to see that all systems are go for AE USA's mailing next day to all its friends and supporters.

6.00 pm Sydney, Australia. Mike Woodall, Heather Valentine and Mehretab Tekie gear up for a late afternoon board meeting as Chairman David Hewetson arrives at the office.

7.00 pm Hilton, South Africa. Michael and Carol Cassidy

have coffee at home and talk about the upcoming ministry tour to USA which will tomorrow take Michael away for three weeks.

8.00 pm Bujumbura, Burundi. Emmanuel Kopwe talks to a church leader about visiting politicians next day to discuss peace initiatives.

9.00 pm Abidjan Airport, Côte d'Ivoire. Ernie Smith and Udo Krueger, after two weeks of mission set-up work preparing for the upcoming mission, gear up to board their plane for South Africa.

10.00 pm Brussels, Belgium. Lynn Badcock takes a late call from a politician about the upcoming AE leadership mission in Brussels. Then again the phone rings – it is a Rwandan refugee in desperate need.

11.00 pm London, England. Jean Wilson is still at her desk trying to get AE international finance records in shape.

Midnight: Harare, Zimbabwe. Late-night owl, Simukayi Mutumangira, Zimbabwe Team Leader, lays down his pen and finishes his talk for the business breakfast next morning.

All in all, it has been a typical day at the office for the African Enterprise evangelists. Forty of them. Black, white, brown. Divided into ten teams, in ten countries. Covering Africa from Cairo to the Cape, helping churches with missions the length and breadth of Africa. Reaching hundreds of thousands of people a year for Christ...

But we are getting way ahead of our story.

PART ONE

The Ordinary Becoming Extraordinary

Chapter 1

Out to Africa

The story of African Enterprise began with Michael Cassidy and is infused with his life. So this story must also begin with him and his roots, and the family background which so shaped his future.

Charles Michael Ardagh Cassidy was born in Johannesburg on 24 September 1936. His mother, Mary, was a gifted musician, but knew nothing about babies. Her doctor, on a check-up visit to the Cassidys' small house in a pleasant suburb of Johannesburg, enlightened Mary as to the reason why her frantic infant never stopped squalling. She wasn't giving him enough food! After that, Michael thrived.

Michael Cassidy was the first-born child of Charles and Mary Cassidy, and only the second generation of the family to be born in South Africa. Michael's mother's parents had both come from England, both rather by accident, and both without intending to settle permanently in South Africa.

Molly Craufurd, Michael's grandmother, came from a grand family. They had an enormous townhouse near London's Portland Place, and rented a private train to take the family – father, mother, Molly, and her younger sister – to Baden-Baden in Germany each summer.

Molly adored her father, but tragically he died while she was still in her teens. Her mother, Kate, then rapidly spent the family fortune until she was faced with genteel poverty or remarriage.

She chose remarriage, but to attract a husband when she was in her forties, she decided she would have to knock at least five years off her age. That meant she could own up to having a daughter the age of Molly's younger sister, Helen (barely 20).

But it also meant that Molly, well into her twenties, was an embarrassment. And so Kate Craufurd suggested her eldest daughter go far away, and never return.

Molly decided to follow her younger sister to South Africa, where Helen had just married Gordon Buchan, an engineer working on the Colonial government's new railway line from the Cape to Cairo. Molly could get work as a governess, and was given letters of introduction and recommendation to the Pauling family. Pauling was then the well known construction engineer.

Mafeking

On arrival in South Africa, Molly decided to visit her sister in the northern Cape before joining the Paulings. This decision turned her life upside down yet again. For it was 1898, and Molly found Helen and the railway engineers in a remote British garrison town called Mafeking, just as the Second Boer War broke out between the British and the Afrikaners. For seven months the Siege of Mafeking made world headlines, as General Robert Baden-Powell, who later founded the Boy Scouts, and his British garrison held out against the legendary Boer (or Afrikaner) siege.

Helen and Gordon Buchan knew General Baden-Powell and of course, during the siege, everyone got to know everyone a whole lot better. Baden-Powell found Molly had some basic nursing skills, and put her in charge of the children's hospital of Mafeking. As the months went by, Molly also made several forays out under Boer fire to pick up wounded men, whether British or Boer, and to nurse them in the little makeshift hospital.

At the end of the siege, Lord Kitchener awarded Molly the Royal Red Cross – the women's equivalent of the Victoria Cross – for highest bravery. Later, at Baden-Powell's request, Molly went to Bloemfontein where she was assigned to nurse the Boer women and children in one of the notorious "concentration camps" set up by the British to house the dependents of the Boers.

Molly never did get to be a governess in Cape Town. She had by now met an Englishman, Captain Edward Reading, who had been badly wounded in the knee while fighting the Boers at the battle of Paardeberg. Like her, he was from an extremely good family, and well educated. Like her, he had got caught up in the Boer War quite by chance.

Edward, or Ted, Reading, came from Sussex, but had gone to Canada to join the Royal Canadian Cavalry. Then in 1898 his regiment had been sent to South Africa to help fight on the side of the British on the eve of the Boer War.

Ted Reading and Molly Craufurd married, and Ted joined the British South African Civil Service. They bitterly regretted the Boer War as a needless tragedy brought about by Britain's greed for empire. It had only succeeded in turning the Afrikaner nation into an implacable enemy of the British. One day they would impress this upon their young grandson, Michael, who recalled: "It was to put into my young soul at a tender age the conviction that war, alienation, vendetta and bitterness were not the way."

Orange River Colony

Meanwhile, in early 1906, in Heilbron in the Orange River Colony, Molly Reading gave birth to twin girls, Mary Tyrell and Mary Craufurd. A magnificent double baptism was held, with General Baden-Powell as the godfather. The girls, nicknamed Tweedle Dum and Tweedle Dee, were inseparable until the age of six, when Dum (Mary Tyrell) died tragically of pneumonia. Molly, Ted and Dee were inconsolable. Dee would feel this loss acutely all her days.

In Heilbron, Ted and Molly developed a deep friendship with Deneys Reitz, the legendary Boer general. The two former war combatants would learn much from this friendship about the importance of reconciliation, forgiveness and good relationships between different peoples. Ted later played a significant part in persuading Reitz to return to South Africa after a time of self-imposed exile in Madagascar. Ted also knew Louis Botha, later to be the first Prime Minister of South Africa, as well as General Jan Smuts (another Boer general and also later another South African Prime Minister), with whom he corresponded from time to time.

In due time, Ted Reading became Chief Travelling

Magistrate for South Africa, and so the family was constantly on the move. Michael Cassidy's mother grew up travelling the roads of South Africa in a horse-drawn carriage, with an oxcart following with all their worldly possessions. She found it a wretched existence.

Dee's salvation lay in boarding school. When she was old enough, Molly and Ted sent Dee to Roedean in Johannesburg, possibly the top girls' school in Southern Africa, where the girl quickly excelled, especially in music. So prolific was her talent that she was sent on to the Royal College of Music in London. It was a time of great flowering of musical talent, and Dee's fellow students included Benjamin Britten, Peter Pears, Imogen Holst (daughter of Gustav), Ralph Vaughan Williams and Malcolm Sargeant, among other luminaries. Even amongst such burgeoning talent as this, the young Dee could hold her own. Her large hands spanned ten notes, to over an octave on the piano, a reach that gave her strong advantage in playing her two best-loved musicians – Chopin and Liszt. She really was extraordinarily gifted.

What she lacked was the self-confidence to make the most of her talent as a performer. When college was over, therefore, Dee returned to South Africa and decided to become not a professional performing musician, but a music teacher. She secured a job teaching at her old school, Roedean.

Then, at 23, Dee's world fell apart. It was 1929, and the stock markets collapsed. Ted Reading lost everything. Soon he and Molly were nearly as penniless as the day they had arrived in South Africa, all those years before. Dee moved her parents to a tiny farm bungalow at Ravenshill, a farming area in the northern Transvaal. She struggled to support them both on her meagre salary as a music teacher.

The despair of his position overwhelmed Ted Reading, and he took to drink. Life became a nightmare for Dee and her mother Molly. Father would disappear, and mother and daughter would search the district together, looking everywhere and anywhere. They found him in obscure hospital wards several times, overwhelmed with the DTs. Yet Molly never gave up on her husband. Her perseverance seemed at last to pay off when some Christian Scientists ran across the struggling couple. With their support and friendship, Ted stopped drinking, and returned to a normal life, working for many years as a magistrate in Parys in the Orange Free State, where he was much loved and respected.

Meanwhile, Dee continued teaching, and was grateful for weekend house parties in Johannesburg spent with a friendly family, whose garden included a rather splendid tennis court. This made them enormously popular with the twenty-somethings of Joburg. Dee loved games. As a schoolgirl she had opened the batting for the school's first cricket team. She was also very good at tennis. So too was a young electrical engineer from England, who also enjoyed the weekend house parties. His name was Charles Stuart Cassidy. He, like Dee's parents, had also ended up in South Africa quite by chance.

Catherine Cassidy

Charles Stuart Cassidy was one of three brothers who had grown up in Glasgow, Scotland. Their mother, Catherine Startin, came from a wealthy family – who had promptly disowned her when she married "beneath her", a ship's captain, Charles Cassidy, of the Union Castle line. Sadly, Catherine was widowed early, and had to raise the three boys herself. But "Granny-in-England", as she would always be known to Michael and his sisters, continued to embarrass deeply her estranged parents and ten siblings. Her political and social conscience was positively "shocking" in a woman of her social standing. She took in a variety of people in trouble: the poor, a succession of single mothers, and ex-prisoners (one of whom stole the family silver). Catherine had a lot of wealthy friends, and was always asking them for clothes to give to "her" unmarried mothers – who in those days were totally beyond the pale.

Catherine was an extraordinary and prayerful Christian woman – a "real lady", said those who knew her. Her social span was enormous, so Michael Cassidy's father grew up in a house that was never dull. Supper parties were lively affairs: if there wasn't the odd ex-convict knocking about, there was usually a peer of the realm, a clergyman, a missionary travelling through, and an MP with social concerns and political improvements on his mind. Catherine loved people, and mixed them up with a fine disregard for status. If they were good-hearted, generous-minded, or in genuine need themselves, they were welcome at her table.

William Gladstone, the then British Prime Minister, was a close friend and colleague in her various exploits and gave her an inscribed Bible as a token of their friendship. Catherine attended Holy Communion almost daily all her life, and almost certainly prayed that one of her sons would enter the ministry. In the end, it was to be her grandson, Michael, who would become an evangelist.

Catherine sent her boys, Mark, Michael and Charles, to the acclaimed Morrison's Academy in Glasgow. Charles had a mechanical bent, and went on to Glasgow University, where he trained as an electrical engineer – one of the youngest ever to qualify at the university. Charles did his apprenticeship in the River Clyde shipyard, which at the time was building some of the best ships in the world.

Then, in 1929, when the world stock markets crashed and nearly destroyed Dee and her parents far away in South Africa, the same ill wind swept through the shipyards of Britain. Charles Stuart Cassidy was laid off, along with about 1,000 other engineers. There was no such thing as unemployment benefit, and no social security in those days. Charles trailed weary miles around Britain looking for work, but without success.

He finally went to sea, like his father before him: not as a captain, but in the engine room of a ship, this being the only work he could secure. The experience, harsh as it was, left him with a great respect for the working man. *"They* are the ones who really make the world go round," he would later tell his young son, Michael.

Then Charles heard that qualified engineers were wanted in Africa, in the Copper Belt mines of Northern Rhodesia, now Zambia. Leaving his mother was a huge wrench. By now she had lost Mark to illness contracted in the trenches of World War I, and Michael, a gynaecologist, had gone to America. But indomitable as ever, Catherine Cassidy bade her youngest son Godspeed, and urged him to go and find his life, wherever God should take him. She had great faith, and committed both him and herself to divine providence. Sadly, Charles saw her only once again, in 1947, when he made the long journey by sea and met up with brother Michael, his wife and son for a long-awaited visit.

So Charles went to the Copper Belt and worked in the mines. The region was called the White Man's Grave with good reason: yellow fever, cholera and typhoid abounded. When a man did not appear for breakfast, nobody bothered to call a doctor. They just summoned instead the black servant who dug the graves.

Charles and Dee

Yet Charles somehow survived, until in the early 1930s an engineering company called Reunert and Lenz advertised for an engineer, to be based in Johannesburg. Charles grabbed his chance to leave the mines, and was warmly welcomed by the Johannesburg community. A friend's parents owned a house with a large garden and the wonderful tennis court, which was where Charles met Dee, the brilliant young piano teacher at Roedean.

By 1933 Charles and Dee's friendship was warming into love. It was Dee's first big romance, and she loved with all the fiery passion of someone with an artistic nature. Charles was an exceptionally good-looking man, with the unconventional attitudes of his mother, and a great capacity for fun and perceptiveness. The marriage was to be a very happy and satisfying one, built on a firm and deep love, regard and friendship. If Charles could not match Dee's passionate nature and longing for romantic highs, he could offer her a sincere love of total honesty. He was a man of decency, dependability and consummate integrity.

Charles and Dee were 31 and 29, respectively, when they married in 1934. There was a simple wedding in Ravenshill under the trees. Granny-Cassidy-in-England sent her congratulations and love from Glasgow by long letter. Ted and Molly Reading were delighted to welcome Charles into the family, as they loved him like a son already.

Michael arrived nearly two years later. By then Dee and Charles had set up home in a modest little house in a suburb of Johannesburg called Orange Grove. It was built of white stone, had a painted roof of corrugated iron, and stood in a small garden with palm trees.

Dee had given up her job teaching at Roedean the term

before the arrival of Michael, and was now to devote the rest of her life to being a mother. Her intense emotional warmth and empathetic nature would make motherhood a natural delight, even if a bit stormy at times.

Charles was doing well – so well that he was soon offered a major promotion. The job would have moved him and Dee well up the social ladder. Dee, with her insecurities from childhood, was appalled. She feared the social demands that would be made of her. Johannesburg was the centre of gold-mining in Africa, and there were a lot of extremely prosperous people about. Dee was apprehensive of social or financial success, much preferring the safety of obscurity. She persuaded Charles to turn down the offer.

Next he was offered a job helping to run a large electrical generating plant in Basutoland (now Lesotho). Basutoland was a land-locked British protectorate within South Africa, situated between Natal and the Orange Free State. It was a good job, but socially fairly obscure. With Dee's agreement, Charles accepted it. In due time he would become the Senior Electrical, Mechanical and Water Engineer in the territory.

And so in 1939 Charles, Dee and Michael moved to the Basutoland capital of Maseru. It was here that Michael grew up.

Chapter 2

Naughtiest Boy in Town

Basutoland (now Lesotho) lies at a high altitude, nestling in the northwest shoulder of the South African province of Natal (now KwaZulu-Natal) and adjacent to the Orange Free State province (now the Free State). It is a lovely region, sometimes called the Switzerland of Africa because of its majestic mountains, vast skies and undulating grasslands punctuated with rocky outcrops. Dotted around are expansive fields of wheat and maize. It is cold in winter, hot in summer. There are far horizons – held up by the magnificent surrounding peaks of the Maluti and Drakensberg mountains – snow-covered in winter.

Basutoland had become a British protectorate in 1861, when Southern Africa was bristling with tensions between the Boers, or Afrikaners, and the British. Then King Moshoeshoe of the Basotho had appealed for British protection in a memorable way by politely enquiring if he might be permitted to be "a flea in Queen Victoria's blanket". The great lady had given her assent, and so Basutoland came into existence – to be developed for the Basotho. The whites were there to serve the protectorate through colonial administration and technical development. Their job was to prepare Basutoland for eventual independence.

In 1939, when the Cassidys arrived, Maseru consisted of one main road of shops, unpaved, with hitching rails all along, where the Basotho tied their horses. Cars were few and far between. Not until 1947, when King George VI and Queen Elizabeth paid a visit, was the main street finally tarred.

Homes and shops alike were one-storey high, built of stone, with corrugated iron roofs. There was a small Anglican church, St John's, with a red corrugated iron roof. There was a big high school for blacks and a small school for the white community's children – Maseru Preparatory School. Older white children went away to boarding schools. There was a small railway station – the main link with the outside world. There was no cinema. Such was the capital of Basutoland.

Relations between the indigenous Basotho, dignified in their hand-woven blankets and tall, shapely conical straw hats, and the resident white South African and British were good with a relaxed "live and let live" attitude on both sides. Many Basotho looked to the white community for local employment in domestic jobs and in the government; and the whites employed as many as they could. Large numbers worked in the mines of the Witwatersrand around Johannesburg. The whites rarely locked their doors, even when leaving on holiday.

The white community in Maseru was small when the Cassidy family joined it – numbering no more than 400 in all. It was ruled by the Resident Commissioner, as well as the British High Commissioner in Pretoria and, by extension, the faraway British government in London. Under them were staff responsible for the colonial administration and a number of engineers, such as Charles Cassidy, and others involved in technological development. They were there to do a professional job to serve the Protectorate; none expected to settle permanently, except for the white trader families.

It was thus a pleasant, stable community in which the Cassidys found themselves. As an electrical engineer for the British colonial administration, Charles was respected, while Mary's warm friendliness, which resulted in lovely musical evenings at the Cassidy home, soon won them many friends. Michael thus grew up in a home which followed the pattern set by his great-grandparents and grandparents, where a wide variety of people were welcomed, ensuring a constant stream of stimulating conversations. Books, music, politics, social issues of the day – the Cassidys' home life was never dull.

Charles and Mary could only afford a tiny bungalow, though it had a large garden, on the outskirts of Maseru. It was of stone, painted white, with a green roof of corrugated iron. One delightful discovery for the Cassidys was that their neighbour across the road was Lady Duncan, widow of Sir Patrick Duncan, the last Governor General of South Africa. She and her sons, Pat and John Duncan, would become close friends of the Cassidy family.

The Cassidy household was not luxurious, but comfortable.

With no labour-saving devices available, much effort had to be expended on housekeeping, and so Charles and Dee employed a cook, nanny, housemaid, gardener and washer-woman – all Basotho. The cook, housemaid and a gardener lived on the property. It was a contented household, competently run by Dee, who reckoned on making one article for the children per day, as it was impossible to buy children's clothes. Children's coats had to be cut down from adults' coats, because material was unobtainable during the war.

War

Charles, Mary and Michael Cassidy settled into this peaceful home and community at a time when much of the world was bracing itself for war. On 3 September 1939, Charles's birthday, war was declared. Michael remembers a grim, tall and very straight-backed man walking past his parents saying: "Well, it's come." Little Michael sensed something momentous being said. "That happening was my first conscious memory as a human being," he later commented.

In later months and years, he would often sit on a little hill-side near the house and watch as, down below, about 200 metres away, and 60 feet below the outcrop, battalion after battalion of black Basotho soldiers would march by, crisp and disciplined, headed for the railway station, the trains, and on to North Africa. They were going seemingly cheerfully to fight a war whose parameters they couldn't even begin at that time to comprehend. Their disciplined marching made a deep impression on the youngster. People caught up in socio-political events involving conflict and a striving for peace – all these were significant memories for young Michael.

At three, Michael was just becoming aware of his parents as people. In the years to come, he would often pay tribute to them both. Charles was an excellent father. He had total integrity, and was unfailingly patient, gentle and consistent with them. He was in every sense a "gentleman", a man of his "word". He was also a wonderful storyteller, to his children's delight. If he was less demonstrative than their mother, this was due to his natural reserve.

He said to Michael once: "I think I have been doomed to

work hard all my life." The comment had a profound effect on Michael – first, because his father's self-revealing comments were few, but also because he led by example. Michael grew up hearing family stories of his father's own early struggles in the shipyards of Glasgow, the copper mines of Northern Rhodesia, and now in Maseru, and would later say that his father's dedication to fulfil the responsibilities of his jobs had engraved the work ethic on him at an early age. Willingness to work hard became a lodestar in Michael's own life.

Family Faith

Charles had a real Christian faith. It was he who gave Michael his first nudge towards God. The family were regular attendees of St John's Anglican Church in Maseru, though personal faith was rarely talked about at home. Charles lived his life in deep reverence of God, but would have found talking about him acutely embarrassing. To Charles, as with many sincere men of his time, faith was an ultra-personal and private subject, not discussed lightly.

And so he deeply startled his young son one evening when Michael was about seven. Charles was tucking Michael into bed when he suddenly said: "I think you should pray every night."

"For him, this was a major speech, because he was very shy of moralising on any subject," Michael later recalled. "So his words made a tremendous impression on me." The youngster began that very night a litany of prayers which he continued for years: "God bless Mummy and Daddy, Olave and Judy (his sisters), Punch (his horse), Dingo (his dog), Jackie (his cat), and Uncle Roger (his godfather)." And all in that order! Poor Uncle Roger – after all the household animals!

If Charles influenced his son deeply through unconscious example, Dee loved Michael (and soon Olave and Judy) with "a kind of elemental love that was very intense. She was very solicitous in caring for us – nothing ever too much trouble. We were first, along with Dad, in her life."

Dee's influence on Michael was enormous and she would be a real, true and intimate friend to him all her days. Her sheer zest for life, her sense of humour, and her sensitivity for people were profound building blocks in Michael's childhood. He gained facility in talking about feelings through her. "I could bare my soul to her as to no other, and feel safe in doing so." From Dee, Michael thus learned early the art of talking to people, and the intense joy of friendship. These skills were to enrich him all his life.

But Dee's passionate nature did not suit all the demands of motherhood. She adored her children, but she had been deeply damaged by the death of her twin sister as a child, by the death when she was seven of her closest childhood friend, by her father's alcoholism and by the financial ruin which had hit the family. Loss, loss, loss – of all that she'd ever held dear and immutable. So now, as a mother, her love for Michael, and later Olave and Judy, was tinged with the dread of losing them as well. This lack of confidence made Dee tend to be overly protective which, as they grew older, became a source of family strain at times. Olave would later say: "The whole of our childhood was affected by the fact that Mum did not have confidence in herself."

Although she released her children to ride, climb, swim rivers, hike or go shooting, which Michael loved, it made Dee incredibly anxious nevertheless when any of the children were ill or had an accident – and accidents were very much a feature of life in Basutoland. "We were constantly being thrown off horses, tumbling off bicycles, falling out of trees, off cliffs and rocks, into rivers – and we had all the childhood illnesses. So there was a good number of broken limbs and plenty to worry about," Olave and Judy remembered later. Raising three children tries the patience of anyone. Not surprisingly, given her temperament, Dee often reacted to parenthood's strains and stresses with nervous anger.

Anger

Michael was later to say that his mother's one great weakness was "her shattering and devastating temper. She certainly did not like being crossed – that is for sure. If she were ever crossed, instead of being able to take it quietly, she would explode. The lid would come off like a volcano." Her hot, searing anger would overwhelm the children. "Our reaction was only ever one of appeasement – at any price. Mother was devastating when angry."

This anger had a profound effect on Michael, Olave and Judy. Michael would later remember, "My mother's scathing temper had the effect of making it difficult for me to cope with anger – my own, or anyone else's." For years – well into adult life, anger was the one emotion he simply could not give voice to. And in late middle age, when he suddenly displayed a flash of anger at a colleague who infuriated him, and dressed him down comprehensively, he afterwards congratulated himself, feeling incredulous: "I felt a sense of Wow! I did that! I got really angry and let him have it! Wonderful! Amazing!"

But as with many handicaps, the weakness was compensated for in other ways. Michael developed an extraordinary perception of anger in other people. "As I grew up, I decided that I hated having people fighting. I craved relational peace around me." His craving gave him a rare skill in facilitating good relations around him: "When Mum blew up, I always desperately wanted everything to calm down, and for there to be no hostility." Thus Michael desired reconciliation rather than confrontation from his earliest years. He was later to speculate: "Perhaps in the strange, sovereign ways of God, it led me to have the temperament of a reconciler and a peacemaker. On the other hand I often wished I had the skills and abilities to be more creatively confrontational!"

Doubting Thomas

Dee had another side to her that was again to serve Michael well in future life. Dee had problems believing in traditional Christianity. Most of her life she called herself a Doubting Thomas. Her parents' conversion to Christian Science had had a profound effect on her. She found she could not accept that Christ was the Son of God. She went to St John's Church, played the organ there and believed that there was certainly a God somewhere, but she was content to leave it at that. She was profoundly suspicious of all "religious" people. A bad experience in early life had left her deeply disillusioned with the clergy. She also suspected hypocrisy, and worse, of anyone who claimed to have all the answers to life. Any hint of jargon, religious "in-language" or a "holier-than-thou" outlook sent shivers down her spine.

This would not prevent Michael from forming his own faith in later years, but it would be a constant corrective to any temptation ever to indulge in "super-spiritual" language or mannerisms. It curtailed him from ever straying down the path of mindless enthusiasm. Throughout his ministry, his mother's honest scepticism would serve as an ever-present, inner critic of all he said. He would always preach with his mother's sceptical questions ringing in his inner ear. If he didn't think that what he said, or how he said it, would get past her, he didn't say it.

Michael would later say that his mother had given him a profound understanding of people who are Doubting Thomases: "I knew the honest perplexity of my mother, and so I have always had the greatest sympathy with people who doubt and struggle with their faith, though that particular struggle was never my own."

When Michael was four, in 1940, his sister Olave was born. General Baden-Powell's widow, Olave, became her godmother, and the baby girl was given her name; but she was soon nicknamed Poll, or Polly.

Naughtiest Boy

While his mother was busy with her new baby, Michael began to stray into trouble as he explored the boundaries of his small world. He devised novel, if naughty, ways of enjoying himself. It was by and large a thoroughly good-natured form of misbehaviour and mischief. Michael believed that social conventions were there not so much to be defied as to be *improved* upon. As Olave grew older, Michael involved her in some of his antics.

Thus, when Michael and Olave sat together in St John's each Sunday morning, Michael explained to her that the collection plate wasn't just for putting money in, but for taking change out as well. This pleasant arrangement financed their weekly visits after church to the sweet shop, their own "threepence bit", given for collection, also going on sweets.

At school he could not resist the long plaits of the girls in front of him: like many a schoolboy before and since, he tied them to their chairs with their own hair. One day his arithmetic teacher stopped him just in time from trying to find out what would happen if he held a lit match to a big bottle of methylated spirits. This bottle of "meths" Michael had cadged off Lady Duncan, who lived just across the road, on the pretext that his mother needed some.

The headmistress was also exasperated with Michael time and again, but forgave him because of the lovely bunches of flowers with which he would suddenly present her. She was unaware that he had stolen them from her own garden on his way to school that morning! She did, however, institute a school rule that "No one is allowed with Michael Cassidy when he has his bicycle because he is so dangerous!" Parents had complained that Michael was taking three other children at a time on his bike "at high speed down steep hills"!

Family and friends remember Michael as a lively, friendly child, brimming with fun, and "very, very naughty. He enjoyed his misdeeds exceedingly," said Olave. Probably because he had thought them up himself, and they had mostly worked in his favour.

Years later in Johannesburg in 1970 when Michael was leading a mission to the city, John Duncan, brother of Pat, introduced Michael at a tennis party saying: "This was the naughtiest boy in all Basutoland. And even if he'd lived in New York, he'd have been the naughtiest boy there too!"

The Maseru Prep School had about 60 pupils of the white community, and was run along British lines. Michael's teachers noted he was very bright – and that he loved both words and people in action. At the suggestion of a Mrs Dodd, a favourite teacher, he began a scrapbook of the war, based on newspaper clippings. "Soon I had very vivid pictures in my mind of Stalin, Roosevelt, Churchill, Hitler, George VI and Goebbels. I could name most of the German generals as well as the British and American ones."

His school scrapbook was the first of many dozens of scrapbooks, as his interest in people and events continued. People in action, things happening, and why, interested him first and foremost. He began a diary in 1948, aged eleven. Both scrapbooks and diaries are still faithfully kept today.

Arithmetic was something else again. Figures – impersonal, inert numbers on a page, held scant excitement for Michael. What could you do with a figure on a page? It was lifeless.

Numbers meant little to him, and he found he had limited interest in working with them. Throughout his life, he would find little to change his mind about this.

When in 1944 his mother gave birth to another daughter, Judy, and was again very absorbed in the new baby, eight-year-old Michael became even more naughty. He took his high spirits out on little Olave, or Poll, but was very protective of baby Judy.

Poll was an easy target for Michael's teasing attacks. Her arms were constantly covered with the welts and bruises of "Chinese bangles" and other childhood tortures. But Michael's attacks were always done in a spirit of experimentation, not malice. Certainly Poll never felt fear, just a bit overwhelmed: "I did my best to cope, and I was not frightened of him, because he also made me laugh. He used to hurt me, and then be very funny and make me laugh – that made me *furious*."

Boarding School and Holidays

But the pummelling began to have a physical effect on Olave. Finally the family doctor, sadly surveying Olave's collections of bruises and abrasions, advised the Cassidys that it was time their high-spirited son was packed off to boarding school: "This is deleterious on your daughter, Mrs Cassidy, very deleterious."

And so, when Michael was nine, Olave five and Judy one, he was packed off to school. From school he wrote home following the train journey: "You will be glad to know I did nothing hare-razing." In September of 1946 Michael arrived at Parktown School, or PTS. It was a well-known all-boys school in Johannesburg, not far up some cliffs from his first home in Orange Grove. PTS was frequented by the sons of those in the colonial service, or working for large companies in South Africa. The education standard was good, but the school was not well supervised, and a lot of bullying took place, along with fierce initiation practices. When a boy reached the senior dormitory, for example, he was required to run the gauntlet through the dormitory as each boy lashed him on a bare back with either a belt or a wet knotted tie. The thing of course was never to cry. That would prove fatal.

At PTS Michael first met the raw brutality of bullying. "Life there was very much based on the law of the jungle." At PTS a particularly brutal practice called "rorfing" involved punching, kicking, pulling the victim's hair till tears and fury in the helpless victim finally extracted some mercy from the gang. Michael recalled later:

> During the day the word would go round that someone had been picked out to be "rorfed" that evening. Shivers of terror ran everywhere. It was like the secret police were coming to get you. The attack would usually come before supper – the victim would be pulled out onto the veranda. Twenty or 30 boys would then kick and bash him to the ground and unleash the shattering assault. It was a horrendous business, and reduced any boy to a complete pulp of desperate tears and terror. I never forgot the day when I realised I was to be the victim. It was a nightmare experience.

At lessons, Michael achieved high grades and won many subject prizes. He also took to sport, especially soccer and cricket. He was quickly promoted to the first teams for both sports. He excelled as a goalkeeper and was an accomplished batsman and wicketkeeper. He made quite a few 50s in cricket matches against other schools, and became famous for diving the length of the soccer goal, and making some spectacular saves. During one cricket game, he stumped seven out of the ten batsmen and was hailed as a wicketkeeper with a future.

Back at home during the holidays, the absence of any local theatre, concert hall or cinema meant that the white community made its own entertainments. They enjoyed a Shakespearean reading circle, amateur dramatics, Scottish dancing, tennis, swimming, horseback riding, and squash. Anyone with any gift was pressed into service, and so a brigadier from the Indian army found himself teaching the children to ride – and soon had them sailing over jumps bareback. "Every Sunday morning after church there was an organised ride through the beautiful countryside, when neighbours and friends would sally forth." Usually there were drag-hunts lasting two or three hectic hours with hounds chasing artificially laid trails of "fox scent" and everyone galloping behind like a cavalry charge. Michael won the so-called Stanley-Clarke Cup one year for being the "Best Rider Under 16" in Basutoland. Olave and Judy likewise excelled and often won cups for showjumping, as did Michael. In fact daily rides, some-times twice daily, were highlights of a golden childhood.

For music many turned to Dee, for the Cassidy home was always filled with melody. The Cassidy children grew up with the works of the great classical composers ringing through the house. Dee installed two pianos – a grand piano and an upright in the living room, so that they could make attempts at playing Beethoven's symphonies and many other works for two pianos. Dee excelled at Chopin, Liszt and Beethoven. Several of the Cassidys' friends had exceedingly good voices, and many an evening was spent in singing well-loved pieces by Schumann, Schubert, Wolf, all the great song cycles and Lieder.

If Charles and Mary gave Olave some respite from Michael by sending him away to school, there was a downside, for at PTS Michael had also discovered boxing, and took to it passionately. Joe Louis, then world heavyweight boxing champion, became such a major hero that Michael once approached his parents and asked: "Do you think you could adopt Joe Louis into our family?" History does not relate the details of their response! Boxing of course was fine during term time, but at home Michael needed a sparring partner – and so he trained Olave! To his delight, "she became really good!"

So good, that "I always sent her in first, to fight any elimi-nating rounds with the few boys around – like my friend Jeremy – before they fought me." Olave, doughty as ever, sailed bravely into boys much taller and stronger – and gave some "fearful bloody noses" as well as almost knocking others out cold. Her newly acquired skill came in handy one afternoon when she was on her way home from school alone and ran into a local boy, Johnny, a friend of the family. (And five decades later unbeliev-ably still a friend and even a donor to African Enterprise!) Young Johnny made the highly unwise decision to tease Olave – and got a tremendous right hook which pretty well floored him. He went roaring home, screaming to his mother that Olave Cassidy was picking on him!

Adventures

Michael also became a major nuisance to the mothers of Maseru. They would organise birthday parties for their children, and serve out lots of cake and jellies. Then later, while the mothers were having their own tea as the children went outside, that Cassidy boy would quickly organise an impromptu boxing tournament, ignoring the normal party games. The prize for the winner was to fight Michael in the final. The casualties along the way were torn dresses, cuts, bruises, bloody noses, tears and children all wanting to go home. "So birthday party after birthday party in Maseru was ruined by my boxing tournaments. Finally I was banned from birthday parties!" reported Michael, looking back with a slightly repentant chuckle.

Maseru was a small community, and together the children shared the adventures and scrapes of growing up. Some of these included Jock and Gordon McClean. Gordon would grow up to become one of South Africa's top ornithologists and a professor at the University of Natal. Their father owned a mill on the Caledon River, and the boys had a wonderful time playing in the grain and oat bins. Of course, they took blood-curdling chances with grinders and other machinery and a broken arm and several injuries were the result. It was terrific adventure. Later when Jock and Gordon's dad moved to a farm in the Orange Free State, Michael visited the boys and had a wonderful, if illegal, time driving the tractor, and ploughing fields – even once late into the night.

A more sedate early friendship was with a local girl, Derryn Powell. Many years later, married as Derryn Hurry, she would work with Michael as editor and research assistant on several of his books.

As Michael entered his early teens, he and his friends ventured further and further afield on horseback on their own. They'd cross the Caledon River into the Orange Free State, trying to knock each other off their horses into the water, and then ride for many miles in the open countryside. They'd hunt guinea fowl and even korhaan, the royal game bird, with .22 rifles, shooting from the saddle as they rode at speed. Michael and John Leckie, still a close friend and now living in Scotland, climbed trees and either robbed birds' nests or pretended they were bombing Germans from the highest branches. Michael and John were also mad about collecting birds' eggs. Michael would often raid the turkey pen of a nearby neighbour and, having painted or dotted the turkey eggs with colour, would swop them for other young collectors' rarest eggs, passing off Mr Gordon's turkey eggs as those "of a rare vulture".

Perhaps the most significant friendship of Michael's youth was with the family's close neighbour, Pat Duncan. He lived in the house next door, with a gap in the garden wall for easy access. Visits back and forth were frequent. Michael remembers Pat as "one of the most charismatic people on earth, with a deep social conscience, and a deep commitment to ending the injustice of the apartheid system. Surely the most interesting and stimulating human I ever knew."

As son of the last Governor General of South Africa, under General Jan Smuts, Pat had grown up in Government House in Pretoria in the thick of the political arena, and early on engaged in what would be called "the struggle" by black politicians. Eighteen years Michael's senior, he was bursting with energy and, in spite of having a stiff leg from osteomyelitis, would involve himself in daredevil exploits with the young Michael. Pat had been to Winchester School and Oxford in England and brought his erudition to bear on fighting the cause of the underdog. His involvement in anti-apartheid politics was the biggest single sociopolitical influence on the youngster, and undoubtedly shaped Michael's concern for justice and his growing understanding of the fiendishly complex maelstrom of South African politics.

Michael would later write: Pat had "passionate political commitments to justice... He abominated apartheid... I became a childhood convert. Discrimination was wrong. Justice was right. Apartheid would doom South Africa. I was glad and proud when Pat joined Peter Brown and Alan Paton in founding the South African Liberal Party." When in later life Pat became one of the few whites in the Pan-Africanist Congress and embraced violence as a political tool to end apartheid, Michael was forced to distance himself from this position, though the friendship remained intact until Pat's untimely death as an exile in Algeria in 1967. Michael had tried to visit Pat in Algeria without success.

Girls and Games

By the late 1940s, Michael began to notice girls in a new way. He developed a fancy for the daughters of the British Resident Commissioners of Basutoland, and "fell" for a succession of those.

His diary in 1949 also reveals a twelve-year-old boy who was meticulous in noting down all the small events that made up his daily life. He felt every day counted, and kept busy playing with his dog, riding his horse, seeing his friends, giving his sisters break-neck rides in the wheelbarrow or on his bicycle and playing the piano with his mother. There was very little time lost; each day had a purpose. The triumphs of cricket games were especially carefully noted in his diary: "We won with 124 for 6. Played wickie (wicketkeeper) – let through no byes." The names of the books he read, and people he met, were also faithfully recorded.

Michael was also awakening spiritually. He had faithfully said his nighttime prayers since his father had advised this, and had always considered himself a Christian. He dearly loved Padre Ernest Lean, the local vicar, who encouraged him a great deal in his cricket, even getting him to play wicketkeeper in the Maseru men's team, and who faithfully sent him ten shillings a term all his years at prep school. All in all, God was a good sort of friend to have, because he could be counted on to keep a benevolent heavenly eye out for you.

Chapter 3

Michaelhouse

In January 1950, fourteen-year-old Michael was sent to Michaelhouse – one of the finest all-boys' private schools in South Africa, located about 65 km north-west of Pietermaritzburg in the Natal Midlands, and a 16-hour train journey from Maseru. His parents had made immense financial sacrifices so that Michael could go. They were not to know that, although the school had an excellent academic programme, it was also something of a jungle in those years. Many pupils were from rich and sophisticated homes. Some were also hard and pitiless. Michaelhouse would thus give Michael Cassidy several of both the happiest and unhappiest years of his young life. "My first and last years at Michaelhouse were blissful. The three in between were wretched," he recalled later.

At first, Michael discovered that he was one of the natural leaders of the pack, and that many of the boys in his boarding house would follow him. But in time, as the boys got to know one another better, Michael found the pack turning against him. There were reasons for this.

First of all, in spite of his childhood naughtiness, Michael had had some values drummed into him at home. But these values clashed with the prevailing values of some of his peers in Pascoe House, who prized four things: muscles, of which the slim Michael had none; a deep suntan, which Michael neither had nor wanted; girls, with whom Michael still felt awkward; and alcohol, of which Michael was particularly wary (he'd heard the horror stories about his once heavy-drinking grandfather). Also, anyone who was physically a late developer, as was Michael, was doomed for torment. "Anyone not hairy by age 14," chuckled Michael years later, "was an object of daily ridicule in the communal showers. That was rough." So when some of the

sun-tanned, muscled fellow students boasted of sexual con-
quests or heavy alcohol consumption, Michael frowned disap-
provingly. When boys experimented homosexually in pairs or
even groups, Michael was horrified and appalled. And of course
he could do nothing about his physical development. That was
up to nature.

And so many in the pack turned against him. Endless teasing and verbal bullying started in his second year. For the next
three years, though he never spoke to anyone at school about it,
Michael was "persecuted out of my mind", as he put it, "and I
came to dread school, and to know the paralysing fear and loneliness of being a victim. I felt totally isolated and quite desperate. I knew of no way out. Indeed there was none."

Michael was teased fearfully through C-block, B-block, and
even part of A-block (i.e., grades 10, 11 and 12) "for things about
myself that I could not change. I was not big physically, but
rather weedy, and thin and not physically developed." Michael
learned then the bitterness of what millions of people in South
Africa knew: being discriminated against for your very self. "If
your writing is bad, you can improve it. If your manners are
poor, you can work on them. But when what is wrong is your
colour or your size, or your physical development, what can you
do?

What you end up with, of course, is a loss of all confidence,
and you start to loathe yourself. You wish you were different,
and you hate yourself because your peers reject you."

The unhappy teenager at first continued with his mischievous streak. This led him into many and varied scrapes, including shoplifting, which made him the despair of his parents and
the school, until an older friend one day said to him, "If you go
on like this, you'll be stealing a car next." Then Langdon
Ibbotson, his house tutor and acting house master, astound-
ingly, but with excellent psychology, began to give him a few
responsibilities around the hostel. Both incidents served to
bring the young teenager to his senses. He made a decision then
and there to do an about-face, and start becoming more responsible and co-operative with authority. His wild rebellion ended
almost as suddenly and mysteriously as it had begun.

Of the teasing and persecution, Michael commented later:

The only benefit of it all was that it started to cast me on to God. The intense, inner loneliness in those middle high school years of having few friends in my own house – I had some good ones in other houses – broke me. Yet perhaps in the strange economy of God, I needed to be broken at that point, because I had been becoming a very wild guy. But to be sure, my Michaelhouse years deeply damaged me as much as they signally equipped me at other levels.

Gone was the cheeky, self-confident, assured young boy. An unhappy, lonely teenager had taken his place. In later years the experience would give Michael a great sense of compassion for other people who had been "broken". When in later years he did missions in various schools and unhappy boys came to him for counselling, "I could respond out of deep comprehension of what they were going through, because I had gone through it myself."

Michael clung to his childhood faith, plus what he had learned in being prepared for confirmation by Fred Snell, his headmaster. He also continued with his now desperate daily prayers. In fact, with a couple of other friends who were being similarly battered, he began a little prayer meeting in the school's crypt-chapel after evening homework.

Time Changes Things

Time, however, changes all things, especially in schools. After three years of hell, Michael reached his post-matric (or post-high school graduation) year, and life changed once again. Most of the gang who had made his life miserable departed, and lo and behold, Michael was made Senior Prefect and House Captain of Pascoe House. It was a decision of genius on behalf of his intuitive house tutor (then acting for the house master, Jim Chutter, who was away on long leave) who sensed there was more to Michael Cassidy than anyone had yet seen. He should be given a chance. "Yes," said Michael, "I owe the world and one of the most important breaks I ever had to Langdon Ibbotson."

So in one fortuitous moment Michael found himself at last on top of the pile, and with some real authority to change and reform his house.

Michael set about the task like an avenging angel. "I resolved to clean the house up, purge it of bullying and persecution, and to get some kind of values and kindness going. Whenever younger boys were persecuted, I pulled the wolves off, and refused to sanction it. I was a very tough reformer actually – much tougher than I have been able to be subsequently!"

Michael insisted on justice and fair play. The bullies were soon smarting under the uncompromising discipline, and many small boys whose lives had been hell began to smile once more. "It was the most fulfilling year of my life to that date." As House Captain and then one of the school's three senior prefects, Michael was blissfully happy. Something of both the pastor and the reformer was emerging in him. "That's when I first discovered that my major interest was people," he said later.

Suddenly, he found friends, laughter and fun again. His little prayer group of one or two boys expanded steadily, until 40 out of the 60 boys in his house were coming along each evening. None of the boys – including Michael – could articulate their incipient faith, but all had a deep reverence for God, and felt that meeting together was a worthy thing to do.

As well as administering strong discipline and justice in his house, Michael had plenty of opportunity that year to think about the national issues of political and social justice. South Africa in the 1950s – indeed all of Africa at that time – was a good example of the ancient Jewish "curse": *May you live in exciting times!*

Emerging Africa

To appreciate the need for the initiative that would become African Enterprise, it is important to grasp the turmoil that was rising throughout the continent of Africa, and lapping at the feet of South Africa's ruling elite: a turmoil of which Michael himself was growing rapidly aware. There were people with black skins on the thrones and in the presidential palaces of Africa's emerging nations. Yet there were people with black skins in South Africa who were not even allowed on the same buses as whites. Everyone was in a headlong rush – some in wider Africa to fulfilment and human dignity and others in South Africa to humiliation, marginalisation and despair.

With well over 30 new, free, independent African nations soon to be born out of old European colonies and protectorates, it is easy to understand why that vast continent was a seething cauldron of change. Old tribal ways of life were breaking down as millions of people left their rural homelands and flooded into the new, burgeoning cities.

Urban Africa was growing fast and chaotically, even out of control, feared many people. The battle was on for its soul: everywhere ideology clashed with political self-interest, while men with selfish ambitions vied for power. Where in all this colourful, pulsating, energetic, disorganised chaos was an answer, a unifying factor that could provide the vast continent with a framework upon which to build its future, and to tackle its problems?

How do you form modern democracies or sovereign states out of clusters of competing tribes with passionate and long rivalries? Meanwhile, the communist Soviet bloc was pouring in propaganda and armaments, and the West was urging development, pouring in billions of dollars in aid, and more armaments.

In terms of religion, Africa was also a free-for-all. Centuries-old traditional witchcraft and all manner of occult practices were endemic. On top of this, Islam was on the march, broadcasting its message with militant fervour, and gaining thousands of converts.

Christianity had been planted the previous century, and had taken root across the continent. But churches and mission stations were often isolated, poorly resourced, and separated by denominational divides imported from the West. Christians desperately needed encouragement, teaching and grounding in their faith and unity, which in many cases simply did not exist.

Exciting times, indeed.

On top of all that, South Africa's turbulent history had left her one of the most fractured societies in the world. White was uneasy with white: the Boer War had left a profound bitterness between the Afrikaners and British. So much so, that white Afrikaner Christians from the Dutch Reformed churches had little or no contact with white English-speaking Christians from the Anglican and other churches.

White was even more uneasy with black. This was the age of apartheid, when discrimination against black people was built into the laws of the country. And the vast majority of white Christians had little or nothing to do with black Christians.

Forum for Debate

Michaelhouse provided a forum for the boys to debate the stormy issues facing South Africa, and had invited South African writer and politician Alan Paton to visit the school in the early 1950s. His message as a guest speaker that day was not a comfortable one for the boys to hear. It concerned the injustice of apartheid, and the dangers it would bring to South African society.

Paton prophesied that apartheid would result in black hatred on an unimaginable scale, which would come to a head just when whites started to think of change and reform. He repeated the words of old Msimangu, as written at the end of his classic novel, *Cry the Beloved Country*: "I have one great fear in my heart, that one day when they turn to loving they will find we are turned to hating."

Many of the boys were deaf to Paton's words, but the anguish in his message made a big impression on Michael. Already sensitised by his family background and family friends, especially Pat Duncan, he knew that the words had a clear prophetic ring to them. Even from the safety of Michaelhouse, he found it impossible not to be aware of the tensions in the country. For in 1954 the clouds of political confrontation were looming on the horizon. Enmities and resentments were stacking up like giant thunderclouds. White, black, mixed race, Asian. All in collision. Where did the answers lie?

The teenager could only hope that "beyond goodwill and hard work in personal relationships, the political process was the way to get things set right in South Africa, so that English–Afrikaner alienation and black–white racism could be removed, and love of all for all take its place".

Love and forgiveness were qualities Michael admired. But these were in short supply in South Africa. So the problem of racial tension continued to "exercise my mind day and night". South Africa's anguish awakened the deepest sympathies of his heart. Being realistic, he felt "It was all very well to talk of love, but whence the capacity?" Cassidy had no idea, and so his deep concern for South Africa remained unfocused with regard to action.

Michael Cassidy never dreamed that the reconciliation of the people of South Africa would one day become a major driving force in his own life.

Future

Meanwhile, he had to plan his future. As a senior schoolboy in his last year at school, it bothered Michael deeply when people endlessly asked him what he was going to do or be. All he could say was: "I don't know," or "I'm not sure."

His childhood dream of being a world heavyweight boxing champion, like Joe Louis, was of course long dead. Another fancy, joining the colonial service, was impossible: the Empire was over and done with. Pat Duncan, apart from politicising Michael, had filled him with a love of birds and nature and so he thought about working for *National Geographic* or doing photography. At one point he even toyed with a career at Shell Oil, geology having become another interest through Pat Duncan.

The Rev Bill Burnett, his school chaplain (and later Archbishop of Cape Town) whispered in Michael's ear that he thought the boy should go into the ministry. His mother was appalled. "I'd rather be dead before seeing you in the church," she said one day. "Do something useful. Why not go into politics or the law?" By the 1950s it was clear that politics in South Africa would never be boring.

Michael's father had once hoped his son would become an engineer. "But seeing me all thumbs with the simplest spanner, he quickly despaired," Michael related.

It was all very confusing, and Michael did not really know what to do. He later suspected that "the good Lord, by this time, must have been wondering if he would ever get a word in edgeways about this preaching business"!

In any event, Michael's post-matric year at Michaelhouse was blissful.

It was very redemptive – more relaxed studies, playing sport in some school teams, having time for art, poetry, music and piano under my great music master, John Hodgson, being able to read more widely in history, philosophy, religion and politics, learning to lead and take authority and responsibility as Prefect and House Captain, plus discovering the pastoral joys of caring for the guys in my house – all this saved me. When I came to leave school, I shed tears of sadness. What a turnaround!

And Langdon Ibbotson, his house master, John Hodgson, his music master, and Bill Burnett, his chaplain, would remain close and life-long friends. Likewise some of the persecutors, with whom he became reconciled in later years.

So, against the odds, Michael left Michaelhouse with very positive feelings about both his school and his schooldays, notwithstanding the painful and shattering things.

Leaving School

In any event, now he was bound for England, the land of his grandparents, to study law at Cambridge University. But first he'd do a nine-month spell teaching 10- to 13-year-olds at PTS, his old school in Johannesburg.

Those prep school months of teaching were a revelation to Michael: "I found teaching intoxicatingly joyful and satisfying." He realised that he was definitely a "people person" rather than a "thing person", and that spending his career arguing complex legal minutiae would probably drive him mad. His intention now was to go into teaching. He knew he was good at it and he really loved it. He taught Latin, French, divinity, cricket, field hockey, soccer and boxing! Life was all fun and delight. He also enjoyed the adult freedom to smoke! But self-doubt about his worth and ability suddenly raised its awful head again. Psychological ghosts out of Michaelhouse days seemed to resurrect themselves in the months that followed in 1955, even while he was still teaching at PTS. It was as if he was experiencing some kind of delayed emotional shock as a result of the hammering he'd received in his schooldays. "A personal crisis hit me. Suddenly, it was as if my whole personality was imploding." All Michael's incipient self-confidence, gained since his post-matric year at Michaelhouse, seeped away, leaving self-doubt and anxiety. Only his daily delight in teaching the boys convinced him that he was actually good for anything at all. The thought of ever venturing beyond a junior school classroom, to tackle anything involving greater leadership and wider horizons, filled him with dread and horror. These wounds were very deep, and would be slow to heal.

Finally, in September 1955, Michael said his goodbyes to PTS, Basutoland, his precious family and Africa for four long years, boarded the *Stirling Castle* and set sail for England and Cambridge University. Michael's mother had insisted he go to either Oxford or Cambridge. The famously hilarious Jim Chutter, a Cambridge man and at that point Michael's house master, now back from his long leave, opened the way for Michael as "a really good all-rounder" to get into St Catherine's, Chutter's old college.

The idea was still that he would read law, but Michael hoped to change the course of his studies as soon as he could.

Chapter 4

Cambrídge

Arriving in England, Michael visited John Hodgson, his old Michaelhouse music master in Preston, Lancashire, and also Roger Haldane, his godfather.

Then came the big moment: Cambridge, October 1955. Autumn was ending and the first chill winds of winter were beginning to blow as Michael settled contentedly into student life at the great university in St Catherine's College, affectionately known as "Cat's". He sensed at once that his life here was going to be good.

Michael moved into digs with Alasdair Macaulay, an old Michaelhouse friend, at 45 Newnham Road, Cambridge, and the same day he welcomed his first visitor, Chris Wilson, a student from the Cambridge Inter-Collegiate Christian Union, or CICCU, for short. He invited Michael to the Freshers' Sermon, and in the days that followed, Michael made friends with other CICCU members.

But the big thing for the moment was to get out of law. Law had been a fall-back option when he was told at school he could not do Classics, as he did not have Greek to go with his Latin. Nor could he do Modern Languages, as he did not have German or Italian or Spanish to go with his French. But in his first few days at Cambridge he heard of another degree option which brought together both Latin and French.

After pleading with his senior college tutor at St Catherine's, and bluffing another two tutors that he knew more Latin and French than he did, Michael extracted himself from Law and enlisted in the elitist sounding tripos, as a degree course is called at Cambridge, of Modern and Mediaeval Languages. This tripos focused on Modern French and Mediaeval French, Classical Latin and Mediaeval Latin, and, of all things, Provençal!

It was to prove a fearfully difficult uphill academic battle, particularly as his standard in languages, coming from South Africa, was far below that of English public schools. Even so, the thought of teaching thrilled him.

Robert Footner

But there were other things to think about beyond Cicero, Balzac and the mediaeval troubadours of Provence. So it was that on Sunday, 23 October 1955, only three weeks after Michael's arrival at Cambridge, Robert Footner, an Anglican and a law student, invited him to Holy Communion at the Round Church. After church, there were still 20 minutes before breakfast and, as the streets of Cambridge were decidedly wet and chilly, Robert invited Michael up to his room for a chat.

Robert closed the door rather firmly and both young men sat down. Michael later discovered that Robert's chief goal that morning was to head off his announced intentions of joining the CICCU, until Michael knew a bit more of what real Christianity was all about.

Robert began by asking Michael how he had enjoyed the Holy Communion service. "I replied that it had been a good experience but not perhaps as meaningful as it should or could be. I noted that Rome was not built in a day, and that if I pressed on with determination my faith would one day come to mean something to me," Michael recalled. Robert did not appear impressed with this line. "He then asked me straight out: 'Michael, do you know Christ?'"

For a moment Michael was dumbfounded. "I imagine I looked as confused as I felt. I made a few rather lame comments about going to church, and all that, and not being quite sure what he meant."

Robert's next question was equally abrupt. "Michael, have you ever surrendered your life to Christ?" If Michael had missed the import or meaning of the first question, he could scarcely mistake that of the second.

"I knew immediately that he had struck at my weakest point. I knew in my heart of hearts that I had done everything possible in the religious life but that."

Michael took a deep breath. This was getting serious! No

one had talked like this to him before, ever. His mother would have branded Robert a dangerous "religious fanatic", and for a moment or two Michael also felt his hackles rise. Yet he sensed that Robert really cared, and was not just "out to get him". After all, his question was a serious one: *Where did Michael stand with regard to Jesus Christ?*

Put like that, it was a valid point, and required some sort of answer. "On reflection, I realised that, like the rich young man who approaches Jesus in Mark 10:17–22, who wanted to know what he had to do to gain eternal life, I had done everything in the religious life as I then understood it, *except give myself to Christ.*" Thoughtfully, Michael admitted this to his friend.

"Would you like to ask Christ into your life right now, right here?" Robert said simply. "We can just kneel down here. Don't be embarrassed."

Michael was appalled. They'd only come to this room to wait for breakfast! A flood of embarrassment and some anger rushed over him. "Who *the blazes* was this fellow to talk to me like this? Besides, what ridiculous fanaticism! Who had ever heard of kneeling down in a bedroom with a friend and *praying*? Besides, we'd *just been to church*, and except for my two or three minutes each evening, my praying for the weekend was over!" Michael swallowed hard, composing himself, and decided "No, I'd just tell him I'd rather not, but thank you all the same."

Meanwhile, Robert was just quietly looking at Michael, waiting:

> He guessed the struggle that was going on in me in those few moments. My pride was raging and reigning victor – overwhelming all my finer feelings. Then, as I returned his gaze, I saw in his eyes the most penetrating sympathy, love and sincerity begging me to respond. I was quite vanquished, and I knew it. I reasoned that if what he said was not true, I had nothing to lose by responding to it. However, if it was true, it was the heart of the universe, and I had everything to gain by embracing it.

Michael smiled hesitantly, and Robert went on: "Do you know the verse in Revelation 3:20: 'Behold I stand at the door and knock. If any man hear my voice and open the door, I will come in and I will sup with him, and he with me'? You see that is a promise to you from Jesus. He is knocking on the door to your heart."

If Michael opened the door to him, he would come in: "It seemed too marvellous to be true. I resolved there and then to take the plunge."

Feeling a bit of a fool, Michael knelt down. Robert knelt beside him. Rather embarrassed, Michael listened to his friend's short prayer. Then he mouthed a few words to the Lord to the effect that "I wanted him in my heart as my Ruler and Friend – would he come in and be with me?"

Michael, warming to his task, asked this of God in all sincerity: "That I do know, but it was certainly in rather *blind* sincerity, for I did not quite understand what it was all about or what it was that was going to happen to me."

The two young men rose, and Robert turned to Michael, his face a picture of thrilled joy and satisfied delight. "Now you really *have* asked Christ into your life!" Robert said. "Isn't that grand!"

And that was it. "We left the room and I felt much the same as before – perhaps just a little more hungry than usual!"

A New Creature

Michael and Robert walked into breakfast. Soon, over the toast and coffee, it began to dawn on Michael what he had done: "I began to realise this was a momentous test. If this worked, then there really was a Lord whom you could personally know." In those moments Michael felt a little like an anxious chemistry master mixing chemicals in a grand experiment before his class: hoping for a spectacular reaction when the chemicals mixed, yet fearful of total anticlimax, or that nothing would happen at all.

The morning wore on, and then, as Michael realised

the true wonder of the promise, things began happening within me with an almost alarming rapidity. It was as though I was having a "radio wave" of joy beaming through me. It was a radiant surge of new and wonderful life – and above all, a new, and hitherto unknown feeling of his presence. All this over the span of a day – a few hours. That very same day I became aware of his presence. It has never left me since – not ever.

That evening Michael was back in church at Holy Trinity to hear the weekly CICCU sermon, as it was known. This time, "I heard a sermon which for once *meant* something to me – for the first time I understood what it *all* meant. And I understood the words of the blessing – 'The peace of God, which passes all understanding' – because for the first time in my life, I was experiencing true fellowship with God."

Michael left church, leapt on his bicycle and tore round to tell Mike Snell, one of his former Michaelhouse friends, all about it, such was his joy.

As Michael poured out his experience, Snell's eyes grew bigger and bigger. He stammered: "Mike, I have never been hit so hard in my life. Do you know that you are saying almost word for word what another fellow, describing his conversion, was saying to me the other day – *word for word!* So, there's something in it after all!"

Something in it?! "By the end of that day, my life had changed forever," Michael recalled. "Jesus had become real to me. He was in my heart as personal Friend, Saviour and Lord. Nothing could ever be the same again."

The following Sunday Michael saw on a church billboard the text of 2 Corinthians 5:17: "If any man be in Christ, he is a new creature; old things are passed away; behold all things are become new" (KJV). That summed it up perfectly. Michael grinned to himself: "So even St Paul found what I have found!"

Filled to Overflowing

Now life at Cambridge really fell into place for Michael. His days and evenings were filled to overflowing: "In between studying, writing essays and attending lectures, playing squash and hockey for my college, I was roaring around evangelising the whole place – undoubtedly scaring the living daylights out of a wide variety of people, probably offending the chaplain and many others with my bad manners and awkward judgements on their spiritual condition. I meant well, but I was probably a spiritual pain in the neck to many at Cambridge!"

The fact was that Michael that autumn was now caught up in a deep reaction against nominal Christianity: "To think that I could have gone through Sunday school, confirmation and church up to the age of 19 and *never* felt I had really heard the gospel clearly enough to have responded to it!" It made him hotly indignant. So CICCU welcomed a keen new member. Michael felt deep perplexity with the entire established Anglican Church and public school scene: "I had been raised in it, and tried to be religious, and though some kind of foundation had been laid, I had *not* heard the gospel in such a way that I could comprehend or respond to."

"Maybe it was my fault more than the church's or the school's," commented Michael later with hindsight. What he did know was that "religion" was not enough. There had to be a relationship with Christ.

Ordinary Men

In any event, a few weeks later a friend lent him a book. Just a little book, and only about other students from Cambridge University: normal young Englishmen, from a variety of backgrounds; unremarkable, except for brilliance at sport. One of them, C. T. Studd, had been captain of the English cricket team in his day. But *The Cambridge Seven*, by John Pollock, was not about cricket. It was the story of what had happened when seven young men had taken their faith seriously, had sought God's will for their young lives, and had then decided to go to China as missionaries. In doing so, these seven Cambridge men had touched tens of thousands of lives.

Cambridge men! Christians! Wanting God's will for their lives! Being given a tremendous task to do for him: to evangelise a vast country! And rising to the challenge! Though only seven in number, going on to make a profound impact for good on a vast, desperately needy country!

Michael read the book and felt dizzy with the possibilities it implied. "This is the story of ordinary men and thus may be repeated," author John Pollock said very matter-of-factly at the end of his little book.

A story of *ordinary* men – which *may be repeated*.

Michael felt as if he'd been pole-axed.

"What struck me so mightily," he said, "was the word *ordinary*. It seemed God could actually use ordinary people. If that was so, it was magnificent. It was in fact almost unbelievable. He could use ordinary men. That meant he could use even me!"

Michael felt a profound, yet still very faraway, wakeup call. Something far in the distance, still on the very outermost reaches of his consciousness, was stirring. Could God actually have a similar purpose in mind for his life? "For the first time I thought of a team and doing something for Africa in the way the Cambridge Seven had gone to China to share Christ."

Such an idea seemed too wonderful, but too tremendous, to be true. Michael strained to see more, to pierce the mists of his future. But there were too many irreconcilables. He knew he loved teaching, and had a real talent for it. He wanted to teach. But how could he think of evangelising Africa when his career would be spent teaching boys in a classroom somewhere? It didn't make sense. In the end he gave up puzzling: "I tucked the thought away and pondered on the new turn of events in my life."

A few weeks after this, Robert Footner burst into Michael's room. "Billy Graham is coming to Cambridge next term!" he said excitedly.

Michael sat back from his books and stretched. "That's nice," he said. "Who's Billy Graham?"

Robert gaped in disbelief, took a deep breath, and explained about the famous American evangelist. He added that he himself had become a Christian at Billy Graham's Crusade at Harringay Arena in London in 1954.

"Okay, then, when he gets here, let's go hear him," Michael agreed. As he was already a Christian, he didn't see what difference this evangelist would make to him. He thought no more about it.

Over-zealous Witness

Instead, Michael continued his own efforts at personal evangelism and witnessing. "I was immensely, continuously excited about sharing with others the personal discovery of Jesus Christ which I had made." So ardent was Michael becoming, and so zealous, "that I scared the wits out of even my Christian friends"!

There was one memorable message brought to him by an

"ever-so-English" English student and CICCU member before a tea party with the college chaplain. The emissary arrived at his door to say that others in CICCU formally requested that Michael should not come along: "You'll only upset the chaplain. After all, Michael, you are rather a Hot Prot, you know!"

"Oh!" said Michael. The tea party happened without him.

Michael knew he was becoming one-track-minded, but could not help it: "Something was happening to me. I was finding myself inexplicably constrained to tell others of Jesus Christ. Unbeknown to me, my call to preach was being birthed midst the panting and often insensitive enthusiasm of a student zealot."

However, although Michael could witness boldly and fearlessly to any one person, he had developed a problem that sometimes made him laugh bitterly when he even thought of the Cambridge Seven. For his traumatic three years of being hammered at Michaelhouse were still having their delayed effects. So damaged had been his basic self-confidence that "I was plagued with a sense of inadequacy and with a terrible fear of doing anything in front of even a few people other than Christians". True, a dear and very close South African friend, Michael Nuttall (later Bishop of Natal), and he were by now teaching a little Sunday school in Grantchester, but that was talking only to a few well-mannered children.

Speaking in front of adults was another matter: "My anxiety about any public speaking was paralysing. I was so gripped with nerves that, in three years of CICCU studies and discussion groups at Cambridge, I don't believe I uttered a single sentence."

Thus Michael's private inner world was in constant turmoil. "I oscillated between grand resolutions for repeating the story of the Cambridge Seven, and the most unimaginably painful struggle with self-doubt." When at college drinks parties he found himself blushing if someone spoke to him, or when he realised he was dreading even shaking the vicar's hand on the way out of church, he sometimes feared that "my psyche had collapsed totally".

Then he would think of John Pollock's book and feel abysmally low. "I was a complete nervous wreck! How could I ever preach, let alone mount any sort of Cambridge Seven for

Africa? The idea was preposterous!" He felt more inadequate than ever.

In due course, Billy Graham arrived in Cambridge for his mission. Michael went to the meetings and was astonished by the power of what he saw and heard. This American preacher was something else! Michael felt "joy and total admiration at Billy's ability to preach the gospel. I longed with all my heart to be able to preach like that. But I knew it would not be for me. I was bound for a life of teaching boys French, Latin and Divinity in a prep-school." Michael felt torn apart at times. He loved teaching and could do it; yet he yearned to preach, and could not.

All he knew for sure was that Billy Graham was marvellous: "I had a new hero!"

If becoming a Christian had rather complicated Michael's desires for his own future, his newfound faith had begun to solve another long-puzzling problem he'd had. As with every thoughtful South African, his country's racial tensions had been a source of real heart-searching and concern. Now that he had discovered the transforming love and power of God, "at once my perception of the South African problem changed. It was Jesus who could enable people to love each other. Surely then, no final political solutions could come, unless out of the matrix of spiritual awakening and renewal. But people would have to be won to Christ – in their hundreds and thousands. That meant evangelism."

Would evangelism then really be a necessary, key factor in the healing of South Africa? Michael became intrigued and excited by the idea. Although his mind was still set on a teaching career, "I nevertheless experienced almost immediately a sense also of spiritual calling to South Africa. I had no idea of its shape or form, except that my life was being redirected."

Which led him right back to his own dilemma. The need for evangelism in Africa was there, for the ultimate answer was Christ. Now, what was he *going to do about it?*

Madison Square Garden

In the meantime, undergraduate life swept him along. Then came June 1957, and an invitation from relatives in New York.

Michael booked a cheap flight, and boarded a student charter plane for the United States in great excitement.

By this time he had decided he would do theological studies after his undergraduate training, mainly to help him teach Divinity well in a school. School teaching still seemed the sensible thing to be aiming for, with perhaps some kind of direct Christian ministry during the vacations. Where was best for theological studies? British Anglican theological colleges required scholarship-seekers to pledge ordination upon graduation, a commitment Michael did not feel able to make. And he was unaware, at that stage, of any good theological institutions in America, South Africa or even in the UK. So where could he go? He decided to write a short letter to the only Christian he knew of in the United States: Billy Graham. To Michael's delight, he had discovered that the great evangelist was busy conducting a mammoth three-month crusade at the Madison Square Garden arena in Manhattan. So he sent his letter there.

The letter arrived in one of the many dozens of different mailbags containing thousands of letters that daily poured into the crusade headquarters. Michael's letter landed on the desk of a Japanese-American student, Harry Kawahara, from Fuller Theological Seminary in California, who was helping with the crusade, and who happened to be sorting mail that day. He read the enquiry about theological colleges, and promptly phoned Michael. Michael was warmly invited down to the crusade in Madison Square Garden, and enthusiastically advised to go to Fuller Seminary. Both suggestions seemed excellent. Michael's life was now turning on one letter landing on one particular desk out of one particular mailbag!

Michael was overwhelmed with the Madison Square Garden meetings – a far larger crusade than he had seen at Cambridge, involving tens of thousands of people each night. "I was fascinated by what I saw. Night after night I attended the meetings and was more and more moved each time." For, despite the vastness of the arena, Billy Graham's message came across as brilliantly clear and simple and, above all, personal. It was clear to Michael that God was using Graham to speak directly and individually to the hearts of the many thousands there each night. Michael found the whole experience electrifying. He had never been to New York before, never mind a mass evangelistic crusade, but in some indefinable way, he felt he had "come home".

Then one night at Madison Square Garden, after the main meeting was over, Michael was pacing restlessly up and down one of the long, dusty rooms below the main arena, down at the basement level where hundreds of inquirers were being counselled. Upstairs he could hear the organ music still softly playing, and around him the murmur of thousands of voices as people prayed, were counselled or were preparing to go home. He felt too restless, too inspired by all that he had seen, to keep still.

Suddenly, an inner voice said clearly: "Why not in Africa? You are to work for me in evangelising the cities of Africa." Michael stopped dead. He felt awe-struck. He knew at that moment that he had received a direct call from God. "The voice within me came as clear as a bell. I was stunned."

Excited, shaken, bewildered and deeply pensive, Michael left Madison Square Garden that night in a daze. "All I knew for certain was that I had been called to preach. Yet, Lord, you know my terrors at public speaking. Aren't you for once fumbling the ball and getting it wrong big-time in calling still-broken me?"

In the weeks that followed he felt very confused. He was still aiming at a teaching career, and did not understand where evangelism might fit into this, least of all through him. Evangelising the cities of Africa was an enormous task, but could God perhaps be calling him to do it during the school holidays? "I was seeking to respond, but did not understand it all. And still of course deep within me were all these fears and psychological insecurities." Public preaching? Surely that could never really be for him.

Eventually he decided, still in some confusion, that he would in any case go on to Fuller Seminary and see where that took him. At least it would prepare him to teach religious studies in the classroom. He would apply now to begin studies at Fuller in the autumn of 1959.

Intense Inner Life

Back at Cambridge that autumn, Michael's spiritual commitment did not falter. Entries from his diaries at this time reveal a most intense inner life of the spirit. Thus:

> Today – a grand time with the Lord. Have resolved to try and witness for the Lord to at least one man a day.
>
> A grand day spiritually and the work went well, as I had prayed about it. But many opportunities for witness were missed. This must be remedied.

Michael was surprised when others commented on his single-mindedness:

> I met E's parents for the first time today – and was surprised to learn later that they had thought me a "little serious".
>
> I'm told some people think I am getting fanatical. But single-mindedness will bear dividends in eternal if not temporal terms. I am constantly being made aware of the fact that one cannot serve God and mammon. Moreover, if I am ever to be a man of spiritual power then I must settle down now to the long years of spiritual discipline and training. Every good thing in life is costly.

Extremely hard academic work, constant Bible study and earnest discussion about friends' spiritual condition over endless cups of Earl Grey tea were by now a way of life. Michael's room seems to have become a hotbed for many serious student inquirers. Theological discussions with them were interspersed with determined evangelistic endeavours aimed at any visiting non-Christian or half-committed friends. No one crossing Michael's threshold could expect to leave unchallenged. When the friends were absent, Michael laboured on their behalf: "Wrote out verses on assurance for F and M and others who came to coffee after lunch."

Friends who dithered and dallied were marched up in prayer to the gates of heaven: "I think we should pray that he is converted before the end of term." "John, who has quite fallen away from the Lord came round to coffee. I told him he had no peace with the Lord and I am going to urge and urge him to repent until he does."

Michael was as tough on himself as others: "I am still dissatisfied though with my witness and my life. I need much more boldness and, above all charity, charity and more charity."

The 3 March 1958 entry in Michael's diary reveals:

The vision of my mission at home in South Africa becomes clearer and sharper by the day; 1957–58 has seen the Lord convince us in our hearts that we are the men He has chosen. [Michael had several South African friends, such as Michael Nuttall, who also yearned for a ministry in Africa.] Oh what an unspeakable privilege! But I feel of all men the most utterly unworthy to accept it. However, for what my life is worth I put it at his disposal and I am willing to be used if He will make me usable.

All this from a man still only 21.

That 24 September, his 22nd birthday, he notes: "My first 22 years have been full enough. I wonder what the next 22 hold?" He still struggled with his problem of shyness:

Witness today has not been all it might be. I need deliverance from timidity.

What a strange bundle of paradoxes I am! One minute believing I can do things that no one has done before, and the next blushing like a schoolgirl in the face of some trivial circumstance. One minute seeing myself as a sort of Saviour of South Africa, the next cringing with fear before a happy friendly crowd of friends who do not mean me the least bit of ill.

In May 1958 Michael prepared to leave Cambridge. For him Cambridge had been "about getting converted, being discipled and learning to work incredibly hard". He had gained his honours degree in Modern and Mediaeval Languages and now spent six months teaching in a little prep school in north London. In December that year came a final holiday with some fellow students at the invitation of Francis and Edith Schaeffer, whom Michael had met through a friend, at L'Abri in Huémoz Sur Ollon in Switzerland. At that time, the Schaeffers were not well known and Michael had invited Francis Schaeffer to lead a Bible study in Cambridge, one of the first meetings he had led in England. Here, high in the Alps, some words of wisdom came to Michael in his struggle with fear.

"In some way the Lord has used this trip... to heal my sub-conscious. During my first evenings at the Schaeffers I was very nervous, but gradually this wore off and soon I felt able to contribute to the discussion without any nervous inhibition." When he shared his problem with Dr Schaeffer, he was advised to claim moment-by-moment victory over this thing, rather than struggling to achieve a complete, exhaustive and once-for-all victory. It was excellent advice, and in the months and years that followed this would prove the way through for Michael.

On 17 January 1959 Fuller Seminary wrote to say Michael had been accepted for entry there in September that year. But there was no news about the scholarship that would make it possible.

Back to South Africa

On 29 January 1959 Michael sailed from England for Cape Town. He wrote in his diary:

> I return a very different person to the immature little schoolboy who steamed into these waters three and a half years ago. I arrived without God. I return to Africa with him. I arrived to get academic knowledge. I return to impart spiritual knowledge. I arrived without orders. I return a commissioned man. I arrived a wanderer. I return an apostle for the gospel.

In later years, Michael Cassidy would look back on his call, and see his life as "a story of God's utter grace. It is as if God had looked around South Africa and said: 'Let's look for the weakest, the most crushed, demoralised and decimated thing, and make something of that.'"

Meanwhile, Michael decided to use the spring and summer that lay before him in South Africa as "an exploratory period when the field of battle is surveyed and the plan of campaign formulated. Politically, certainly Christ is the answer. But before He can be the answer to South Africa the country, He must be the answer to South Africans, the individuals."

On board ship Michael met some missionaries from the Belgian Congo (later Zaïre and now the Democratic Republic of Congo) and a British family from Northern Rhodesia who made an enormous impact on him. The husband, Jack Holmes, contracted meningitis on board and had to be put off in Sierra Leone in West Africa, critically ill. His wife, Ruth, with five children, had to continue on board ship to Cape Town. Michael was impressed by Mrs Holmes' calm acceptance and spiritual serenity in the face of such trouble and anguish. He and Mrs Holmes struck up an immediate friendship, and he shared with her his hopes for the future. She gave him an article written by an American evangelist called Merv Rosell that contained a quote from Sir John Foster Fraser. The quote read: "When God desires to shake, shock or shape any age in order to save sinners, He always chooses a man – not a system, not a plan, not an organisation, but a man."

The words hit Michael like a thunderbolt. He wrote in his diary: "When God leads out to a new victory, He chooses a man. Be that man! Be that man!" The words tumbled back and forth in Michael's mind for days. "Certainly I feel as though I have it in me to do the work – or at least to be the Lord's spokesman as He does it."

And yet the next day, recalled Michael,

Mrs Holmes suggested we put on a Sunday School on deck for the children. The ship's purser suggested the tourist dance deck at 2.30! My heart leapt. Preaching on the deck of a luxury liner filled with luxury loving people frightened me! But then I thought of the words "Be that man." If I was going to be the man for South Africa, I might as well begin now on the dance deck! About 15 children and about 20 adults came, and I was staggered to find that I only felt the very slightest tinge of nervousness and no fear. Truly God does deliver.

On Thursday, 12 February 1959 the ship steamed towards Cape Town harbour, with Michael up in the bow of the ship looking across the Cape rollers towards land: "I surveyed Table Mountain and wondered at what Africa held for me. I felt very much an ordinary, feeble, inadequate sinner. The job of making a dent on this country, so full of sin and prejudice, seemed too great a thing for me. But then I remembered that 'If God be for us, who can be against us?'"

Michael did not hang about. The very next day he went to

see the Anglican Archbishop of Cape Town, Dr Joost de Blank, who gave him a fair hearing. Michael wrote later:

> Joost mentioned the evangelicals' neglect of "incarnational responsibilities", that was indicated in their failure to condemn social and political evils and I said that I too felt this to be a real failing on our part. Then Joost said that if only a man would arise who could confront the country with the necessity of synthesising the spiritual as well as political and social responsibilities of the gospel, then the church would make real progress here. He added, "Perhaps you are the man to do this."

This was so flattering that Michael could hardly feel he meant it: "All the same it reiterated what I felt *inside*." Michael left an hour later, deeply impressed with the man and his humility and rather suspecting that this was not the last he would see of this fine archbishop.

Home Again in Basutoland

Michael spent the next eight months back in Maseru with his family. After nearly four years away, he had a rapturous reunion with his parents and sisters, looked up dozens of old friends and let the beauty and vastness of Africa seep back into him. He also visited a wide variety of Christian leaders.

He wrote in his mid-1959 diary:

> I am staggered by the immensity and complexity of the problem here. It takes a very great amount of faith to believe that anything can be done here at all. The whole problem seems quite out of hand. A tidal wave of nationalism is sweeping Africa and most Europeans fail to see that they must ride on the crest of the wave and not allow it to fall with a crash on them. One must get in alongside the African, win him to oneself by a demonstration of indiscriminate love, and then ride his revolution with him. Anything other than this can only lead to disaster.
>
> But indiscriminate love only flows from the regenerate heart. And it is Christ who regenerates. So one comes back to the fact to which I shall cling with all my being: that Jesus Christ is the only answer. The trouble is that everyone thinks He has been tried and found wanting. But the one found wanting is "another Jesus", and not the One I know.

I do pray with all my being that in this insidious atmosphere of nominal religion, racial prejudice and blinded minds I should retain undulled my vision that He can change the future of this country and that he means to do it for himself through me. "Make me usable, then use me, O Lord."

Said Michael many years later: "I blush now when I read this spiritual bravado mixed in with these illusions of grandeur in all my diaries of those years. But I was an immature though spiritually ambitious young believer grappling with the unknown contours of a call."

Michael also read book after book, immersing himself especially in endless biographies of every sort, while waiting on word from Fuller Seminary as to scholarships: "The insights, mistakes, achievements, agonies and ecstasies of other men all helped to focus my mind on what it meant to live meaningfully during this one mysterious opportunity which each of our lives represents as we walk across the planet."

At last, good news: a letter from Fuller informed him that he'd been given a scholarship for *double* the value of the one he'd applied for. But the Fulbright travel grant was rejected. Now Michael had a student place in seminary and funds waiting for him in California, but he was stranded in South Africa.

Dee Cassidy was still very much against the idea of her son doing theological training, and so Michael felt it was out of the question to ask his parents for financial help. The summer wore on and, having no job at the time, Michael saw clearly that he would never raise the money in time.

He kept praying, and wrote in his diary: "I still feel God wants me to go this year, and feel this is a test... but I cannot for the life of me see where the money might come from."

Meanwhile, he had booked to sail on a Union Castle liner on 7 August 1959. But the money did not come in, and the ship sailed without him.

Some missionaries assured him God would still undertake and gave him Philippians 4:19: "My God shall supply all your need according to his riches in glory by Christ Jesus" (NKJV).

Then it all happened: an amazing and miraculous last-minute supply. Michael's Cambridge friend from South Africa, Tom Barlow, whom he had led to Christian commitment and who had played polo for Cambridge in the tradition of his famous businessman father, Punch, phoned Michael. "I am selling my polo ponies and feel the Lord wants me to give the money to you." Michael went through the roof with excitement, especially when his dear Mum, now reconciled at the last minute by his determination to go, unselfishly put in the balance of the funds needed.

Michael was on his way. By air, no less! He knew he had a story to tell, but would he ever have the courage to tell it publicly?

He would soon be tested on this.

Chapter 5

Fuller Theological Seminary

A panting, excited and grateful Michael finally reached Fuller Theological Seminary in Pasadena, California, in September 1959. His first experience of southern California was one of culture shock: the crew-cuts, coloured shorts, loud voices, flashy shirts, wild accents and above all, casual blue-jeaned students who called the lecturers "Prof", gave this dignified young graduate of Cambridge University a healthy dose of culture shock!

Fuller Seminary, just a few miles from Los Angeles, began its autumn term with a weekend retreat up in the nearby San Bernardino Mountains for nearly 100 new students. Michael was thoroughly enjoying himself until it was announced one morning that that evening would be "testimony night", when any of the first-year students could share with the rest anything about themselves and how they had come to be at Fuller.

Here Michael's torment began: "I immediately felt prompted by God that I should share the amazing way provision had come so I could be there. But the idea of standing up before all those students absolutely terrified me." The other students enjoyed an active day in the beautiful mountain conference centre. But Michael slipped away, and had an afternoon of hell on his own in the forest. He wanted to obey the inner prompting and share that evening, but felt that, if he did, he would probably faint. This would be the dreaded public speaking in front of adults.

In due course, in between some wonderful singing, the testimony night got underway. Student after student calmly shared their stories of how they had been called to come to Fuller, and what they hoped to do in their future ministry. Michael sat in a cold sweat and an anguish of fear. The hour grew late, and the inner urging did not let up: "Finally, with a massive effort of courage, I hurled myself to my feet – just as another student did, and he was spotted." Michael sat down now in a total panic, feeling he simply could not take that step again. In a few minutes the student finished, and Michael sat, blushing and breathless, for ten to fifteen seconds "battling everything in my psyche". Then, light-headed, he stood, was called on, and began. "I think I flushed brilliant red, and my throat constricted. It felt as if my dying moment had come."

Then suddenly, he found that his voice somehow still worked, and a flow of words began:

> I simply told how God had made it possible for me to come to Fuller. I explained that by the time the ship had left South Africa, I still had had not enough money, and so had missed it. But then a friend whom I'd met at Cambridge, whose father was a big industrialist in South Africa, and whom I had had the privilege of leading to the Lord at Cambridge, contacted me at zero hour. He said that he had had the strongest feeling for several days that he was to sell his polo ponies and give me the money towards my fare.
>
> Then my mother, who had opposed my going to America (You'll marry some Hollywood girl and never come back!) suddenly changed her mind and agreed to put in the rest of the money I needed. So I jumped on a plane and flew out here to California. [That was just not done in those days: people went by sea.] I arrived only two days ago and here I am. Praise God.

When Michael finished, he sat down totally played out and emotionally drained. No one spoke or moved. There was a hush over the whole auditorium. Finally, Dr Carlton Booth, the Fuller professor who had been leading the evening, said quietly, "After that, nothing more can be said tonight. We end it here." Michael realised then with awe that his words had touched his fellow students. "God had anointed my fearful and simple testimony. It was overwhelming." Years later he would have tears in his eyes when he recalled this first public testimony in America concerning his faith. "No one was more mind-boggled than I."

He went to his room in a daze, asking himself: "What has happened here? But I knew in my heart: God had come down."

Thrust into Leadership

Back at Fuller, the professors announced that they had chosen two of the incoming students to share their testimonies with the entire seminary. To his horror, Michael found he was one. This was worse than anything he could possibly have imagined.

Michael went through the whole process of dread all over again. Again, he was amazed at the reaction his words produced. The seminary was spellbound. "I found it quite incredible – this was not from me consciously." Then a small delegation from the Fuller Seminary Student Missions Fellowship (FMF) arrived on his doorstep. It was an important body in the seminary that promoted mission concern and co-ordinated missions work. The delegation told Michael that the unanimous feeling was that for the very first time ever, FMF should be chaired by a freshman, namely, him.

So less than a week after arriving from South Africa, Michael, who'd thought he could cope with no more than teaching boys, found he was in leadership over mature, young graduate men, some of whom had fought in the Korean War. He was to speak in chapel on a regular basis, and chair committees. He was appalled.

> Somehow, I did it, but it was always a trial by fire beforehand. I was never conscious of any ability. When people told me I had it, I did not believe them. In homiletics class, where we had to preach to our fellow students, I went through agonies. People got torn apart in there. But all they said to me was: "why not go into preaching? You have a gift." I could not accept this as honest advice for months. I simply could not believe it.

Nevertheless, as the first year sped by, Michael began to gain more self-confidence, and to share with people his embryonic vision for evangelism in Africa. The founder of Fuller Seminary, Dr Charles Fuller, who was also one of the great radio and mass evangelists of his day through his worldwide radio programme, had taken an immediate interest in Michael, and listened thoughtfully. Another strong supporter was Carlton Booth, Professor of Evangelism, and the man who had picked Michael out to testify. A group of fellow students began to pray with Michael, and to get excited over the possibility of future ministry in Africa. One was Ed Gregory, the other student chosen to testify before the seminary at the beginning of term. Michael found their interest highly encouraging.

Inspired by a book he had read on how Dawson Trotman, the founder of the Navigators' ministry, had prayed for different areas of the world, Michael made a decision as the summer of 1960 arrived. He got out an atlas, and made a list of the 31 major cities of Africa. He decided he was going to pray for one each day of the month for the whole summer. Ed Gregory agreed to join him in this prayer vigil, asking God for the chance one day to minister in each city.

Meanwhile, numerous opportunities came along for doing evangelism. When the summer term of 1960 ended, a prominent Pasadena businessman financed five of the students (including Michael) to go and work in the 1960 Billy Graham Crusade in Washington, DC. Michael met Billy Graham briefly, as well as Doug Coe, then in the early phases of working with the legendary Dr Abraham Vereide in his great outreach to the political leadership sectors of Washington. Then the students travelled, doing evangelism in local churches throughout the New England states, and on down into Kentucky amongst the mountain people. All the experiences – and some of them were hilarious (Michael and his Greek Orthodox/Baptist bodybuilding roommate Alex Aronis laughed about these the whole following year) – only confirmed to Michael that he loved mixing with people, and was beginning to enjoy doing the work of an evangelist.

All the while he faithfully prayed for his 31 cities, and kept mulling over this vision of evangelising the cities of Africa. What exactly was God calling him to? To offer himself as a missionary to an established organisation, or... what? Said his journal: "The vision was beginning to take hold, but how should it be expressed? Should even a separate agency be formed? I was at a real crossroads of my life." Especially as Bill Bright was showing interest in Michael's going on to establish the Campus Crusade for Christ work in South Africa – a marvellous opportunity for an unknown seminary student. Should he take it, or what?

An opportunity for quiet reflection came when Bright invited Michael to spend some time that summer at a three-week Campus Crusade Training Institute on Lake Minnetonka in Minnesota. Michael shared his developing crisis and crossroads with Bright, who then allowed him to spend the first week in personal solitude and prayer, away from the classes. His whole desire was "to seek to ascertain once and for all whether the Lord wanted me to move forward on the developing vision. And in what way?"

Michael had early on in his Christian life developed the habit of waiting on God through long hours of private, solitary prayer. He did so now. He was only too aware of the enormity of the vision and impending decision that had somehow come to overshadow him, and conscious that if he did not handle this "call" correctly, it could ruin his life. Too many Christians set out on projects that crashed on them.

Decision to Proceed

However, by the end of that week of "waiting on God", Michael felt a deep assurance that it was right to proceed with a new agency for evangelism. It was not that he did not respect the agencies already at work in Africa. It was simply that he felt his particular vision was unique, and that no other agency quite shared it. His sense that he was now on the right path was confirmed to him when he was suddenly handed a tract by Mary Jane Smith, the wife of Dr Wilbur Smith, the celebrated American Bible teacher and one of the founding professors at Fuller. She said only: "Michael, I was praying for you, and felt that you should have this."

The tract was entitled "This thing is from me". On the back page were these words: "Are you called upon to launch out upon a great and demanding undertaking? This thing is from me. Therefore launch out on Me, *for I have given you the possession of difficulties.*"

"That did it. I knew then what I had to do," said Michael. "But I also heeded the advance warning – it would be the possession of *difficulties.*" A thousand times in the years that followed, Michael would go back to God and say, "Well you did underline it would be difficult!" "Without that warning right at the beginning, I would probably have given up at key times in the work to come."

Michael's vision for Africa was well expressed in a letter he wrote that summer of 1960 to *Eternity* magazine, after they'd accepted an article of his for publication.

You asked about my future plans. Since the time of my conversion, I have felt there to be an urgent need for a new work in Africa that would seek to reach the influential people of this continent for Jesus Christ.

These people, the most *influential*, are also the most *untouched* by the transforming message of the gospel. And it has greatly thrilled me that the Lord has drawn closer to me quite a number of young men and women of exceptional ability who are very serious about joining me in this work. But we do not seek only to reach the leaders in the various African parliaments, but would also seek to reach the masses by means of mass evangelism.

In addition, we desire to have a social emphasis in our ministry as well, because we are conscious that evangelical Christians in Africa have failed seriously in this area, and have presented a lop-sided message that has greatly ignored the social implications of the Lord's teachings. Consequently, to quite a great extent, they have lost the hearing of the people they are trying to reach; therefore, we feel it important to have a ministry to the physical needs of these people, as well as to their spiritual needs.

We also have in mind to do everything we can to promote understanding amongst people of all races; and this could be accomplished, to some extent, by supporting interracial conferences, house parties, camps, etc.

We are, of course, aware that there are many other organisations already at work in Africa, and there is nothing we want less than to become just another small group stumbling blindly around the continent. I am very aware, as the psalmist said, "That except the Lord build the house, they labour in vain that build it."

I am being extremely cautious in all of this, but so far, have had nothing but the encouraging signs to go ahead. A number of businessmen are showing a genuine interest, and prayer support is very readily forthcoming. You also asked me for my age. I am 23, going on 24 in September.

African Enterprise

Meanwhile, what to call his new "agency"? And when to start it? Michael and a South African friend, Murray Albertyn, were driving into the desert one day to preach in a church near Palm

Springs, several hours east of Los Angeles, and were mulling things over together. Murray was sure of one thing:

> Mike, you must not wait for years to get this going. You are in America for four years – utilise this time. Get some friends together and draw up a mailing list of supporters. Don't leave it until you are out of Fuller, and on your own. As you preach in churches here as a student, begin to collect a mailing list of supporters.

Michael nodded. It was good advice. "But what should I call it?" For some time he had been vaguely toying with "African Leadership" because Vereide's great work in Washington, DC, was called ICL – International Christian Leadership. But Michael was talking about Africa. So why not African Christian Leadership? No. Africa for Christ? No. With the memory of his mother's reactions to hyper-religious phraseology, Michael was cautious not to adopt anything that might sound "corny" to a non-Christian.

"My strategy for the name was not to have anything that could alienate anyone, or offend anyone." Names such as "Revival Gospel Crusade" would tie some folk in knots, never mind the name of some of the missions he had worked with in the southern states, for example the Beefhide Gospel Mission, or with the congregation improbably labelled "Hell for Certain" – named after the swampy creek that ran behind it. "When I thought of telling my mother that I was working with the Beefhide Gospel Mission, or preaching at Hell for Certain, I knew she'd have walked on broken glass to get me out of the place. But those amazing folks, mainly tough Bible- and gun-carrying single women working in those dangerous mountains of Kentucky, were really something." But not a name like that for his work! So he decided to have a name that was free from any Christian sub-culture.

Murray Albertyn was silent for a bit and then said: "You know, there is a ship that sails from Africa to the States called the *African Enterprise*. What about that?"

They drove on about half a mile. Why not indeed? Michael rolled it around in his head for a few more minutes and said, "Yes, why not?"

So that was that! African Enterprise. It sounded good. Nice ring to it. Rolled easily off the tongue.

Back at Fuller Seminary the following week, Michael told the Africa prayer group of the Students Mission Fellowship that he'd finally named the "work". He was going to call it African Enterprise. But he forgot to say where he had got the name from. The following week one of the girls in the group was driving near Los Angeles harbour and was astonished to see a vast warehouse with "African Enterprise" painted in four-foot-high letters along about 100 yards of its side. She jumped to a hasty conclusion: "Wow, that Michael Cassidy with his African Enterprise is really a mover!"

Well, he was, but not quite that fast. Nevertheless Michael had become aware that it was time to take the next step. After his many weeks of prayer that summer, "I had a deeper walk with God, and I began to find that God would sometimes speak to me in very clear ways – not exactly audible, but clear. Now the prompting came: 'Next summer, I want you to *go* around the cities of Africa.'"

So out came the atlas again. Michael pinpointed the major cities and sat back with a deep breath. This trip would take him clear round the African continent. Where was the money coming from to pay for all this? He had no idea. He was working each night in the seminary library for $14 a week just to earn pocket money for things like razor blades and toothpaste.

"Well, I need to test this out." Was this his imagination, or a leading from God? So as not to be swayed by anyone's enthusiasm, he decided: "I won't tell anyone." Instead, he went along to a travel agent in Pasadena and explained he wanted to book two tickets that would take him and a companion to Africa. If he was going to go on such a reconnaisance trip, he knew he shouldn't go alone.

"Fine," said the travel agent, pencil poised. "Where do you want to go?"

Michael handed him his list: Tripoli, Tunis, Casablanca, Dakar, Conakry, Freetown, Monrovia, Abidjan, Accra, Lagos, Léopoldville, Elisabethville, Johannesburg, Salisbury, Zomba, Blantyre, Nairobi, Addis Ababa, Asmara, Cairo, London, and then back to Los Angeles.

Bill Lescher, the travel agent, swallowed hard, put down his pencil, and then said slowly: "All these cities. You want to go *all the way around Africa?*"

"Yep."

Lescher blinked. "Fine. Yes. Okay. Of course. Er – where do you want to start?"

"Well," Michael thought for a moment, "why not at the top?"

"Ah – what's up there?"

They dug out a map.

Libya. "We'll begin our trip round Africa at Tripoli," Michael announced coolly, as if it were something one did every day.

Tripoli, the agent wrote down. Then he hesitated again. "Er – which way next – do you want to go clockwise or anti-clockwise?"

Michael shrugged. "Why not anti-clockwise?"

And so the trip was planned. From Los Angeles to Washington, DC, to London, to Rome, and then on to Tripoli and Tunis, before dropping down through the capitals of the West and Central African countries, into South Africa, before heading north through East Africa, and finally out through Addis Ababa, Asmara and Cairo.

Lescher scribbled furiously away, perplexity and amazement etched into the lines of his friendly face. He began to look strained by the time he totalled up the cost. He at last gave Michael a look that said that though he might be a seminary student, it was obvious that John D. Rockefeller or some other millionaire must be his father.

Michael didn't disillusion him. Nevertheless, "I walked out of there feeling heady. I had just booked a trip that would cost thousands, and I hadn't got a dime."

One person who was a constant recipient of Michael's almost daily confidences was his professor Carlton Booth, who would become a member of the AE board. Thus a 1961 diary entry recorded: "Shared God's working with dear Dr Booth. His ecstatic response was a joy and encouragement to witness. That man means so much to me." Booth was to remain a board member, wise counsellor, and great friend of Michael's until his death more than 30 years later.

Trip to Africa

For the next few months, Michael continued to pray for his 31 cities, and to pray also about the proposed trip. Nothing much happened. Then one day his friend Ed Gregory drew him to one side, looking excited and slightly apprehensive at the same time.

"Mike, I need to talk to you." Ed took a deep breath and then announced with tremendous importance and gravity: "Mike, I believe God wants us to go to Africa next summer."

Michael sat there poker-faced for a moment. Then he said: "Well, actually, Ed, we're already booked!" As his face gave way to a great mischievous grin, Ed exploded with joy.

As a throwaway reply, it had dramatic effect. "Ed's face! He thought he was bringing me a mighty revelation. In fact all he was doing was confirming my feeling that he would indeed be my travelling companion." Though Michael enjoyed playing it cool, inside he was tremendously thankful to God for such an obvious confirmation that he was indeed on the right track. "I needed that, because at the moment in my life, I could not afford to make any mistakes."

Of course, two penniless seminary students being convinced that they should travel around Africa did not actually bring either of them any closer to being able to afford it.

With his excitement increasing daily, Michael wrote in his diary: "It is my most fervent prayer that African Enterprise should stand as a living testimony to the reality of a miracle-working God in the 20th century and beyond, if the Lord tarry."

Then he added a doxology of spiritual devotion: "My Jesus, I am thine, for the intelligence of it, for the safety of it, and for the sheer delight of it."

In the months that followed, Michael and Ed told people about their proposed 50,000 km trip, but purposely did not mention their urgent need for money. That was a matter between them and God alone. Nobody else mentioned money either – only poor Bill Lescher, the travel agent, who kept asking when they intended to pay. Michael smiled and said Bill should relax. The situation finally became critical, as the day for their departure sped closer. Finally, with only 48 hours to go, Charles Fuller called for Michael. Curious, Michael went along to his office.

Fuller came out from behind his desk, and stood facing Michael. He had a sombre smile on his face: "Michael, I don't know about your finances for this trip, but the Lord has laid it on my heart to pay for your tickets to Africa." Michael could scarcely believe the news, and was dazed as Dr Fuller presented him with a cheque for several thousand dollars.

"After I'd thanked him best I could, I grabbed Ed, and we raced round to the travel agent. 'Bill,' we said, 'come at once, we are taking you to lunch.' So we took him to a café, told him the story, and handed him the cheque we had been given that morning. Bill burst into tears. Right there in the restaurant!"

Two days later Michael and Ed left California and made one important visit in Washington, DC before heading overseas. It happened that, after the brief 1960 meeting in Washington, Dr Abraham Vereide, head of International Christian Leadership, had written to Michael and said: "Come to DC and address a luncheon of all African ambassadors to the United States."

Dr Vereide had taken to the young South African immediately, delighted to meet a young man of such promise who shared his call to minister to the *leaders* of a country. He had been excited by Michael's vision for a work aimed specifically at the leadership of urban Africa. He had accordingly invited Michael in early 1961 to attend the Presidential Prayer Breakfast to be addressed by the new young President, John F. Kennedy, who had just taken office, and by Billy Graham. The day after the breakfast Vereide called Michael to meet with him privately. He looked at him with solemn, far-seeing eyes.

Vereide said slowly and deliberately: "Michael, you are a man of destiny. The leaders of Africa, you must never forget them." The words came almost as a divine injunction. "Oh! How my heart sang to my God as I saw His hand opening 'undreamable about' doors," said an entry in Michael's journal.

Michael had been confused and embarrassed, yet overwhelmed, sensing Dr Vereide really meant what he said. "It baffled me. I was only 25." Michael told no one of this meeting but wondered long and hard what it might all mean.

Now, as Michael and Ed prepared to leave on their tour of Africa, Dr Vereide was making contact again and putting forth every effort to speed them on their way with the best support possible. Incredibly, considering they were no more than a couple of seminary students in their early twenties, he organised a luncheon in the US Senate dining room for the African ambassadors. Lieutenant General Silverthorn and Admiral Morris led the meeting and then turned it over to young Michael Cassidy.

Michael stood up, took a deep breath, and shared his vision for what African Enterprise would try to do. He began by saying that the destiny of Africa would be settled by its leaders and the twelve per cent of people at that time who lived in its cities: "I told them we wanted to serve Africa and to serve Christ, and Africa was in danger from communism. I never thought about African Enterprise as merely an individual soul-saving exercise, but as a strategy to win a continent and its leadership for Christ, and so ideologically influence millions of its people for good."

The response of the African ambassadors was "quite mind-boggling... I felt like a spectator to something God was doing." They opened up their countries to the two students, giving them contacts that would ensure they could get straight through to the top. Abraham Vereide and Doug Coe filled out the list with many astonishing contacts and open doors.

Four days after arriving in Washington, on 18 June 1961, Michael and Ed flew to London. There they caught the flight for Rome, and then south to Africa, their first stop being Tripoli in Libya. During the next three months, Michael and Ed travelled some 50,000 km around Africa, visiting virtually every major city on the continent. During June and July alone, they went on to visit Tunis in Tunisia, Casablanca in Morocco, Dakar in Senegal, Conakry in Guinea, Freetown in Sierra Leone, Monrovia in Liberia, Abidjan in Côte d'Ivoire, Accra in Ghana, Lagos in Nigeria, Léopoldville (now Kinshasa) and Elisabethville (now Lubumbashi) in the Congo, Brazzaville in the Republic of the Congo, and ending up in Johannesburg. They spent all of August in South Africa, and in early September continued up to Central and East Africa: Salisbury in Rhodesia (now Harare, Zimbabwe), Blantyre and Zomba in Malawi, Nairobi in Kenya, Addis Ababa in Ethiopia, Asmara in Eritrea and finally Cairo in Egypt.

The strategy was always the same: on arrival in a city, Michael and Ed would try and seek out any politicians or other leaders they had been told about. Nothing whatever was set up in advance, and to any foreign diplomat the scheme would have seemed mad. Never mind. It worked. Especially in Sierra Leone, where Michael simply rang the foreign minister and the prime minister, Sir Milton Margai, dropped the right names – and was invited round straight away. "We walked straight in – it was totally wild!" In Kenya it was the famous Tom Mboya, leader of the opposition. In Ethiopia it was the crown prince, heir to the throne of Emperor Haile Selassie. Once in, Michael and Ed would introduce themselves as a couple of young seminary students who felt they wanted to come and make a contribution to mission in Africa. How did their host, as a political leader, or a royal, see the situation in his own country, and how could such a contribution meaningfully be made to his own people?

Almost always, the leader would say that any Christian work needed to be done in the cities, because all traditional missionary work had been in the rural areas, and important and fine as that had been, the need was now in the cities of Africa. This was said to Michael time after time after time. It filled him with great inward excitement: "I was getting the sustained reassurance coming from these political leaders that what I thought was my call from God was right." What he heard about South Africa's reputation in black Africa, though, deeply saddened him. One foreign minister told Michael that the South African so-called "Christian" government had seriously harmed the name of Christianity throughout the continent, and had won much sympathy for Islam.

Michael and Ed also searched out the cities' leading businessmen, church leaders and missionaries. Some of the situations in which Christians toiled away touched the two young men deeply. In Tripoli they could find only two missionaries, a man and wife, who had soldiered on quietly for years, at "incredible sacrifice" to themselves, and with little visible fruit.

As the weeks and cities sped by, Michael filled page after page in his diary and notebooks with observations and comments. "My eyes and ears were very tuned to watch for any signals. I wanted to hear anything God was saying to me." Certainly the tumultuous life of these great African cities filled both Michael and Ed with excited anticipation. "We looked at the needs, the opportunities, and were challenged to the depths of our beings. So many opportunities!" The rate of development in black Africa was phenomenal. Michael wrote in his diary: "The South African nationalists are crazy if they really think the clock can stand still!"

The potential for effecting change if the leadership circles within those cities could be reached was clearly "enormous". And what an unparalleled chance the media would give one! Everywhere people had transistor radios, and were eager to read anything they could get hold of. "Here was a continent still largely uncommitted. It had not yet chosen its ultimate spiritual and ideological destiny. It was still mightily and profoundly open to the Gospel of Christ."

By the end of that summer, Michael wrote in his diary of "much excitement and gratitude in my heart that we have pulled it off, this African tour, due to His power and mercy". He also knew: "I can never be the same again, for God has made his call irrevocably and indelibly clear to me."

50 Years of Ministry

On the morning of 18 July 1961, while staying at Radio ELWA in Liberia, as the team had a strong developing interest in Christian radio, Michael went for a long solitary walk along the beach. When he and Ed weren't actually meeting people or travelling, Michael spent a lot of time by himself. "The Lord had become so real to me that summer, that I wanted hours alone with him in prayer." In his diary, Michael wrote: "I know he has called us, and heard our prayers, and that we stand on the edge of something enormous."

Suddenly, on impulse, Michael drew a vast outline of Africa in the sand. He scrawled: "Claimed for Jesus Christ" inside it. He stepped back – it looked great, but also an enormous challenge. So as he resumed his walk, "I also asked God for 50 years of ministry in Africa – a year for every state then on the African continent. As I walked along I jabbed a trail of 50 marks on the sand – a mark for every year of ministry I wanted in Africa from God."

But where in all of Africa should they have their first city-wide campaign? In which one of these 31 major cities should they first focus? Michael and Ed had no idea, and again made it a matter of prayer. As they reached Lagos, Nigeria, on the tour,

Michael was considering the matter afresh and praying constantly, "Lord – where will the first city for us be?"

On 1 August 1961, in a round thatched hut in Lagos, during a torrential tropical thunderstorm, the answer was suddenly shot back at him, almost audibly: "Pietermaritzburg". Michael had been reading in Acts 18 about Paul standing frightened and nervous before the challenge of the pagan city of Corinth. Then the Lord of Power and of the Great Commission speaks to him: "Do not be afraid, but speak and do not be silent: for I am with you and no man shall attack you to harm you: for I have many people in this city" (vv. 9–10).

It was a confirming word and a defining moment. Cities were to be the focus of Michael's call. He had first got this word in the basement of Madison Square Garden in 1957.

Which would be the first? "Pietermaritzburg," came back the Inner Voice. "Maseru," Michael's hometown in Basutoland, was also somewhere in the whisper. But "Pietermaritzburg" was the louder word. Michael wrote "Maseru and Pietermaritzburg – 1st August 1961" in the margin of his Bible. Maseru would come in 1966. But Pietermaritzburg would happen the following year. Michael, in his rain-drenched hut in Lagos, was not to know that just yet.

Michael was at first astonished. "After all those weird and wonderful cities we'd seen!" Pietermaritzburg was not even on his list of 31 cities at all. It was the capital of the South African province of Natal, but rather off the beaten track, one hour inland from the much larger city of Durban and relatively near the southern tip of Africa, about as far away from Lagos and Central Africa as you could get.

Three Students and Calvin Cook

As it happened, the tour did take Michael and Ed to Pietermaritzburg, where some students had invited Michael to speak at the university. Though so terrified he couldn't eat for days beforehand, the meeting with a jammed auditorium turned out to be electrifying. So much so that the three inviting students: Jenny Comrie, Ivor Glass and Marjorie Watling, rushed out the next day on impulse and in extravagant faith booked the Pietermaritzburg City Hall for two weeks the following 10–24 August, with the city stadium booked for a final rally on August 25. "We want you back next year for a citywide mission," said the three intrepid young adventurers.

They then took the startled Michael and Ed to meet Dr Calvin Cook, the local Presbyterian pastor, who on the strength of the students' urging invited Michael to preach in his church that Sunday. The young fellow did alright.

Weeks later at the ministers' fraternal, Dr Cook would tell the ministers, who had been exploring the idea of a citywide mission, "I think the time has come for the churches of Pietermaritzburg to take a major risk. Let's not go for the big names we've been thinking of inviting. Let's invite this kid and his friends!"

Calvin Cook, set in due time to become AE's longest-standing friend and counsellor in South Africa, then sat back to see what would become of this wildest of ideas.

At the end of the tour, Michael and Ed parted company in Cairo, Ed having to hurry home for family reasons, while Michael made two other stops. The first was to Trans World Radio (TWR) in Monte Carlo to connect again with Paul Freed, founder of TWR, who along with Bob Bowman of Far Eastern Broadcasting Corporation (FEBC) was firing the young AE team with a vision for Christian Radio. The second stop was in France at the Palace of Versailles to join Abraham Vereide and Doug Coe at a conference for European leadership. Each experience further fired Michael's dreams and visions for the African ministry.

Returning to Pasadena

Returning to Fuller Seminary that autumn of 1961, Michael felt like he'd stepped back into another universe. Pasadena was a far cry from the teeming streets of Tripoli, Casablanca, Accra and Cairo. Much as Michael loved his studies at Fuller, it was difficult at times that winter to concentrate completely on them, as he was faced with the continual challenge of getting the fledgling African Enterprise ministry off the ground.

He had two main priorities for his remaining two years at seminary: to establish a financial support base and to lay the foundations of an administrative infrastructure in the USA that could support the work. One of his professors, Dr George Ladd, noticing these priorities, commented, "Don't forget, Mike, you are here primarily to study!" No, he didn't forget that and resolved to keep up a good B+ average, which he did!

One day he received another summons to go and see Dr Fuller, who had something amazing to say to him.

> Mike, I have received an unusual leading from God. I feel burdened to help you get started with this vision of yours for Africa. So I am making you this offer: I will put the administrative services of my office at your disposal, lend you a little money, which you can pay back when you can, and I have three people in mind who could be the core of a little board – two Christian businessmen who are friends of mine, Bruce Bare and James Gorton, and my secretary, Rose Baessler. You add to the board as you want to, then get a leaflet out saying what you want to do, and then go to it!

Michael asked Dr Fuller for time in which to reflect on his astonishing offer. Was this to be the way forward? Six weeks later in the Christmas vacation and while at an InterVarsity house party at Lake Tahoe in northern California, Michael stood late one night in prayer by the lapping water's edge. The moon was shining brightly over the Sierra Nevada Mountains. The Lord seemed very present. Prompting. Positive. Suddenly Michael knew. He felt that, yes, this was the right thing to do. He would gratefully accept Dr Fuller's offer. The old evangelist beamed approval when Michael told him some weeks later. They proceeded to set up a board along the lines Dr Fuller had suggested, for sketching out the future administrative infrastructure for African Enterprise. In future years, AE was to be incredibly grateful for the wisdom, guidance and help that these three people gave it. Bruce Bare, who was an insurance man and a deeply dedicated Christian, became known as the "Father" of AE in the USA, and was to make nearly 60 trips to Africa at his own expense over the following 35 years.

In the meantime, it seemed that African Enterprise was going to have some more members on its actual working team. For four other students at Fuller were growing more and more convinced that this was to be their future work as well.

Paul Birch was a Canadian with degrees in English literature from the University of British Columbia, an education diploma in English and mathematics and a licentiate degree in music from the University of Toronto. He was also an associate of the Royal Conservatory of Toronto and an accomplished pianist and organist. Rightly believing that music was vital to any outreach ministry, he was keen to put his musical talents to the use of AE missions by directing the music, as well as taking part in follow-up teaching.

Dick Peace and his wife Judy were from Detroit, Michigan. Dick had graduated *cum laude* with a degree in electrical engineering from Yale University, where he also did geological research. After some secular work, the call had come to him to go into fulltime Christian ministry, and so Dick had come to Fuller to work on a theology degree. His main interests would focus on pre- and post-mission lay training. A very gifted speaker, Dick was also keenly interested in modern communications media.

Christian Smith was from Princeton, New Jersey, and his wife Barbara had been Miss Arizona and placed third in the Miss America contest! Chris, as he was known, held a Masters degree in electronics from Rutgers University in New Jersey, and had taught it at university level, before going into engineering research with the Jet Propulsion Laboratory in Pasadena, where he had worked on the Mariner space probe to Mars. In AE missions he would serve as general administrator and also as master of ceremonies, choir director and inspirational song-leader on the missions.

Then there was Donald Ehat, from Boston, Massachusetts, and his wife Joyce. Don was a brilliant organiser who had received extensive crusade training under Jerry Bevan of the Billy Graham team. He had a magic way with people and could inspire teamwork and co-ordination planning as he helped the fledgling team think through on its goals and strategies.

All were high-fliers and independent-minded men. They saw themselves not as going to work for Michael in any way, but as a group who had been called by God to come alongside Michael to do a specific job and share in the task. They would soon discover that they were, in fact, a team with complementary gifts, and with a good deal of interdependence.

All five young men now set to with ferocious energy to gather financial and prayer support for African Enterprise. To do this, they would need to approach as many churches as possible, asking for a chance to speak to the congregations, and then to leave with them leaflets setting forth their vision for the ministry, and what supporters could do to help. So the first task was to write down the AE vision in a mission statement that would tell people what they were about, and thus set out their stall in the most coherent, professional manner possible. All five had a passion for excellence, and were determined that their organisation would be run along the most professional lines possible.

So, throughout the autumn of 1961 and into early 1962, Michael and the new AE team were out talking wherever they could about AE, and handing out leaflets that introduced and explained the work.

Charles Fuller backed AE publicly, saying, "The AE team has a unique approach to the missionary thrust in Africa as a whole. I am convinced this project is truly of God, and I commend these young men to you." This commendation from such a famous evangelist and household name gave the five young beginners the leg-up they often needed.

It wasn't long before invitations from churches in the area began to pour in, and soon Michael and the team were almost over-busy with speaking engagements at many Presbyterian, Baptist and independent churches in the Los Angeles area.

Michael in his talks would begin by describing modern Africa. He would project a slide of an ultra-modern city that many in the congregation would mistake for New York or Chicago and then be amazed to learn it was Africa. For modern Africa was more than "grass huts, spears, and the cries of Tarzan. Of course much in Africa is primitive, dark and precarious, but this is very emphatically only part of the story. Modern Africa is where the stone age and the jet age walk hand in hand. In Conakry, Guinea, one sweeping glance can take in mud streets, shanty bazaars and the towering splendour of the Hôtel de France."

Modern Africa was certainly on the move – some cities had increased in population by 30 per cent in as little as ten years, with people seeking a better life away from their tribal homelands. But what these semi-Westernised Africans actually found were immense social and spiritual problems. They'd lost their tribal society, but had no way of integrating into the complexity of industrial life. The result was broken families, widespread crime and promiscuity, alcoholism, violence, and almost total social breakdown. The city-dwellers of modern Africa also became natural candidates for communist and other exploitation.

As for African leaders, they faced enormous burdens – and temptations. Michael outlined these for his audiences:

> For them, country often means more than conscience, the political more than the spiritual, the temporal more than the eternal. In Africa today the rise of many leaders has been meteoric. Men have been catapulted into power by one of the most rapid social and political revolutions of all time. It has been an intoxicating and sometimes unbalancing experience, and resisting temptations to a grandiloquence not far short of deity has not been easy.

For example, Kwame Nkrumah of Ghana had called himself "Osagyefo" or Redeemer, and announced that he would not mind if some Christian hymns were used to praise him, substituting his name for Christ's. His statue in Accra was inscribed: "Seek first the political kingdom and all other things will be added unto you."

"In the light, then, of the fact that so few are influencing the ideological allegiance of so many, it becomes startlingly evident that the winning of the leadership circles to Christ is a task of the utmost urgency and significance," Michael would stress again and again.

"We believe that it is just at this point that Christianity's greatest relevance to African nationalism can be demonstrated. If the leader is committed to Christ, he will see to it that his nationalism, as well as that of his followers, is expressed within the ethical limits prescribed by this Christian commitment."

Many of those Californian Presbyterian, Baptist and independent churches saw the point of what the budding young evangelists were saying. As the months went by, the list of people willing to support AE began to grow.

Chapter 6

The Mission to Maritzburg Turning Point

By now Michael had talked about African Enterprise for two years. Then, near the end of 1961, an invitation suddenly came – to *act*.

A letter arrived from the Ministers' Fraternal of Pietermaritzburg. It was written by Dr Calvin Cook, the Presbyterian minister of that city (and later Moderator of the Presbyterian Church of Southern Africa and Professor of Ecclesiastical History at Rhodes University in Grahamstown, South Africa), who the previous summer had daringly proposed to the Ministers' Fraternal that Michael and his little team come to the city for a major interdenominational evangelistic campaign. Now Dr Cook was writing to ask if African Enterprise would instead come and conduct, on behalf of all the churches in the city, a citywide mission.

Michael felt tremendous excitement, and a sense of how right this was: God had given him the city-focused vision for AE, and had told him Pietermaritzburg would be the city for the first mission. The team were electrified. This was it!

In the months that followed, Michael Cassidy, Dick Peace, Paul Birch, Chris Smith and Don Ehat spent all their spare time in between arduous studies preparing for the mission. Ehat was a crucial ally, having had experience of being an intern with the Billy Graham Evangelistic Association. Don was an administrative genius, trained by Jerry Bevan, the man who had built the Graham ministry's amazing organisational structures. Don's gifts also tied in splendidly with those of the mission chairman in Pietermaritzburg, Archie Hart, the assistant city engineer, and one day to become Dean of the School of Psychology at Fuller Seminary. His links to Fuller in fact started with this encounter with the AE team. Many years later he would chair the AE board in the United States.

The mission was to be held the following 11–25 August 1962. It was the first-ever citywide mission Pietermaritzburg had ever attempted and possibly the first of its kind ever in South Africa. It was clearly of fundamental importance for the fledgling AE. It was their big chance. If they got this wrong, their reputation would be tarnished and they would be rendered ineffectual before they even began.

Objectives

Objectives for the mission were drawn up with meticulous care. The team did not want a mission that would go off like a firecracker but leave little trace of its existence afterwards. They wanted something that would kickstart the churches in Pietermaritzburg into growth, but also help set in place church programmes that would nurture the young Christians born in the mission. The team would leave nothing to chance. Their list, so revealing in its professional approach to mission, is worth reprinting here in full.

It ran as follows:

a. All AE promotional, evangelistic, and contact work has one basic objective – to help men and women develop a personal sense of responsibility for sharing the Gospel within the context of their normal, everyday lives.
b. AE believes that to realise this objective the Christians of Pietermaritzburg will need to receive help to:
   1. develop confidence in the use of the Bible
   2. develop close personal Christian friendships
   3. schedule fellowship with men and women of like understanding
   4. help their early converts experience "success" in their early Christian experience
   5. identify with a church
   6. identify with AE
   7. understand the concept of stewardship of time and money

 c. AE seeks to establish a favourable public image in the eyes of:
  1. South African denominations
  2. South African national government
  3. South African missions, both interdenominational and denominationally oriented
  4. South African universities and professional educational groups
  5. American support within churches, etc.
 d. AE seeks to build a working group of faithful indigenous African supporters
 e. AE seeks a broad base of popular support within Africa, through personal relationships with African nationals of all races
 f. AE seeks to develop an extensive mailing list of interested persons in Africa, Europe and the US
 g. AE seeks to establish good precedents for city missions in the minds of church leaders throughout Africa. It is hoped that what has been done successfully in one place will be adopted in similar situations in other places.

It was a big list, with big ambitions. Meanwhile, the donkey work for the Pietermaritzburg mission was underway. There is more to mission than preaching: the team set about securing passports, tourist visas and vaccinations. Poor Bill Lescher, the travel agent, now had to take a deeper breath than ever as the impecunious young Michael came in, this time booking not two tickets to Africa and back, but five! Bill's faith in both God and man was about to be taxed again to its outer limits.

As the preparations proceeded, the North Americans began reading up on South Africa, continued to seek churches to support them financially and in prayer, copied in duplicate and then in triplicate their slideshow for itineration, and planned tentative routes and dates.

This was the age, of course, of the great Billy Graham Crusades, where one personality was used to attract people into coming to a large rally. Don Ehat decided therefore to "personalise" their mission, and a photograph of Michael was printed on large fliers posted up all over Pietermaritzburg. They announced:

The Churches of Maritzburg invite you to hear

MICHAEL CASSIDY
A Man With A Message

each evening at 7.45
from 13–25 August in the City Hall
*a message relevant to our time
*something vital for you
* all are invited to attend
Don't miss an evening!
United Churches Mission to PIETERMARITZBURG – UCMM

Other fliers announced Michael as "A Man for the Heart of Africa".

Sometimes the team paused to wonder exactly what they had taken on: "It seemed the height of presumption for a team of students who had never done anything like this before to take the City Hall of Maritzburg for two weeks when it had never been previously filled for more than two days! But the embryonic vision needed a good lift off to give it substance and truly launch it on its way."

Departure

With summer exams at Fuller over and the panting Bill Lescher satisfactorily paid in full, the Lord having worked this amazing provision once again, the team flew out to Africa, and flung themselves into last-minute preparation – and cultural acclimatisation. None but Michael had even been in Africa before, and Pietermaritzburg was very different from Los Angeles! Day after day leading up to the mission the advance team were rushed around Pietermaritzburg, meeting church leaders, speaking at small church meetings, and getting a feel for the city until they felt almost dazed. Michael, needing time to rest, recover from the term, and prepare all his mission talks, came later by sea from Southampton via Cape Town and Durban.

As the *Cape Town Castle* liner left Southampton, God gave Michael a verse for the summer which he excitedly recorded in his diary. It was the prayer of Jabez from 1 Chronicles 4:10: "And

Jabez called on the God of Israel saying, Oh that thou wouldst bless me indeed and enlarge my coast, and that thine hand might be with me and that thou wouldst keep me from evil, that it may not grieve me! And God granted his request." In the margin of his Bible by the reference he wrote: "*Cape Town Castle* – July 1962." That was to be the prayer for him – for blessing, the enlarging of his coast, the hand of God, and protection from evil.

The day the ship finally docked in Durban, the readings in Michael's little *Daily Light* devotional book included Acts 18:10, the verse about Paul and Corinth given to Michael the previous year during the torrential thunderstorm in Lagos: "Do not be afraid, but speak and do not be silent: for I am with you and no man shall attack you to harm you; for I have many people in this city."

For the inevitably anxious young beginner evangelist it was confirmation, if ever there was one, and a word to calm his involuntary nerves.

Michael's faith, however, was strong. On arriving in Maritzburg, one lady from a local church alarmingly said to him: "You've booked this City Hall for two whole weeks. Sheer madness! Young man, you don't know Pietermaritzburg!"

"Madam," replied Michael in one of his cheekier responses, "you don't know God!"

Curiously enough the first-ever evangelistic meeting the team were to hold was in the Durban City Hall some days before the Mission to Maritzburg began. The invitation had come from Youth for Christ (YFC).

The occasion was an inauspicious baptism of fire for one and all in the AE team, especially Michael.

The Durban City Hall was packed out with 3,000 young people and it looked to Michael to be a nightmare. YFC wanted an "open appeal", inviting people to come forward and commit themselves to Christ publicly on the spot at the end of the meeting. It was not a method with which Michael at that stage felt comfortable. He did not think he could pull it off. He was, at that point, more in favour of John Stott's method. This famous Anglican clergyman of All Souls Church, Langham Place, in London, favoured a low-key approach and, after preaching, simply said that anyone who wanted to know more about the

Christian faith was welcome to stay behind after the service for further information. This seemed to work well and required less audacity!

Reluctantly, Michael finally agreed to the insistent YFC wishes, and after "preaching my heart out", gave the appeal while the choir sang "Just As I Am", which had already become Billy Graham's trademark appeal hymn. No one came forward. Feeling he was being hanged in public, Michael asked the choir to sing it again. No one in all that crowd of 3,000 moved. In desperation, Michael did what he never thought he would be forced to stoop to, as he croaked: "We are going to sing 'Just as I Am' for the last time."

In the very last line of the very last verse of that final, desperate appeal, with Michael just about dying at every syllable, two people at the back of the hall finally stumbled forward to the front. One was an amiable rolling drunk, and one was a skinny little schoolboy.

Michael went back to Pietermaritzburg that night depressed and so utterly shaken by the experience that he just wanted to crawl into a deep hole and die. Years later, in the mid-1980s, he met a dynamic pastor at an AE conference who bounded up to him and reminded him of that terrible night back in 1962 when only two people came forward. The last thing Michael wanted was to remember that nightmarish evening. "I was the young boy that came forward that night!" the pastor exclaimed. "I went on into the ministry and now I train evangelists!" Added a chastened Michael: "It was a reminder to me never to despise the smallest response, and never forget the scriptural principle that God's Word which goes forth does not return void. You may not see the result, but it is there. The Lord is faithful."

Opening Night

Finally came the opening night of African Enterprise's first ever mission. It was a solemn moment. Michael spent most of the day in prayer. Tonight was what he had been working towards for the past two years. Could he really succeed as an evangelist? Especially after the disaster of Durban just a few days previously?

Over and over in his head that summer, Michael had tested

each link of the chain that had led him to this evening. Each one held fast and strong. As far as he knew, there had been no mis-judgements, no wrong decisions. He had no doubt that this was where he belonged, and that God had indeed called AE into exis-tence for just such an event. As the hours sped by towards the first evening meeting, Michael was keyed up, but mercifully not terrified. He felt he was on the verge of the beginning of the rest of his life. This was what he had been born to do.

By early evening Pietermaritzburg was convulsed with a traffic jam at an unusual hour, and in an unusual direction: the roads leading *down* to the City Hall were streaming with people. Cars coasted slowly through the crowds, seeking a place to park. By 7 pm the place was filled to capacity, and still people were cramming themselves in. Every seat was taken, every ledge, every spare inch of standing room. People of all denominations, of no denomination and no faith at all, and of all races were there. Incredibly, the city authorities turned a blind eye to the mixed-race event.

This was it: AE was at last open for business. As 7.30 pm arrived, the team sprang into action. Chris Smith bounced on to the stage to take his place as the irrepressible, warm-hearted master of ceremonies. Paul Birch supported him with an exu-berant selection of music that had the people singing with enthusiasm and gusto. And finally, at the appropriate moment, the mood was calmed and stilled, and Michael came on stage to preach his heart out on "The Person and Claims of Christ".

That first night was an overwhelming success. Dozens of people came forward after the meeting was over, making enquiries about becoming a Christian. The counsellors pro-vided by the local churches were kept very busy. Better still, that first night was not a freak event, for all the meetings through-out the mission were jammed. Night after night for two weeks people of all races and denominations came to the City Hall, generally filling it beyond capacity.

If the team were delighted, so were the local churches, who knew all too well that this was an extraordinary response for this particular city, and put the success of the mission down to the great amount of prayer, planning and dedication that had gone into it.

The team were especially touched to find their efforts had

reached into every stratum of Pietermaritzburg society, from household servants to university students and professors to professional men and women. Hundreds made commitments to Christ. This in turn encouraged the Pietermaritzburg churches, which woke up to find they now shared a common sense of purpose and unity.

Meanwhile, the AE team wrote home, saying: "How glorious it was to see the faithfulness of God. What we saw here went beyond all our expectations. Before the main meetings ever started, half our follow-up material was used up, and further orders had to be hurried out from England!"

Even those who had not intended to come to the meetings were caught up. One lad was on his way to a Scout meeting when he heard singing at the city hall. So he popped inside to see what was going on, committed his life to Christ, and later went into the ministry.

Chemistry professor George Quicke, chemist Milton Anley, lawyer Garnett Venn and housewife Sybil Jackson were among the many who responded and who would stand by the team for decades to come. Choirmaster and lecturer Ebenezer Sikakane brought his choir. One day he would join the team. So would David Peters, an Indian petrol station attendant, and his brother-in-law, Derick Bruce.

Unbeknown to the team at the time were two other conversions out of the mission which were to play a leading role in the future of African Enterprise itself. A couple called Rona and John Tooke were converted, and their friendship and support was to bring great riches to AE in the years ahead. John Tooke would become a leading player in the AE team and director one day of the AE Centre.

Mission Over

With the Pietermaritzburg mission over, the team visited many people including Alan Paton and Peter Brown, founders of the South African Liberal Party, and then in secret up the north coast of Natal with Albert Luthuli, the banned leader of the African National Congress. "The answer for South Africa," Luthuli told the young evangelists, "is the way of the Master."

Michael made a quick and heartwarming visit to Maseru to

see his family, and then travelled to Nairobi, Kenya, and Kampala, Uganda. Here he made three more key contacts for the future of African Enterprise. The first was with Rev Tom Houston, pastor of the Nairobi Baptist Church, who later headed the British and Foreign Bible Society, then World Vision and finally the Lausanne Movement. Tom would always be a good friend and astute counsellor to Michael and the team. The second contact was with William Nagenda, a leader in the famous East African Revival movement of Uganda. The third was with the Archbishop of Uganda, Leslie Brown.

The Revival movement had been a great force for revitalising the East African church and Michael wanted to know if AE might work with the leaders of the Revival at some future date. Michael admired much about the Revival, but thought some of its teaching had become too rule-driven. (For example, taking out insurance was seen as worldly and having a watchdog was seen as a failure of faith.)

But he was delighted with what he found in William Nagenda. Far from putting up barriers, Nagenda was natural and down to earth and astute enough to say that any AE evangelists to Kampala should be "men of God, well educated, well brought up and well able to handle themselves with politicians and diplomats". The gospel, William emphasised, should commend itself to the educated and cultured and not appear as if intended only for the poor and uneducated.

"I considered this a highly significant comment in the light of our own calling," Michael wrote in his diary. "These clearly are men we *can* work with." Just how closely AE would work with Ugandans converted through the Revival he never dreamed.

The Anglican Archbishop, Leslie Brown, was certainly not of the Revival movement, and indeed had "suffered at their hands", as he put it. (Some revivalists tended to dismiss those who were not wholeheartedly in the movement.) He greeted Michael politely, though warily, as behoves archbishops interviewing young Christians with big ideas! He asked Michael just exactly what were his intentions for this new organisation? After Michael had spoken for some minutes, the Archbishop leaned forward and interrupted him with a broad grin: "Look, I had a polite speech all prepared to decline you my help.

However, after what you've said, I want you to know that you have my support 100 per cent."

Michael was further challenged about the need for Christian radio in Africa when the archbishop reported to him that, while on safari recently, he had tried to get the BBC on his little transistor radio. No success. "However," he said, "I got Radio Moscow clearly in English on three separate wavelengths." Yes, the battle was on for the heart of Africa.

Michael was further astonished by the next stage in the conversation. As he wrote in his diary later:

> I then got on to my relationship with the Anglican Church, and my desire to get licensed as an Anglican lay-reader and thus have an Anglican credential for work in the denomination. I was astounded when the Archbishop said that on the basis of this conversation alone he would happily license me to preach anywhere in Uganda. This will give me a useful lever to use with South African Anglicans! Praise the Lord. We ended with prayer together and I went on my way rejoicing.

As Michael left Africa, his diary records that back in his heart again was the prayer of Jabez. Yes, they had certainly seen God bless and enlarge their coast and expand their territory. How faithful too had been his protective hand on the little team!

Back to California

Autumn 1962 was by now closing in, and it was time to head back to Pasadena for the final year at Fuller Seminary. That autumn, winter and then spring of 1963 was a time of intense and impatient activity as Michael, Chris, Paul, Dick and Don continued the task of laying a foundation of prayer and financial giving in the US and Canada – as well as keeping up with their academic work. A wide assortment of churches agreed to support the young work.

By the early summer 1963, four happy years of seminary were drawing to a close. All the team were awarded their Bachelor of Divinity degrees. The little team of five now had twelve degrees between them! In worldly terms they were qualified. But were they spiritually ready?

With studies and exams finally over, the relief was immense. At last the team were free to throw themselves entirely into getting AE up and running. Their tiny office just off the Fuller Seminary campus was now the headquarters of African Enterprise and became a scene of frenzied activity.

By June AE was a proper, legal corporation, with a list of bylaws, an executive director, eight board members, and five on the team. It looked like this:

Executive Director: Eugene Parks: Gene was a student at Fuller who wanted a part-time job. He was gearing up to be a military chaplain and once took Michael to preach at the Fort Lewis Army base in Washington state to young troops preparing to go out, probably as cannon fodder, to Vietnam

Board Members: Bruce Bare: Director of an insurance company

Miss Rose Baessler: Secretary to Dr Charles Fuller

Dr Carlton Booth: Professor of Evangelism at Fuller Seminary

Dr John Crouthamel: Senior Pastor of Central Baptist Church in downtown Los Angeles

James Gorton: Industrialist

Bill Gwinn: Director of Mount Hermon Christian Conference Centre near Santa Cruz, in northern California

Paul Winter: Civil Engineer

Team Members: Michael Cassidy, Paul Birch, Don Ehat, Dick Peace, Chris Smith

August 1963 went by in a blur of preparation. Michael reported for AE to its several hundred supporters:

With the smog struggling in vain to choke our enthusiasm, we are vigorously assaulting the mountain of things that must be done before the new year arrives, what with visas to acquire, support to raise, a small office to establish, the Canadian deputation trip to plan and a follow-up programme to develop for us in Africa, we are certainly being kept busy. However, in spite of all there is to do, each of us, I think, is conscious of the fact that all this activity and all this preparation will be nothing more than the "chariots of Egypt" (Isaiah 31:1) unless our basic trust is in God and his enabling power.

Midsummer brought more heat and smog – but also opportunities to gain more experience in evangelism. Michael joined in with the special evangelistic endeavours of Dr Leighton Ford of the Billy Graham team in eastern Canada and later the whole team involved itself with the Billy Graham team in the Los Angeles Crusade. It was instructive, inspiring and valuable on-the-job training in evangelism, even though they did many menial jobs, from chauffeuring and stamp-licking to typing. In the closing rally, with well over 100,000 people in the Los Angeles Coliseum, Michael prayed: "Lord, how wonderful it would be one day to preach to a crowd like this!"

Yet the team longed most of all to get back to South Africa. As they told their supporters, they felt that "God is calling us to South Africa at a very crucial time in its history". An article in the *New York Times* had said, "We must face up to the incredible complexity of factors which make for disunity in this really exciting country, and be generous enough in our criticism to recognise that solutions must be found in evolution, not in revolution."

But Michael sadly added: "What strikes us, however, is the grim fact that the movement of evolution seems to be irrevocably set towards revolution. Some people give South Africa ten years, others are less optimistic."

Many questioning letters came in to the AE office that summer, as people tried to understand what this new little organisation was all about. In reply to one quite critical note, Michael wrote:

You ask whether AE will be "just another" Christian organisation. Yes, in that it is Christian and an organisation and made up of finite human beings who will not be exempt from temptations and failures. We can make no claim to any sort of spiritual infallibility. In another sense, I think we are fairly unique in our target, namely, the leadership circles of the African continent. At present no one else, as far as I know, has a real vision or concern for this section of the society.

Secondly, we are fairly unique in the personnel on the team. All are not only highly qualified men, but also independent thinkers who are constantly willing to evaluate and adapt. The team members will always insure that the message of Christ be presented in a way which is calculated to earn the serious consideration of thinking people. The team, as I see it, is dedicated both to scholarly principles and to simple piety, a combination which I believe is entirely biblical and proper.

In the third place, AE has some degree of uniqueness in its attitudes of openness, sanity, unconditional acceptance of others, and in its strong desire to unite rather than divide God's people.

As the autumn of 1963 sped by, the team's growing popularity with other evangelists could have been a great distraction. Thus Michael reluctantly refused an invitation from Leighton Ford to join him and work for Billy Graham Evangelistic Association (BGEA). Said Leighton: "Michael, everything Billy has given and opened up to me I will give and open up to you." The offer was overwhelming. But Michael knew he had to head to Africa and start from scratch and without the huge resources of the BGEA. Chris Smith, for his part, also reluctantly refused an offer of an internship with the Billy Graham team in Boston. Both felt their priority now must be to raise enough support to get back to Africa.

The Problem of Finances

For the African Enterprise team were up against a major problem with which they were to become all too familiar over the years to come: lack of money, and the difficulty of raising support. There were a number of reasons for this.

First of all, African Enterprise was interdenominational. That meant that no one powerful body of churches "owned" it, and when it came to missionary budgets, the vast majority of churches simply gave to their own denomination's work.

Second, AE's focus on evangelism did not have the sheer

heart-tug of relief work: there were no starving babies on the front of AE literature. And evangelism in association with many denominations was not seen as a great need for, in America, the denominations tended to support their own denominational evangelistic programmes.

Third, African Enterprise was so young and unknown compared with the great number of other Christian agencies, that most people tended to stick with giving to agencies they'd known for years, rather than switch loyalties, or increase their giving.

It was all very frustrating at times. Michael and the team knew how comparatively little they needed compared to other Christian work. In all the United States, only 300 people giving $10 a month would have underwritten AE for all of 1964, but could they find them?

These aspiring and gifted young men, who would have been on high salaries if they had used their skills in the secular job market, found themselves again and again brought up short by simple lack of money. In other walks of life, hard work and commitment usually bring financial reward, and a freedom to enjoy life free of financial worry. This would be a luxury unknown to the AE team. They would work long hours, month after month, year after year, for little financial reward, and certainly without long-term financial security. One of the problems was that Christians in South Africa would always assume Americans were funding AE, and Americans would feel South African churches should be doing much more.

So the appeal letters sent out to supporters in December 1963 were only the first of many to follow down the years: "Won't you consider your own part in this crucial ministry, and interest at least one friend and your church in AE?" For 1964/65, the total salaries for the whole team and their families ran to approximately $2,000 a month, plus $8,000 for the year's operating costs. "The weight of this financial undertaking is pressing hard upon us, so we are hopeful that our friends will consider this a most worthwhile investment in the Lord's work."

As late as April 1964 only a quarter of the sum needed had been pledged.

The AE team had great faith in God, but had decided to keep strict financial discipline and not return to Africa until their financial backing was in place: "We feel most acutely the urgency to return, but cannot do so until our support has been secured." The team were determined not to run into debt.

By now, several more churches had joined the AE support group, and things were looking more hopeful.

Two months to go, and with an enormous effort, somehow the pledged monthly support needed was raised. "We are grateful for God's faithfulness. We have just enough to manage, no more. We appreciate very much that which is given, none of which do we take for granted."

Setting Forth in Faith

Slowly, family by family, that spring and summer of 1964, the little AE team set forth in faith and began to move itself out to Pietermaritzburg. Five young men determined to preach the Christian gospel to the cities of Africa. So few – for so many. It seemed an absurdly extravagant dream. Michael knew his life's work was about to begin.

And faith was certainly needed, for they were leaving without the required residence visas from the South African authorities, which were still not forthcoming, even after months of waiting in the USA for them to be issued. This departure seemed folly to many, but Michael believed the team should press forward in faith. They sailed from New York on the SS *United States* with all their crates of belongings and household goods. While Chris and Barbie Smith and Paul Birch sailed through the Suez Canal to Beira in Mozambique, and thence overland to Salisbury to await their visas, Michael and Dick and Judy Peace travelled by air to Cairo, Khartoum, Addis Ababa (where Michael contracted the potentially deadly typhus), Nairobi and Salisbury. Without visas, they could not yet enter South Africa. Michael, still feeling weak and wretched from the typhus, flew on to Johannesburg to explore the visa situation in Pretoria.

The dream looked as if it could abort on a documentation problem.

No word about the visas from anywhere. They held on to Hebrews 11:8: "By faith Abraham obeyed when he was called to go out to a place which he was to receive as an inheritance: and he went out not knowing where he was to go."

Chapter 7   # Underway in Africa

On 6 October 1964, Michael Cassidy woke up feeling ill and desperate, in a little hotel in Johannesburg. His team were stranded far to the north in Salisbury, Rhodesia. He was very unwell. He had to gear up to go up to Pretoria to find out what was happening about the visas.

Hope and rescue came from his devotional reading for that morning, which was Deuteronomy 8. The whole chapter was reassuring, especially verses 5–10:

> Know then in your heart that, as a man disciplines his son, the Lord your God disciplines you. So you shall keep the commandments of the Lord your God, by walking in his ways and by fearing him. For the Lord your God is bringing you into a good land, a land of brooks of water, of fountains and springs, flowing forth in valleys and hills, a land of wheat and barley, of vines and fig trees and pomegranates, a land of olive trees and honey, a land in which you will eat bread without scarcity, in which you will lack nothing, from whose hills you can dig copper. And you shall eat and be full, and you shall bless the Lord your God for the good land he has given you.

Then there was a warning which Michael forever took to heart:

> Take heed lest you forget the Lord your God, by not keeping his commandments and his ordinances and his statutes, which I command you this day: lest, when you have eaten and are full, and have built goodly houses and live in them, and when your herds and flocks multiply, and your silver and gold is multiplied, and all that you have is multiplied, then your heart be lifted up, and you forget the Lord your God, who brought you out of the land of Egypt, out of the house of bondage (Deuteronomy 8:11–15).

A long three-week visa saga followed. On 9 October, Michael wrote desperately in his diary: "This is perhaps the deepest test of my life to date – and being so physically down I don't feel I am weathering it frightfully well. May He deliver me from anxiety, fatigue, doubt and confusion. Oh, how I need Him! I still have just enough faith to believe for a miracle on these visas. 'If thou wilt, thou canst.'" The saga ended with a member of parliament in Natal, Howard Odell, taking up the team's cause. Finally, permanent residence visas for the foreigners on the team were granted by Jan de Klerk, then Minister of the Interior, whose son, F. W. de Klerk, would later be President of South Africa.

By autumn 1964, African Enterprise was able to hang up its new sign in Pietermaritzburg and declare itself "ready for business". The first headquarters of AE was a little office in Longmarket Street, discovered by Chris Smith, and consisting simply of two tiny rooms with a connecting door. But it was a start, for there were desks, a telephone, a typewriter, stamps and envelopes. Esther Kuun joined as a secretary. AE was now in business.

It was a very small beginning for a very big dream. Just four young men setting out to evangelise the cities of Africa. (Don Ehat did not join them, as he was pursuing further studies in Boston, and Ed Gregory, who had toured Africa with Michael in 1961, decided his long-term call was in the United States.) The young team, however, like the biblical David before them, was not daunted by the Goliath that stood before them. They had a profound faith in God and were confident that, because God had called them, they would win the confidence of the many hundreds of churches with which they would have to work in order to achieve their dream.

Theology of the Itinerant

This, in fact, became their first challenge, thrown at them by Dr Calvin Cook, the Presbyterian pastor who had given them their first big break with the Pietermaritzburg mission and who would become a lifelong friend and counsellor to Michael and the team and a board member from the beginning.

He had written to Michael at Fuller and asked simply: "What is your theology of the itinerant?"

It was theological shorthand for a very serious question that was now demanding an answer: "Your AE team has arrived as a group of Christians bent on evangelism. But Africa has already got Christians, grouped into many denominations and churches. How are you going to relate to them? How will you choose where to have missions? Will you pick likely spots on the map, move in and evangelise, and then group your converts into AE churches? Or abandon them without anything, or advise them to find a church, or what?" AE were loose cannons, at present owning no master. What would they do?

Calvin Cook was soon to be leaving his Presbyterian church in Pietermaritzburg to take up a lectureship in Johannesburg at the University of the Witwatersrand – or Wits, as it is informally called – but he was still concerned for the welfare of this little group of young enthusiasts whom he had helped, in signal measure, to bring to Pietermaritzburg. Dr Cook was well qualified to ask the young team to think the matter through. Born to missionary parents in China, he had studied theology at Cambridge University and Princeton Theological Seminary, and would one day become Professor of Ecclesiastical History at Rhodes University in Grahamstown, South Africa. His vast knowledge of the church past and present meant he knew well the pitfalls even keen, dedicated Christians could fall into without due care.

So he threw out his challenge to Michael: "What is your theology of the itinerant?" As evangelists, they would not be settled, but constantly on the move from place to place. How did they see their calling as fitting in with the calling of the local pastor and the local congregation? How did they see their gift as evangelists finding its place in the more settled Body of Christ in a given locality, i.e., the local churches?

Certainly in Pietermaritzburg, the capital of Natal, there was a long-established church tradition. For one thing, Pietermaritzburg was the home of the famous Church of the Vow, commemorating the solemn pledge made to God by the Voortrekkers on the eve of the battle of Blood River in 1838. The Vow had integrated the religious, cultural and political elements of Afrikaner life, all of which later contributed to the birth of apartheid. But Pietermaritzburg was also becoming a national centre for theological training. There were theological courses at the University of Natal and the Union Bible Institute. Later would come Federal Seminary, the Cedara Catholic Training Centre, the Evangelical Seminary of Southern Africa and the Evangelical Theological House of Studies (ETHOS).

Dr Cook had put his finger on the most crucial issue facing the AE team, and they knew it:

Who did they think they were in relation to all these other churches and Christian groups?

Michael later recalled:

Thinking through this one, we quickly came face to face with St Paul's picture of the Church as Body with many members, but one head and one Spirit uniting all in all. And as "There are varieties of gifts, but the same Spirit" (1 Corinthians 12:4), so our gift and calling as evangelists *had to be related to and recognised by the local church or it could not function.*

This made us very dependent upon the local church and upon local congregational and ecclesiastical authority. If we wanted them to take us seriously, then we had to take them seriously. There could be no bypassing of the local church. No hit-and-run evangelism of the sort that had complicated the lives of local clergy in many places for many years. No rushing into a town, setting up an ad hoc committee of self-selected friends, having a preaching jamboree and then leaving town equally promptly, leaving the local ministers to try and pick up the pieces.

So we agreed before each other and before God to wait until we were invited and wanted by the churches or properly constituted Christian authorities in any given locale.

It was one of the most important decisions AE ever took. It may have made their pace of initiative a bit slower, but it would pay off a hundred-fold in the years to come, as church leaders and denominations gradually came really to believe that African Enterprise was there to serve them, encourage them and be enriched by them: "We wanted to be mutually supportive."

Soon local invitations to speak even at Pietermaritzburg Anglican churches drifted in, even though the Anglican Church had distanced itself from the AE team and the Mission to Maritzburg in 1962. Michael accepted, but before he went, he rang the local Anglican bishop. To Bishop Vernon Inman's

pleased astonishment, Michael was observing the strict protocol that said that it was appropriate for a layman always to get
episcopal permission before preaching from an Anglican pulpit.
Willingly, the bishop gave it, again and again and again, finally
deciding to authorise Michael to preach anywhere in his diocese. In 1973, Bishop Inman licensed Michael as a lay minister
in his home parish of Hilton, just north of Pietermaritzburg, "to
instruct and prepare candidates for Holy Baptism and
Confirmation, to preach, to assist in the administration of Holy
Communion, and to perform such other pastoral duties as are
not reserved to the ordained ministry".

Ladysmith

Also in the autumn of 1964, just over two years after the successful mission to Pietermaritzburg, came a letter from a group
of churches in another South African city, Ladysmith, about 150
km north of Pietermaritzburg. Would African Enterprise come
and help them hold a mission? The team were delighted and
accepted at once. It was the first major invitation from a city's
churches since AE had arrived in South Africa several months
before. This was their first great opportunity to put into action
all they had learned about citywide evangelism in the last five
years across America.

Earnest, systematic preparation quickly began. There were
courses on pre-evangelism to arrange for the Christians who
wanted to be involved, there were venues for little meetings to
find, venues for the bigger rallies to choose, music to select, services to plan, sermons to write, follow-up material to order.
Who had time to eat or sleep?

The team had made it over many hurdles to get this far:
from a group of students at Fuller Seminary with a dream, they
now ran an organisation based in Africa, and at last they had a
citywide mission to plan, organise and lead. They might have
been forgiven for thinking all their major troubles were behind
them. They were wrong.

Ladysmith, in northern Natal, was a city full of history for
any South African. Just two miles away, Andries Pretorius and
the Voortrekkers had prayed for victory over the mighty African
warrior Dingane, and made their famous Vow in 1838, promis-

ing to commemorate the day forever if God would give them victory over the overwhelming numbers of opposing Zulu warriors. Sixty years later, the Boers were shelling the city during the famous siege in the Boer War. The city remained a microcosm of the tensions between the main groupings of South Africa, i.e., blacks and whites, English and Afrikaans. The AE team was soon to learn they could not ignore these tensions.

Nineteen-sixty-five was the beginning of a steep learning curve for African Enterprise – unsurprising, when you consider AE was attempting to evangelise and unite people in one of the most fractured societies in the world. While it was the high ambition of Michael and his team always to co-operate with all the Christians of a city, what would happen when the Christians of the city were not co-operating with each other? In Ladysmith there were three distinct church groupings. First, there were the English-speaking churches, which had extended the invitation to AE. Second, there were the larger number of Afrikaans churches, who gave AE the cold shoulder, and would not co-operate in the mission. Finally, there were groupings of black Christians, who were keen to come to the mission, but both white church groupings wanted to ignore them altogether.

So how do you preach the gospel message of reconciliation and love to non-Christians when an evangelistic mission is being organised by Christians who will not speak to each other? The history of South Africa made it culturally almost impossible for the Christians of Ladysmith to see this, never mind change anything.

African Enterprise did not want to get caught up in any of this. "Our desire was to see the Gospel proclaimed by every means possible and people won to Christ. We had no desire at all to be caught up in anything which would detract or distract from that primary commitment," Michael wrote later. "However, it quickly became evident that there was no way we could avoid confrontation and collision with the racial set-up in South Africa. Not if we would be true to the gospel."

This came home to them the moment they arrived in Ladysmith. Abruptly they realised that while the first mission to Pietermaritzburg in 1962 had been inter-racial, apparently without too much problem, "We quickly discovered that that apparent lack of complication was to be the exception rather than the rule." For AE was confronted with the unqualified pro-hibition of inter-racial meetings in the town hall. Neither the mayor, nor the town clerk, nor the city council seemed willing or able to do anything about it. "No blacks in our town hall, Sir. That's the law. Sorry. We can do nothing about it," was the blunt official line.

The team sat back, appalled. They quite literally did not know what to do. They had committed to the mission. They were beginners, feeling their way, anxious to hold the mission, already over-stretched with work, and now uncertain of how to cope on this issue. There was only one town hall and only one racial group was permitted to use it.

After prayer and much discussion, they finally secured per-mission to run a relay line from the Ladysmith City Hall to a nearby Methodist church where blacks could gather to listen to the service. It was the first and last time AE would ever agree to hold meetings under such a restriction. Forever after, the mem-ory of it "sends shivers of embarrassment and shame through me," Michael wrote later. "To think we allowed ourselves to be thus bludgeoned and compromised!"

To register AE's protest at this absurdity, Michael would often go over to the Methodist church and sit as a solitary white person with the blacks through the first part of the service and then hurry back to the city hall during the hymn before the ser-mon, which he would then preach with both gusto and sadness, also telling the whites of the absurdity of the set-up.

Response

The mission meetings, which were held every night for three weeks, were well attended but, everyone agreed, were harder going and less spectacular in response than the Pietermaritzburg mission of 1962. The AE team were especially glad to see that professional people – the local leaders of Ladysmith – were happy to come along, and that a good few responded and became Christians. One businessman spoke publicly of "a spirit and peace of mind unknown to me before". "It's interesting, isn't it, how people, young and old, white or black, educated or illiterate, always mention this thing of peace," Michael mused. "It accords so well with Jesus' promise:

'Peace I leave with you; my peace I give to you'" (John 14:27). A local leading sportsman said: "What a wonderful change Christ has made to my life!" Many people sat up and took notice of what the team preached, and the team were glad to see that their theory of influencing a city through its leaders was already working.

One Rhodesian businessman, whose wife had been praying for years for his conversion, found himself stranded in the town with a broken-down car waiting for spare parts. With nothing to do each evening he came to the meetings. Before the end, to his wife's ecstatic delight in a prayer-answering God, he came to a deep and lasting conversion experience.

Many of Ladysmith's "tough characters" melted before Christ's love, to the joy of many local Christians. "What a joy it was to see scores of Africans come to a knowledge of Christ!" said one man. Another said: "As I sat and listened on a Sunday afternoon I felt as though my body had been electrified. I could not sleep that night. I then committed my life to Christ. Now I know that I am a new creation in Him." There was good follow-up with help from the Union Bible Institute team, for which AE was very grateful. In the end, every home in the locality was visited, and Bible studies made available for anyone who wanted them.

But the guilt of not being able to welcome blacks to the city hall haunted Michael, Chris, Paul and Dick. So they resolved to venture out into the black township for an extended series of meetings. They hired a large tent, which was packed each evening despite the winter weather. Then disaster struck again: the tent blew down in the wind. Still undaunted, the team hired a large school hall. Hundreds of people packed into it for each meeting, where Chris energetically led the meeting, Paul organised the music, and Michael preached with the help of a Zulu interpreter, one Ebenezer Sikakane.

Ebenezer was a lecturer at the Union Bible Institute, and had helped Michael before, bringing a choir with him to the Pietermaritzburg City Hall in 1962. He was superb – the best Zulu translator in the country – and seemed to understand Michael's approach so well that soon the two men preached seamlessly together.

At the end of the Ladysmith mission, AE had many mixed

feelings. Their main work, with the English-speaking churches, had unquestionably resulted in new church unity, although the main Afrikaans church, the Dutch Reformed Church (DRC) had kept its distance, and a new vision for reaching the outsiders. Commitments had been solid and prayer and Bible study meetings had doubled in size. In fact, people would go on deciding for Christ weeks after the mission was over. Against that, there were two regrets: not having the Afrikaans churches on board hurt the mission, as Ladysmith was largely Afrikaans. And most of all, to have had blacks banned from the meetings was a disastrous disappointment.

Other Invitations

A number of smaller invitations to hold "missionettes" here and there followed the Ladysmith mission. The team was kept more than busy speaking at these, as well as making new contacts, studying Afrikaans and preparing material for future outreaches. They loved the work, and getting to know the Christians in the region was a delight. Everything was going fine, except that finances to fund the work itself were quite desperate. It was a problem that would follow them for years. Back in the States, the American Christians were still assuming that the South African churches were supporting AE, and the South Africans were still assuming that, as the AE team was mostly American, and had been "conceived" in the States, that the "rich" Americans were looking after this new kind of missionary society. And as it is a universal human failing not to hear what you don't really want to hear, both American and South African Christians seemed curiously deaf to AE's repeated pleas for help.

By early summer, when African Enterprise celebrated its first "birthday" the team were in real trouble. Michael wrote to the American supporters, telling them that, while "certainly doors are opening faster than we can go through them, and we've just had to turn down an invitation to Addis Ababa next year, at this present moment we are standing in genuine need".

For Michael and the team, it was real anguish to be in such a position: "The task of getting out the gospel of Christ is more urgent than ever. We in African Enterprise count it a rich privilege to be having a small part in God's programme for this. But we need your continued gifts and prayers if our particular contribution is to go ahead."

First University

Meanwhile, African Enterprise was about to make a small bit of South African church history. They were leading the first-ever evangelistic mission to a university campus in South Africa. The small but lively Christian Union of the University of Natal in Durban had invited African Enterprise to come and "have a go" at preaching the gospel to some of the most sophisticated and sceptical young people in all South Africa.

Michael, Paul, Dick and Chris were delighted at the opportunity: university students had been part of AE's concern and interest from the start. After all, they were the leaders of tomorrow. But university students required careful "handling". They were for the most part sceptical over the existence of God, and cynical over the claims of Christians to have found new life in Christ. Such students were always ready to argue about the meaning of life, but rarely disposed to believe anything just because someone sincere told it to them.

Thus AE decided that its approach would focus on presenting one basic conviction: that the historically risen Jesus is indeed the Truth seeking men and women in need. The team would argue that Truth is personal and not simply propositional. Truth, the team would say, lies primarily in a *person*, not a system, making Christianity the faith best able to make sense of all the data of life. It builds coherence into an otherwise absurd, empty and godless universe. The theme of the mission was "Christianity – Fact or Fairy Tale?"

On the eve of the mission, the team were all too aware of the challenge: the student world is not easy to reach, but the needs within it are immense. Michael and the team felt a compassionate concern for these young people, so soon to take up key jobs and responsibility and leadership in such a fractured, violent society. "So pray for a deep and extensive moving of the Holy Spirit among the students," they asked their supporters and prayer partners.

AE may have tiptoed on to the campus feeling like Daniel

entering the lions' den, but to their delight, none of the lions tried to eat them. The Christians on campus had done a superb job of preparation under the direction and training of Dick Peace and, as a result, Michael was heartened to find that the student response surpassed all expectations.

One beautiful spring day a student, Alan Chattaway, still a friend to AE and now in Canada, bounded up to Michael and said: "I have found Jesus. And guess what I noticed today for the first time?"

"The signature of God in creation," replied Michael without batting an eyelid.

"How on earth did you know?" answered the astonished student.

"Ah!" said Michael surveying the bursting spring blossoms all round, "that's one of the real consequences of true conversion: we see the Lord's hand in creation as never before."

"We received a very fair hearing" was the happy verdict on the mission. And it reinforced AE's conviction that thorough preparation by Christians on the ground ahead of time was going to be absolutely vital to the success of any mission.

Vryheid

That September, the combined churches of Vryheid, a town in northern Natal, invited African Enterprise to lead what would be AE's third interchurch mission. The invitation was backed up by a warm welcome from the civic and business communities, a heartwarming encouragement for the team, who were so keen to get the attention of just these sort of local leaders. Apart from the Dutch Reformed churches (DRC), all the churches, including the Roman Catholic, were in. The DRC leadership had declined, saying "the communists had sent this team".

Vryheid's Christians were certainly not out to sensationalise the mission. Fliers announced simply: "A series of meetings at which the credentials of Christianity will be presented in a way that will command the respect and interest of the modern mind."

Nevertheless, the crowds poured in, black as well as white, this time. AE made sure of this, for the memory of segregation in Ladysmith had haunted them. "The pathetic incongruity, indeed sinfulness, of what we had allowed in Ladysmith had not been lost on us, and when we got to Vryheid, we took a firmer stand." After some feisty discussion, the church leaders relented so far as to allow blacks into the hall, but only in the gallery. It was almost as degrading, but not quite. The main thing was that everyone was in the same hall. It *was* progress.

But Michael recalled:

> Even though this was progress, it was still far from satisfactory. We resolved never again to compromise the gospel of our Lord Jesus, who had broken down the barriers between people and shown that in Him there is neither Jew nor Greek, bond nor free, male nor female, but all are one in Him.
>
> More than that, we recognised the futility of seeking to proclaim a God who loves all people, indeed the whole world, from a platform which showed more loudly, indeed deafeningly, that He loved some more than others. The message had to be incarnated. The word had to become flesh. Otherwise it would literally be incredible to our black listeners.

The mission, held in the Memorial Hall, went so well that the meetings had to be extended for nearly a week. There were also "Movie Munches" – free lunchtime film shows with a Christian flavour. Even the Roman Catholics were thoroughly enjoying themselves, to AE's surprise and delight, and the priest and a number of nuns were deeply touched by the endeavour. It all ended in a cheerful, noisy rally in the Church Square, and a month later with a weekend retreat for all the new Christians.

By October, after a "missionette" to the town of Harrismith in the Orange Free State, where the meetings were almost snowed out by an unseasonal snow blizzard, the team got busy with preparatory trips to Durban, Pretoria, Port Elizabeth and Basutoland, where a major thrust the following year was planned, on the eve of the country's independence.

Looking Back

Looking back, AE's first year of fulltime ministry had been encouraging. More invitations were arriving now for the next year, most from ministers' fraternals in various cities, from Wynberg in the southern suburbs of Cape Town, to Port

Elizabeth, Grahamstown and East London in the Eastern Cape. AE only went into cities when invited by the churches, so the meeting of the fraternals was always the first step.

One interesting feature of that first year was that AE's interest in reaching leaders bore fruit on the ground in every mission where the team seemed able to connect to the business, civic, professional and academic circles of every community they visited. Usually evangelism bypassed this sector, but the AE team did not and their labours were fruitful here.

With the links back to the Washington, DC, fellowship, it was not surprising that the year had been opened for Michael and Dick Peace with a visit to the National Parliament in Cape Town, along with British Conservative Party MP, Sir Cyril Black, whom Michael had met previously in London through Abraham Vereide.

The aim was to try and get a prayer group going in the South African Parliament. Mr H. J. Klopper, Speaker of the House, and a founding member of the Afrikaner secret society, the Broederbond, told Sir Cyril, Michael and Dick that a prayer group for MPs in Parliament and to pray for Parliamentarians was not necessary "as we are all Christians". Whether old man Klopper registered his visitors' decidedly raised eyebrows, history does not relate. Getting a prayer group going in Parliament, Michael thought, would have to wait for another time. The day of the visit – 24 January 1965 – was also the day Winston Churchill died, and Sir Cyril, who had known Churchill well, regaled Michael and Dick with fascinating stories of the great statesman. He also said he believed Sir Winston had a real faith in Christ by the time he died. Churchill's former secretary once said something similar to Michael when some of the Cassidys visited Chartwell House in Kent where the great man had lived.

Differences

All these experiences in contacts and missions had been wonderfully interesting and fulfilling. But while things were going well with the team in public, in private they were finding that their honeymoon with each other was over. A year of living and working so closely together had served to highlight just how different the team members were in temperament, family backgrounds, Christian tradition, and simple cultural preferences. While back at Fuller, where each team member had a wide circle of friends and space to be himself, they had been drawn together by their great desire to evangelise in Africa. Now, a year into the work in Africa, they still had their total commitment to their work, but they were finding that, in living and working on top of each other, they could all get on one another's nerves pretty quickly.

These differences cropped up daily. For instance, how do you publicise a mission? One team member wanted to "puff" Michael into a big personality and use the personal touch to draw the crowds, as the Billy Graham organisation did. He felt that people related better to one person than to an organisation or an announced series of mission meetings. Another team member found this appalling, and was adamant that no names should be pushed, just the fact of the mission advertised.

Or again, what sort of music should be used in missions? One team member was for all the American choruses with lyrical melodies and rhythm. Another found them trite and wanted more substantial and traditional hymns.

Again, another team member was culturally "middle America", with an uncomplicated faith that was very strict about smoking, drinking, dancing and such. Another was much more English and oblique in approach, admired "literary" Christians such as C. S. Lewis, and even smoked a pipe on rare occasions!

Each team member in his way was enormously talented, and each was a thoroughly dedicated Christian, but their ideas often clashed, as did their personalities, which ranged from buoyantly optimistic and boisterous to gentle restraint with a craving for quietness.

Here again, as in his childhood, Michael found himself desperate for reconciliation, for what he called relational peace around him. He was in human terms the major common denominator among them all, with a deep and private friendship with each one. The others weren't "natural" close friends to one another. Sometimes Michael cried out to God in desperation: why such a diverse team? We are doing evangelism in one of the most fractured societies in the world, with all the churches splintered from each other, and our own team can't even work together without getting on each other's nerves! Sometimes it felt as if the great dream to preach the gospel to the leadership of Africa was at risk through daily edginess and frayed nerves.

"The tensions in the team were terrible at times. It was almost as if the devil had thrown the book at us from day one of our arrival." These constantly fractured relationships were exhausting, with patience and understanding often stretched to breaking point. Never mind healing the rifts of South Africa, the team found that they had a constant struggle for reconciliation among themselves. At times it seemed as if their only alternative was to give up and die as an organisation.

In later years, Michael came to understand what was going on within African Enterprise in those early years:

> The Kingdom of God is all about relationships, because it is based on unity and love in Christ. So it is precisely the relational aspects of the work which the devil has always attacked. If he can destroy the relationships, he can destroy what the whole thing is all about, namely, *shalom*, which is all about right relationships with God, with ourselves, our families, our governing authority, even our ecological environment! Yes, *shalom* – Hebrew for peace – sums this up: wishing "peace" on the totality of a person's relationships. We had gone to Africa to preach the Kingdom of God. We were proclaiming the Kingdom of right relationships, and therefore in our own world, our relationships came under attack. In the spiritual things of God, Calvary is at the heart of all reality, for Jesus was "the lamb slain from the foundation of the world".

It is a law of the universe that Resurrection and Pentecost are impossible without Gethsemane and Calvary. Everything is birthed by falling like a grain of wheat into the ground and dying. You lose your life to save it.

Calvary pain brings forth resurrection power, but resurrection ministry will and must have Calvary pain. And the pain, and the strain of keeping a diverse team together so that they could minister to diverse churches in a fractured society was real and deep.

Many times over the years, Michael would cry out to God: "This business of Christian ministry is too much for me. I am too feeble, too inadequate, too sinful. Send someone else!" Like Moses in the Bible, Michael felt simply inadequate for the task.

"God always came back to me," recalled Michael later. "Firstly, I have never worked with any other kind of people than the likes of you: frail, fallible, sinful and faltering, in fits and starts. I only work with sinners. Second, you volunteered for the job, and you've got it, so no backing out now. Go for it!"

Mercifully, the team kept working on their own relationships, often via team meetings which lasted for hours, as differences, approaches and attitudes were worked on. These struggles helped the team to minister sympathetically into many of the divisions endlessly encountered in the churches.

In the meantime, one very bright bit of news was the friendship the team was forming with John and Rona Tooke of Pietermaritzburg, both of whom had been converted in the Mission to Maritzburg in 1962. John was one of the first South Africans other than Michael really to be gripped by the vision of what the team was trying to achieve. Gradually, over the months, the Tookes were coming closer to the team. It would be a strategic friendship for the team and for Michael one of the special and most treasured relationships of his life.

Chapter 8

Missions Galore

The African Enterprise team packed its bags in January 1966 and headed for the mountains of Basutoland where Michael had grown up. AE had been invited to lead the churches in a six-month mission to the whole nation. It was a critical time for the people, as they were on the eve of independence, when they would cease to be the British protectorate of Basutoland, and become the independent nation of Lesotho (pronounced le-SOO-too, where the language is Sesotho, the people are collectively called the Basotho and an individual person is a Mosotho).

The churches that had invited African Enterprise proved eager to help, so much so that even before the mission began, they managed to distribute some 250,000 pieces of Christian literature provided by AE. However some communists said: "Beware, Verwoerd (the Afrikaner President of South Africa at the time) has sent them."

"Goodness," commented Michael. "In Vryheid the Afrikaners said the communists had sent us. Here the communists say the Afrikaners have sent us. We must be doing something right!"

For six months, from January to June, the team, along with American intern Dick Avery, lived, ate, breathed and dreamed Basutoland. "We preached our hearts out in situation after situation, stood trembling before university audiences, or rode on horseback through rivers and streams to isolated mountain villages in the backwoods of Basutoland. Sometimes we were speaking to tens and twenties, often to hundreds, and sometimes, praise God, to thousands," Michael wrote later. "Experience upon experience of the faithfulness of God came to us in those months."

One night Michael and Chris Smith found themselves in the

remote Basotho village of Mokhotlong. Once their horses were safely paddocked, the two men were entertained by the school-children, to whom they had preached that afternoon. Then the villagers produced a feast under the stars with haunting African music and singing.

"That night the dear minister and his wife insisted on vacating their double bed in a two-roomed dwelling so Chris and I could be comfortable," Michael told friends later. "Then very early next morning, in our little hut on that mountainside in Mokhotlong, in the middle of nowhere, we were woken by the BBC News from a transistor radio, plus a steaming cup of hot coffee! Also as we woke we heard the chorus 'Give me oil in my lamp, keep me burning' wafting over the mountainsides from youngsters who'd learned it from us round a village fire the night before!"

Of course, there were headaches too. Finances were still a constant worry, with some hair-raising rescues. One time the team needed R1,000 urgently, and had nothing. Next day a cheque arrived from a nurse in a remote corner of South-West Africa (now Namibia) for R1,000. Second, living on the road for so long was also quite hard on all team members, especially on the wives – Barbie Smith and Judy Peace – for whom coping with all this movement and travel and changing lodgings con-stantly was becoming a real strain. In reality they coped amaz-ingly. And there was all that suspicion to overcome, as to who had sent them. Was it the communists, the Afrikaners – or maybe even God?

Even so, the mission ultimately provided the young evan-gelists with "nothing but a gracious forward movement in the ministry. Even more important, we knew it was mercy and not merit, for our fumbling and mistakes were many and various!" said Michael.

But on one issue the team were no longer fumbling. They had decided to make their public stand on racism clearer, more overt and more specific. "Repentance from racist attitudes seemed to us to belong equally clearly with repentance from immorality or drunkenness. And we preached it, disconcerting though it was to many of our white leaders," remembered Michael.

As if to practise what they preached, African Enterprise

went further that summer and made plans to take on a new team member, Abiel Thipanyane. Abiel was a Sesotho-speaking South African from the Orange Free State and had been one of the main interpreters and preachers in the six-month endeavour. It was an extremely important Rubicon for the team to cross and the integration process thereafter would continue as other black evangelists and staff workers joined AE. It was agreed that Abiel should join AE fulltime the following March. To do so, he amazingly turned down a job to become the official interpreter to the new Lesotho Parliament, a post offered him after some members of Parliament had heard him interpreting for Michael.

At the great closing rally with 10,000 or more present, Abiel interpreted again for Michael. It was the beginning of a great partnership and friendship that is still in place today, almost four decades later.

Safely back in Pietermaritzburg by July, the AE team were able to sleep at home for a few weeks while they conducted a mission to the University of Natal, as well as the local teacher's training college. Preparation had been good, and in the end 200–300 students attended every lecture that AE held on everything from "Conflicting Ideologies in Emerging Africa", to "Christian Evidences for the Resurrection".

Berlin Congress

Of course, no white Christians in South Africa could make such a stand as African Enterprise had, in insisting on non-racialism, and not expect a backlash in South Africa. The attack came that October 1966 in Berlin, of all places.

Hundreds of Christians from all over the world had been invited to attend the Berlin Congress on Evangelism, organised by the Billy Graham Evangelistic Association, and Michael Cassidy was among those asked to present a paper. His assignment was "Political Nationalism as an Obstacle to Evangelism". In a sense, the subject was: "Does racism or runaway nationalism stop people becoming Christians?" Three Dutch Reformed leaders, who'd seen an advance précis of the paper, forbade Michael to deliver it, saying: "If you do, we will tell five million people you are a traitor to the country." "Strange," thought

Michael, "I thought there were 25 million people in South Africa. Oh yes, the other 20 million are black!" It was of course dynamite as a subject, but Michael ignored the threat and did not hesitate to light the fuse. The subject had haunted him for several years, and this was his chance to set down the conclusions he and the AE team had reached on the issue. "I hammered both white and black nationalisms when they elevated themselves above the Scriptures and nullified biblical social ethics on the basis of a majority vote," he remembered. "I challenged the *vox populi vox dei* – the voice of the people is the voice of God – line and urged sociopolitical submission to the Word of God."

There were three reactions to Michael's paper. First, predictable fury among the Dutch Reformed leaders and several other white South Africans, who demanded that Michael's paper be expunged from the record. It wasn't. British pastor, author and theologian John Stott put his arm on Michael's shoulder and said: "Maybe there are some people whose support you shouldn't have." Said American theologian Carl Henry, who had been a founding professor at Fuller Seminary: "I always knew you had problems in South Africa, but I didn't know the half of it."

Second, AE gained great friendliness and an increased credibility not only from South African blacks, but from African-Americans. Third, there was overwhelming affirmation from the worldwide evangelical community. Michael returned to South Africa convinced that AE was on the right track.

Nevertheless, many evangelicals in South Africa did not think so. They insisted that as evangelical Christians they should have nothing to do with anything so tacky as politics, and condemned African Enterprise for calling for political change. And yet all the while these elite evangelical white South Africans were enjoying the privileges and lifestyle of apartheid. Again and again, Michael would say that just accepting the status quo because it suited them was as much a political action as protesting against it. "How could they say opposing apartheid was political, but supporting it was not?" he asked the team endlessly.

That autumn the African Enterprise team discovered they had another major difference with the evangelical churches of

South Africa, namely, a willingness to relate warmly to the wider church. These were the days when evangelicals, in defending their high view of the Bible, had become defensive, withdrawn and suspicious of the more theologically liberal, mainline denominations. The mainline denominations, for their part, had fallen into the habit of discounting evangelicals altogether, finding them rather rude and condemnatory. African Enterprise attempted a different approach, having no desire to wage war on the non-evangelicals, but to win them over with good manners and hopefully a gracious spirit. Polite friendliness and common courtesy won AE many friends in the mainline denominations in those early years and this was to prove very important for the team's later impact and witness.

Other Projects and More Journeys

That December, Michael flew back to Pasadena to report to his board and the many churches that were supporting the ministry on the tremendous progress AE had made. Aside from the citywide missions, the university work had continued and, with outside help, the AE team had even managed to produce a film on the Lesotho Mission entitled "Freedom 66". Now the hugely versatile Dick Peace and Archie Hart, the chairman of the Mission to Maritzburg committee in 1962, were thinking of a second film based on the parable of the Lost Sheep, to be filmed in Lesotho, a land of many sheep and shepherds. Chris and Paul were hard at work on music projects and dreaming of the day when AE would own its own conference centre. Michael himself had been delighted to be asked to speak at an Anglican pastors' conference. The "mainliners" were warming up to AE more and more.

Invitations and enquiries for missions in other parts of South Africa were coming in, and even for missions right across the continent. The work was gathering pace, and the team was eager to expand its membership to meet the demands and develop its ministry to all sections of society, especially leadership circles.

February 1967 brought a 35,000 km trip for Michael Cassidy. After weeks of meetings and speaking in California, he left for other engagements in churches across America, before flying on to London, and then on to East Africa – Addis Ababa and Nairobi. Michael had spent the past two years in South Africa, and was curious to see independent Africa again. He was struck by the sheer energy and drive of modern independent Africa, as symbolised by Africa Hall, the headquarters of the Organisation of African Unity in Addis. Michael was also impressed once again in both Addis and Nairobi with the power and militancy of African nationalism. He was told of the concern in Kenya over leftist trends in Tanzania, and wrote to friends: "The ready availability of communist literature all through East Africa reminded one of the ideological and spiritual battle for the heart of Africa." It made him long to expand his African Enterprise, to reach as many of these people as he could with the gospel message.

Meanwhile, March 1967 was an historic month for the young African Enterprise team: it nearly doubled in size. Abiel Thipanyane, John Tooke, a Pietermaritzburg graphic design artist and public relations man, and Shirley Reynolds, a great youth worker, singer and guitarist, officially joined the team. The count now was: three white South Africans, one black South African, three Americans and one Canadian.

The team had great hopes for their first black African teammate, Abiel. They saw him as vital in initiating a ministry to African people. For this, they wanted to give him some support. The team had already approached Ebenezer Sikakane of the Union Bible Institute, and was planning to bring him on the team fulltime by the end of 1968. They would meet "a very specialised need both linguistically and culturally" in African Enterprise's outreaches.

Spearhead

The very next month, April, saw an opportunity for Michael, Chris, Paul, and Dick to put their new ideas – and new teammates – to the test. They were due in Cape Town to lead the four-month Spearhead Youth Mission, the ambitious brainchild of the Wynberg Ministers' Fraternal led by Anglican rectors Stanley Wakely and Bruce Evans. These ministers were deeply concerned for the young people of all races of the southern suburbs of Cape Town, who were largely unreached by Christianity.

It was a major challenge: there were at least 18,000 potential listeners between 14 and 25 years of age.

Nothing was going to be easy. For starters, the Security Police, who by now were entertaining perennial suspicions of AE because of its disregard for apartheid ideology, were alerted by some conservative Christians to the mission symbol which included a spear, interpreted by them as a military symbol. Surely this AE must be linked to *Mkhonto weSizwe*, the armed wing of the African National Congress! They accordingly tried, though vainly, to block AE's non-racial meetings. Then African Enterprise and the churches had agreed that the original contacts with the young people would have to be made outside the church buildings themselves. There had been churches in the area for years, and their impact on non-Christians was minimal. It was useless to imagine that young people of the southern Cape suburbs would suddenly wake up one morning and say, "Hey, let's really enjoy ourselves – let's go to church!"

No. The place to get in touch with the unchurched youth of the area was where *they already were* – in their homes. This was a new idea for African Enterprise to try out. So CHUM groups (Christian Home Unit Method) were founded and set up. They were based in the homes of 30 different Christian families from Diep River to Plumstead, from Wynberg and Kenilworth to Ottery. Christians able to lead such groups needed very special skills, and the AE team trawled over 25 congregations looking for just the right people. The team then trained their 30 CHUM leaders in a series of preparatory classes. Then there was the backup needed: each CHUM group also needed hosts, speakers, song-leaders and general staff. The task involved was gigantic, as most of the people were quite unfamiliar with such programmes.

So Spearhead kicked off with 30 small groups meeting informally for several months in people's homes. Christians invited their non-Christian friends and schoolmates. The CHUM evenings followed a pattern of fun singing, food, and skits to produce a congenial atmosphere. Gradually, it would finally move on to a non-threatening proclamation of the gospel.

Chris, Dick, Paul, Michael, Abiel, John and Shirley worked around the clock. They were meticulous, thorough and would accept no shortcuts. Their second great challenge in getting the

Spearhead Mission off the ground was the law that only outdoor venues could allow inter-racial participation. So the AE team, while in confrontation with local police over the desired venues for non-racial meetings, finally opted for a large tent on the Plumstead Cricket Ground, which, the local police commandant had reluctantly to admit, was not covered by apartheid restrictions.

Meetings in homes all over the place? A tent going up? A mass inter-racial youth crusade planned? The city's press were intrigued, then friendly, then determined to give the mission good coverage. Soon Spearhead was in the headlines. This had a fortunate snowball effect, and by the time the main week of meetings in the tent began, there were nearly 800 young people inside. For the following ten nights between 600 and 800 people came each night. The tent in the Plumstead Cricket Ground was filled to overflowing, and Chris and Paul outdid themselves by providing the most varied musical programme yet. Soon several hundred extra seats had to be added outside. Skits and drama featured regularly. Some conservative Christians complained about "guitars" being used. "If you compare the Psalmist's orchestra in Psalm 150," replied Michael in a magazine article, "you'll find the Spearhead orchestra conservative by comparison!"

A positive feature of the campaign was the degree of racial co-operation. "The thing that impressed me was the way people of different races banded together to see these meetings go ahead," a young mixed-race boy said.

Apart from these large meetings, the six team members of African Enterprise gave nearly 400 separate messages during the following five months of the mission. Among these were several golden opportunities to speak in public high schools. One heartwarming response was when 120 boys came forward after one such morning assembly. One young man much impacted was Brian Helsby, later to become national director for Youth for Christ.

Doris Riederer, a mixed-race girl who had lost both her legs when she threw herself suicidally under a train, had come radiantly to Christ in the aftermath of this tragedy. She gave herself wholeheartedly to the Spearhead Mission and remained a friend to AE ever after.

The team were thrilled that so many complete outsiders came to the meetings, and in the weeks of follow-up concentrated on getting the young people back into the 40 or so home groups which had now developed.

By September the South African Baptist newspaper concluded: "For many churches and Christians in the Cape Town suburbs, Spearhead has lived up to its name. It has made a strong thrust into the life of the community's young people with the news of Jesus Christ. The job is not yet finished, but Spearhead has been one more step on the road to this goal."

Results

Yet the team, after so much work, was often depressed and even disappointed. They had hoped to make even more impact on the area after five months of such concentrated work. By September they were so exhausted they felt like failures when they saw that not all young converts were sticking to their CHUM groups and growing deeply in their faith.

The problem of securing adequate long-term results always challenged AE. If these results seemed not to be forthcoming, the team wondered where they were going wrong. Some felt AE had stumbled or failed due to unresolved tensions within the team, inadequate prayer together or excessive dependence on good organisation. All these were thought to be possible reasons for the spiritual anaemia the team thought it detected in itself.

But Michael, looking around at his exhausted and dispirited teammates, felt they needed comfort and encouragement more than anything. While accepting that "we must always be ready for self-examination and evaluation", Michael also insisted: "We must be careful not to project our own expectations on to a situation, and then define whether God has or hasn't worked in terms of those expectations." Especially as the team had not had time to find out very specifically what was going on, "there was the temptation to think that nothing was happening".

Looking back over Spearhead, Michael reminded his colleagues: "You have given fully of yourselves and sought to be faithful in proclamation." So what was success? In terms of results, it then became a matter of the sovereign moving of the

Holy Spirit. Also, he reminded them, "except very exceptionally, it was the experience of all God's workers today that 'results' and 'numerical success' were becoming harder and harder to achieve. We are living in ruptured times and should not be surprised to find the going hard."

Meanwhile, that June, AE had launched Africa's first indigenous religious film unit. Funded by American and Canadian Christians, it was headed by a British TV cameraman, Tony Taylor, and his wife. Their first production was *One in the Night* – the parable of the lost sheep. Filmed on location in Mokhotlong, Lesotho, high in the Drakensberg mountains, the film actually used 100 real and unwittingly "acting" sheep for two days, along with one human actor: the ever-obliging Abiel as the shepherd. The hope was that a series of parables could be produced in film version, aimed at the African market, "for whom precious little exists at the moment," said John Tooke. As John told a reporter, "We are now furiously busy preparing scripts, not only for TV but for radio as well. Our aim is to produce material of first-class quality, material that stations in Africa will be only too happy to air."

Wits University

By July 1967, when AE was on the eve of its biggest university mission yet, it had attracted the attention of some large secular papers. Among them was the Johannesburg *Rand Daily Mail*, which promptly nicknamed them "the Commandos". Columnist Hugh Carruthers noted Michael Casssidy's "boundless enthusiasm" and said of the team and its efforts: "They were a brash bunch, but they enjoyed a high degree of success."

The "brash bunch" of "commandos" were actually very nervous when August arrived, and with it a two-month mission to Wits, the University of Witwatersrand, in Johannesburg – the largest English-language university in Africa, and to the Johannesburg College of Education.

As the AE team told its supporters, "It is one thing to preach in cities and churches, and another thing to tackle what is unquestionably the academic hub of the country!"

The team knew that, spiritually, Wits was "like an insuperable mountain, hard and apathetic to the gospel". The student body was nearly 45 per cent Jewish, from well-to-do, highly sophisticated backgrounds. To the team of AE evangelists, "the whole thing is a veritable Goliath and we feel very small Davids". So they appealed to their supporters: "If you have prayed for no other mission we've ever done, please pray for this one!"

The mission was the ambitious idea of the Christian students on campus, supported by various professors. All ten Christian societies on campus, including the Anglicans, Methodists, Roman Catholics and Universities Christian Movement (UCM), were united in wanting AE to lead them in an attempt to get the gospel talked about and embraced. No one thought it would be easy – indeed, they knew it was "one of the most ambitious Christian endeavours ever held at a South African university".

As usual with African Enterprise, the groundwork for the mission was the result of long and prayerful preparation, with Dick Peace spearheading deep and extensive training in basic apologetics and follow-up. Nothing was left to chance. The initial advertising and promotion of the mission was carefully done. Instead of posters proclaiming Christian truths or the fact of the mission, a stylised epigram of the face of Christ with a pair of eyes and a cross, the brainchild of John Tooke, and later, cartoon creatures, peered down at students from walls all over the campus. Tooke's background in PR and graphics was coming in handy, as he decided at this point merely to catch the students' attention by puzzling them. The eyes, he said, like the eyes of Christ, "would look down at the spiritual wasteland and hopefully worry its inhabitants into thinking".

Meanwhile, five American university interns who had volunteered their summer holidays to work for AE were quietly moved on to the campus to live in residence and promote discussions among the students about the Christian faith. David Bliss, a big fellow from Princeton University, was asked by the students to stand in at a boxing tournament for their heavyweight boxing champion, who was sick. "Well I've never boxed before," replied Dave, thinking his co-operation would further the cause of the mission, "but I have seen it on television. Alright, but I have to lead a Bible study tonight, then I'll come to the gym." And thus it was. Sadly, however, Dave only lasted a few seconds before being knocked out stone cold by his giant, semi-professional opponent. The scar on his lip 35 years later testifies that it was all for real. In any event, he was a hero the next day for his courage, the mission was more on the map than ever, and many were now ready to listen to Dave's and the team's testimony for Christ!

Years later Dave would return with his wife Debbie to give their lives to mission work in South Africa.

The aim of the mission was realistic and attainable. As John Tooke told reporters, "It is not to rush students into conversion. It is to present our side as believers, and get students to think about it, and only then seek to secure their response."

Indeed, the whole pitch of the mission was as low-key and non-threatening as possible. When news of it began to spread across the campus, AE's explanation of what they were doing was completely non-emotional:

> Why a mission? Out of the conflicting ideologies to which students are exposed at university a worldview slowly emerges. But there are problems in this process. Perhaps the main one is lack of complete data, which is a result of incomplete exposure to various worldviews. This is where a mission fits into the university picture in presenting the Christian worldview as the most "reasonable" option to explain the realities around us of an orderly universe with spiritual, rational creatures called humans in it. AE believes that Christianity is relevant to students here and in situations and environments that are making Africa the fulcrum of contemporary history.

Dick Peace, a genius in apologetics and discipleship, produced a brilliant and provocative booklet called *Dangerous Christian Books No Atheist Should Dare to Read*. Then he listed some of the best books on basic apologetics that students could buy from the mission bookstand.

The focal point of the mission was a series of lectures given by Michael Cassidy in the university's Great Hall. To everyone's delight, the pitch of the mission, with its emphasis on rational discussion, had worked: thousands of students attended the lectures over the week.

And here Michael's gifting for presenting the gospel to academic leadership circles came into its own. For one thing, he knew his audience. His own mother had struggled with doubts for years. Further, all Michael's schooldays had been spent among intelligent and generally agnostic public schoolboys. So in speaking about Christianity, he automatically filtered what he said and, by stressing the historic intellectual rationality of it, not the emotion, Michael could connect with those sorts of people: "I knew where they were coming from." His background had ensured he would never make the mistake of using emotional Christian jargon on such non-believers. "My own mother hated it!" Michael was grateful now for such a childhood, seeing in it "the sovereignty of God at work. Through our life experiences, God equips us for what He asks us to do, though it may be painful at the time!"

By the end of the lectures, more than 500 books explaining Christian faith and commitment had been sold. The mailing list for students requesting more literature soon stretched to more than 400 names.

As well as the lectures, AE set up symposia where major issues could be debated from all sides. The Death Symposium proved of astonishing interest and insured a full house, as a Hindu, a Jew, a sceptical doctor and Michael Cassidy presented different views. "It suggested that young people think a lot more about the ultimate rendezvous and destiny of man than we realise," Michael observed. A symposium on "Jesus as Messiah" also attracted a great number of students at the Wits medical school, where Michael and Rabbi Apt, the Senior Rabbi of Johannesburg, put the Christian and Jewish perspectives on this theme to a full-house audience. Many others challenged the exclusiveness of the Christian claims, but Michael, Dick and the other missioners ably held their ground and made their case.

The AE evangelists were fascinated to discover that questions on science and politics were actually quite infrequent. Most students were preoccupied with the nature, mystery and mastery of evil. "What's going on in the world is bearing in on people more and more as a theological question," Michael told a newspaper reporter covering the mission.

As the weeks of the mission went by, hundreds of students sought out the AE team for counselling, wanting to know more about Christianity. The team did their best to provide them with information and literature, and to put them in contact with Christians on the campus who could talk to them further, if they so wished.

Rest and Change

By September, Michael, Dick, Paul, Chris, John, and Abiel were exhausted. They had had enough of meetings and rallies. They had argued themselves in and through and out the other side of dozens of debates. They wanted a break from the major issues of their time. What they really wanted was some peace and quiet. So after hoarse goodbyes to all their new friends on the Wits campus, the team retreated to a small hotel in the Drakensberg mountains of Natal for a few days of rest, prayer, fellowship and assessment. Five years had already passed since that first mission in Pietermaritzburg! It didn't seem possible.

As well as catching up on sleep and enjoying ordinary home life again, it was a time for the men to step back and assess the whole AE endeavour, to dream a little. Back in the office in Pietermaritzburg, it was so easy to become swamped with the administration and office work that went into each mission and the constant need to try and raise more money. Such details were an ever-present frustration to these young men, who in an ideal world wanted to be let loose to preach, teach, write, broadcast, edit magazines, lead missions, and generally come alongside churches in Africa to proclaim the gospel.

So they began by each reviewing their own individual responsibilities in the team. The results were highly indicative of each personality.

Michael saw his gifts as in "preaching, writing, initiation and dreaming dreams..." but reluctantly guessed that "I should do more fundraising".

Paul Birch yearned for more time to "spend on music and with people, and in radio work", but admitted "I should help others when they are overwhelmed by mission work".

Chris Smith was a ball of fire: he wanted to "disciple lay people, organise conferences for pastors and Christians, teach pastors, teach programme directors and song leaders, and organise and establish a Christian conference centre for evangelism". Instead, he was busy "handling AE organisation of missions, administration, all finance, and acting as programme director. I am desperate to drop finance and mission organisation!"

Dick Peace wanted to lecture and do other university-based work, as well as write articles, books, and training materials. He also wanted to train the laity, study more himself, and develop the film and radio side of AE. He was anxious to drop as much general organisation as he could, as soon as possible.

John Tooke, with his background in PR, was aiming high: he only wanted "to help modernise the image of the church in South Africa"! Meanwhile, he was busy in administration, raising funds, running the PR for AE, and helping with their newsletter called *Update*.

Abiel also had specific, ambitious dreams. He wanted "to help non-evangelical churches be evangelical, to speak at pastors' conferences, to preach the gospel, to further my studies, and to write Sesotho language religious books, and salvation tracts".

Also now in the equation on a visit to South Africa was another new face, Bob Bason, an American graduate from Fuller Seminary who had joined AE to run the expanding American office as Gene Parks moved on into the military chaplaincy. He was unique in AE in that he was the only one who really *enjoyed* administration! His sights were set on fundraising, office management, liaison between the US board and the AE office in Pietermaritzburg, and so on. He also kept the overall financial picture clear, managed the books, made arrangements for team deputation to the United States and helped with the production of the AE-USA publication called *Outlook*.

Reflections on the First Five Years

After a long hard look at themselves, the team set down what it thought African Enterprise had accomplished in the first five years of its ministry.

To begin with, its main aim had not deviated. Evangelism, in all its forms, was the first reason for AE's existence. And in the past five years, AE had tried every method used in the book of Acts for handing on the message of Christ.

First, of course, there was person-to-person method, as in Philip's discussion with the Ethiopian eunuch. The members of the AE team had all used this approach many times with interested people.

Second, there was the group method, as in Peter's conversation with the group at Cornelius's home in Acts 10. The idea for the CHUM groups during the Spearhead Mission came from this.

Third, as AE now knew well, they could employ dialogue and disputation, as in Acts 17 when Paul disputes with the Jews at Thessalonica. After a summer spent in debates at Wits University, the AE team reckoned it had fully exploited this famous Pauline methodology.

Fourth, there was simple mass proclamation, as at Pentecost or on Mars Hill. This was the big meeting approach, when the team preached to hundreds or even thousands in mass rallies organised by the churches' fraternals.

"These are the biblical ways, and still to be used today," the AE team concluded, adding that they were also very happy to make use of the "insights of modern sociology, adult education, psychology, group dynamics, as well as the techniques of modern science as they relate to mass communication".

It all added up to being "both ancient and modern, both biblical and progressive, both simple and complex, both divine and human. These are difficult tensions to maintain but we do want under the Lord to have a stab at it."

At the same time, AE hoped that the churches would not stop at evangelising their neighbourhoods. For giving birth to new Christians was really just the beginning, not the end. Young Christians needed instruction and encouragement to live like responsible Christians. This was discipleship, and such work "obviously cannot be the work of a few days". It needed thorough planning and execution and a "considerable duration of time". Dick Peace was masterful at producing material for this and a follow-up programme to compete with the best anywhere.

AE wanted to serve as a catalyst in this process of evangelism, not imposing the activity or programme from outside, but rather stirring it up and inspiring it from within the context in which it is called to serve. Even beyond that, the team had a further hope: to stimulate the vitality and effectiveness of the church.

So, as 1967 drew to a close, where was AE five years on? In one of their last sessions before they headed back to Pietermaritzburg from their mountain retreat, the team agreed that "AE is beginning to have a good and disturbing influence within the South African theological context".

AE had again and again challenged the church on two flanks – on the one hand, the poor testimony of many conservative attitudes, and on the other the biblical unsoundness of much liberal theology. Therefore, "our ministry is directed at evangelicals in terms of influencing some narrow attitudes and at liberals in an attempt to redirect their over-broad theology."

African Enterprise walked an unusual path because "as a group we seek to be liberal in our attitudes, and conservative in our theology".

Certainly one heartwarming outcome of this was the way in which a great diversity of individual Christians and denominations was welcoming AE. Already God had given them some unprecedented opportunities in evangelism with both Pentecostals and Roman Catholics working together jointly in the Wits mission. This was a good sign for the future.

Of course, 1967 had also been a year of great expansion for the team – 17 new mouths to feed by addition and procreation! This meant major new expenses – and more financial headaches. Unfortunately, the film unit had not worked out, and that work had to be abandoned for the present.

Future

As for the future, there were three main hopes for 1968 and beyond. The first was Michael's keen desire to continue to break into leadership circles. Leadership letters aimed at business and politicians was one way, but what about discussion groups and trial prayer breakfasts?

Second, what about more support for the clergy and Christian leadership? Why couldn't AE provide a tape library, clergy newsletters, seminars, pastors' conferences – and even, one day, a conference centre?

Finally, the team members were honest, and admitted they needed more help. It was impossible for the team in its present form to minister to the 31 key African cities in their lifetime. A second team was required. East Africa seemed an ideal place for it to be based. It was agreed in broad principle that there would be many advantages in having an inter-racial team based in and operating out of East Africa. The need for other associated groups was quite apparent. In their present form they didn't have the sufficient breadth in gifts, language, and cultural understanding to minister effectively in all sections of the African community and continent.

Neither did they have the money. Financing the work continued to be a real problem. People tended to give only once or twice, and the team was now continually in danger of slipping into the red. By that autumn of 1967, each month's income was falling $1,500 below expenses and the bank account was going into overdraft. Even worse, the income for the first six months of 1967 had been some $3,000 over that of 1966, but the same period had seen expenses rise from $25,000 to $40,000. The reality was stark and simple: the figures indicated that, by the beginning of 1968, they must either increase their income or cut back their activities.

It was the same old problem: people thought AE was well-off and subsidised from America for general operations as well as salaries. But their needs were either not being heeded or not being understood by the vast number of people with whom they had established contact in South Africa. They decided to try once again to establish better communication with their present donors, revive their former donors and increase support from churches, which was again a problem, as AE was interdenominational, and so fell between the lines.

AE made one last decision that was to have enormous repercussions on the work for years to come: they would set up prayer groups around the country that would both pray and give, made up of Christians who were willing to assist AE both spiritually and materially, but most especially with intercessory prayer. In due time those groups would number in the hundreds.

Prayer was becoming ever more central to the work. It was a healthy development.

Chapter 9

Two Mighty Encounters

The year 1969 was to prove a momentous one for Michael, with two mighty encounters. He was to connect deeply in ministry with a Ugandan, Festo Kivengere, who would join AE and become co-leader of the ministry, and he was to meet Carol Bam, who would become his wife.

The year, however, began for Michael with a walk down memory lane: a visit to Michaelhouse, the school he had left just over fourteen years before. The school had graciously invited Michael to come in on his own as an Old Boy of the school and conduct a mission. Michael was delighted to accept.

Last time he'd been there, for a brief preaching engagement in chapel several years earlier, the teachers had teasingly reminded him of his naughty school days, and wondered aloud what *he* could possibly have to say in chapel. But the visit had gone well, and now the school felt ready for this novel idea of a mission that would invite the students to think through the claims of Christianity in a deeper way for themselves.

It was a real breakthrough. Missions to South Africa's private schools had not happened before. So this would be a pioneering effort. If it succeeded, what a tremendously important way of reaching the future leaders of the country with the gospel!

It could – and in the end, did – open what would be one of the most fruitful dimensions of the entire AE ministry.

The format of the mission to Michaelhouse involved Michael leading the chapel service each morning. After chapel, Michael was given the chance to teach all the divinity classes during the day. Afternoons were devoted to counselling individual boys, hour after hour. Several boys shyly came to Michael and were astounded at his depth of comprehension of their various problems. "But I *knew* their life – I had been there!" he said. So it meant that all that pain from his own schooldays was at last of some use to him: "The Lord brought it all back to me, and transformed it so that I was able to use it to help others. I learned a great lesson: nothing is wasted in the sovereignty of God. What He allows to happen to you can all be part of the training process for your future work. Nothing is lost."

Finally, the mission held voluntary services in the chapel each evening. To the astonishment of all, most of the school attended every night, and a quarter of the entire school said they wanted to become Christians and stayed as enquirers for the after-meetings held after each service. Some staff were critical, saying this staying afterwards had divided and polarised the school into categories of sheep and goats, the haves and the have-nots. Michael said later: "I think there was some validity to this criticism and I decided not to use that form of appeal again in schools." But Tommy Norwood, the Headmaster, or Rector, of the school, said in both public and in writing: "It was in my view the greatest week in the history of the school and certainly the high-point of my time as Rector." Norwood would, soon after the mission, come to a new and life-transforming Christian commitment of his own that shaped his life profoundly to the end of his days.

Michael left the school rather uncertain as to how successful he had been in this solo endeavour which he would not repeat, always insisting thereafter on taking a team from AE. "I don't know how I pulled that off," he would say years later. "I guess I was young!" How does one measure the results of a school mission? Often, of course, such a mission is a seed-sowing time, which paves the way for a more adult, measured response later on. Of the boys who become Christians, a number of these might or might not be still committed to their faith a year later. But one thing could be seen already, and it pleased everyone: there was a general air of what can only be described as a new "kindness" in the school. Even the rugby scrums were cleaner, said one observer! In the weeks that followed, the senior chaplain, Harold Clarke, now on the AE board in New Zealand four decades later, let new enquirers know that prayer and Bible study meetings had begun. These flourished wonderfully. Much later, in years to come, Michael had the satisfaction of seeing seven or eight of the boys who professed a faith in Christ at that mission going on into fulltime Christian service in a wide assortment of ministries, from work with parliamentarians, to the pastorate, to denominational leadership, to Christian radio, youth work and so on.

Throughout the mission, the headmaster, chaplain and most of the staff had been invaluable in their help. Even those masters who had reservations about the mission had shown admirable restraint in not damaging the faith of boys who had responded. All in all, Michael and the team concluded that this new kind of mission for South Africa had been significantly blessed by the Spirit of God.

Yet somehow, it still wasn't enough. As the year wore on, the dream of somehow widening the AE net continued to haunt Michael and the team. After all, what about the rest of Africa? Since Madison Square Garden in 1957, Michael had believed that God had laid on him the burden for the evangelisation of the *cities of Africa*. Now it was 1968, over eleven years later, and it had become very clear that the present African Enterprise team by itself was never going to achieve this goal. The formation of other teams would be necessary.

Nigeria and Festo

Michael was praying about what to do when, in early July, he flew to Nigeria to attend the ten-day West African Congress on Evangelisation being held at the University of Ibadan. The Biafran war was on, and the bus journey from the airport to Ibadan had been punctuated by regular hold-ups at military checkpoints. Cocky teenage soldiers would clamber menacingly aboard the bus, rifles at the ready, and precariously anchored hand-grenades hanging from their belts. They kept demanding to see everyone's passports. Africa was indeed a cauldron of political turmoil. After the umpteenth checkpoint, the bus finally pulled up outside the university.

Michael got off and was greeted with a truly African incongruity: a young Nigerian book vendor was sitting outside the registration office of a Christian conference on evangelism, selling glossy Red Chinese literature. A couple of days later Michael saw him again, still surrounded by little Red booklets on the "Thoughts of Chairman Mao", only this time he was avidly devouring *Tortured for Christ* by Richard Wurmbrand, a book obviously given to him by one of the congress delegates and which told the autobiographical story of a Romanian Christian imprisoned unjustly for years for his faith.

The book vendor made a big impression on Michael. The lad seemed the personification of all the need of the cities of black Africa. He and his two books "spoke parabolic volumes about Africa, first of all as a continent in political upheaval and internal alienation and then as a continent still searching for an ideological and spiritual commitment." Commented Michael, "This was uncommitted Africa! This was Africa the question mark! How else could a vendor ardently peddle Chairman Mao one day, then devour Richard Wurmbrand the next?"

It made Michael wild with impatience over his desire to expand African Enterprise, for the gospel was the answer. Jesus was the way forward! The pan-African microcosm of that congress dramatically showed it to be true as people from many parts of Africa found unity in Christ.

Among the panel of speakers for the congress was a celebrated and already famous Ugandan lay preacher called Festo Kivengere. Michael had first met Festo back in 1961 when Festo and William Nagenda, another famous spokesperson for the East African Revival, had visited Fuller Seminary. Festo had made a profound impression on Michael and the two men out of Africa had connected deeply in heart and spirit. Festo had been converted in the great East African Revival of the 1930s and 1940s, and was a teacher-turned-evangelist who was now of international standing, with preaching engagements all over the world. The two men reminisced warmly about their 1961 encounter at Fuller.

When Festo Kivengere learned that Michael was now also a fulltime evangelist, they got talking, and soon the hours slipped away. Finally, Michael reluctantly returned to his room: "As I entered the door one of those precious moments of seemingly divine illumination overwhelmed me: '*Africa – the cities of Africa – and Festo. That's it – build another team around Festo.*'"

"I barrelled right back out the door and down to Festo's room, flinging open the door," recalled Michael. "'Brother,' I burst out. 'I think I've had a word from the Lord! We need to build another AE team *around you* for ministry in the great cities of independent Africa!'"

Festo Kivengere turned round in amazement. "Well, brother," he said cautiously, "won't you come in?" But Michael was already in, and thinking fast.

"You'll want to try it out, of course," he rushed on. "We have a mission to Nairobi coming up – our first in independent Africa. Why not come and join us, and see how we get along preaching together? We could take it from there." Unbeknown to Michael, Tom Houston and the Nairobi mission committee had already been thinking of inviting Festo to join Michael and the team for the citywide mission they had invited AE to conduct.

"Ah, ah..." Festo was clearly overwhelmed. But his response was cautious. "I'll have to think about that, brother." He told Michael later the thought of teaming up with a *white South African*, however Christian, really shook him. He dearly loved the white missionaries he had come to know in Uganda, but they were not South Africans. Festo also feared that linking up with Michael might also do him damage or even play havoc with his reputation in black Africa. Other Africans might well despise him, think him a traitor to his race, or wonder what was in it for him.

Fortunately, nothing had to be decided that moment. After further talk, the two men prayed and then laughed over Michael's impetuosity and left it at that. But it was obvious that Festo had not dismissed the possibility.

Michael remembers that, later in that congress, Festo gave a talk on the origins of the East African Revival. The text was Ezekiel 37 and it was entitled: "Can These Bones Live?" Michael thought it possibly the most powerful Christian address he had ever heard in his life. The congress was electrified.

Meanwhile, after some meetings in Nairobi to plan the big effort for the following year, Michael flew back to South Africa and joined the rest of the team for finance meetings. At last the news was not all bad: for once, income equalled expenditure.

In August a second major South African private school opened its doors to AE, this time Hilton College, a prep school rival of Michaelhouse located near where Michael lived.

Headmaster Raymond Slater said: "We've heard about the amazing thing at Michaelhouse. Won't you come here too?" Going this time with others from the team, Michael again followed the simple format of leading morning chapel, having daily discussions in the classrooms, counselling in the afternoons and holding voluntary meetings each evening. Again, the response was overwhelming: nearly 95 per cent of the whole school attending the voluntary evening meetings. Again nearly a quarter of the school professed response in Christian commitment. Friendships were also struck up between AE team members and the teaching staff. Promises were made for further missions in years to come.

Nairobi

With the Hilton College mission over and September quickly passing, the AE team flung itself into planning the pre-mission set-up in Nairobi. The mission office there became a hive of activity with evangelists buzzing in and out laden with lists and literature and cups of tea, fighting to get hold of the phone before the next person did. Chris Smith, leading the administrative work, also trained a mass choir and produced a songbook for the mission. "It was almost a religious experience watching Chris Smith come to town and lick the churches into shape and into pulling together," chuckled prime mover Tom Houston, pastor of the Nairobi Baptist Church.

Dick Peace and Paul Birch had desks awash with Bible study courses, training papers, lists of churches and contact addresses for prospective mission counsellors. Michael shut himself away to write and prepare: he had dozens of evangelistic sermons to compose. Abiel was also busy writing sermons, aimed at the smaller evangelistic meetings. John Tooke was working on PR and planning a publicity campaign that would grab the attention of the citizens of downtown Nairobi. The mission, named "Crossroads" or "Njia Ipi?" – "Which Way?" in Swahili – was going to run for nearly six months, and would be the most intensive campaign ever attempted in Nairobi. Chairman John Mpaayei, Kenya's first black Cambridge graduate and director of the Bible Society, encouraged them with almost daily visits to the office. One day, over lunch with

Michael in a little café, he suddenly blurted out: "You know, Michael, this must be for *all of Africa*." Michael told him of his dream of working long-term with Festo, who had by now accepted the invitation to come and preach in the mission. Mpaayei beamed: "I want to be part of that!" He would later become the first Chairman of the AE Kenya board.

As news of the mission spread, newspaper reporters started ringing. Michael was delighted to take their calls. The press had picked up on the fact that Crossroads was another historical first for Africa, with the combined churches of a black African capital asking a mainly white, South Africa-based group to conduct a mission in their city.

This was mind-boggling! It was quite literally the "beginning of Christian Africa's gracious attempts to forge a spiritual link with South Africa", as Michael put it.

By December the whole team was in Nairobi. Michael, Paul, Dick and Judy and little daughter Lisa, Chris and Barbie, John Tooke and Abiel were all there, having crammed their suitcases full of sermons, training material, follow-up material, hymn sheets and even a few clothes. Film director Tony Taylor also had all his tripods and cameras. The warm-up for the citywide outreach to Nairobi was in full swing. The team was ready. The churches were poised. The whole thing was incredible: the team's first mission outside South Africa! Invited by churches in independent Africa! Unbelievable! Momentous! Visions and dreams were coming true.

Or so it seemed in January 1969. None of them realised that, within a couple of years, massive changes would rock the team and even threaten their dreams. The time would come for a parting of the ways and for new, unexpected horizons. By 1971, just two years away, African Enterprise would be just about unrecognisable.

But all that lay well down the road. Meanwhile, the AE team got busy with an extensive lay training programme in Nairobi. Here Christians of all races, and in churches throughout the city, were taught the basics of personal evangelism. A few weeks after that, the church leaders took a collective deep breath, and the larger meetings were ready to roll.

By March the Crossroads United Christian Mission was officially launched in Nairobi. To everyone's delight, Festo

Kivengere had finally agreed to come alongside and preach with Michael. Festo was widely regarded as one of the finest preachers in independent Africa, and so would be invaluable to the mission.

The mission came at a critical time for Kenya. President Jomo Kenyatta's regime was weakening and a number of politicians were jockeying for power. Who would win? No one knew, but Kenya boasted one of the strongest indigenous churches in Africa. "The church here is strategically placed to make a real contribution to the country's future," people said, and the Nairobi mission became all the more vital against this background. The realisation of this gave Michael and the team great satisfaction. This is what they had been called by God to do: reach the leaders who would in turn influence the lives of their people.

Stratified Evangelism

This time the team had enough resources and Christians on hand to try an approach known as "stratified evangelism". Specific targeting with appropriate methodologies of all sectors, or strata, of Nairobi society was planned, including schools, businesses, universities, housewives, political leaders and the Asian community. Not even the city's prisons were forgotten: at one meeting alone Festo spoke to more than 100 prisoners.

"We've 'struck oil' with the stratified evangelism programme," Michael told AE prayer partners later. The idea had worked splendidly, whether in homes, offices, prisons, marketplaces, hotels, hospitals, schools, or colleges. African Enterprise's problem now was urging lay folk to take a bold Christian initiative in their own spheres of influence.

In the end, literally hundreds of evangelistic meetings were held. Michael wrote in the AE newsletter: "No one knows what a free evening is, such is the proliferation of opportunities and open doors."

Larger events were also laid on. The biggest cinema in Nairobi was taken over and Christian films shown daily at lunch time. It was packed out every day for three weeks – more than 20,000 people in all went along. This led to 700 enquiries about Christian commitment, 170 of them after one showing of the AE "lost sheep" film, *One in the Night*, starring the celebrated actor Abiel Thipanyane and his 100 sheep!

The city's media loved Crossroads: it gave them lots of good copy and photographs. Newspaper, radio and TV reporters followed the AE team and Nairobi's church leaders to major events. The popular TV station Voice of Kenya gave them airtime.

On top of everything, of course, were the huge rallies which ran every day for weeks. Late each afternoon Michael and Festo found themselves in Kamakunji, a large open space between the city centre and the suburbs which caught everyone on the way home from work. Festo preached in Swahili one day with missionary Don Jacobs, later to join the AE International Board, interpreting into English. The next day Michael would preach in English with a Swahili interpreter.

People said: "That Festo-Michael combination is powerful."

After Kamakunji, the meetings moved into the central park in the middle of Nairobi for a few more weeks. Crowds varied from a low of 800 on one midweek afternoon to 3,000, with 6,000 at weekends. "Preaching," Michael wrote later, "for both Festo and me, felt easy and relaxed through the Spirit's help. We were delighted with the approximately 3,200 who responded as inquirers. This is certainly a greater response than we have ever seen before."

As Michael later wrote to AE's supporters: "I wouldn't say we have turned the city upside down, but I do think we can, without falling prey to evangelistic hyperbole, say that we have made a real dent on the place." In reality the mission would be talked about for years afterwards.

Certainly the follow-up department was absolutely swamped, while the AE mission office in Nairobi had earned the nickname of "Kenya's leading active volcano".

After one of the open-air evangelistic meetings, Norm Riddel, a missionary from Congo, came up to Michael and said: "This kind of city evangelism, not the hit-and-miss stuff, is what the whole of Africa needs."

Michael and Festo

Meanwhile, behind the scenes, Michael and Festo were both praying about the future. "So blessed was our ministry together that we could not but sense that God must have something more in mind," Michael felt.

A visit from a founding member of the AE USA board, Bruce Bare, and his wife Adeline, gave Michael a chance to discuss with them the possibility of building a second team around Festo. Bruce was very enthusiastic. By this time Bruce had become a special friend to Michael, a real father of the work, one might say, at the American end. He would, over the next three decades, visit the work in Africa 57 times at his own expense. "Never, ever will we adequately be able to calculate what Bruce Bare has brought to the AE ministry," said Michael. But back in Nairobi, with Bruce on his first visit to Africa, Michael knew that World Vision was also in talks with Festo and wanted to work with him in some way. The same was true of the Billy Graham Evangelistic Association. Michael thought that, if Festo had the choice between AE and World Vision or the BGEA, struggling little AE would surely lose out.

By the end of March, Michael's involvement in the Crossroads mission was coming to an end, and so he and Chris Smith accepted an invitation from Festo to go to Kampala, and see grassroots evangelism "Ugandan style" at the Greater Kampala Mission.

Kampala was a real eye-opener for Michael and Chris. Both had known in their hearts that the Nairobi mission had been weak in really grassroots African lay involvement. Not so Kampala! Here was mission strongly indigenous in nature and in which the involvement of the African church was truly deep.

The effect on Michael was immense:

> The Kampala visit underlined dramatically in my own mind that the AE team as presently constituted is totally unsuitable for ministry in the fully African cities. Nairobi is more cosmopolitan than truly African. This is in sharp contrast to Kampala, where my impression was that as we are we could not possibly lead a mission here, even if we were invited to do so.

For one thing, the Ugandan church had been heavily influenced by the mighty East African Revival. The "Revival Brethren", as they were called, had developed a very definite Christian "sub-culture". In their enthusiasm for Christianity, they could sometimes fall into the trap of thinking that the specific, outward revival experiences that had so blessed them were the only true form of Christianity. For example, unless Christians described themselves as "walking in the light" and "awakened", and confessed their private sins regularly in public, your average Ugandan revivalist would seriously doubt that they could be "truly saved".

This was not true of the Ugandan Christians who had had a chance to travel and mix with Christians from other backgrounds, such as John Wilson, whom Michael met at Namirembe Cathedral on a hill in central Kampala, and with whom he sensed a natural affinity straight away. John Wilson was a polished and well-educated businessman, a key figure among Kampala's Christians. He worked with Caltex Oil, and had been on the executive committee of the mission, to advise the Bishop on how best to reach Kampala. So far so good, but even John admitted that once the mission got underway, a particular group of revivalists or "Revival Brethren" had more or less taken over, and wanted things run according to their strict rules.

The problem regarding the culture was confirmed to Michael by the now-famous missionary, Dr Joe Church, who, with several Africans in the late 1920s, had been used under God as catalysts of the East African Revival. The Ugandans had been profoundly blessed by the revival. For so many it was their only knowledge of Christianity – many having come straight from animism – and they could not bear to change anything about this way of expressing their faith. Many of them were very suspicious of formal education and overseas influences. Another revival tendency, which would not have gone down well with AE's American board, was that there was no thought of working to a budget and little idea of giving proper account of money spent!

Festo had grown up amongst, been converted by, and become a leader in the East African Revival before moving on and embracing a wider, more Western evangelical approach.

Michael could only admire a man who could leap such a cultural chasm, and still be loved and accepted by the Revival Brethren of East Africa.

It all confirmed to Michael and Chris that, if a second AE team was ever going to be launched in East Africa, they needed a man of stature and breadth of experience like Festo, who had the confidence of all the revivalists and the mainline church leadership, to lead it. Only Festo would have a chance to introduce other Christians to the city, and get them eventually accepted by the Brethren.

After several days of talks with leading Christians in the city, Michael was chatting with the Salvation Army leader of Kampala, Major Northwood, who suddenly suggested a united evangelistic effort in the city, along the lines of Crossroads in Nairobi.

"I had one of those strange sensations that that ten minutes of sharing was the germ and seed that would ultimately lead on to an AE mission one day in Kampala," Michael wrote later.

Equatoria Hotel

Meanwhile, later that same week, on 1 April 1969, Festo invited Michael and Chris for lunch at the Equatoria Hotel in Kampala.

Michael shared his findings of Kampala with Festo, admitting that AE, as it then was, could not possibly minister effectively in these cities of independent black Africa.

Then Michael went on to spell out once again his conviction that there was a definite need now for a pan-African team, made up of Africans from different parts of the continent.

"I then talked straight from the shoulder," said Michael, "and told Festo I thought that such a team should be built around him. I then sat back and fastened my seatbelt!"

Festo sat a moment and pondered. Then he said: "It makes sense, brother. My wife Mera and I have been praying much about this since our time together in Nigeria and we feel the Lord does want us to join African Enterprise so we can work together."

"Resisting an inclination to do cartwheels," Michael said later, we proceeded with discussion. As we did so, Festo warmed more and more to the idea. He said the concept of a team had been with him a long time, but nothing had ever materialised, and the Lord seemed to have kept him loose from firm attachment, either to other bodies and teams in the States, or to the Anglican Church in Uganda, who were eyeing him one day to be a bishop. He suspected now that the purpose of the Lord so leading him to be free of attachments was so that he would be available now to assume this new responsibility. I really don't know how Chris and I refrained from shouting "hallelujah!" right there in the hotel dining hall. We certainly said it and felt it within.

Festo then discussed some possible team members, such as Matt Nyagwaswa in Tanzania and especially John Wilson, the Ugandan businessman Michael had met. Wilson had just been made sales manager of Caltex and was on a terrific salary, but nevertheless wanted to leave business for fulltime ministry. His expertise was administration and finance and he could preach and witness capably as well. "It was therefore evident that the basic nucleus of a pan-African team might very well be there already. Naturally time will have to show, but it was all most exciting," said Michael.

After lunch, the three men went upstairs for a time of prayer. Michael recalls:

> I think all of us were on spiritual tip-toe with excitement and anticipation. As we prayed the verse came to mind God gave us at the inception of AE: "And with you in all the work will be every willing man who has skill for any kind of service" (1 Chronicles 28:21). The promise here is not only for the provision of men, but for the provision of willing men equipped with a wide variety of skills. I have also always interpreted this to mean a promise not just of any men, but of the *best* men.

Many wonderful women of course would be added in due time as well.

Later, alone in his room with Chris, Michael wept. They were tears of deep thanksgiving to the Lord. The pan-African vision and dream was moving ahead! Festo would be a major key. In his diary that night, Michael wrote: "April 1, 1969 at the Equatoria Hotel, Kampala, was a landmark event in the history of AE and the Lord's work on this continent. To him be the glory!"

Michael and Festo would keep in touch. Perhaps the following year they would visit the United States together and share their developing dream.

Later, back in South Africa following further ministry in Nairobi, Michael told the rest of the team: "Although it is impossible, alas, to judge infallibly that this whole experience has been of God, yet both Chris and I felt profoundly that the whole situation bore all the marks of authentic divine imprint. Somehow it seemed as if the Spirit witnessed to both of us that this was a genuine moment of truth for the whole future of AE."

Meanwhile, there was the present to worry about. The AE team set about debriefing itself on the Nairobi mission and lessons learned. The first and most obvious was that, although the AE team in South Africa by itself could not reach these African cities, "we still have a tremendous amount to offer in the way of theological balance and outlook, organisation and procedures, and unifying influence. If we can add what we already have to a second and more indigenous team... we will really have a special trump card."

House-to-house visitation had been big in Kampala, carried on by more than 150 people for twelve hours each day. "If this also can be really built into an overall programme, it is a real winner. However, whether this can be done without a group such as the Revival Brethren, remains problematic."

Finally, the team concluded: "God is faithfully fulfilling his promises and plans for AE's destiny. May we be vessels for the Master's use."

Gear Change

But what on earth was God doing with his vessels? Michael may have been forgiven for wondering at times that spring and summer of 1969, for suddenly there was uncertainty in the air and, incredibly, the AE team itself, rock solid for seven years, began to creak and groan and move towards some kind of gear-change. What was God doing? Team members were getting restless, wondering if after six or seven years it was time to go home. Relationships were getting strained.

Paul Birch, homesick for Canada, felt he had probably had enough of the chaotic life of an itinerant evangelist. His thoughts kept turning towards teaching where, in a more structured lifestyle, life would be a bit more normal. Also he could concentrate more on his music. He was now in his early thirties; now if ever was the time to change careers and get established in a new one.

Dick and Judy Peace were also thinking of home. The work was becoming very stressful, especially moving around with children, and relational strains didn't help. With them also was the call of academia. They longed for the lecture room, the library, the chance to study further, produce Bible studies, write books, start on a doctorate. Dick hoped that a professorship might one day open for him and indeed in due course it did, first at Gordon-Conwell Seminary in Massachusetts and then at Fuller.

Yes, uncertainty was in the air.

Michael had no doubt God had given him AE as his life's work. As he prayed anxiously over possible changes in the team that could be imminent, he felt his concern change to peace and acceptance. One door was seemingly closing along with the decade, and another one was opening. Though the loss of some founder members of the team would surely be a grievous blow, as these were uniquely talented people, perhaps God was saying the time was coming for AE to become more truly and wholly African.

Certainly John Tooke was here in the AE family to stay long-term, and growing in enthusiasm and expertise each year. Abiel as well had taken to itinerant evangelism with great joy and total commitment. And for some time now Michael had felt keen to take on Ebenezer Sikakane, the Zulu translator from the Union Bible Institute, and one of the best Zulu preachers in the country. And if Festo came on board in East Africa, and new teams began sprouting around him... It was all very exciting – the sky was the limit in possibilities. But all sensed that times of change and readjustment were on the horizon.

Cape Town University and Carol

Meanwhile, missions went ahead as planned. The next "biggie" on the calendar was one to the University of Cape Town (UCT). It was due to be launched in mid-August. The student preparation had again been splendid, and the pre-mission "enigma" posters, used to such great effect at Wits, had the campus guessing. One student hostile to Christians thought the posters terrific and assumed they came from the art faculty. He taunted the Christians: "The day you Christians can pull off anything like this, I will be tempted to consider Christianity." Well, actually, they had and maybe he did!

Mid-August arrived and Michael wrote to supporters: "Today the final 'explanatory' publicity has gone up, and the campus knows what is coming. Or do they? Or do we? is perhaps more to the point! For one never knows exactly what course a mission will take till it is really underway."

In fact, everything was ready for lift-off. The multimedia light show developed by two American interns, Don Andreson and Eric Miller, had the campus buzzing. Then the lunch-hour symposia with Michael addressing an assortment of issues from comparative religion to "Sex Rules or Free Love" with two or three opposing voices drew 1,200 or more students to pack the Jamieson Hall each lunch hour. And then some 500–600 students came each evening to the more directly evangelistic talks.

But there was another amazing development waiting to happen that would radically change Michael's life. And all because of a mosquito.

It happened like this: AE had placed its male team members to act as assistant missioners in each student residence, to be on hand for personal discussion with students. However, for this UCT mission, AE had asked the student mission committee themselves to pick the lady missioners for the women's residence. Two were duly selected.

Then one got bitten by a mosquito and developed malaria. A substitute had to be found – quickly. Mick Milligan, director of the Student YMCA on campus and guiding light of the mission, decided with Christine, his wife, and the YMCA committee, that Carol Bam, a UCT graduate currently teaching in Cape Town, would make an excellent substitute.

The Sunday before the mission started, Carol walked in the door of the student YMCA where Mick Milligan had all his students stuffing envelopes. Chris Smith was stunned. Michael couldn't but be struck by her, but feigned nonchalance. This was not an arena for mistakes. Like any normal young man of 32, even a Christian one, Michael had had an assortment of romances that had not worked out. In fact he had been caught up for some four years in a traumatic stop-start relationship, full of uncertainties, fumblings and pain. All this made Michael pause before bouncing into a new relationship. He knew he needed both the Lord's mercy and faithfulness if he was not to make more mistakes in this arena of his life. Carol Bam was a dark-haired beauty with great poise and presence. She had style and a certain something in her presence that froze Chris to the spot. He then grabbed Michael and hustled him to one side, whispering feverishly: "Hey, old buddy, if you fumble the ball on this one, you've really had it!"

Although lonely and longing to be married, and with all his friends around him already married, 32-year-old Michael nevertheless dismissed Chris's crazy notion. Chris had a long and distinguished history of trying to line Michael up in each mission with some lovely choir member, counsellor or pianist. This was more of the same. "But just pray about her," Chris pleaded. Michael declined.

However, midstream in the mission two avowed atheists asked Carol if she would connect with them over coffee to challenge this provocative evangelist. This resulted in an encounter in which Michael and Carol combined efforts to try and win over the doubting duo of atheists.

When the formal mission series was over, Chris and Michael went hiking up Table Mountain, Chris insisting all the way that Michael should ask Carol out. Finally he almost demanded that they at least "pray about it" as they reached a high outcrop of rock. Michael finally relented. Chris prayed excitedly. Then, as the two men rose to hike back down, an extraordinary thing happened to Michael. An inner voice, almost like a telegram from on high, resonated into his inner being: "Go right ahead, my son. This is the girl I have for you." Michael was so thunderstruck that he said nothing to Chris. In the early hours of Monday morning, the Lord spoke again to

Michael. There was an urgency in the Spirit's word. Michael got hold of Carol that day and asked her out to dinner. It was their first date. Before it was over Michael had proposed and Carol, to her own astonishment, had accepted. "It was as if the Lord just took over and said to me, 'It is alright. You can accept.'"

"For me," recalled Michael later, "it was probably the single most supernatural thing that ever, in God's merciful grace, happened to me. For I was very undeserving. I also have to tell young people as a cautionary measure, that you can only propose on your first date if you have prayed daily, as I had, for fourteen years for the girl I would marry, and that I should not get it wrong and should know for sure when the right one finally came along!"

"The right girl, Mike, the right girl," Charlie and Honey Fuller always used to say at Fuller Seminary, "that's what we're praying for. The right girl!"

Michael broke the news of his engagement to an ecstatic Chris Smith a week later. The Right Girl had finally arrived! And to think that Michael and Carol would never have met were it not for the mosquito bite that took assistant missioner, Joyce Scott of Kenya, out of the UCT mission! Joyce often chuckled with Michael and Carol in later years about this delicious coincidence.

However, regardless of the excitement of a wedding to plan for the end of the year, there was a lot to sort out that autumn. A sad farewell had been made some months previously to that amazing musician, Paul Birch. This had been a great loss to the team, but he became Chairman of the AE Canada board and continues to serve the ministry with distinction from that end. The fledgling East African team needed more time and energy, as Michael and Festo wrote back and forth. Ebenezer Sikakane was welcomed to the South African team.

The imminence of a new decade was also a good time to pause and re-focus the work. The team felt AE must once again give thought to reaching urban Africa. "We have had all along an increasing involvement with the African situation and I believe our sensitivity has grown to the needs there," wrote Michael. "Now we are getting ready to move out in this arena in a new way, particularly by means of another team based in East Africa."

Another thing Michael wanted to deal with was the "success problem", a hazard to evangelists the world over, who were often overly enthused by measurable response, and overly dejected by the lack of obvious response. Such a roller-coaster attitude to their work had caused AE to misinterpret their efforts. A wiser, saner course, Michael felt, would be to concentrate on faithfulness, rather than success.

Meanwhile, on 16 December 1969, a radiantly happy Michael Cassidy, having driven from Pietermaritzburg to Cape Town on the wings of love – "I hardly needed a car for that journey!" – married Carol Bam in the Congregational Church of Claremont, her parents' home church.

Michael Cassidy had not "fumbled the ball on this one", as Chris Smith had so feared he might.

Chapter 10

From Platform to Superstructure

As 1970 dawned it was almost exactly ten years since the first rather anxious and tentative AE prayer letters had been sent out from Pasadena by the trembling young student at Fuller Seminary.

The decade had seen the birthing and bringing forth of a dream and a vision. The story of that birthing and all that had preceded it, and how God brought it to fruition, has now been told. And we have told the story of how Michael Cassidy, just an "ordinary" man, was called by God to do something pretty "extraordinary", and found African Enterprise. This is the basic platform and foundation for the rest of the story, and the super-structure of the three decades which followed.

Nineteen-seventy brought forth the great Mission '70, a year-long outreach in Johannesburg with some 300 churches participating. More of that later. But suffice it for now to say that with the platform laid in that first decade, the team was ready to move forward and develop on a wide assortment of fronts and in many different ways. But Michael would always feel acutely the departure in 1969 of Paul Birch – "The best piano accompanist I ever knew" – then of the brilliantly gifted Dick and Judy Peace in early 1971 and finally some seven years later of "that grand and versatile lieutenant, Chris Smith" and his lovely wife Barbie with the mellow singing voice that had enchanted thousands over the years. Chris had felt a developing anxiety about raising his daughter in apartheid South Africa, and decided that she should be educated in the USA. When Paul and these two families left, Michael felt that several major limbs of his life and of the AE ministry had been lopped off. How ever would he manage without them? What was God doing? Perhaps he was indigenising the work in Africa and giving it now primarily to those of the African soil. But those who were to come would forever be indebted to those gifted pioneers from North America.

To narrate now the entire subsequent story blow by blow in chronological order would require a volume several times the size of this one.

However, the most important thing is that, since 1970 and the birth of the East Africa team in 1971, many other African Christians have felt called by God to join African Enterprise. Michael's vision for African Enterprise has become *their* vision as well. Like Michael, these African Christians are also just "ordinary" men and women, but with a God-given and often exceptional "gift" for evangelism.

That gift is wonderfully evident wherever they go. Whether it is person-to-person, to small groups, or to large crowds, AE evangelists always seek to proclaim the love of Christ, so that people are irresistibly drawn to him. It seems as if AE evangelists are often used by God to act as his lightning conductors for getting the Good News of Heaven down to earth. Wherever AE evangelists speak about Jesus, their prayer is that the Holy Spirit's lightning of spiritual awakening will strike. Indeed, faith has been earthed deep in countless thousands of people's hearts as the gospel has been proclaimed across Africa. Festo loved to remind the teams: "We are only little donkeys carrying our Lord downtown!"

But that first decade had not always been plain sailing. There had been failures, relational hassles, and always, seemingly, "the possession of difficulties", as "that word from the Lord" in a tract had promised Michael back in Minnesota in the summer of 1960. But the Lord's grace and mercy had held the team. The challenge for the future was to know how to do better, how to fish where the fish are and how to do things the Lord's way, not man's.

Festo loved to preach about the Cross and on grace and mercy, and this would bless all in AE in the years to come, as the ministry entered a new chapter. As he once said when talking about the disciples' encounter with Jesus when they had failed and could not catch fish:

These men were better fishermen than Jesus. They were experts in this business of catching fish, and they thought they knew what to do. Yet they had to confess that, after fishing all night long, they had caught nothing. Their nets remained empty. Without him, even missions and campaigns, despite good methods, remain empty. "No, Lord, we have nothing!" No rebuke came, and it didn't come later. Some of us would have lectured the disciples and given them a long lesson on what they should have done. There was no rebuke from him. Failure itself rebukes better than any sermon. When you fail, you know it. And you don't need a preacher to remind you of it. The Lord understood. He knew the disciples had had enough. What does he say to them? "Will you please put your nets on the right side? Then you will get fish." They were too weak by then not to obey. Some of us are too strong to obey. It takes failure to make some people obedient. Then with failure staring them in the face, give them any suggestion and they lap it up. You see, faith is weakness hanging on to strength. The lessons of failure make us more dependent on the Lord, more obedient than success does. So these men dropped the nets and the fish were caught. So simple! And so wonderful! The nets were alright; the methods were alright. There had been something else lacking, something more essential. It was the power of him who rose from the dead, enabling the weak to cope with whatever needed to be done.

Yes, it takes failure to make some people obey, and AE's failures as well as its successes were pressing the team into that new posture of maturing faith, where "faith is weakness hanging on to strength" and feeling out in new ways for that "power of him who rose from the dead", to make up for all lacks.

Glory Through Grace

Taking lessons like these on board, the team looked to the future and the challenges of growing the ministry through the grace of God. Indeed had not the Apostle said: "Having this ministry by the mercy of God, we do not lose heart" (2 Corinthians 4:1).

Expanding the work of course meant taking on more evangelists, and more evangelists meant more teams. Not surprisingly, then, the African Enterprise teams have grown in number. In Southern Africa there are now permanent AE teams in Malawi, South Africa and Zimbabwe. In East Africa there are teams in Kenya, Rwanda, Tanzania and Uganda. In West Africa there is a team in Ghana, while other younger teams are in place in Congo (DRC) and Ethiopia. Excellent linkages in Egypt may pave the way for a team there. Other teams will inevitably come on-stream to serve other sectors of the continent.

Through these teams, Michael's God-given vision for Africa has begun to come true. AE teams *have* indeed been at the task of evangelising the cities of Africa. Every single one of those 31 cities Michael prayed for in 1961 is still prayed for and the team has conducted missions in many of them.

In fact, since 1970, AE teams have held literally hundreds of missions. The missions have ranged from two evangelists – visiting rural communities by bicycle or on foot to preach under trees – to nearly 100 evangelists blitzing modern African cities. They have preached to thousands in soccer stadiums and even once to 300,000 people on a racecourse, as with the closing Addis Ababa mission rally in 1995.

AE evangelists have led every kind of person imaginable to Christ: murderers in prison, prostitutes in slums, witch-doctors, street sweepers, miners, factory workers, public school-boys, university professors, lawyers, doctors, presidents of major corporations, senior politicians and even members of royal families.

Yet African Enterprise's impact on the churches of Africa has not just been through the missions. AE has never wanted just "converts" to Christ. Its aim has been to make *disciples* for Christ, people who will think through what it means to be a Christian in every area of their lives. In Africa, especially hot issues have been the social and political implications of following Christ.

Initiatives

With this end in view, AE has launched a number of other initiatives over the past three decades or so, including:

- A series of major pan-African conferences to bring together the leading Christians of the continent. Unity among Christians is fundamental if they are to be truly the Body of Christ.

- Extensive use of clergy seminars and conferences to build up thousands of pastors, clergy and lay workers in countries right across Africa. You can't expect isolated, discouraged and untrained men and women, however sincere, to build healthy, dynamic churches.

- Two conference centres, one in South Africa and one in Kenya, to provide thousands of people with training and encouragement in the Christian faith.

- Major political reconciliation initiatives, such as those spearheaded by Michael Cassidy in his attempt to bring the calming voice of Christ into the maelstrom of South African politics, and by Reconciliation Ministries Director Emmanuel Kopwe, with his intense reconciliation endeavours in Burundi, and by AE Rwanda team leader Antoine Rutayisire in the aftermath of the Rwandan genocide.

- A great number of other "reconciliation initiatives" that have brought together estranged people, especially from political circles, to seek reconciliation before God.

- A number of books, written by Michael Cassidy, AE Malawi team leader Stephen Lungu and Antoine Rutayisire on the gospel's witness and application in African contexts.

- Extensive relief aid to Uganda, following the terrible years of dictators Idi Amin and Milton Obote.

- An extensive feeding programme for schoolchildren in the townships of South Africa.

- Humanitarian aid to the refugee camps in Rwanda.

Of course, African Enterprise evangelists have not done all this on their own. Over the years a vast network of Christians around the world have felt called by God to give AE vital back-up support.

The boards which govern AE include more wise minds than you could shake a stick at. These include an impressive assortment of bishops, deans of faculties of universities, professors of theology, clergy from major churches, senior business and management figures and financial experts. Powerful and concerned Christians around the world back AE.

Support groups in countries such as Australia, New Zealand, USA, Canada, the UK, Switzerland, Germany, Belgium, Ireland and Norway offer vital prayer and financial support through supporting churches and individuals. Michael Cassidy's dream is to extend the network of AE linkages to Asia and Latin America so that AE becomes a truly global partnership, blessing the worldwide church and being in turn blessed by it.

But the unsung members of the AE family are perhaps the most heroic of all: the quiet lay Christians who never get to see the excitement of a mission, who may never even meet an evangelist, but who all the same pray faithfully and give regularly to support the work. They are found singly and in pairs all over the world, from California to the Cape to Sydney to Lausanne. A little old lady in Melbourne who had taken public transport to get to one of Michael's meetings, and whom he had never met, said: "I pray for you every day." In the USA a family said to Ugandan team leader Edward Muhima: "We pray for you faithfully and our children call you 'Uncle Edward'." At the end of the day, it is only the faithful stewardship of such as these in terms of prayers and finance that makes it possible to keep the AE show on the road.

And what a show!

Between 1970 and 2002, African Enterprise's ministry took hundreds of evangelists on hundreds of missions from Cairo to the Cape and back again. In any one monthly issue of *AE Update*, a newsletter for supporters, you can find AE evangelists reporting back from schools, universities, hospitals, prisons, factories, mines, various business, commerce and financial circles, and even occasionally presidential palaces. They've just returned from villages, towns, cities in various countries across Africa, or even from overseas. They tell stories of lives changed, suicides averted, and people radiant with joy to learn that their life has meaning and purpose after all – that someone cares about them.

When you scan the decades of such joyful activity, the AE

story becomes a dazzling kaleidoscope. The colours are always the same, but the picture is endlessly changing. New patterns form every month as missions are held and people reached. Then – whoosh – a shake and all is changed. New missions, new ventures to new cities, different countries – yet more new people finding at last the answer to their life's longing: the love of Christ for them personally. Month by month, down 40 years, the kaleidoscopic picture forms, dazzles, is shaken, is re-formed, and shines radiant once again. Each beautiful picture is iridescent, glowing with the love of Christ in action across the vastness of Africa.

How to tell such a story without making the reader's head spin with endless names and places? Even in this fairly substantial volume, one can highlight a mere cross-section and sample of the highlights of the AE story as it unfolded from 1970 onwards.

A good way to start is to meet some of the extraordinary "ordinary" men and women who have made up the AE teams. Their stories and experiences all speak of a God who still uses weak vessels to do amazing things. And maybe even now, "we ain't seen nothing yet"!

Chapter 11

A Team Together

An entire book could be written about the lives and testimonies of the AE evangelists alone. Sadly, it is not possible to introduce everyone – or even most of them. There is room only to tell a few of the stories of these AE evangelists, all either national, regional or local team leaders, who have come in over the years.

Festo Kivengere

Festo Kivengere has already featured heavily in the AE story. So here we can be brief. But what a career he had! Festo Kivengere had been born about 1918 in the hinterland of southwest Uganda. His family were of a royal clan and were cattle herders. Festo grew up, like all the tribe, believing in animism and drinking cow's blood for food. He was nine years old before he even knew that white people existed. When he saw his first white missionary, in 1929, he was terrified and hid in the grass. In due course, the missionaries persuaded Festo's parents to let him attend their little school, where he learned to write using banana leaves for paper. Festo learned about Christianity through his schooling, but remained uncommitted. After further training to become a teacher himself, he was notorious for being against the Christians. But the East African Revival eventually caught up with him, and one night in his home village of Rukungiri, a village in south-west Uganda, he experienced a dramatic, life-changing conversion.

The very next morning he became an evangelist, for his electrifying testimony brought several of the boys in his class to faith in Christ within the hour. Festo, a natural leader, soon became one of the local leaders of the revival, until he felt God calling him to take the revival to Tanzania. He and his wife

Mera and daughters spent a number of years teaching in Dodoma, where they helped establish the revival, and Festo's fame as an evangelist spread. In due course, Festo returned to be schools inspector for Kigezi Diocese in Uganda and then a few years later went to Pittsburgh, Pennsylvania, to study for ordination. An international ministry as an outstanding evangelist quickly developed until, by the late 1960s, Festo was loved in church circles all around the world.

Festo teamed up with Michael Cassidy in 1970–71 to launch the East African team of African Enterprise. He began with a team in Uganda, and Christians in Kenya and Tanzania were soon interested as well. Early missions were warmly received but life became much complicated first by Ugandan dictator Idi Amin's brutal regime, which spread terror and widespread disruption of travel and communications across the country, and then by the Church of Uganda making Festo Bishop of Kigezi in 1972. He was greatly loved as Bishop, but inevitably the time he gave to the diocese was time lost to that early team. But he rode the two horses as only Festo could.

Festo's testimony and stand nearly got him killed in 1978 when the Archbishop of Uganda, and also incidentally chairman of AE, Janani Luwum, was assassinated by Idi Amin, who then sent his Nubian guerrillas after Festo. Festo and Mera escaped on foot through the mountains into Rwanda and on into exile until late 1979. Bishop Festo in exile became a potent force for Uganda, for Christ and for AE as he travelled extensively around the world, preaching and raising support for the Ugandan refugees. By the time of his return in 1979, Bishop Festo had achieved "superstar" status within Uganda and in many places across the world.

Sadly, in late 1987 Festo fell ill with leukaemia, and died in Nairobi in May 1988. Uganda gave a state funeral to this beloved son, and many thousands attended the funeral and memorial services across Uganda. Michael Cassidy felt specially privileged to preach at the huge memorial service for his friend Festo in Namirembe Cathedral in Kampala.

David Peters

Another of the additions to AE in the early 1970s , this time in South Africa, as some of the North American team members left, was David Peters. David was born of Indian Hindu parents in Pietermaritzburg in 1934 and is one of the best-known and most enthusiastic evangelists on the AE team. His preaching ministry, counsel, and healing ministries are sought out widely by people all across South Africa. David grew up effectively as an orphan and found his most congenial company amongst gangsters. Not just a gangster but a prankster, he would some-times steal food offered to the idols in the Hindu temple and then chuckle no end when rejoicing worshippers said the gods had eaten their offerings. He was passionately anti-white and identified with the politically militant Natal Indian Congress, which struggled for decades to overthrow the South African apartheid regime. His formal education was minimal and when the team first encountered him it was as a petrol attendant in the Valley Service Station in Pietermaritzburg, where Chris Smith and other members of the team periodically filled their cars. Chris and Michael always remembered this vibrant per-sonality at the station who always wore the widest of smiles and attended to your car better than anyone else in town.

A point came in David's life when he was involved in a major gang fight and received a serious head wound, which landed him in hospital. While there, some Christians doing hos-pital calling ministered to him and the way was opened up for him to come to Christ, particularly when the healing power of Jesus touched him in his injury and also brought to an end fear-ful headaches which had become part of his life. "I had to get a hole in the head," said David, "for the Lord's light to come in!" In 1972 David was invited into the AE team. Then in 1973 he participated with the team in the Congress on Mission and Evangelism in Durban to which Dr Billy Graham had been invited. Natal being a home to many Indians, the AE team decided that it would be appropriate for David and his beloved wife Edna to be right up front in the welcoming party when the great evangelist arrived in South Africa.

David began his life in AE as a backroom worker running the mimeograph machine. It soon became apparent that David had a gift for befriending and counselling people who came by the team office. Before long he was giving his testimony in meetings, then preaching, and in no time at all an outstanding evangelistic gift began to emerge which has taken him all over South Africa and around the world. He also exercised amazing gifts of healing, counselling and supernatural knowledge.

Once he went to Michael and Carol's home to help counsel a domestic who had become caught up in witchcraft. After David had ministered to her, he asked whether she had surrendered all her witchcraft paraphernalia. She said she had. Then the Lord spoke to him and said: "What about the things that are in the bottom right-hand drawer of your wardrobe?" David had not even been into her room, but he then insisted on doing so. She began to shake. When they got to the room and opened the door, they indeed found all sorts of witchcraft paraphernalia in the bottom right-hand drawer of the wardrobe. The gift of "knowledge" had operated supernaturally.

In 1995 when AE set up several regional teamlets in different cities, David took charge of the Pietermaritzburg teamlet and established the Lord's Counselling Room in an arcade of downtown Pietermaritzburg, of which more will be said later. Very sadly David lost his beloved wife Edna a number of years ago and, with his five children, has continued to feel that loss acutely.

John Wilson

One of the most special additions to AE in the early 1970s was John Wilson of Uganda, often described by Michael as "one of the best and most loyal friends I ever had in Africa. Certainly he was a key with Festo in getting our East African teams up and running and keeping us all together."

John Wilson was born on Christmas Day, 1922, in Butakula, Uganda. He was the eldest son of Edward John Wilson, a wealthy timber contractor who had seven children with John's mother, and fourteen with his second wife. Edward Wilson, however, did not put a high premium on the education of his children, so the determined young John saw his own way through school, finding teachers and mentors along the way who saw his eagerness to learn and gave him the help and encouragement he needed. He eventually made his way to Makerere University where he "discovered" and embraced evolution. He renounced God, adopted the philosophy that man was a product of chance, and set out on a journey of drinking and making merry. John soon became a heavy smoker and drinker and was caught up in an immoral lifestyle. But a chance meeting with a young woman by the name of Mary Mukasa changed his life forever and led finally to his conversion in June 1955.

John Wilson worked in many different arenas of life, eventually winding up at Caltex Petroleum, where he started as a salesperson and ended up as one of the directors. It was during his years at Caltex that John, already close friends with Festo Kivengere, met Michael Cassidy in 1969. Everywhere Michael went in Kampala on that early visit he heard about this most unusual Christian businessman called John Wilson. The two men met, clicked and formed an immediate bond.

Although very effective and much in demand as a Christian businessman giving his testimony here, there and everywhere, John began to feel more and more that God might be calling him into fulltime Christian service. However his wife Mary was not at all sure about this. She had comfort and financial security and wondered what the uncertainties of fulltime Christian ministry might bring. There were also seven children to educate.

In the meantime Michael Cassidy had been popping in and out of Uganda to see Festo and meet with the developing local AE board. In 1973, there was something of a crisis in the Uganda team and board and Michael came to Uganda with Keith Jesson to meet with Festo, his colleague Zebulini Kabaza and the board. However, at immigration, Michael was denied entry not for being a South African but because his passport occupation was "missionary". Idi Amin had said missionaries were no longer welcome in Uganda. Michael was told he must catch the next plane out of Uganda. Sitting in the airport lounge and praying hard to "the God of open doors", Michael decided to challenge the immigration official as to whether he was a Christian! The official answered in the affirmative to which Michael said: "How then, my brother, can you keep a fellow Christian brother out of your country?"

Reeling under what Michael later called this "rather low blow", he relented and let the South African in. The next day Michael and Keith were in John Wilson's office at Caltex when Amin's security people arrived and asked the rather startled John Wilson whether he had in his offices "a certain gentleman called Michael Cassidy".

John Wilson said yes, he had. He became very anxious because this was the Uganda of "people getting disappeared", and many awful brutalities were occurring. John was thoroughly alarmed that his friend should be picked up by Amin's security police. John accordingly, along with Keith Jesson, accompanied the police who took him to the Department of Foreign Affairs where his category was declared "UP". Michael assumed it meant Undesirable Person! The official said Michael must leave by the next plane out of Uganda. Michael said he would only leave by a plane taking him to Nairobi, and then home, not one flying that night to London. The official agreed, which allowed Michael, John, Keith, Festo and the team to meet in an extended session with the board that night with the great Archbishop Erica Sabite in the chair. The problems the team were facing were resolved that evening and Michael left the next day rejoicing.

This whole episode shook the Wilson family considerably and Mary, who had been so anxious about John going into full-time ministry, came to her husband and said: "My dear, if Amin can put people like Michael out of Uganda, then I believe that people like you should move fulltime into the Lord's work. I therefore release you to do so." Amin's drastic hand had been the devil overreaching himself and becoming the means by which John's call into the fulltime ministry could be fulfilled.

A few months later John was in AE as Deputy Regional Team Leader under Bishop Festo. After a year at Fuller Theological Seminary, John graduated with a Masters in Missiology and returned to Africa to begin an incredible ministry of peace and reconciliation that took him to every country in Africa, to most nations of the Middle East and several times around the world. In recognition of his outstanding efforts towards peace, he was awarded the St Andrew's Cross by the Archbishop of Canterbury, and was made a Companion of the Cross of Nails at Coventry Cathedral.

John Wilson's achievements with AE spanned over 17 years and are too numerous to list here but some of the highlights include PACLA (the Pan-African Christian Leadership Assembly, of which he was the co-ordinator), his relief efforts to the war-torn areas of Uganda, the RETURN programme (Relief, Education and Training for Ugandan Refugees Now) that helped many exiled Ugandan students to receive an education abroad, the Greater Kampala Mission, and MECLA (Middle East Christian Leadership Assembly), on which he was working so hard before his untimely death at the hands of gunmen in Uganda on 16 March 1986.

It was while trying to reconcile the warring factions in his beloved Uganda that John Wilson was martyred, leaving behind a legacy that is being continued today by his wife Mary and their seven children. The story of this outstanding man of God can be found in a very moving book by his daughter, Victoria Wilson Darrah, entitled *My Father's Daughter: Continuing the Dream for Peace and Reconciliation*.

Orpheus Hove

Orpheus was born in 1940 in the Mberengwa District of Zimbabwe, of non-Christian parents. His father was a polygamist and Orpheus was born of the younger wife, second-born of eight children from his mother and one of the many children from his father. His native name was Muzwondiwa Zivengwa, meaning "the hated one". The name was given by his mother as she was hated by other wives when he was born. The family worshipped ancestors and consulted witch-doctors and spirit mediums. Orpheus only heard of church when he joined a mission school at the age of fourteen. He then joined a church and did a three-year catechumen class, was baptised, and partook of Holy Communion and all other church activities, but without the Lord in his heart. He continued a life of ancestor worship and church at the same time, while preparing to take over from his father the leadership of the ancestor-worship ceremonies. He was taught how to call and appease the spirits, beat the drums and dance for the spirits till they manifested themselves.

At church he joined a youth group and church choir for fun and because his friends were members. In these groups he had fallen in love with several girls whom he was stringing along with promises of marriage. In 1961 there was a youth camp out in the mountains and one of these girls invited Orpheus to come. By now, he had left school and was herding a neighbour's cattle, as his father, with so many children, could no longer finance his education. On the first day of the camp, a Good Friday, a film of the crucifixion of Jesus was shown. Orpheus' heart was melted and after many struggles he finally confessed his sins and opened his heart for Jesus to come in. "Jesus met me that very day and saved me," testifies Orpheus.

For a while his parents could not understand Orpheus as he sought to cut himself free from ancestor worship, an immoral life, witchcraft and drinking of animals' blood. He also had to separate from at least a dozen girlfriends. He was then expelled from home for six months because of his newfound faith, and not allowed to go back to his workplace because he had supposedly betrayed the family. Through help from other spiritually grown-up youths he broke away from his old life and continued to grow in the Lord. "It's only by God's grace that I became a Christian and have remained one, considering the dark family from which I came," says Orpheus today.

He then started to testify and preach at school, at work, in buses and on trains. Later in 1963 he joined a Bible School with the Dorothea Mission, a tent ministry, and did three years of Bible training after which he worked with the organisation as a team member, Bible School teacher, Bible School Principal and finally the ministry's National Director until 1984. Interestingly enough, one of those who helped to disciple Orpheus was Robert Footner, who had led Michael into Christian commitment back in Cambridge in 1955. Robert himself, having become interested in Africa through Michael, later joined the Dorothea Mission, where he came into close contact with Orpheus and indeed also Stephen Lungu, whom likewise he helped to disciple and who would become such a pivotal figure in the AE ministry. For Michael and many in AE, Robert Footner is a special and unsung hero.

In 1983 Chris Sewell, then team leader of AE Zimbabwe, invited Orpheus to lead devotions in their offices and it was after this that Orpheus began to feel strongly drawn, as he put it, "by their worldview of evangelism which expressed my own heartbeat". Knowing also that Lungu was going with AE, he joined the team in Zimbabwe in 1984, serving as its team leader from 1991 to 2001. During this time he also became one of Michael's deputy international team leaders. Today Orpheus has travelled all over Africa and finds it difficult to believe that he came from a background of pagan beliefs and practices. Not only Michael, but his teammates and all who know him say: "Now if you want to see a real Christian gentleman, look at Orpheus Hove!"

Stephen Lungu

Steve Lungu was born in Malawi in 1942. His mother and father had a very difficult time of it and finally divorced when Stephen and his brothers and sisters were quite small. What made it all worse was that neither of the parents wanted the children, who therefore felt totally rejected. Stephen puts it this way:

> All I knew was beatings every day and that I had to feed myself somehow. I never experienced the love of a father or mother. I also denied the existence of God. I thought Jesus Christ was a white man; and if there was a God, I hated him for bringing me into this world. I hated myself and I hated the frightening tomorrow. I said to myself, "The only way is to end my life." The fact is I didn't want to wake up the next day and face more suffering so one day I took a rope and tried to hang myself, but somehow didn't succeed properly. People later found me and saved my life.

In the coming years, he took to drugs, glue and spirits and joined a gang of young thugs called the Black Shadows, who would roam the streets at night robbing people or breaking into houses. But none of this was spiritually or emotionally satisfying. Said Steve later: "There was always a vacuum and an emptiness in my life. I tried to fill it with girls, with drink, with cigarettes, with coveting flashy clothes and so on but still the emptiness was there."

On top of this were the political tensions of the situation in pre-independence Rhodesia, where Steve Lungu was now living. In fact, in Salisbury, Rhodesia, in the spring of 1962 peace and comfort were rare commodities for any blacks. In the preface to his autobiography *Out of the Black Shadows*, Steve writes:

> The whites had the army, the police, and plenty of guns to maintain the right-wing government and the status quo. But they did not have all the fighters and all the guns. The city was riddled with left-wing factions, financed by the Eastern block countries. They wanted control of Rhodesia and so mobilised a second, secret army and armed it with petrol bombs, hand grenades, Russian rifles and pistols. Local political agitators urged the Black Shadows and hundreds like us to cause more trouble.

By the late 1950s and into the 1960s the Black Shadows were hard at work in the townships of Salisbury. Their instructions were to cause maximum public terror and civil unrest. For Steve, this produced some satisfaction and enjoyment. He had grown up frightened and angry and at last he was getting his own back. But then one Sunday evening early in 1962 his gang decided to bomb a bank in a nearby shopping centre. Soon after the group set out with their little bags of home-made explosive devices, petrol bombs and knives, they came across an evangelistic tent meeting being conducted by the Dorothea Mission from South Africa. Stephen could hardly believe his luck. To petrol bomb a tent filled with hundreds of Christians was much better than blowing up a mere bank!

Interestingly enough, one of the people participating in the service that night was Tom Barlow, Michael's friend from Cambridge whom he had the privilege of leading into Christian commitment back in 1956. Here now again was Barlow sharing his testimony before the main speaker. This was the man who had sold his polo ponies and given Michael the money so he could fly to Fuller Seminary in late 1959.

Steve was staggered when a beautiful young girl from Soweto gave her testimony about finding Christ. This was riveting. In the meantime he was planning his attack and gearing up to throw his flaming petrol bottles. But somehow in the process of all of this, as he sat with his gangster friend at the back of the tent the words of the preacher, Shadrach Moloka, seemed to pierce Stephen's heart and whenever he pointed his finger it seemed to be pointed straight at Stephen. At one point the preacher quoted 2 Corinthians 8:9: "For you know the grace of our Lord Jesus Christ, that though he was rich, yet for your sakes he became poor, so that you through his poverty might become rich."

Stephen, however, was particularly startled when the preacher began weeping and put fresh urgency into his words when he said: "I am crying because I know that there are people here tonight who may die without Christ." When the preacher gave the gospel appeal at the end of his sermon, Steve knew this was his moment, a moment to be delivered from the intolerable burden of pain and hurt and evil that had haunted him all his days. "So, clutching my bag of petrol bombs, I stumbled through the little group of people around me and began to make my way forward. I had never been to a service like this, and I had no idea that the preacher intended to invite people forward at the end of the service in any case. I simply wanted to be near him. He would help me find this Jesus." Stephen found himself sobbing at the preacher's feet.

But just at that moment an avalanche of stones flew into the tent. People screamed and panic broke out. A minor explosion also followed as a petrol bomb was flung on to the outside canvas of the tent, setting it ablaze. Little sheets of flame sprang up, but fortunately did not spread. People screamed. A moment later dozens of stones were hurled against the tent and many of them came inside, injuring some people. But by this time Stephen had made the greatest decision ever of his life, the decision to follow Christ. The sense of transformation and the presence of Jesus powerfully and quickly overtook Stephen. Before long he was sharing his testimony with everyone he met, and even on buses. Anyone hearing him might quickly have decided that here was a born preacher. Stephen got to know members of the Dorothea Mission, including the famous Patrick Johnstone of Operation World, who encouraged and discipled him, in due time inviting him to become part of their ministry. Years later, as an evangelist for the Dorothea Mission, Steve met Michael Cassidy when the South African was the main speaker in 1982 at the Keswick Convention Conference in Blantyre, Malawi.

Says Stephen in his autobiography *Out of the Black Shadows*, "In May 1982, after nineteen very happy years with the

Dorothea Mission, I joined African Enterprise. I knew a new life was about to begin: I was excited at the prospect of wider horizons." Since that time Stephen has become one of the most powerful evangelists, not only in Africa but around the world. His testimony in both spoken and written form has gone far and wide. As leader of the Malawi team, he has had endless opportunities of gospel witness in his own country and he is always a hit in AE's major African campaigns. In other parts of the world people are, not surprisingly, riveted by his story.

In 1998 Michael made Stephen one of his four deputy international team leaders with a roving international assignment in addition to his local role as team leader in his own country.

Israel Havugimana

Not long after Steve Lungu came into AE, another very remarkable young man was joining the work in Rwanda at the instigation and encouragement of Festo Kivengere, who knew him well. He would lead AE Rwanda from 1984 to 1994. His name was Israel Havugimana. His service to the ministry would be distinguished indeed. And for his witness he would pay the supreme price with his life in April 1994.

Israel Havugimana was born in 1954 in the Gikongoro Prefecture of Rwanda. The East African Revival, which swept the landscape in the 1930s, made a second visit in the 1960s to the East African countries of Rwanda, Uganda, Burundi and Congo. Israel was a secondary student attending a teacher training college when he came to a saving knowledge of the Lord Jesus Christ. This second Revival hit mainly the youth population, and Israel was one of its products.

However, it wasn't until his days at the National University in Butare where Israel took ownership of his faith and really started serving the Lord. After graduating from Butare, Israel pursued further studies in Belgium. He then returned to Rwanda and worked for Scripture Union as the Evangelism Coordinator for Rwanda, Burundi and Congo. He began the work of an itinerant evangelist and his reputation spread nationwide.

Concurrently, Festo Kivengere and AE were seeking to start a new team which would reach the francophone countries of

Rwanda, Burundi and Congo in East Africa. Bishops Festo Kivengere, Emmanuel Kolini of Congo (later to become Archbishop of Rwanda) and Sindamuka of Burundi all agreed that Israel was the man to lead this new team called African Evangelistic Enterprise (AEE) with "Evangelistic" inserted to clarify the central activity. The organisation would be based in Kigali, Rwanda. Israel became AEE's first team leader in 1984. Two years later, Israel was married to Jacqueline and they quickly began a family.

In 1990, Jacqueline died. While others would have folded under the pressure and pain of losing a spouse, Israel's determination kept the ministry of AEE going. His determination was fuelled mainly by his passion for reconciliation. In 1988 and 1989, ethnic problems rapidly began to rise between the Hutus and Tutsis in Rwanda. Although Israel was part of the Hutu ethnic group, he did not take sides in the ethnic conflict and, as a peacemaker, he was not afraid to speak prophetically to both government and people about many of the Hutu injustices. He organised ethnically mixed prayer groups and conferences for the clergy and the top leadership of the country with the theme of reconciliation. AEE's passion and commitment for reconciliation were birthed in these meetings. Because Israel proved by his actions to be genuinely impartial during this time, both sides disliked him and were suspicious of him. As ethnic tensions rose, Israel became even more determined to bring reconciliation to the land. AEE became famous, said one Rwandan, and well known for their reconciliation endeavours.

By 1993, Israel was beginning to pay the price for his unswerving stand against the hostility and hatred which ruled the day. In the early 1990s, he had many opportunities to leave Rwanda in the face of potential danger to him and his three young children. Israel, however, cared deeply for the people of his country and would not leave without furthering his crusade of reconciliation. Late one night in 1993, Israel and his son had been watching television when a grenade was thrown through the window of his home. Providentially both Israel and his son had just moved out of the room, the lad to go to bed and Israel to attend to a chore. Mercifully both escaped injury or death. A second grenade was thrown into the home of a woman who was part of Israel's prayer group. She was not killed either.

In February 1994, following an AE International Partnership Board meeting in Uganda, Michael, Malcolm Graham, David Hewetson and Don Jacobs visited Israel and saw the shrapnel holes all round his sitting room. It had been a very close shave. But Israel was undaunted. At that time, Israel also took the visiting IPB members down to displacee camps in the southern part of the country where there were some 300,000 displacees who had fled their homes to take shelter in these improvised tent "mini-cities". AE had also had the privilege of putting up some classrooms for refugee kids to learn in during the day.

At that same time, Israel opened up for Michael the opportunity to address the leadership and membership of most of the Christian organisations of Kigali, where a brilliant young interpreter did the honours for Michael. His name was Antoine Rutayisire and, unbeknown to him or to Michael, he would soon take over the leadership of the AE team in Rwanda. To the NGO heads and church leaders, Michael said: "I believe the church here has all the trump-cards if it will only play them. Indeed, the church is the sleeping giant." To which everybody chorused, "Amen." Said Michael afterwards: "Was this the church talking in its sleep?"

On 7 April 1994, the plane carrying the presidents of Rwanda and Burundi was shot down in Rwanda. The Hutus blamed the Tutsis and in the next 100 days almost one million Tutsis and sympathetic Hutus were slaughtered. Israel was one of the first targets in the killings. The armed militia came to his home and took his money and belongings. They returned the same day, lined up Israel and two of his three children and shot them dead.

One may look at the life of Israel Havugimana and only think of tragedy. Christians, however, know the story does not end with mortal death.

Yes, the spirit of Israel Havugimana and his passion for reconciliation lives on. Deo Gloria!

Antoine Rutayisire

By a wonderful provision of God, when Israel died there was someone of outstanding gifts and spiritual stature ready to be raised up to lead the AE Rwanda team. Antoine Rutayisire was born in 1958 in the eastern part of Rwanda to a country family. His father was a very industrious "jack of all trades" running a fishing business and a small shop as well as tending his fields and cows when he was not out selling something. This comfortable life was not to last as Rwanda witnessed the first waves of ethnic massacres against the Tutsis from 1959 to 1964.

That was when Antoine lost his father. In his book, *Faith Under Fire*, he records that:

> when I was five years old my father was seemingly butchered in broad daylight, before our very eyes, and left for dead in front of our house. He later on recovered, but was taken once more, and we never saw him again.
>
> We never even saw his body, we were never able to bury it. This kept us in a state of suspense for many years, hoping that maybe he had managed to escape and would come back some day. The death of a dear one is very difficult to accept when you have not witnessed it, or at least have evidence like a grave to prove it. I grew up thinking maybe my father was somewhere and would come back. When they talked of his death my young heart and mind could not accept it.
>
> When I finally came to accept my father's death I turned my anger on all people I had seen beating my father and looting our possessions. Every time I had a problem I always remembered the massacre scene, and blamed my problem on the people. "If they had not killed my father, I wouldn't be faced with such a problem," was my simplified way of thinking. I grew to hate even their children and I remember I used to persecute one of them who was with me in secondary school. He was far younger and did not even know what his father had done to mine. He could not understand why I hated him and I never took pains to explain... Then during the massacres of 1972–73 we had to undergo a series of humiliating escapes, spending sleepless nights in hiding, uncertain of the future. I survived the experience, but this added to my list of enemies to hate. The tree of ethnic hatred in my heart was growing branches. (*Faith Under Fire*: pp. 105–106)

With the death of his father, Antoine now had to shoulder many family responsibilities with his mum, then only 25, who was now a widow with four children. Not surprisingly, Antoine says he often feels he never had a childhood.

The calling of the Lord started at the age of seven when, for the first time, Antoine went to church. The first thing he went home with was the image of the priest in his majestic robes. And Antoine felt that perhaps he would be called to become a priest when he grew up. At the end of his elementary school, at age twelve, he was registered in a Roman Catholic junior seminary to train for the priesthood. The Catholic junior seminaries are very elitist schools offering classical studies in Latin, as well as lots of lessons in modern languages and sciences. Antoine was very good at all those and when he finished that level of schooling, he had outgrown his ambition to become a priest. He went to the National University of Rwanda, where he graduated with a Masters in Modern Literature (English and French). He was then recruited to become a lecturer at the same university, but after one year of service he lost his position because the government had come up with an "apartheid" policy under which Tutsi were not allowed to occupy positions of influence in government-run services.

It was during that time of disappointment that Antoine started reading the Bible and became convicted of his sins and gave his life to the Lord. He committed himself to read the Bible at least three times from cover to cover in six months before declaring his faith in the open. After that period he wrote to his friends and informed them of the decision he had taken to live according to the Bible, "calling right what the Bible calls right and calling wrong what the Bible calls wrong". Antoine started telling others about the great changes that Jesus brings into your life when you allow him. His ministry as an evangelist had started. In the school where he had been sent to teach he started Bible study, prayer, and social action groups that deeply impacted the school. He was then promoted to the position of deputy headmaster.

The call to fulltime ministry came in 1990 when, with a group of university graduates, Antoine came up with the idea of starting the work among the university students. He was chosen to pioneer that movement, which today has spread over all the campuses of the country, numbering around 2,000 Christian students among the 8,000 that attend the higher institutes of Rwanda. Antoine still ministers to the students and is the chairman of the Union des Groupes Bibliques du

Rwanda (Fellowship of Evangelical Students), a branch of the International Fellowship of Evangelical Students (IFES). It was during his time of service with the IFES that Antoine came into contact with AE. Israel Havugimana and four other members on his team were among the pioneers of the movement. Antoine became an associate evangelist with AE. Later on he was elected to the board as secretary.

When the genocide began in April 1994, Antoine, his wife Peninah and his children found their lives immediately threatened. A group of Hutu soldiers approached their house. They were discussing whether first to throw a hand grenade into the compound or just break in. Antoine remembers it all vividly:

"This is our turn," I told myself. Immediately wild and weird thoughts whirled in my mind at a flashing speed. "Am I going to let them rape my wife, kill my child and all these young women and men in my home under my very eyes without even some attempt to protect them? What type of death are we going to die? Are they going to shoot us or to cut us into pieces?" I shuddered.

Then the idea crossed my mind: "Why don't you grab a stick or any other weapon at hand and go out and fight them? Can't you die like a man?" This was a spontaneous, human reaction. I could recognise my old self surging up, as in the past I would never have tolerated any ill-treatment without some reaction.

I was then deeply convicted in my heart as I remembered all the past efforts I had made to keep my heart pure of anger and bitterness. So I made this short prayer of confession: "Lord, forgive me for thinking of making my own defence and give me grace to obey you even unto death. I ask for your blessing on these people, and if it is your will that we die, have them give me time to die praying for them, as You did on the cross." At that very moment, a feeling of deep peace that I had never experienced before flooded through me, and I felt so light inside that a breeze could have swept me off the ground. I had accepted death, and I knew what I would do when the killers came. Everything else did not matter anymore. I was ready to face death with a Christ-like attitude, and I was even curious to know how it feels after death. (*Faith Under Fire*: pp. 25–29).

Mercifully and inexplicably, the soldiers suddenly turned away from Antoine and Peninah's home. It seemed God had spared the Rutayisires. Later they would learn of Israel's death and that of other members of the staff and board of AEE, and Antoine would answer the call to relaunch the ministry in Rwanda. From the ashes of the original team has risen a new team which is today ministering to more than 2,000 orphans and their families, carrying out a healing and reconciliation ministry to all the corners of the country and ministering through evangelistic outreaches and seminars to all the layers of the community from government ministers and parliamentarians down to the people in the villages.

Not surprisingly, Antoine is called on to speak in reconciliation conferences all across Africa and around the world.

Edward Muhima

In neighbouring Uganda, a mere hour's flight from Kigali, lives Edward Muhima and his wife, Vasta, and their family, along with "Kaaka", Edward's old mum. Kaaka must find it strange that this boy of hers is now not just Edward Muhima, but the Rev Canon Dr Edward Muhima, senior Anglican minister and international evangelist!

After all, she remembers that she gave birth to Edward, all by herself, under a banana tree beneath which she had laid some banana leaves. She remembers too the little boy growing up and serving as a herdboy for some five or six years looking after sheep, goats and cattle. He would not get the opportunity to go to school until he was ten. She also remembers that his home had been a simple little African hut in a simple little African village.

Edward's place of birth was in fact Kigezi in south-west Uganda, and his early life was in the very large family of his polygamous father. Not just a polygamist, his father was also a priest in the traditional religion and a chief in the then colonial administration. After he died in 1954, each of his many wives became responsible for her own children. Edward's mother, Kaaka, being the youngest of the wives, had the youngest lot of children to take care of and she had a deep desire for her children to go to school. Even though she herself was illiterate, she knew that educated people became important and rich and that was what she wanted for her own children.

In 1956 she was able to send Edward to a church school as

he turned ten. That same year Edward was baptised and took the name of Edward rather than his Mukiga tribal name, Bakaitwako. Three years later he was confirmed and had access to Holy Communion, but it meant little to him and did not affect his life. "I was the same after they were carried out as I was before."

Not surprisingly, growing up without a father around, Edward became quite a wild character with what he called "lots of smoking, drinking and womanising". In the middle of all of that he also became a champion athlete and was a star in the 100 yards and 220 yards races and the high jump. In fact, he was a reserve for the national team of Uganda and was due to represent his country at the Commonwealth Games in Perth in 1966, but at the last minute could not go because of his school exams.

He had enjoyed his high school education at the Nyakasura School in Fort Portal, western Uganda, near the Ruwenzori Mountains, the legendary "Mountains of the Moon". While at Bishop Tucker College, where he was doing his first extension degree from Makerere University, Edward found his heart more and more hungry and finally in 1969 committed his life to Jesus Christ. "I was never the same from that time on," said Edward. "I became a new creature."

In 1972 he was ordained a Deacon in the Kigezi Diocese of the Anglican Church of Uganda by Bishop Festo. Edward was then posted to a high school as a teacher and chaplain. In 1973, when Edward protested against the killing of one of his students by a firing squad of Idi Amin's people, Bishop Festo sensed that he might be in danger and decided to send him to the United States for further studies. Michael Cassidy remembers Bishop Festo saying to him once: "I have this brilliant young student that I want to send for further training. He has tremendous potential, possibly even for the future of our ministry."

Edward studied at Trinity Evangelical Divinity School and Northwestern University in Chicago, Illinois, earning in his eight years in the Windy City a Diploma in Christian Education, a Master of Divinity, a Master of Arts in Old Testament, and a PhD, writing a dissertation on "The Fellowship of Suffering – A Theological Interpretation of Christian Suffering Under Idi Amin". After the overthrow of Amin, he returned to Uganda.

He then taught at the Bishop Tucker Theological College, now the Uganda Christian University, for seven years after which he felt called more specifically into the ministry of evangelism. Bishop Festo invited him to join him in African Evangelistic Enterprise where Edward has served since 1987, becoming the Team Leader of AEE Uganda in April 1988 after the death of his famous and much-loved mentor, Bishop Festo.

Edward has participated in many AE missions, both national and pan-African since he joined AE and his highlight memory is that of the Dar es Salaam "Back to God" mission in 1991 in Tanzania, where he first became a witness to the power of God to cast out demons. Although he had always believed that God's people had authority to cast demons out of people, he had never witnessed this before. A startling moment came during the Dar mission when God used him actually to cast demons out of a young lady who has since become a powerful evangelist in Tanzania. Another highlight Edward remembers was when he preached in a church in Chicago and two homosexuals came forward to receive Christ and were delivered out of the gay lifestyle. One of them has also now become an evangelist.

God has given Edward a strong relationship with President Yoweri Museveni and his wife Janet, the First Lady of Uganda. As the Aids pandemic swept across Uganda with devastating consequences, Edward was one of the prominent voices appealing to the authorities of Uganda not just to teach and preach a condom culture but a change in sexual behaviour along the lines of Christian morality amongst the people of Uganda. This message in due course registered strongly with both the President and First Lady and Ugandan government policy became that of proclaiming a Judaeo-Christian view of sexual behaviour, namely abstinence before marriage and faithfulness within it. It is this message, in the view of many observers across Africa and around the world, which has resulted in Uganda being one of the very few places where the HIV/Aids pandemic has been turned back and where its incidence has dropped from 30 per cent to 9 per cent.

When Kaaka thinks of her son's accomplishments and recalls the banana tree and the banana leaves on which he arrived in the world, she must surely stand amazed and feel deep gratitude to her God!

Grace Kalambo

Not far from Edward's bailiwick in Uganda is the lovely land of Tanzania from which Grace Bayona Kalambo comes. Affectionately known as "Amazing Grace", this multi-gifted dynamic woman with the gifts of teaching, preaching, counselling and administration, is the only woman team leader at this time in African Enterprise. In this regard and in many others, she has been a trail-blazer of note.

Grace was born in the western part of Tanzania in a place called Bukoba. Her parents are committed Lutheran Christians, and she was brought up in that Christian atmosphere. She comes from a big family of twelve children, with four sisters and seven brothers. Her parents were very concerned with the welfare of their children so they both worked hard to enable all of them to go through formal education.

Although she grew up in a Christian home, Grace did not know Christ personally until she was 16 years old. The Holy Spirit challenged her about "following Jesus at a distance", as the Apostle Peter had done. The Holy Spirit told her to stop that hypocrisy, she made a deliberate confession of her secret sins, and she accepted Christ as her Lord and Saviour. Now, after more than two decades of walking with Christ, she still marvels at God's provision of mercies and grace.

When she completed high school Grace was offered places at two colleges of higher education, but by this time she had made a vow that she would serve the Lord. Her interest was to minister among youth. She decided to wait upon God, for she felt strongly that he had a place for her to serve him, even though she had no idea about the existence of African Enterprise. It didn't take long before someone from AE approached her and asked her to join the team and establish a youth desk. Grace praises God that, though she was unskilled then in 1985, God began to use her wonderfully all across Tanzania, especially with young people.

In her youth work, Grace increasingly felt that she needed to get some further qualifications in order to be maximally effective. Therefore in 1988 she went to Daystar University in Nairobi, Kenya, to study Communications and Christian Ministries. She got involved in youth ministries in Kenya and every weekend would be out doing evangelism in schools, colleges and churches. People around Grace quickly saw that no grass grew under the feet of this young dynamo. In spite of all her many evangelistic activities on the side, Grace nevertheless was able to apply herself diligently to her studies and was Best Student of the Year. Everybody knew that Grace was destined for leadership.

Finishing up at Daystar, Grace went back to AE in Tanzania and set up a communications desk and got going once again with all vigour in her much loved youth ministries. Her great desire and passion was to see African young people come to Christ. Indeed she could see no hope either for her country or her continent unless young people in the multiplied thousands and indeed millions turned to the living God in Christ.

She worked as a communications and youth officer in AE Tanzania until 1994 when she was appointed as office director for that team. This she carried out in addition to her evangelistic ministries which increasingly now had a new component in them, namely training others to do evangelism.

Says Grace: "The great need in Africa is training. There are many people who are willing and eager to do things for the Lord, but they lack training, and this is no less true of the field of evangelism than any other. People have to be taught and trained how to do evangelism with maximum impact." This realisation led Grace to feel that she should go to Wheaton College near Chicago and pursue a Master's Degree in Training and Education.

Michael well remembers talking to Grace by phone when she was in the middle of these studies in the States. He asked her how it was all going. "It is going wonderfully, but, Daddy, sometimes I am quite lonely and I wish I had a husband."

When Grace began calling Michael "Daddy" he started praying for her to find the right husband. That was always the deal thereafter. Grace would work hard at her studies for her ministry, while Michael prayed for her to find the right life partner! Grace returned to AE in Tanzania in 1997 when she was appointed team leader and remains in that role now. How "Daddy" Michael rejoiced when she married Anglican pastor Peter Kalambo, with whom she has had two children!

In her twelve years of ministry with AE Grace has seen

Happiness for Michael is a day at the sea during a "once-in-a-childhood" family holiday to Durban.

Michael's Mum and Dad, Dee and Charles Cassidy.

Robert Footner, who led Michael Cassidy into Christian commitment at Cambridge. (October 1955)

Three South African musketeers at Cambridge: Alasdair Macaulay, Michael Cassidy and Michael Nuttall.

Graduation Day 1958 – the Cassidy family comes to town: (Left-right) Judy, Charles, Michael, Dee and Olave.

The original team in 1962/63 with Dr Charles Fuller (centre) in Pasadena. (Left-right) Chris Smith, Paul Birch, Ed Gregory, Michael Cassidy, Dick Peace, Don Ehat (seated). *(Photo courtesy of the Billy Graham Evangelistic Association)*

The team – 1970: (Left-right) Chris Smith, Abiel Thipanyane, Michael Cassidy, Ebenezer Sikakane, John Tooke.

Two great South Africans are the first two chairmen of AE South Africa: Dr Edgar Brookes (left), and Bishop Alphaeus Zulu (right).

A great AE moment on 1st April 1969. Festo Kivengere and Michael Cassidy outside the Equatoria Hotel in Kampala, Uganda on the day Festo decided to join AE.

Michael and Carol get married in Cape Town, December 1969.

Billy Graham gives Michael the podium during St Louis, Missouri Crusade in 1973.

"On the spot." PACLA Press conference, Nairobi (December 1976). (Left-right) Michael Cassidy, Gottfried Osei-Mensah (PACLA Chairman) and John Wilson.

Historic meeting in Limuru, 1971, for launching of East African teams. Front row: Canon Elijah Gachanja, Archbishop Erica Sabiti, Rev. Yowasi Kinuuka, Lilian Clark, Helen Rufenacht. Standing: Gilbert Ngaywa, John Wilson, Bishop Gresford Chitemo, Zebulini Kabaza, Canon Yowasi Musajjakawa, Don Jacobs, Graham Carr, John Mpaayei, Festo Kivengere, Michael Cassidy, Matt Nyagwaswa.

Israel Havugimana, first Rwanda Team Leader, ministers in Kigali Mission 1989. Martyred in April 1984 during Rwandan genocide.

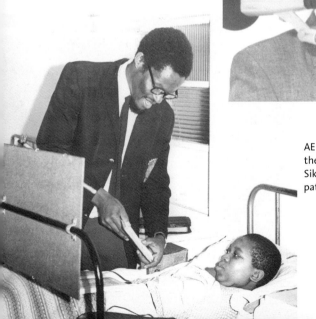

AE hospital missions began in the '70s. Here Ebenezer Sikakane ministers to a patient. (1974).

Pan-African AE teamlet at Peta-Tikvah, Israel (1983) when the biggest gathering yet of Jewish and Palestinian believers came together. L-R: Don Jacobs, Carol & Michael Cassidy, Steve Mung'oma, David Peters, John & Mary Wilson, Mera & Festo Kivengere.

"There's a Great Hallelujah Meeting over there" – Matt Nyagwaswa of Tanzania captivates King's School youngsters, Paramatta, Australia (1981).

AE/NIR teamlet inspects devastated black township on the edge of Port Elizabeth (March 1986). An hour after this picture was taken, the teamlet was arrested by security police for questioning. L-R: American AE intern Gary Haugen, Michael Cassidy, unidentified local pastor, Abiel Thipanyane, David Richardson.

Press conference at National Initiative for Reconciliation (NIR). (Left-right) Michael Cassidy, David Bosch, Desmond Tutu (1985).

International Partnership Board (IPB) meets in Harare (1986).

Bishop Festo's successor, Bishop Gresford Chitemo, visits with Coptic Pope Shenouda during AE ministry visit to Cyprus (1989).

thousands of people from different backgrounds come to Christ. There is nothing she loves more than seeing the acts of the Holy Spirit during AE missions. In one of the more recent missions conducted in Arusha, Tanzania, Grace was thrilled when a couple came together again after 20 years of separation and committed their lives to Christ after seeing their daughter wonderfully delivered from demonic oppression. "This sort of thing really thrills me," she says.

In Tanzania, which is 35 per cent Muslim on the mainland and 98 per cent Muslim on the island of Zanzibar, the AE ministry feels that one of its greatest challenges in the upcoming years is that of attempting to bring Muslims to know Christ as Saviour and Lord. Imagine Grace's delight when one young Muslim man came to Christ in one of the missions to Dar es Salaam. This same man is now an African Inland Church pastor who has also done theological training. Grace's team sees this kind of thing quite often.

A special challenge for Grace is Zanzibar, where the team has been trying to set up a mission for some time in spite of incredible difficulties, complications and opposition within that fully Muslim controlled island with its slave trading past, and its romantic and exotic associations in the eyes of foreigners.

"I know the Lord is going to open up Zanzibar for us," says Grace. "We came so close a couple of years ago to getting a mission up and running there and then political troubles torpedoed us. But it will come to pass. You watch." Thus the language of a leader – Amazing Grace of Tanzania.

Nii Amoo Darku

On the opposite side of the continent is Ghana, home of the Rev Dr Nii Amoo Darku, AE's Team Leader in that country. With a PhD in Urban Mission and Evangelism, and being a superb evangelistic preacher on the top of that, Nii Amoo Darku is perfectly placed and qualified to lead an evangelistic team whose focus is reaching the cities of Africa and doing it "through Word and deed in partnership with the church".

Nii Amoo was born into a Muslim family nearly 50 years ago. Although raised in the Muslim faith, he always felt that there was something missing and that he had not yet truly and fully found God. His restive heart was always yearning for more in spite of carrying out all the Muslim religious duties and rituals.

When he looks back, Nii Amoo says: "I believe that God is truly sovereign and that's why I believe He had this foreknowledge of me and how He would bring me to himself and make me one of His agents of change for our generation and the world."

In 1969, while in secondary school, Nii Amoo was brought face-to-face with the claims and challenges of Jesus Christ when he was invited to a Scripture Union meeting in his school.

In 1980 he found himself involved in a citywide evangelistic outreach and involved with a team of eager young evangelists. During this time he received his own call into fulltime ministry.

From that point on, nothing could hold him back. He served eagerly in an assortment of assignments and capacities, first as a Missions Director, and then as a pastor responsible for evangelism in a church that, at the time, had only 500 members. Such was Nii Amoo's zeal as Evangelism Director that when he left the church seven years later there were 4,000 members.

Nii Amoo also worked in the Missions Department of the Billy Graham Evangelistic Association in Ghana, where he served alongside the Director, Bob Williams, "a man of blessed memory for me," says Nii Amoo. By this time Nii Amoo had been a freelance evangelist for seven years and his passion was intensifying for ministry in his nation and across the continent. In fact when he was studying for his doctorate in the United States, someone spoke a prophetic word to him and said "One day you will be involved in gospel ministries for all of Africa."

This began to come to pass in the early 1990s. Michael and the African Enterprise International Partnership Board had asked Gottfried Osei-Mensah, himself a Ghanaian, to take whatever initiatives were necessary to set up a new AE team in Ghana which would reach out around West Africa. Gottfried knew this rising young star called Nii Amoo and invited him to become the National Team Leader for AE Ghana. Little did anyone know at that time that before long he would become one of the four Deputy International Team Leaders under Michael and then find himself being appointed to succeed Ernie Smith as AE's pan-African Missions' Director.

"In my seven years of service with AE," says Nii Amoo, "I have seen some wonderful changes taking place in the lives of so very many people in all kinds of missions in which our team has been involved. I am especially thankful for the ministry we have been able to have to street children and prostitutes and it has been wonderful seeing the Lord rehabilitate so many of these and equip them to have a meaningful lifestyle." Nii Amoo feels that only now, with his appointment to this pan-African position, is he going to start seeing the fullest fulfilment of that prophetic utterance given him more than eleven years ago that his ministry "would be for all of Africa".

His wife Margaret and their children are with him all the way in this.

Time Fails Us to Tell...

In the famous Hebrews 11 chapter about the heroes of faith, the writer, having presented his famous catalogue, finally runs out of space and time and says (verse 32): "And what more shall I say? For the time would fail me to tell of Gideon, Barak..." etc, etc as he lists their exploits. While the many other AE team members across the continent and around the world might shrink from being ranked with or compared to the famous catalogue in the book of Hebrews, nevertheless they stand as people who have made, are making or are set to make wonderful contributions to the future of the AE ministry and for the Kingdom and in the name of the Lord they love so much.

Time fails to tell all their stories though you will hear about many of them as this story proceeds. But in all of these, Michael Cassidy and all in AE rejoice, most especially in each of the ministry's other team-leaders whom we note briefly here.

Thus they rejoiced when a major AE need was met in the late 1980s with the addition of a real star in the person of Berhanu Deresse of Ethiopia, in due time to become Ethiopian team leader in Addis Ababa. Berhanu is a specialist, with several American university degrees, in training and helping Christian leaders and in organisational and human resources development. He began with the ministry in East Africa and helped get the East African Leadership Training Centre in Karen, Nairobi, up and running. Pastors from all over East Africa and Congo came there for training courses and were the beneficiaries of Berhanu's courses. At other times he took those same courses out to where the pastors were in their various countries. After he became the leader of the Ethiopian team, AE reaped the benefits of his astonishing gifts in mission set-up as one city mission after another followed in Ethiopia.

Also much celebrated was the way Phambu Babaka, the Belgian-trained lawyer and pastor, got the AE Congo team up and running in the middle of incredible adversity and the context of civil war. As a new team leader, Nico Nteme takes the work forward, and many in AE stand amazed at how much he has been able to achieve with resources so few and slender. His crew of largely volunteer helpers constantly amaze everyone with what they achieve.

"I remember going to Congo a few years ago," says Michael Cassidy. "Ernie Smith and I were there together and we came away profoundly humbled by what we saw. So few were achieving so much for so many with so little by way of resources. In fact the impact of this little team was evident right across Kinshasa and well beyond."

As much as these other colleagues have rejoiced Michael's heart, so more recently has he rejoiced as the Lord has brought Mark Manley in to take over the leadership of the South African team. Michael's longstanding prayer for AE South Africa was that the Lord would bring into the work there a visionary and a proactive leader who would birth again in the work the spirit of the entrepreneurial.

Mark came into the work in early 2002 out of a background as one of South Africa's high-profile Christian personalities through radio and television ministries and programmes. He has had extensive involvement in Christian leadership training, peace and reconciliation endeavours and wide experience in marketing and business. To cap it all he has a tremendous heart for evangelism and has helped organise many campaigns and missions. "It's quite something," says Michael,

> when a man who has been the Mayor of Randburg (a suburb of Johannesburg) and is familiar with everyone in the world of politics, business and the media also turns out to be a preacher, teacher, worship leader, activist, guitarist, singer and minstrel, as

well as lecturer in strategic planning, conflict management and even local government. Where do the man's gifts end? Certainly this brother is a real answer to our prayers as he takes over AE South Africa.

Just to the north, the Very Rev Simukayi Mutamangira recently became the new team leader of AE Zimbabwe. A big man of impressive gravitas, yet with a gracious and friendly warmth, Simukayi's booming voice is capable of conveying the good news of Christ across Africa whether amplification is available or not. Simukayi, a man of high and varied academic qualifications, who came to AE after serving as the Dean of the Anglican Cathedral in Harare, has courageously let his powerful voice be heard also in speaking out against the violence and injustices being perpetrated in Zimbabwe in recent years. It is his heart for evangelism and for winning people to Christ across the continent, though, that attracted this gentle giant to African Enterprise.

The Rev Stephen Mbogo, AE's Kenya team leader, is one of the rising young stars of the AE ministry. His predecessor, Jason Nyaga, died tragically just after the Amsterdam 2000 evangelists' conference when he came down with pneumonia. Jason, an accountant and an effective evangelist, left big shoes to fill, but the energetic and able Stephen has risen to the challenge, impressing audiences in Washington, DC, and Singapore in some of his first forays into the worldwide ministry opportunities AE's international partnership has offered him, as well as taking teams of Kenyan evangelists to minister in Egypt.

The Promise of Long Ago

As Michael Cassidy thinks of these and so many other colleagues in the ministry in evangelistic teams across Africa and in the support offices, he reflects back nostalgically and with thanksgiving on the promise given him long ago in 1 Chronicles 28:21 when he was still a young student at Fuller Seminary and exploring the first glimmers of the African Enterprise call: "And with you in all the work will be every willing, skilful person for any manner of service."

Says Michael:

Yes, the Lord has certainly been true to his Word and fulfilled it most amazingly. How can I ever thank him adequately for those he has brought in to share in this ministry? This has been a team effort from day one. And it still is. It is not an individual thing. I am just one of many in a team. Without these many wonderful brothers and sisters who have come alongside me in this ministry, we could never have got anywhere. We are in this together. In fact, I can rejoice with all my heart that at this stage, 40 years on from the beginning of the work, probably 99 per cent of all evangelism done by AE is done by others. I do my bit. I still love to preach and will always love to preach and evangelise. But it is others who are doing the lion's share of it all and this is something I celebrate with deep thanksgiving to God.

PART TWO

To Jerusalem, Judea and Samaría

Chapter 12

Calling Campuses to Their True Centre

Michael Cassidy had become a Christian at Cambridge University. Festo Kivengere was constantly challenged by Christians during his years at Bishop Tucker College in Uganda.

So, not unreasonably, university students were part of AE's concern and interest from the start. But the team had no idea whether opportunities for campus ministry would ever come their way. It was one thing to get the co-operation of school chaplains and heads, quite another to win the confidence of university Christian unions.

However, AE did not have to wait long. In their first year of fulltime ministry, 1965, the University of Natal in Durban invited them, then the University of Basutoland, Bechuanaland and Swaziland (UBBS), as it was then called, in 1966, and the University of Natal later that same year. Wits followed in 1967, along with its Medical School, and the University of Cape Town in 1969. Wits asked AE back again in 1970, and the team ministered to Rhodes University in 1972, the University of Natal again in 1974 and a modest input was managed at the University of Zululand in 1978. Teachers' training colleges in Durban, Pietermaritzburg, Johannesburg, Grahamstown and Cape Town followed suit. Wits would again open in 1984. Makerere University, the University of Dar es Salaam, Nairobi University, Kenyatta College, plus the Universities of Legon in Accra and of the Cape Coast in Ghana called for missions. University student ministries have also been held in Kigali in Rwanda, Harare in Zimbabwe, and elsewhere.

For Michael and Festo, the challenge of university missions was to call the modern campus back to its true centre in the person of Jesus, who is the Truth.

From his own experience of Cambridge and the Cambridge Inter-Collegiate Christian Union, Michael knew from the start that:

> our approach in most of the campus missions must focus on presenting one basic conviction: that Christianity is true and that the historically risen Jesus is indeed the Truth seeking man's needs. Truth is personal and not simply prepositional. It lies primarily in a person, not a system, although the Christian system as such is the one best able to make sense of all the data of life. It "saves the phenomena", as the saying goes, and builds coherence into an otherwise absurd, empty and godless universe.

Michael and his team also attempted to help students see that their problems of lostness, alienation and meaninglessness could find their best answer in Jesus as "the friend and Saviour of sinners".

A major key to making a university mission a success was not just how well AE ministered as a team, but how well the Christian students did themselves. How committed were they to the mission? How much training in evangelism had they had? Another vital element for the AE team was to discover what the issues really were on each campus. Then the team could prepare themselves to deal with these questions, and share how the gospel spoke to that particular situation.

Lausanne Congress and Student Evangelism

In 1974 at the Lausanne Congress on World Evangelisation, which drew 4,000 evangelical leaders from across the globe, Michael was chosen to lead the seminar and give the main address on University Evangelism. In his paper he noted, among other things, that:

> the Christian has a unique right to be on the campus, not simply as an agent of evangelism, but as an agent of reminder that the university as we know it is really a uniquely Christian creation. It was born out of the mediaeval synthesis with its unified Christian

worldview. The original scholastic guild was based on the Christian presupposition that man lived in a "universe" – a reality which cohered as unity, and was turned (*versus*) into one (*unus*). Such a presupposition was theological through and through. Reality was all of a piece, a single coherent whole, regular and predictable. It could therefore be systemically studied and would yield itself intelligibly to man's intelligence, being the creation of an Ultimate Intelligence.

Not only that – the earliest universities like Oxford, Paris, Bologna and Salerno were avowedly "vocational". They came into existence not primarily to train people for a job or to earn a living, but to supply persons "fit to serve God in church or State". Underlying all academic pursuits was the notion *Dominus Illuminatio Mea* (God My Illumination). Theology, as the Queen of the Sciences, controlled and co-ordinated the whole academic enterprise. Jesus, as heart of the universe, was the key to everything.

This basic view, and its relation to academic studies, was later articulated by Edward Pusey, the famous 19th century spokesman for the Oxford Movement: "History without God is a chaos without design or end or aim. Political economy without God would be a selfish teaching about the acquisition of wealth. Physics without God would be a dull inquiry into certain meaningless phenomena. Ethics without God would be a varying rule, without principle or substance or centre or regulating hand. Metaphysics without God would make man his own temporary God, to be resolved after his brief hour into the nothingness out of which he proceeded."

In fact, what we are on to here is the *logos* doctrine of John's prologue. Theologically put, the university is in a sense the offspring of the *logos* doctrine, "for in Him are hid all the treasures of Wisdom and Knowledge" (Colossians 2:3). Truth is personal before propositional. Small wonder that, centuries before, Justin Martyr (Second Apology XIII) could say of Plato and the Stoics that "whatever things were rightly said among (them) are the property of us Christians". They shared in the *logos*.

Michael went on to note that:

the same is true today. Whatever real truth is found on the modern university campus belongs to us and to our God and to His Christ. It is this which enables us to step on to the campus with our heads held high. Indeed, the Christian has not only the special right, but the deep obligation to speak the gospel into the modern university in such a way as to help restore that structure of inner meaning which has collapsed in secular society. It is only as the modern anthropocentric university rediscovers its theocentric origins in the *logos* that it has any hope of achieving its true destiny and purpose. F.R. Barry observes that "we must not forget the warning of what happened when Roman education became 'rhetoric', teaching people how to be clever and get on in a careerist society, while it gave up teaching them how to be good".

The Christian therefore can and must approach the modern university, erected as a shrine "To An Unknown God", and declare, "What therefore you worship as unknown, this I proclaim to you" (Acts 17:23). We then proclaim Jesus not just to lost individuals, but to the university as a lost institution. (*Let the Earth Hear His Voice*: pp. 749–750)

It was with this kind of theological and philosophical understanding that AE strategised for its university missions across the continent. The university was seen as having lost its metaphysical centre and point of reference. In consequence it was lost and needed Christ once again as its centre.

Following the Lausanne Congress, the next main mission proposed was to the famous Fort Hare in the Eastern Cape.

Fort Hare and Biko

The Mission to Fort Hare University early in 1975 looked like becoming a major landmark for African Enterprise. It was AE's first major mission on a *black* South African university campus. Campuses at that time were often seething cauldrons of political and social unrest, and thus the idea of a mission there was daunting to even the two experienced evangelists who led the team: Michael Cassidy and Maurice Ngakane, then a national student worker and later General Secretary of the South African Council of Churches. En route to the campus to meet both faculty and students, Michael and Maurice stopped near King William's Town to meet in secret with the famous black activist, Steve Biko, then living under the dread banning orders imposed by the apartheid courts and police on those who opposed them. Michael remembers the powerful presence and passionate convictions of Biko, then widely known as the country's leading young exponent of the Black Consciousness movement. Neither Michael nor Maurice were to guess at the horrific and tragic death by torture in a South African prison which was in due time to befall Steve Biko, thereby inflaming the racial passions of South Africa to new intensity. Did Biko view with scepticism Michael and Maurice's proposed venture on the Fort Hare campus? One wonders.

In any event the whole thing looked fraught with complexity. And it was.

Michael alerted all of AE's prayer support worldwide well ahead of time: "We need prayer! This black university near East London has the extremes of South Africa wrapped up in it; a government-controlled administration and the 'home of black power'. The seriousness of the situation should not be underestimated."

Michael's gravity beforehand was not misplaced. The tensions between the administration and the student body made the campus such a maelstrom of unrest that, shortly before the mission, the rector of Fort Hare asked the AE team to postpone the mission. Reluctantly, they accepted his decision. "If you come here the campus might so explode that we would have to close it down," he said. A while later, Maurice Ngakane, fearing imminent detention himself, and feeling he could never face torture, would leave the country for a life in exile.

Things went better in the summer of 1975 at the University of the North, in Turfloop near Pietersburg. Ebenezer Sikakane and Rev David Gitari, later Archbishop of Kenya, visited while on a Student Christian Movement (SCM) conference and led Bible studies and spoke to 800 students. One hundred people professed commitment to Christ.

The AE evangelists never took such warm responses for granted, and it always touched them. After Ebenezer spoke at a youth rally in Gaborone, Botswana, about 100 youngsters also decided for Christ. It was quite a sight to see them scattered all over the field in small groups while counsellors helped them.

East Africa

In East Africa, Bishop Festo and his East African AE team also tackled the universities – with much the same caution and thorough preparation. In February 1974, in the midst of Uganda's agony under the ruthless dictator Idi Amin, Zebulon Kabaza and John Wilson joined forces with Rev John Stott to visit Makerere University in Kampala. Large numbers of students and staff attended night after night for the five days of the mission. There was a good response, and in those desperate times for Uganda, the team were happy to see a number of Christian students filled with new enthusiasm.

Tanzanian students also wanted a firm reality to underpin their lives. When, in July 1975, Titus Lwebandiza spoke to a convention in Singida of 350 Christian students from all over Tanzania, his invitation at the end of the meeting drew "a great rush of people, many pushing as they moved forward. Faces everywhere were wet, but joyous as the revival praise hymns burst from the whole hall." Sunday afternoon had been reserved for testimonies, but so many wanted to hear the gospel that the AE evangelists preached for an hour or so first. Then testimonies began and continued until dusk, even though each one was limited to two minutes.

Later in Kenya Michael Cassidy, via Gershon Mwiti and Daniel Serwanga's set-up, spoke at both the University of Nairobi and in the Sunday morning service of Kenyatta University College, where a staggering 2,000 students were in attendance. "Where in any Western university," Michael asked Gershon and Dan, "would you find 2,000 students out for a Sunday morning campus service? This is why I believe Africa is one day going to be the major fulcrum of Christian world mission."

Other Campuses

In April 1976, the Fort Hare University Mission was back on the agenda. Yet a few weeks before it was due to kick off, Michael, Ebenezer and others visited the campus and ran into insurmountable resistance from some of the students. This was no time for evangelism, they said. It was only a time for politics and the liberation struggle. Sure enough, the Fort Hare mission was cancelled a second time. This resistance to having the gospel on campus was so strong that the team suspected there was a spiritual conflict, much as they supported the liberation impulse and struggle. An urgent request went out to ask friends to stand with them in prayer for the "breaking down of the stronghold", to quote St Paul, and the victory of Christ. "The Lord loves those university students and the faculty. He will win and an entrance will be made in his time."

Meanwhile, there were other campuses. In September 1976 the South African team held a mission to the Teachers' Training College in Mowbray, Cape Town. It was the best yet to a teachers' college, and AE was grateful to the Christian students on campus who prepared thoroughly for the mission in a fervency of prayer. The main thrust of outreach was held during lunch-hour lectures of apologetics and proclamation, followed by evening concerts. Twenty young women professed commitment to Christ, and follow-up with each one was through correspondence, talks and even a retreat. Michael was thrilled to meet a woman who had become a Christian during an earlier AE mission in 1970, and also a teacher who'd been converted through AE at a mission in 1967.

Other missions included ones to the University of Nairobi and to the University of Natal once more, both in 1981. In each case, the Christian students worked very hard ahead of time, preparing the ground. But university campuses were never easy and the AE team coveted extra special prayer.

Stellenbosch Joy and Sadness

In hopes of prompting a mission to Stellenbosch University, near Cape Town, Michael and Festo visited the famous Afrikaans university in November 1980. For many this was seen as quite historic, for Michael and Festo were together as a black and a white, preaching as equals in an Afrikaner stronghold where the National Party's apartheid philosophy had been born and nurtured. Bishop Festo was on his first-ever visit to South Africa for some dual ministry with Michael. And Michael, being of English heritage, had never been invited there. But the novelty value of the black-white evangelistic combo attracted the interest of the Christians on campus. When they arrived, the chaplain was apologetic, warning that only a few students would show up. But 1,300 packed the hall, along with faculty members. "We had a wonderful opportunity to share Christ's love," remembered Michael. After hearing Festo speak, one Afrikaans student rushed up and said: "I feel I have today been liberated from racism. Thank you, thank you, Bishop Kivengere!"

Excitement in the Christian group at the prospect of a mission to the university led by Festo and Michael was immense and it was only a matter of timing. When could the AE duo come?

But other, more sinister, forces of opposition were also at work both on and off the campus. Such a mission would strike at the heart of the separatist apartheid philosophy.

The head of the student Christian group received an anonymous phone call, suspected by the university chaplain to be from a secret police agent in the Bureau of State Security (BOSS). Said the anonymous voice: "Is it true you are planning to have Cassidy and Kivengere for a mission to the university?" "Yes indeed," said the student Christian leader. "Well," said the voice, "I want to warn you about that, as Cassidy is a terrible man and has left his wife and is living with another woman." The shocked student went at once to the chaplain. "Oh, my goodness," said the chaplain, "they never try anything new. They put out a story like that on me to try and discredit my ministry when I first came on this campus."

Michael was of course appalled and distressed when the chaplain told him the libellous story. However, whether it was ongoing efforts like this or others, opposition to the mission built up and it never took place. "Maybe you should go on your own," Michael told Festo. "No, brother. We either go together or not at all," replied the Ugandan bishop. Sadly it turned out in the end to be "not at all".

When an embarrassed Michael told Carol this story she just laughed: "Once when I was still a student, I was talking with Beyers Naude of the Christian Institute and he told me he was always getting threats or anonymous calls or faked letters as if from some mysterious black lover, and he'd just go straight down to the police with the letter and give it to them. Perhaps they guessed he was trying to say to them: 'I think this is from you. Would you just stop playing your silly games!'"

Spiritual Hunger

Things were a bit easier at Makerere University in Kampala when Festo and the East African team went there in April 1984. Not just the students turned out for the various meetings, but also senior staff, professors' wives, their children, cooks and all the workforce on camps. "I have been to several missions on this campus but I've never seen anything like it," James Katarikawe said afterwards. "The students were really *hungry* for the gospel." One student cried so hard that as he walked up to the front, he collapsed in Bishop Festo's arms. But later, when he had accepted Christ, "he was so full of joy". Even outsiders were affected. Like the businesswoman who confessed she had been buying articles and selling them at inflated prices. She stood in public and said: "I am not going to overcharge anymore. So, come to my shop if you want. I will sell to you at the correct price." By the end of that mission, not only had 100 people made a decision for Christ, but the Christians on campus themselves were "warmed up" spiritually, and ready to reach out more than ever to their friends.

In June 1984 Vasco Seleoane, assistant to David Richardson in the mission set-up department, visited the Students' Christian Movement at Indumiso College in Imbali Township, Pietermaritzburg. Vasco's talk generated such enthusiasm that he, David Peters and Mbulelo Hina, were then invited for a mission. The three men ministered to over 250 at each meeting with about 50 students responding. At least a dozen seemed to have genuine life-changing experiences. Vasco was "deeply moved" to see those young people come in tears "as they recognised their need for Christ".

Destiny '84

Any chapter on AE's university work must include the "Destiny '84" mission to the University of the Witwatersrand in August 1984. It was a troubled campus, with 17,000 students in the mire of mounting tensions between left-wing and right-wing, Muslims and Jews, whites and blacks. To meet such a challenge, the Christians banded together, with support from the Students' Christian Association, Campus Crusade for Christ, the Anglican

Society, the Methodist Society, the Catholic Society and Wits Christian Fellowship. There was also input from overseas. Actor Nigel Goodwin and mime artist Geoffrey Stevenson, both British Christians, commandeered the Great Hall piazza, an enormous open space on central campus, for poetry recitals and mime acts that drew the crowds. They were supported by painted clowns and banners, plus a colourful dance and drama team from Youth With a Mission, helping to turn the hallowed portals of learning into something more closely resembling a fairground.

The AE team had arrived on campus in some wariness. Michael wrote later:

> We had been led to expect that we would almost be eaten alive on South Africa's toughest and most strategic campus. So we felt a lot like weak, timid Gideons facing the Midianites at the beginning of this mission. But the team had generated massive prayer around the country and around the world for this mission. It was so strange. It was as if the devil's teeth, like those of a roaring lion, had somehow been pulled. The much vaunted and prophesied opposition came to naught. It was as if we were being given a free ride in the Spirit. Students were just amazingly open and responsive in every situation. The Lord just seemed to give us favour.

The Christians fanned out across the campus, the Great Hall piazza, the swimming pool, amphitheatre – all places where students would meet in leisure moments. After a public performance, the team members would mingle, armed with coffee, to strike up conversations. After a presentation of Christian dance, poetry and music, a young ballet dancer in the crowd was so captivated she made a decision for Christ on the spot.

Lunchtime lectures were taken by Michael and the Rev Frank Chikane, General Secretary of the Institute of Contextual Theology and a leader of the United Democratic Front. When he and Michael tackled "Must the Beloved Country Cry?" alluding to Alan Paton's classic novel, it drew much comment and discussion. Chikane was to become in the late 1990s a chief advisor to President Thabo Mbeki. At this stage in his life, his clear Christian cries for justice and a new deal for blacks in South Africa were strong, sure and uncompromising. Other guest lecturers, including Dr Louw Alberts, South Africa's Director General of Mineral and Energy Affairs and President of Youth

For Christ, and Professor David Bosch, Professor of Missiology at the University of South Africa (UNISA), joined the AE team to help tackle issues such as Marxism, evolution and the Christian's responsibility within his state. After Dr Philip Le Feuvre, Dean of St Paul's Theological College in Grahamstown and a close friend of the university, had spoken on "A Christian critique of Marxism", he led one of the professors to Christ. It was all happening on all fronts.

Open Responses

Meanwhile, some of the AE team moved into the student residences. After one meeting, a young student shot up to his room where he posted a note on the door: "I need Jesus." A mission worker passing down the corridor later that night saw the note, went in and led him to Jesus. A rugby player told Brian Gibson, the minstrel for the mission, "During this week twelve of my close friends have become Christians." At the Glyn Thomas residence for black students in Soweto, the TV in the big lounge was switched off so that the AE team could hold a meeting. Every single student filed out in disgust. But when the audiovisual show was switched on, every single student came back in to see what was happening. Hearts were opening. Responses were coming.

Interestingly enough, Jews made up the largest ethnic group on campus. An AE team member had a long conversation with one young Jew, who grew extremely excited when he suddenly saw that Jesus was God incarnate communicating with man. "So, he's not a God way out there, he actually understands us!" David Block, a Jewish astrophysicist who had become a Christian and a powerful apologist, remarked at one meeting for faculty members and professors: "There are more science people here than we can get to turn up to our faculty meetings!" A lecturer in the engineering department told his students: "I'm not a Christian, and you are probably not Christians, but something significant is happening here, and I think we should all be attending these meetings."

Stephen Mung'oma, from the Ugandan team, spent the week among the black Christian students on campus. They were able to share with him their pain and dilemma over where their allegiance should lie: with Christ or with the liberation struggle for South Africa. Could one bring the two together? Stephen encouraged the white Christians on campus to develop strong ties with these young black Christians and together seek answers in the power of Christ to the dilemmas of the nation.

All in all, Michael summed up the mission saying: "We found astonishing openness and receptivity. It was one of the best campus missions we have had in a long while."

A Jewish girl said: "It is hard for me to accept a Christian mission. But I can't deny that something beautiful has been happening on campus this week."

By the end of an exhilarating week of teamwork and much prayer, the team felt that the huge campus had been genuinely impacted for Christ. The mission would go on to provide the Christian groups based on campus with a wonderful springboard for witness and follow-up in the months and years ahead.

Results

Many other university missions have been held down the years. Always these conversions on campus, won from such hostile territory, give the AE team good reason to rejoice.

More recently, in 1998, AE's Ghana team leader, Dr Nii Amoo Darku, was the main missioner in a mission to the University of Cape Coast with the theme "Is There Any Hope?" The response overwhelmed Nii Amoo. In fact, he reported, "in our final meeting the auditorium was jammed to capacity and student listeners even overflowed into adjacent classrooms to view by closed-circuit TV, while still others who could not get in at all stood under trees outside and listened from loudspeakers." The local FM radio station interviewed Nii Amoo afterwards for an hour on spiritual, theological and political issues.

Then, in 2001 in Addis Ababa the Evangelical Students' Union of Ethiopia (EvaSUE) asked Berhanu Deresse and the AE team there to support them in training their leaders. The purpose of the training was to equip student leaders who come from campuses all over the country to help them minister effectively, and set up a national forum for student leaders to share their vision, discuss issues, and set strategies to accomplish their dreams of serving God on campus.

Openness among the young in Ethiopia is amazing and in November 2001 Berhanu said:

> Last night and this morning we reached about 5,500 young people in six church centres and at the National Theatre Hall. The National Theatre was again filled to its brim and probably over 1,000 young people had to be turned away and directed to other mission centres. The Lord brought as many as 113 young people to himself. These were the ones courageous enough to come forward in public commitment. There were others who put their hands up but were not brave enough to come forward.
>
> In our approach at the Theatre Hall we had professional young Christian actors who did a wonderful drama that brought many youngsters to the Lord. One young man gave a dramatic testimony to the huge audience of young people. He said he had been a member of the so-called Chinese Gang Group who were fighting with other groups and killing each other and doing all sorts of ugly things and unimaginable robberies – very drastic things. They were a great threat to the society. Then he told how the Lord had met him through the testimony of a girl whom he wanted to rape. His testimony helped bring as many as 40 young people to the Lord.
>
> A girl of perhaps 20 came forward and gave her testimony that she had rat poison in her hand and she was going around every day gearing up to kill herself. She said, "Jesus has met me and I am handing over the poison to you. I now have hope, peace and life eternal through Jesus. I do not need to commit suicide." As she was saying this, her face was filled with tears. This is really a real miracle. Praise the Lord with us.

As in other contexts, spiritual results, whether long-term or short-term, are always hard to gauge. But they are always there. Sometimes overwhelmingly, as at Makerere University when Festo was there for a week in 1976, or at UCT in Cape Town in 1969 or at Wits in 1984, or at West Coast University, Ghana, in 1998, or in the outreaches in Ethiopia in 2001.

At other times results are less obvious.

Thus, Michael thought the 1974 mission to the University of Natal in Pietermaritzburg was "a roughie, a tough one, not much fruit there. Rather a heart-break time." Then one day at a pastors' luncheon in Harare an Anglican minister leaned across to him and said: "At last I can say thank you to you. I've always wanted to do it. You see, I came to Christ in that 1974 mission to the University of Natal in Pietermaritzburg. Later the Lord led me into the ministry."

"Over the years this sort of thing has happened so often," commented Michael, "that I have learned pretty deeply that, regardless of how barren any outreach may seem, if one has faithfully proclaimed the gospel, there is always fruit."

And this has been as deeply true of university and campus ministry as of any other. Yes, the truth, which is always personal in Jesus, before it is propositional in statements, still sets people free.

Even students! Deo Gloria!

And Christian witness can still help campuses find their true centre in Jesus who is not only the Way, and the Life, but the *Truth*.

Chapter 13

"Good Luck, Sir"

Though universities had opened first to AE, hard on their heels came schools.

Reaching schoolchildren has always been key in AE's vision and programme. In fact, Michael Cassidy held his first-ever prayer meeting while still at school. Festo Kivengere first heard the gospel in a little mud and grass schoolhouse in Rukungiri, high in the Kigezi hinterland of southwest Uganda. He had warmed to it, and left the animism of his tribe behind. Years later, when he was a teacher in Kabale, his electrifying testimony in school on the morning after his conversion had galvanised his little class. Two of his students who came to faith in Christ were Stanley Kashillingi and James Katarikawe, both of whom would later become Church of Uganda clergymen, and then AE evangelists in East Africa.

So both Michael and Festo knew, from first-hand experience, as did other AE evangelists, that many teenagers are spiritually hungry. Young people ask questions about the major issues in life, and want answers that make sense.

Both Michael and Festo also had a strategic reason for targeting the schools. The future leaders of Africa would come from those schools, with the power to shape Africa for good or ill. So when Michael founded African Enterprise, school missions were a high priority. When Festo began the East African AE team, school missions again were a high priority. Happily, both men found that the schools were only too happy to welcome them as African Enterprise evangelists. Both Michael and Festo had the perfect credentials.

Michael's background as a student in Michaelhouse opened doors in the public school network right across South Africa and Rhodesia (now Zimbabwe).

Festo's background as a schoolteacher in both Kabale, Uganda, and Dodoma, Tanzania, and then as chief schools inspector for Kigezi Diocese in southwest Uganda, also opened doors for the AE team, right across East Africa.

In many cases, Michael and Festo found that the heads and teachers at these schools knew them personally. They had either taught them, or been their classmates. (Michael, as Prefect and House Captain, had even caned a young lad called Dudley Forde who would one day be a distinguished headmaster of Michaelhouse!) Michael's school mischief, which was both notorious and extensive, was to catch up with him when he went back to preach at his old school. After his first visit to preach at Michaelhouse in 1962, the Old Boys' magazine carried an astonished and cryptic observation; *"If it can happen to Cassidy, it can happen to anyone!"* One master had even said prior to the service: "I can't think what you could be saying in a chapel, but I'm coming along anyway!" Rector Tommy Norwood even tried to get him to confess to an old schoolboy crime of putting butterballs on the roof of the dining hall – a crime of which for once he was innocent, "as if to get me to clear my conscience before entering the pulpit," said Michael later.

Later on came the 1968 invitation to Michaelhouse which brought AE its first real opportunity to do schools missions, and thus began one of the most fruitful dimensions of the entire AE ministry. "Being our first school mission, we inevitably made mistakes." But they must have done most things right, for, as one observer said, "This has been significantly blessed by the Spirit of God." For headmaster Tommy Norwood it was, as previously indicated, the high-point of his years as head. Most of the school attended the meetings every night, and eight or nine of the boys who responded to Christ at that time, as we observed earlier, went on into fulltime Christian service.

Hilton

Soon another invitation arrived, from Hilton College in Natal. Again, the response was remarkable. Nearly 95 per cent of the school attended the voluntary evening meetings. Headmaster Raymond Slater and his wife, Charlotte, joined Michael each evening in discussing the boys who had responded in a special way to the message.

In 1972 Hilton invited African Enterprise back again. Raymond Slater, the headmaster, was intensely amused when little Gavin Sklar-Chik, the youngest and smallest boy in the school, came up to Michael just before the first mission service, and staring up at the tall, tall man proffered his hand and said: "Good luck, Sir." "He spoke as if I was some sort of Daniel entering a den of lions, or was it a lion entering a den of Daniels," chuckled Michael later. This time in the mission no less than 45 per cent of the entire school of 350 boys professed some sort of new response to Christ. Over 1,500 Christian books were purchased. Several Bible study groups were formed by the boys themselves, which not only survived, but grew. "Thank you for changing this school from a mere place of education into a wonderful community, all helping one another," one student wrote to Michael.

Commented Raymond Slater: "The 1972 mission was the most significant and important experience in my entire life as a schoolmaster – both for me personally and for the school."

Unbeknown at that time to either Slater or Michael, the seeds of the gospel were also sown there in the heart of little Gavin Sklar-Chik. A couple of years later, no longer able to resist the clutchings of Christ on his heart, he gave his life to Christ. Soon he experienced a call to the ministry. Hearing of this, and before Gavin headed overseas for theological training, Slater invited him to preach at the school and share his story.

On his way to preach at Hilton College, he called in on Michael at his home. As he left Michael, and still shaking in his boots, Michael turned the tables of yesteryear on the young man, held his hand out solemnly and said: "Good luck, Sir!" "Gavin's sermon," said Raymond Slater later, "was a smash hit!" Gavin's great ministry as a pastor continues to this day.

Michael was also delighted to learn later that that mission produced some outstanding student Christian leadership on South African university campuses in the following five years. Several boys who became Christians through the mission went on to devote themselves extensively to youth work through the Scripture Union Independent Schools' work. Others have shone for Christ as professors at universities. One heads the Human Science Research Institute of South Africa.

Visits to Hilton were to be repeated a good many more times in the years that followed. Meanwhile, that "happiest possible" experience opened private schools all over South Africa, and also in what was then Rhodesia. Some of the private schools which graciously opened their doors to African Enterprise were Bishops, Cape Town, St John's, Johannesburg, Kearsney, Bloemfontein, St Michael's Girls' Collegiate in Bloemfontein, St Andrews in Grahamstown, St Andrews, Bloemfontein, Kingsmead, Johannesburg, St Mary's, Kloof, St Stithians in Johannesburg, and St Johns, and Wykeham Girls' School in Pietermaritzburg. Also, in Rhodesia, Peterhouse and Falcon, plus no fewer than 20 Salisbury schools opened up during a special citywide scholars' push there in 1977.

Generally the schools gave AE the warmest of welcomes. At St Andrew's and St Michael's in Bloemfontein in 1974, virtually all the boarding establishment of both schools attended the voluntary evening meetings. Prayer groups sprang up in all the houses. The boys and girls meant business: one student told Michael near the end of the mission: "I no longer need you to explain to me what is involved in becoming a Christian. Now tell me exactly what is involved in going on as a Christian!"

Rhodesia

Peterhouse, near Salisbury, Rhodesia was an Anglican school of 350 boys, with a dismal Christian fellowship at the time of the mission: it numbered precisely three. A couple of weeks later, 80 boys had made a first-time commitment to Christ. Nearly 120 more wanted to join Bible study groups. Sales of Christian books were phenomenal. The Christian bookshop in Salisbury had been amused when the team first came in wanting a huge number of Christian books for the school mission. They'd packed them in boxes with some scepticism, sure they would be unpacking them again in a few days' time. Their eyes really popped when two days later the team was back saying, "Sorry, we're out of books!"

Weeks later, the headmaster wrote to AE:

The Bible study groups (now running in five dormitories) are organised and run entirely by the boys, and they reveal a level of leadership and inspiration which is heartwarming. Most thrilling of all is a new Sunday evening activity which takes the form of a praise and prayer session in the chapel. The boys take charge and there is a great freedom in extemporary prayer. Peterhouse really seems to have been the scene of a miracle!

This excited Michael for the future: "I believe we are going to see Rhodesia permanently affected out of these two missions. These boys are sure to become leaders." One of the interns on this mission, Peter Twycross, who had come to Christ in the Michaelhouse mission of 1968, found this time decisive in the birth of his own call to fulltime ministry in which he continues to excel to this day, having become a specialist in planting new churches as far afield as Kenya.

A mission to Falcon College, near Bulawayo, right after the Peterhouse mission, brought some open hostility and ridicule. There seemed to be much division among the staff and Christians on campus as to the appropriateness of such a mission. One staff member declined to enter the staff common room if Michael or AE team members were there. Still, more than 200 of the student body of 350 turned out for the voluntary meetings of the mission week. Even so, it was one of the few school missions the team ever did where there appeared to be no visible results at all by the end of the week.

But in general terms, the school missions soon fell into a pattern that was so successful that AE still uses it to this day, where appropriate. The day would begin with the AE team members taking Chapel/assembly each morning, teaching the Religious Education classes during the day, counselling students in the afternoons and then having voluntary services in the evening. Almost invariably the majority of the school turned out, intrigued by the inter-racial make-up of the AE team, if nothing else. Sometimes imaginative skits, drama, music and audio-visual presentations would add extra appeal. When comedian Jack Garratt came on the AE South African team, the added extra of hilarious comedy paved the way amazingly for the serious stuff.

In all these situations, the support of headmaster, chaplain and staff was both essential and invaluable. Where staff members had reservations, they almost always showed restraint and integrity in not undermining the effort in any way.

In each school there were also students in trouble. Michael and his teammates listened and prayed with students who sought them out. One student was able to begin to forgive his father for a traumatic childhood. Another found a way out of deep bitterness to forgive God for the death of some close family members. Another felt his growing cynicism had turned to joy in finding something he could really believe in at last. Michael astonished many a small unhappy boy by being able to identify with being bullied. "Gee, Sir, did that happen to you too?" marvelled one thirteen-year-old.

Follow-up, as ever, was carefully carried through. Members of the AE team made themselves available after each mission to offer counselling and training to the boys who had made a commitment. They made sure Christian fellowships were in place. At one school, so large had been the response that Michael (perhaps thinking of his mother) wrote a letter of calm explanation to the parents of each one of the students who had decided to become a Christian. He did not want to alarm any parent, and thus create needless difficulties for the boys.

Letters poured in from schools after missions. A teacher at Hilton College wrote: "The change in most of the boys who heard you has been immense. It is just wonderful." A student wrote: "I was very wicked. But suddenly now, I don't seem even to want to do those things, and each day I feel taller because I know that Jesus died for us."

Impact at Kearsney

A few lads went a bit over the top in their enthusiasm. Wrote one from Kearsney College in Botha's Hill near Durban:

A few weeks after your mission my friends and I were in the chapel baptizing a couple of boys when this other boy came in and started messing us around. He kept on butting in when we were praying. Mark and I took him into the vestry and told him about Jesus. We challenged him to come with us to the chaplain. He did, and when we all prayed for him, he burst out crying. I suppose that was all the sin coming out.

Another lad wrote: "Your biblical teaching led me to a deeper experience of the Holy Spirit and enriched my relationship with Christ. I shall always be most grateful to God for the ministry of African Enterprise." He went on to become a vicar.

One senior said: "I am so grateful for the magnificent and incredible change you've made to the school. Almost one quarter of the school has become Christian!"

Rev Peter Veysie, now an energetic Pretoria pastor, said:

> The Kearsney mission was key for me. That's when I got called to the ministry... I have had the privilege of having Michael Cassidy as a mentor from 1978 as a young 16-year-old trying to understand the reality of Christianity. Michael came to Kearsney, shared in a morning assembly of the importance of living a day to day walking, living, breathing relationship with Jesus. I found that my spiritual struggle at boarding school revolved around being thrust into chapel daily and twice on Sundays, and of course as boys we had ways and means of avoiding this challenge.
>
> All this changed for me when I heard the simple gospel challenge from a strong evangelical, Michael Cassidy. He spoke into my heart and I felt as if God himself was saying – there is more to me than just religion, I want to have you as a friend.
>
> As a young 10-year-old I had made a simple commitment to Christ at a Billy Graham rally which AE had organised in 1973 in Durban, but now it all became so much clearer. My heart was beating so fast with this call from God and I put up my hand and recommitted my life to Christ. Michael wrote in my small Bible which I bought at the end of the meeting "Anywhere, provided it be forward – David Livingstone". These are my life words now, as well as Romans 12:1 and 2 and Deuteronomy 30:19,20. I had experienced the touch of God like never before.

Peter and a big rugby hero who he had helped into commitment started a 5 am prayer meeting: "We then started to challenge the rest of the school to join us in the early morning meetings, and slowly but surely over a two-year period we grew from a small group of seven or eight to a group of 120 boys, committed to supporting relevant speakers, guitars and prayer. At that stage Kearsney had a total of 400 boys including day scholars."

Michael met another Kearsney boy years later in Jerusalem: "In that mission the seeds were sown for my conversion," he testified.

After a mission to St Andrew's and St Michael's in Bloemfontein Michael wrote: "How tremendously exciting and encouraging these school missions have been! In fact we are constantly amazed at the openness and hunger of so many young people in these private schools."

The turnout for the AE school mission meetings, always voluntary, continued to be phenomenal as year followed year. In later missions to Peterhouse, 75 to 80 per cent of the school turned out, at Falcon, 65 per cent, and at Wykeham, about 95 per cent. The book tables at each school raised enormous interest, and once at Peterhouse "there were almost mob scenes when the books came out".

Peterhouse's Christian fellowship continued to grow. Letters kept coming from staff and scholars, telling of some of the exciting things that continued to happen there. Soon a leading student, the head of school, was converted. Another, a very "hard case" for whom his newly converted head of house had been praying, was then converted. *"I could not believe this boy had become a Christian...!"* commented a master.

In 1975 African Enterprise held a major mission to Pietermaritzburg, targeting about 25 schools of all racial groups. Some evenings the mission drew nearly 4,000 young people to the local Royal Show Grounds. A particularly interesting spin-off of this effort was an annual prefects' meeting hosted by Girls' Collegiate in Maritzburg, when the prefects and Christian leaders from most of the city's schools came together for a creative evening of inter-racial fellowship, dialogue and spiritual challenge.

Black Schools

The African members of the AE South African team used their cultural advantage to gain access to any number of black schools for missions. In spring of 1976 Abiel held a mission to Butha Buthe High School in Lesotho, and a few weeks later Ebenezer held a mission to the Mankayane High School in Swaziland. Both men were warmly received, but the students struggled to separate Christianity from apartheid in their minds. Other black schools also opened their doors to AE. Denton Sibisi pioneered this ministry with dedication and skill, but found increasing resistance from black teenagers because the apartheid system had so often seemed to come to them on the wings of Christian rationalisation. The AE team read the signs of the times, and knew that this presented them with a momentous challenge as they sought to face the deteriorating situation amongst young black people in the country.

One especially happy mission was to Moroka High School, with an AE team of Abiel Thipanyane, Andrew Mohibdu and Michael. The inter-racial make-up of the team intrigued the young people. Sport was big at Moroka, and several wanted to know if a Christian should play sport. "I felt the best answer in this soccer-crazed school was to acquire for them a large silver cup which I called the 'Mojalefa Trophy' (Mojalefa being Michael's Sesotho name) to be presented to the winning team in the annual inter-house soccer contest," remembered Michael. "This was considered a highly satisfactory practical answer to a serious theological question!"

In Windhoek, South-West Africa (later Namibia), Malcolm Graham, David Peters and Andrew Mohibidu spoke at one school where all 20 prefects professed commitment to Christ. All 20 went on to lead daily prayer meetings in their dormitories.

Up in Lesotho, David Peters visited a small village school. Seventy-five young people responded, and many wanted to talk with him afterwards. Life there was an uphill struggle, with poorly equipped schools, drugs, widespread corruption and crime.

Of course it was hard to measure the long-term results of the school missions and inevitably they varied. But there was generally evidence of new kindness in the school, prayer and Bible study meetings sometimes began and occasionally even the rugby scrums became cleaner! Most notable was that many young people professing commitment were still going strong for Christ years later. For others, the mission was seed-sowing time which paved the way for response later on.

Uganda, Kenya and Tanzania

In East Africa, too, the teams had great success in schools throughout the 1970s, 1980s and 1990s. Bishop Festo was about as close as you could get to superstar status in Uganda, and commanded attention wherever he went with the fledgling team. News that he was coming to a school almost anywhere in Uganda or Tanzania drew not only the entire student body as a matter of course, but often the parents, aunts and uncles and grandparents as well! As Festo's AE team became better known, the schools would turn out for them in their hundreds and even thousands. The contacts and links formed with these schools were very special to AE, and continue to the present.

And so it went on, throughout East Africa. Young people in countries torn apart by civil unrest and natural disasters were willing to make time to listen to what the AE team had to say. When Titus Lwebandiza spoke at a girls' school in Dodoma, Tanzania, observers said simply, "The Spirit of the Lord came down." Fifty girls made a decision for Christ that morning, and another 35 did so that evening. Titus left jubilant, with about one-third of the student body now Christian, and some follow-up going on.

In one month alone during 1976, Titus spoke to eleven secondary schools, four teachers' colleges and one nurses' training centre, and took part in crusades or conferences in three widely scattered areas of Tanzania. "I have seen people come to the Lord in scores," he said. In some places magic charms were produced and burnt. "I have never witnessed such spiritual hunger." The turnout of students at the schools, on a voluntary basis, was astonishing.

The Kenya team met with a similar response. When AE held a mission near Nairobi, the Rev Dan Serwanga reported that 300 Masai youth from various schools attended an Ngong rally. Many wanted to know more.

The Rev Stephen Mung'oma went to Mulango Girls Secondary School, and a young girl wrote to him afterwards: "Even though you've been gone some days, there are still students being saved. Many are angry and criticising Christianity, but we like it that way. This is because now they are beginning to think more about God, and soon they are going to join us!"

Gershon Mwiti, visiting Kenya's Highlands Bible College, met a Ugandan student who said he had been planning to go back and fight in Uganda with the anti-government guerrillas. "But Jesus has found me, and now I want to return and have a ministry to young people in the churches."

In the early 1980s, when Uganda's Karamoja region was suffering a terrible drought and the people were bracing themselves for invasions by cattle raiders, Stephen Mung'oma visited Kapenguria High School. If he'd thought the students would be otherwise occupied, he was wrong. They turned out in their hundreds, and by the end of the mission, Stephen found the young people so eager to testify that "it was hard to end the meetings and get them to go home!"

In November 1981 an AE team of three, James Katarikawe, Stanley Kashillingi and Canon Abraham Zaribugire (dean of the cathedral at Kabale) decided to visit French-speaking Rwanda, Burundi and eastern Zaire, to hold brief missions in the schools of Gahini, Kigali, and throughout Butare diocese. No time or opportunity for careful preparation here, but the response to a clear declaration of the gospel was again heartwarming. In one secondary school in eastern Zaire alone nearly half the students responded.

When the Kenya team held a mission to Nyeri in the early 1980s, they visited seven high schools and two teacher training colleges. Voluntary attendance at meetings topped 4,000. Several hundred students made a commitment to Christ, which greatly encouraged the hitherto struggling Christian unions.

When David Peters and Andrew Mohibidu visited Namibia, one school meeting drew very few, but those students who did come included two of the biggest thugs in the school who were then converted, much to their teachers' amazement. And imagine the gospel impact on their peers! For another school meeting in Namibia, Michael asked bearded minstrel, songster and team associate Brian Gibson to accompany him. The 500 kids, with some huge rugby players upfront, looked bored to tears – till Brian, also a karate fighter and bodybuilder, flexed his giant biceps, did a forward and then a backward somersault on the stage, landing neatly on his feet both times, and then, with the shocked audience now riveted, began to sing a gospel song! Said the startled but delighted headmaster afterwards, "No one in the history of our school ever started a Christian meeting that way. No wonder you guys had our kids eating out of your hands!"

Schools Thrust Incorporated into Missions

When the national AE teams of South Africa, Kenya, Uganda and Tanzania and later Zimbabwe and Malawi, began teaming up each year for major pan-African citywide missions, the schools work was incorporated in these larger missions as a key feature.

In May 1987, during the pan-African mission "Lilongwe for Jesus!", Sheckie Masika went to the Robert Blake Secondary School and shared how Jesus had helped heal his drug addiction. Many of the boys present responded by saying they too wanted to make a commitment to Christ, and leave drugs behind. To prove it, they later turned out their pockets and gave Sheckie their secret hoards of dagga or marijuana.

During the "Manzini for Jesus" city mission in 1988 in Swaziland, the team began each morning at 7 am, when they spread out to take assemblies in each of Manzini's schools. "The response was enormous," testified mission set-up director Neil Pagard.

At Mjingo Secondary School in the late 1980s, the irrepressible Jack Garratt gave a presentation of the gospel in dramatic form that was so lively it had the girls gasping and laughing hysterically in turns. Later that day even the science teacher decided to make a commitment to Christ, and then kept Jack busy with many questions. When the driver arrived to fetch Jack, the girls saw the car, but did not tell Jack because they wanted him to stay. When Jack finally rushed out to catch his lift to the next meeting, the driver was fast asleep.

During the July 1982 pan-African mission to Mutare (formerly Umtali), in Zimbabwe, David Peters visited a secondary school where 200 young people responded to his message. One boy who had "borrowed" some geography books brought them back to the school principal in front of his 1,300 schoolmates and testified, much to their amazement. His confession of his theft and his radiant new life in Christ impacted many.

During the tough 1984 Gweru "Back to Jesus" mission in Zimbabwe, when the city was torn with riots, David Peters told the girls of Chaplin High School how he'd turned from Hinduism to Christ. A Hindu girl came up to him afterwards. This was her first-ever Christian meeting, she said. She had no idea why she'd even come, and now she wanted to become a Christian like David.

David told of his conversion from Hinduism at another school in Malawi. At the close of the meeting, he said that those who wanted to become Christians should remain behind. But nobody left. Calling the interpreter, David asked him to explain again in Chichewa: if you want to become a Christian, stay behind, otherwise you may go. Finally, two teenagers left the hall. The rest stayed. David could not believe it, and told the boys to go back to their rooms and think very seriously about such a commitment. If they were still serious they could come to him early the next morning at his lodgings nearby and tell him. Next morning at 6 am there were about 150 young people outside David's bedroom window.

Of course Stephen Lungu's dramatic testimony of being a violent petrol-bomb-throwing rebel in the old Rhodesia, fighting for the end of white rule and then being dramatically converted, always stunned school assemblies. Whether in Malawi, Ghana, Liberia, Kenya or even in South Africa, once Steve had shared this incredible tale, teens would mob him to talk, question or seek private counselling. The same would happen if Steve spoke in Australian, Canadian or American schools.

So incredibly fruitful was the AE schools ministry that in July 1977, a seven-member AE team went on a mission to Salisbury and spent the entire week just in the classrooms of the 20 main schools of the city. The idea had come from the Rhodesia Council for Christian Education and Scripture Union. The mission targeted hundreds of black and white students in central Salisbury and in the townships of Highfield and Harare. As well as conducting school assemblies, helping in RE classes, and holding lunchtime meetings, they held late afternoon and evening rallies, ending with a major Youth Rally at the Salisbury sports centre. Most meetings were full to capacity. Some 8,000 teenagers were contacted, and 600 professed interest to know more.

So it went on, during the 1970s, 1980s and 1990s. The young people of Africa were always of special concern for African Enterprise. As Michael Cassidy once put it: "Here is where our hope and our future lie. What a weight of history and destiny rests on them! And how spiritually hungry and responsive to the gospel they are!"

The AE teams' hearts went out to these young people: they were wrestling with all the usual problems of growing up, dawning romance and career choices, almost always against a background of enormous political tensions, and often also poor education, widespread poverty, violence and corruption. (One girl wrote to them from a township: "Please help me, my boyfriend was murdered last week!")

In response, the AE teams could only ask their supporters for prayer, so that "we may know how to minister to them more effectively".

St John's

And much prayer was surely needed as the team went in early 1991 to St John's, a leading Johannesburg boys' school. This was a major challenge, with potentially enormous repercussions. St John's taught many of the future "captains of industry and commerce" in Johannesburg. For years the school had significantly impacted the South African economy, and would continue to do so. David Richardson wrote to AE supporters. "Youngsters who come to Christ from schools like St John's really can have a major influence. So let's continue to pray that the Lord will consolidate and mature these young folk. So much depends on the follow-up meetings if short-term enthusiasts are to turn into long-term disciples."

During the mission to St John's, shared as AE often did with the wonderful Scripture Union team led by Mike Battison, Michael spoke at extended morning assemblies and voluntary evening meetings for the wider school family, and the team members took the scheduled divinity lessons for the week, as well as counselling and taking part in the everyday life of the school, from sports events to choir rehearsals. The inimitable Jack Garratt kept everyone chuckling from day one. One skit on a minister preaching almost brought the convulsed headmaster into cardiac arrest!

By the end of the mission, 316 boys out of 622 filled out forms indicating either first-time commitments, or rededications, or requests to know more, or to seek further counselling. The chaplain and headmaster were "greatly encouraged" by the response. One student wrote: "I was getting very close to being a Satanist because of Heavy Metal music, but when I stopped listening to it, I started living again. Your mission affirmed my life."

This reference to Satanism was not isolated. African Enterprise had no illusions about what they were doing when they went into schools: St Paul had once described it in Ephesians 6 as "wrestling with principalities and powers".

African Enterprise knew that the students were in a spiritual arena, and that their souls were being fought for. And again and again over the years, the AE teams asked their supporters for back-up prayer.

Michael wrote once: "I really do believe that when we go into these missions we need to know that the battle is won in prayer ahead of time..." And so often there were parent groups around South Africa, officially praying for each school mission for more than six months before the AE team even visited the school. Furthermore, before each mission, prayer supporters all over the world had "adopted" every pupil and had then prayed for them specifically and individually. In the St Stithian's Mission in 2001, the chaplains expressed much appreciation that every pupil and staff member was being individually prayed for by prayer partners all across the nation and overseas.

In Townships Too

This individual prayer was however difficult with missions into some of the townships where student enrolment was huge. In one mission alone in June 1992 in one township 14,000 high school pupils were reached.

The township schools were a particularly marathon effort. In one township school, the AE team took about 40 meetings with pupils each day. Some of the really rugged evangelists took up to 19 classes a day, "most of which was spent standing in front of the class, and sore, tired feet were the order of the day!" The teams had expected a hard time from the pupils, who had a reputation for being difficult, but on the whole there was great openness. About 117 pupils made first-time commitments in one school alone – the Mehlokazulu High School – with 16 recommitments. In another, the Zibukezulu High School, 70 young people gave their lives to Christ for the first time.

One head told the team: "before this outreach by AE, we didn't take RE seriously. We had a real teacher shortage and RE was just not a priority. Now, if we could, we would keep AE here for the whole year..."

Touching Teachers

Of course, another way to reach young people was through the teachers themselves. In June 1987, AE East Africa organised the Dar es Salaam Teacher Prayer Fellowship, to encourage teachers in the secondary schools and colleges in Tanzania. Fifty-three teachers came, some travelling up to four days by train to get to Dar es Salaam. More than 100 across Tanzania had wanted to come, but lack of transport defeated them.

In Ghana, team leader Dr Nii Amoo Darku and his colleagues have also had regular access to schools. Commenting on the recent Akosombo International School Mission in Accra, Nii Amoo said:

> The key to every successful school mission is having the head of the school a committed Christian with a committed believing chaplain. This came home to me when I was invited to this particular school for a weeklong mission.
>
> Because the headmistress and chaplain were committed children of God who see the need for all their students to be exposed to the gospel which alone has the power to save all who believe, they, in collaboration with Christian organisations such as ours, schedule a yearly mission for their students. I was privileged to be the main speaker for this mission. Each evening we saw scores of students coming to the Lord for the first time and others dedicating their lives afresh to Christ.
>
> It was also a significant that during the mission even some teachers came to see me for counselling, with one particular elderly teacher coming to accept the Lord and renouncing some traditional family rituals, ties and covenants. She was also delivered from demonic attacks. A number of Moslem students likewise came to see me for more insight into aspects of what I shared when I gave my testimony as a former Moslem and how I came to know the Lord. Many young ladies, especially, came to see me to be counselled and prayed for on sexually related issues. The joy with which each of them left the counselling sessions spoke for itself as to the great things the Lord had done in their lives. We

give God the glory and thank him for the opportunity to use AE platforms for these life-transforming experiences in schools.

Preparation

If such high response rates across Africa seem hard to comprehend, it must be remembered that African Enterprise did not just drive up to a school on the first day of a mission, and plunge straight in. They spent weeks in meticulous, careful preparation. Before AE entered a school, it also made sure it knew what issues were high on that school's agenda. And the evangelists then addressed those issues: from Christianity and Marxism, to evolution, to racism, to sexual ethics, and marriage, to materialism, or the African Renaissance, or to the future of Africa or whatever. The team usually tried ahead of time to speak informally with the prefects, get them on side, and learn from them the school issues and what made the place tick. If the school staff could be addressed ahead of time that was also done.

In fact the use of testimony and story in preparation, in build-up and in presentation, is increasingly seen in AE as essential and powerful. Missioners must come ready to tell their stories. For example, Caesar Molebatsi of Soweto was a powerful, special addition to the team from time to time: his testimony deeply moved the young people. He had been in a motor accident in which he lost a leg after being knocked down by a white driver. When he was later converted, his forgiveness of the white driver and how he had found this forgiveness in Christ spoke powerfully in healing black-white relations in South Africa. "In one mission the most conversions of that mission occurred after that talk."

When Michaelhouse headmaster Dudley Forde (now recovered from Michael caning him at school), and chaplain Alan Smedley (himself deeply impacted by the 1972 Mission to Hilton) asked Michael and Bishop Philip Le Feuvre in 1999 to do another mission to Michaelhouse, the theme chosen was: "My Story Meeting His Story". Again Scripture Union and its Director Mike Battison were involved but this time there was also a powerful contingent of Michaelhouse Old Boys (graduates) who had become Christians. Everyone invited, including a rock band and dance group, was requested to come prepared to tell their stories to the boys, specially emphasising what happened when the story and person of Jesus intersected with their own story.

"As an actuarial professor, a research scientist, a businessman, a farmer, a dramatist, a rock star, some prominent sportsmen, and the Scripture Union team plus the AE Foxfire team all testified to how Christ had impacted their own lives and stories, the lads kept hearing and seeing the dice roll six all the time," recalls Michael.

> The thing was that in each instance and regardless of background or profession, Jesus had consistently made the decisive difference in each person's life. The power of story is awesome.
>
> "After hearing all these stories all week," said one senior boy, "I believe most of the school really knows there is something to this Christianity thing. Now they have to decide what they will do about it." Michael, Philip and the Scripture Union team were glad they had urged all missioners to "come prepared to tell your own story. And of course that makes you the world expert on your subject. So don't be nervous!"

Imagine likewise the riveted attention when Steve Lungu tells young scholars of his pre-Christian petrol-bomb days when he wanted to blow up all whites in old Rhodesia. Or when Nii Amoo tells of his former life as a Muslim. Or Edward Muhima, PhD, tells of growing up in a polygamous family, getting caught up in "smoking, drinking and womanising", and then finally becoming a new creature in Christ.

Set to Influence Africa

All in all, in 30 years of ministry, the AE teams across Africa have spoken to hundreds of thousands of Africa's young people. Tens of thousands have responded to the gospel with openness and great interest. What these key young people do with their commitment to Jesus Christ in the long term is, of course, varied, but African Enterprise evangelists pray that it will influence the present and future leadership of Africa.

And going into any schools in the years to come they will always still be happy to hear any small boy or girl say – "Go for it, Ma'am."

Or more likely – "Good luck, Sir!"

Chapter 14

Searching for a City Strategy

Evangelise the cities of Africa. That had been at the core of Michael Cassidy's vision for African Enterprise since 1961. In the following 40 years, the vision came true in city after city after city. Dozens of them, hundreds of them, from Cairo to the Cape. Little regional cities, big commercial cities, war-torn and ravaged cities, elegant national capitals, sprawling metropolises.

How the cities responded! Crowds of hundreds, of thousands at any one time and, once, over a quarter of a million, would gather to hear the team as they joyfully proclaimed the good news of Christ's love for that city.

City evangelism, of course, had been where it all began for Michael personally. He had been at the Billy Graham Crusade in Madison Square Garden, New York, the night he felt God say to him: "Why not this for Africa?" "Why not the cities of Africa?"

Cities had also been where Michael began praying for Africa. He and the early team had prayed for the 31 key cities of Africa for a couple of years while at Fuller. He'd visited them all the following summer. Then, through the various teams, AE had spent the following 40 years in evangelising in most of that list of 31 – plus dozens more. A city was even where African Enterprise first began: Pietermaritzburg.

The full story of African Enterprise's ministry to the cities of Africa from 1962 onwards would occupy many hundreds of pages, and is well beyond the scope of this book. These chapters can only attempt to highlight a scattering of the hundreds of city missions which the individual AE teams have tackled within their own regions over the years. (We will also tell the story of some of the pan-African missions, when the AE teams join forces from all over Africa for a mega-push in a major African city.)

The story of AE's early missions in the 1960s has already been outlined in earlier chapters. As the years rolled on, and AE's reputation spread, it became clear that it would not be difficult to get invitations to the many key cities of Africa. News travels far and wide in Christian circles, and as AE missions were held in one city, they were talked about, and dreamed about, in a dozen more. Churches that had worked with AE gave it their personal recommendation – and the word spread fast.

It is easy to understand why so many doors opened so fast for African Enterprise. The churches liked what they heard about AE. Here was an organisation that would never just arrive in their city without an invitation from the churches already there. Once there, African Enterprise would also never set up a rival "AE church" and try to grab Christians from other churches to fill it. AE made it very clear that its role was not to found their "own" churches, but to help churches already established in the task of mission.

Further, African Enterprise offered to work alongside the churches of the host city for months ahead of time, preparing the local congregations for mission, encouraging their pastors, training both them and the laity in the best ways to share their faith in an effective, rational way. Once the mission was over, AE would not simply dump the new converts and run for the hills. They would help the churches co-ordinate their follow-up teaching and support for the fledgling Christians, helping them to settle into local churches, which had been trained as to the best way to nurture their new flocks. The churches in the cities of Africa heard all this, and liked what they heard.

So a firm invitation would arrive at AE headquarters: please come and do a mission.

Preparation

That would initiate step two: the preliminary visit by an AE expert on "set-up". For many years this was the job of Canadian David Richardson, who had grown up in South Africa and had a background in business. His mixture of friendly enthusiasm, plus no-nonsense realism, was ideal when the highly complex logistics of a mission had to be sorted out. Year after year, time after time, David would venture into cities to "spy out the land", to visit the churches, and discover whether a mission here or there would be practicable. David had a mental checklist of things that needed to be in place before a mission was feasible. Commented Michael Cassidy:

> It never ceased to amaze me how David would go into a town of massively divided Christians and churches and begin to cajole, encourage or kick butt, as necessity required, until slowly ecclesiastical or theological enemies were finding each other and gearing up for once to co-operate in evangelistic outreach. It was and is a special gift. And it takes someone with grit and determination and some bull-terrier qualities to pull it off. Yeah, David was a real trooper in this advance stuff ahead of missions.

Travel and Preparations

Preparing for his trips was quite an item for David. Going into one "sensitive" West African country, Liberia, not much enamoured of South Africa, David had to be specially careful on this "scouting, Caleb and Joshua exercise". Said David's report:

> My travel research indicated that there was only one airline that stopped in Liberia. It was Pan American Airlines. They had found a loop-hole that enabled them to carry passengers from South Africa. They simply made out the ticket to appear as if the journey began in Gaborone, Botswana. When I got my ticket the first coupon had already been removed thus making it look like I was just in transit in Johannesburg.
>
> Lesley and the girls helped me to take the SA labels out of my clothing, and to scrape off the "produk van Suid Afrika" print on things like my shaving cream can and toothpaste tube. It would be highly dangerous to be identified as a "permanent resident" of the apartheid regime of the most hated and racist nation in Africa. Many prayed as I departed with both of my Canadian passports. One, issued by the Canadian Embassy in Pretoria, was for leaving from and arriving in South Africa. The other had no stamps indicating any link with SA. From the passport I was just an anonymous Canadian from nowhere. There was no address indicated and it had been issued at my request in Ottawa. The Canadian government understood the sensitive nature of my travel and granted my request for this second passport. I had to renew it every year and pay the usual fee but it was never denied or withdrawn.

We arrived at Robertsfield – the international airport, and former World War 2 US Airforce base, at 2.30 am. I got my hand luggage together and was on my way down the aisle when a weary member of the cabin crew asked me where I was going. I told her that I was getting off in Monrovia. She replied: "Sir, nobody gets off here, it is just a fuelling stop." I assured her that I was getting off here as I had business in Liberia. "Have you been here before, sir?" she asked. I replied that this was my first visit. She asked me to wait while she called the senior cabin person. He came quickly and checked the facts of my story. He asked me if I had a visa for Liberia, pointing out that it was under a military dictatorship at that time. I assured him that I expected my visa to be waiting for me at the desk.

He advised me that if I stepped off of the stairway from the aircraft onto Liberian soil they would no longer be able to offer me the security of the USA. I thanked him for his concern and went down the steps to where a soldier in a slouch-hat with a rifle that looked quite ancient met me. He had a bandolier of bullets across his chest but greeted me in an accent that sounded a lot like the southern drawl of the USA, and escorted me into the terminal.

Another AE mission set-up visit was underway.

Comedy

Another such set-up visit David and Stephen Lungu of Malawi paid was to Freetown, Sierra Leone, at the invitation of the Council of Churches. Here the hazards were slightly different. They did however have their comedy component. David's journal records:

Steve and I were put up in single rooms in a second-rate hotel near the Council offices. We unpacked, had a passable meal and went to bed. We had been in airports and on flights for almost two full days. To lie prone with a noisy airconditioner purring in the window was bliss but it didn't seem like more than an hour when someone was banging on my door. I woke up with a start and leapt out of the bed into the wall. I resolved to sleep on the other single bed that was open to the room on the side that I was used to at home.

Dazed, I rolled back and hit the night light as I staggered to the door rubbing my forehead and asking aloud "Who is it?" "Dave, it's me, Steve." I opened the door to find a partially clad Steve. He was not smiling as he entered. "Brother, sorry to call you at this hour but I have problems with these women coming to my door to make themselves available!"

I was wide awake now. "Just tell them no thank you. No, make that no tankee." "But Dave, they just come back and there are many." "Well, brother go down to the lobby and complain to the manager or ask him to call the police."

Steve looked unsure about the strategy but went off to find the manager. I hit the light switch and the pillow at the same time. I was just dozing off when that same bang had me instantly awake again. I jumped out of the right side of the bed this time and opened the door. Steve launched into another diatribe about prostitutes. When he had found the manager, Steve discovered that he was fully occupied with his own string of "ladies" and busy making suggestions as to which door to try next.

At this point Steve moved into David's room and had the rest of his night ruined by Dave's snoring! The team always felt it better for the men to travel two by two if they possibly could. Far safer!

Visiting the Churches

Usually David would begin by visiting the churches that had made the invitation, and finding out a bit more about what they had in mind. He'd also get an idea of what resources would be on offer to the AE team. For example, how many of the city's churches even wanted the mission, and how many would be prepared to back it with money? With manpower? What of the Christians in the city? How many were in government, in banking, in business, in engineering, in medicine, in education, in industry, in commerce? What about the leisure clubs, the tennis, the golf clubs? What about the housewives? What about the domestic workers or slum-dwellers? Every possible grouping of people within the city was considered and the question asked: where are the Christians among them? Would they be willing to help us meet these "stratas" of city society in a manner with which the residents felt comfortable? Could coffee mornings, lunches, dinners, be organised to which professionals could be invited? How about the hospitals, schools, prisons, mines, industries? Would they allow AE in to speak with people informally during break-times? Or even to take short meetings? Would women help organise meetings for any domestic staff?

Next came practicalities: what resources did the city possess? Where could small, medium and large meetings actually be held? Would people be willing to open their own homes? Would the larger churches and cathedral be available? How about school auditoriums and sports fields for rallies? How far ahead did they have to be booked? What did they cost?

What about PA systems? Was the city's electricity supply fairly dependable, or was a rally of several thousand people apt to be silenced and plunged either into total darkness or soundlessness without warning? (Despite assurances, this would happen on several occasions over the years. The AE solution was usually to ask people to keep their seats, and sing choruses in the dark until the power came on again!)

What about transport? This was always a tricky logistical problem. Some African cities are vast and sprawling, with undependable public transport. So how do you physically move people around to meetings, and on time? (Even flexible African time?) AE evangelists in their time have travelled by foot, squeezed into public buses, crawled into the back of open trucks, and even, when desperate, hitched lifts on the back of complete strangers' bicycles.

What about food? What about housing? When a team arrived in a city, it could number up to several dozen people needing bed and board for several weeks. Where to put them? What to feed them? A seemingly trivial matter, but one which had to be organised all the same, if the evangelists weren't to find themselves temporarily homeless. (In one city the churches requested that people donate livestock to feed the AE team. A number of goats and cows arrived, and one facetious report back to HQ at the end of the mission said simply: "We still have a cow and goat left, wandering around, uneaten.")

Such preparation for a Christian mission might seem so elaborate as to put off churches for good. But the problem facing the Christians of the cities of Africa was clear. As Michael Cassidy would describe it:

It is a notoriously difficult task to penetrate a city effectively with the gospel of Christ. The sheer size of a city, the complexity of its problems, and the diversity of the people place such a challenge beyond the scope of any one individual local church.

Yet the cities must be reached. How can this be done? African Enterprise believes that the way is through citywide, co-operative preaching missions. When all the churches in the midst of the city stand together to declare corporately their faith, a spiritual penetration in depth can occur.

This had been abundantly demonstrated in AE's initial city-wide 1962 mission in Pietermaritzburg.

Yet even here, African Enterprise began to realise that there was room for refining and improvement. That first "Mission to Maritzburg" in 1962 had been held in the vigorous tradition of Wesley, Graham, Moody and the other giants of evangelism. The mission was based on large public meetings and a call for the surrender of the person's life in conversion or rededication. It was also strongly influenced by the commitment of ministers of many denominations who'd invited AE to speak on an interdenominational platform. This interdenominational group saw evangelism as the means to express or create unity between the Christians of the city.

In those early days, these influences gave rise to AE's urban evangelism policy. This depended on a central superstructure (the AE team and leading local clergy) imposing a programme (with the full approval of the clergy and mission committees) on the city's churches. The programme focused on large meetings and public rallies.

Training and Enabling

As the years went by, closer relationships developed between the ministers of South Africa's churches and the members of the AE team. It became evident that the laity in the various churches were also eager to help, but required some help in learning the do's and don'ts of effective evangelism. African Enterprise then began to see a new role for itself: as *enablers* in evangelism. The small teams could be best used strategically if they not only preached the gospel themselves, but if through thorough training, they enabled the resident laity of the city to work alongside them. Thus AE developed a new role: serving as the handmaiden of the churches, helping them to learn to do the task of evangelism.

Then along came "Mission '70" to Johannesburg in 1970. This added yet another dimension to the AE role. Large meetings drew the crowds, but who were these crowds? Did they represent a true cross-section of the entire city? Were the uncommitted really there? Highly unlikely! So AE began to devise a scheme for penetrating the city for Christ at all levels. AE called it "stratified evangelism" – evangelism that sought to reach different homogeneous groups in any city with methods and approaches best suited to that group's cultural identity. Thus prayer breakfasts for politicians, and business lunches for business people and small meetings in hospital wards for busy nurses and languishing patients. In all of this, however, AE still continued to design the programme, build the organisational structures of the mission, administer the mission, raise the funds, teach the laity, preach at the main rallies, pray continually, and worry and rejoice by turn more than anyone else.

Mission '70 also saw the development of small home groups used as an evangelistic context. Dick Peace, building on the CHUM groups (Christian Home Unit Method) started in the Spearhead Youth Mission (1967), produced a brilliant twelve-week set of "Witness" studies with lecture tapes by Dick and handbooks attached (much like today's Alpha groups but without videos). Churches were to draw in their uncommitted friends for this twelve-week course. So successful was this in Johannesburg that in some cases the Witness groups were still going twelve or 15 years later. In fact Dick's Witness course pretty much launched the era of home Bible-studies and fellowship groups in South Africa as the manuals and lectures went far and wide for years afterwards.

As to all the other mission labours generally, these were fine and effective as far as they went, except that the AE team were always pushed to the limit, and often utterly exhausted. After several years, the flaws in this approach to the evangelism of whole suburbs or cities became increasingly apparent. Most of these problems surfaced around the concept of "superstructure" – the organisational scaffolding that was erected for each mission, and around which a united programme was created, involving many congregations.

Problems

There were several problems with this approach, and the team grew to know them all too well. First, there was the high cost involved. Organisation was costly, because it involved a number of administrators, office facilities and secretaries. In Mission '70 half the budget had gone simply in maintaining the superstructure. Communications required enormous effort and cost. Advertising the mission was expensive, and printing fliers became prohibitive.

A second problem was identified as "divided commitment". AE found to its dismay that too often the churches that said they would participate in the mission in reality did anything but. These churches meant well, but seldom "owned" the large and wider mission programme. Instead they sought blithely to proceed with their own local agendas. This left members of congregations across the city trying to participate in their own church's programme as well as in the wider programme of the mission. Often these meetings clashed. In some city missions, only a fraction of the participating churches ever really got involved.

A third problem could be called "confused identity". When converts were made, they invariably identified their new faith with the mission which had led them to Christ. But this mission was no more than a temporary identity compounded of the AE team and the participating churches. At the end of the mission, with the dismantlement of the "superstructure", the convert was left with no permanent ongoing relationship with the agency that brought him or her to Christ. AE was haunted by the hundreds of converts who had probably been lost or set back in their Christian walk as a result of this.

Fourth, what about any ongoing evangelism? Because evangelism invariably happened outside the context of congregations, AE discovered that churches were not prepared for an ongoing programme of outreach. The mission came, the mission went, and all was static once again. Missions were thus often anti-climatic.

Fifth, there was the inevitable problem of gaining co-operation from a wide variety of churches across the given city: churches that in many cases had not got along for years. This is a hazard of interdenominational missions, which have always carried the exhausting and difficult problems of getting churches from different disciplines to work effectively together.

Sixth, Michael was concerned that a wrong theological emphasis had crept in here. In the larger city mission it was all too easy to aim for making converts, rather than disciples. A convert is someone who is born into the kingdom of God. A disciple is someone who is not only born into the kingdom but is growing within the context of the church and living under the kingly rule of Christ.

Michael later wrote: "All of these flaws worried us for some time. It was very difficult to break with the old pattern, for everyone expected it and asked for it."

Major Shift

By 1975, however, AE was ready for fresh experiments. Dick Peace had always said: "AE is an ongoing experiment in evangelism." With its "Mission to Maritzburg", AE decided to take the plunge and introduce a major shift in its evangelistic strategy.

In its first phase before the mass meetings, Maritzburg '75 was to take the form of a series of congregational missions. Each congregation was invited to design and execute its own mission, with the help of training and resources provided by AE and other Christian agencies.

This approach emphasised the importance of both homogeneity and diversity in evangelism. In addition, the team organised a number of community projects for city labourers, businessmen, domestic helpers, college students and high schoolers, which were geared specifically to homogeneous audiences. No mission office or big superstructure was to be built. Instead, each church was expected to pay for its own mission, and also make a reasonable contribution to the execution of the community projects.

Once the Maritzburg churches had got over the shock of such a new idea, they decided to take up the challenge. Some 50 churches, from all the racial and fourteen denominational groupings of the city, said they'd be willing to give the new scheme a try. The existing structures of these churches became the vehicles for planning the mission. A small overall mission committee was put together, but its job was only to co-ordinate, not to mandate. The executive power rested with the congregations.

AE knew where it could be of real use, namely in offering the Maritzburg churches a church growth and renewal course for the Christians themselves, to help set the tone for the mission. The course was attended by clergy and leading laymen from over 30 Pietermaritzburg churches, and would prove a vital factor in preparing local church leadership for evangelism from the outset of the mission programme.

The need for dependence upon "the empowering of the Spirit" emerged very clearly during the course. One person explained: "As the session progressed, I had an extraordinary sense of the unifying effect of what was being shared. It was as though the Spirit was saying, 'I am not here to fragment the church, but to make it whole.' For me, the climax of the session was a most marvellous time of prayer."

When dozens of others spoke of the power of these sessions, which always included a lengthy time of prayer, the whole experience was seen as a profound endorsement of James 4:10: "Humble yourselves in the sight of God, and he shall lift you up." As Michael and his team explained to the churches: "There is a danger of starting a mission in a spirit of shallow triumphalism, instead of in a spirit of humble penitence. It is one of those glorious paradoxes of God that his strength is made perfect in the weakness of his people."

Discipleship Course

Soon the team noticed a quickening of enthusiasm as members of 30 churches signed up for the pre-mission Discipleship Course taught by Michael weekly in the City Hall. Soon all 1,400 seats in the City Hall were filled through advance bookings and tickets for each Wednesday evening, with more folk standing at the doors, even though attendance meant a tuition fee, memorising Scripture verses, doing weekly homework and reading and short 20-question tests at the beginning of each session. There were one or two near-misses on the roads while people sought to memorise their verses in the car in anticipation of the exam that night!

In addition, the Pentecostal churches organised a prayer chain for continuous round-the-clock prayer for the eight months leading up to the main mission thrust. Christians across Pietermaritzburg signed up to cover every single hour on the whole rota, sometimes singly, sometimes in groups. They spent a total of 5,856 hours in prayer, asking for wisdom and guidance and blessing on every aspect of the mission.

Dr Paul Walters, a lecturer at the university, later wrote: "Our congregation was encouraged in the Lord to see their ideal as that of a fellowship or shared life, a body, actually growing." The church had learned something about management, too. "We learned the importance of self-evaluation and the setting of clear goals."

In the mass services some 4,000 people attended the meetings at the local show grounds each night, with some 800 responding for Christian commitment the night Michael spoke on the occult. On the Friday night Michael addressed the issue of applying repentance and faith to the South African situation. "We have to repent of racism and apartheid as much as sins like adultery, or greed, or violence, or slander."

"It's a shame," said one little delegation that came up to Michael after the meeting, "that you should now spoil such a good evangelistic series by bringing in politics."

When would South Africa relate its professed faith to the issues of injustice in the land, Michael wondered.

The mission also was one of the first to include a strong component of prayer for healing, as an evangelist with a special healing ministry was allowed to do the main address in one of the meetings.

The closing rally in Woodburn Stadium drew some 10,000 people with nearly 1,000 professing commitment when the appeal was made.

Needless to say, the mission rocked Pietermaritzburg, as the churches welcomed hundreds of new converts, and made sure that they would be taken care of and nurtured in Christian discipleship.

Landmarks

July 1977 was another landmark for AE. For the first time in its history of 15 years, "team members were this month involved in significant opportunities in parts of Africa new to our ministry".

For example, in West Africa that month, Ebenezer Sikakane and Bishop Festo did large rallies in Kumasi, Ghana, alongside the Ghanaian Congress on Evangelism. Ebenezer, fresh from his year of study at Fuller Seminary, also gave three church growth seminars at the congress. The Ghana experience gave AE a valuable new foothold in a part of the continent they were longing to enter, and where they wanted to start a new team. In due time they would do just that.

In North Africa there were other landmark meetings. John Wilson of the Ugandan team was receiving an enthusiastic reception from ministers in the ancient city of Alexandria in Egypt. It was the first step in the organisation of a mission to the cities of Cairo and Alexandria, being planned for Bishop Festo and Michael Cassidy the following year. AE hoped fervently that this door, so kindly opened for them by the Bible Society in Arab Africa, would enable more work to be done in the area. AE also wanted to establish a team in North Africa. John Wilson seemed to be given very special favour in speaking, relating and preaching to Arab people, whether in Egypt, Jordan or Lebanon.

As well as missions to cities, AE tackled some of the sprawling townships of Africa, where tens of thousands of people crowded into densely packed and pitifully poor areas. One such mission was the July 1980 Mission to Edendale and Imbali. Both were sprawling dormitory areas on the outskirts of Pietermaritzburg. A two-week mission was planned, and all the church and parachurch organisations in the area were invited to participate. The response was "wonderful", as local committees covering every aspect "are hard at work to ensure that the Gospel impacts all sections of the community".

The organisers had their work cut out for them: the population of these two areas alone was estimated to be about 60,000, most under 20 years old. So AE developed a specialised youth evangelism team under Nico Kleynhans called "The Ambassadors". They spent the summer before the mission visiting all the schools, teacher training colleges and church youth groups in the townships. In the meantime, Michael Cassidy, Andrew Mohibidu, Abiel Thipanyane, Denton Sibisi, Billy Winter, Hezekiah Langa, and Gershon Mwiti of Kenya prepared their evangelistic addresses.

The mission was held, and many hundreds came. There was only one major problem: none of the 35 church buildings in the townships was big enough to accommodate the numbers of people involved.

A Festival of Faith

African Enterprise tried yet another model when invited to Kimberley in the autumn of 1980. AE, together with the 35 local congregations of this beautiful and historic city, organised a Festival of Faith and Fellowship, which climaxed in a final mass rally at the de Beers Stadium, with drama, worship and exhibitions. The idea for the festival had come from a conversation Michael Cassidy had had in the USA in early 1980 with Dr Ralph Winter, one of the great missionary strategists of our time, and the Director of the United States Center for World Mission. Winter felt the church ought to have periodic and regular moments when it could really experience its togetherness and fly its flag. He suggested AE might try to mount a "sort of combination of a county fair and an evangelistic campaign".

The idea appealed and so AE decided to attempt this at Kimberley. It worked well as the Christians of Kimberley in celebratory mode visited nearly every home in the city to extend an invitation to the meetings. Also, black and white churches worked closely together to reach a wide variety of groups, from businessmen to prisoners. There was especially riveted attention one evening when Michael and Abiel shared together on "White and Black at the Cross and the Crossroads". Abiel's poignant, courageous and uncompromising testimony about what it meant to be a Christian and a black in Apartheid South Africa deeply touched everyone present.

In advance of the Kimberley mission the AE Ambassador Youth Team found itself barricaded into the troubled Galeshewe township for a couple of weeks as the police sealed it off with armoured vehicles and forbade exit or entry. Leaflets were dropped from the air by military helicopters urging one and all to stop rioting. During this time of being locked in the township the Ambassador team got to know and win the trust of the leadership of the young political firebrands. When the AE team came to town Nico and the Ambassadors arranged for Michael to meet in secret with these leaders and hear their grievances, most of which centred on education. Michael was able to get these to Dr Piet Koornhof, then Minister of Education, whom Michael knew.

Luthando

Following the mission, many of these youngsters came to the AE Centre, including a young political "heavy" called Luthando Charlie, sent along to ensure that the "kids did not sell out to whitey". At AE Luthando had a significant conversion experience to Christ.

However, back in Kimberley, Luthando and 19 other friends were detained by the police as "witnesses" against five other young school friends charged with "riotous and destructive behaviour" – i.e. burning schoolbooks and classrooms. Local church leaders phoned Michael to try and do something about these detentions. Michael approached the authorities, but in vain.

Luthando was kept in prison (uncharged) for 19 months, six of them in solitary, and fearfully tortured for information. When he came out Michael and his wife Carol decided: "We can't be responsible for all South Africa's detainees. But we can take responsibility for one we know."

Michael and Carol accordingly made Luthando, who had lost his parents, a sort of temporary foster son, and secured a scholarship for him at Hilton College, one of the country's most prestigious private schools. Over the next few years, with Luthando one of the pioneers at Hilton for non-racial education, the young man caught up on his studies, became the first black boy to play rugby for Hilton, and secured his matric.

His past was kept pretty secret, except for the knowledge of his headmaster and housemaster. This was to prevent him becoming a hero to the school's liberals and a villain to its conservatives.

Michael and Carol also secured scholarships for him for some university and then technikon education. Luthando still calls Michael and Carol periodically to report on his progress as the Alumni Director for his technikon. His witness to Christ remains firm. The Kimberley mission thus lives on!

Festo to South Africa

In the midst of South Africa's racial tension, student riots, black employee strikes and school boycotts, Bishop Festo Kivengere made his first visit to South Africa in late August of 1980. The week of dual ministry fulfilled a twelve-year dream which Festo and Michael had had since their ministry together began. Over 20,000 people in 17 rallies throughout Soweto, Cape Town, Durban and Pietermaritzburg received the message of hope which Michael and Bishop Festo shared. More than 500 committed their lives to Christ.

Both men were astonished at the spiritual receptivity of the black townships, areas of considerable political tension and frustration. This was especially true of Soweto, known for the 1976 Soweto riots. Because of their racial differences, Festo and Michael found many doors opened. "Festo could say many things as a black that I could never say as a white, and vice versa," said Michael. "It was very important for me as a white also to be ministering because many blacks had given up on whites." Conversely, Festo found, as previously mentioned, that after speaking at Stellenbosch University, one Afrikaner could tell him that he had been delivered from a racist posture towards blacks.

Testimonies from Secular Leaders

Meanwhile in Kenya in early 1981, a month-long mission to the city of Kitui, led by Gershon Mwiti, reached a staggering 60,000 people. Gershon Mwiti "praised the Lord" for the full support and attendance of even the Kenya Minister of Labour, the Honourable Titus Mbathi. Titus Mbathi did more than attend: he testified himself as a Christian, and even led a choir composed of the leading men and women of Kitui.

Using this testimony of secular leaders who were Christians became another effective strategy used in AE's city missions.

Chapter 15

Converging from All Corners

If you want to lead a life full of suspense and action, with occasional brushes with danger, that involves constant travel and meeting interesting people, with rewards that are literally out of this world, then what are you waiting for? You should join African Enterprise's pan-African Missions. These are missions which take place once or twice a year when the whole AE pan-African team from all corners of the continent converges on one major city.

Just about everything that *can* happen *has* happened on these missions over the last 30 years. It is, after all, a highly combustible mix: take up to several thousand Christians who are determined that their message should be heard. Place them in any teeming city of Africa. Add a good measure of civil unrest, various other religious groupings, the odd riot and/or epidemic, and a good dollop of electricity strikes, power outages, petrol shortages, and an occasional military coup. Season with sweltering tropical or desert heat and torrential thunderstorms or blinding sandstorms. Stir well, and finish with only a dash of reliable transport, a pinch of effective communications, and a thin scraping of money. Offer the result to African Enterprise and say: This city is ready for you now! Come and help us hold a united churches citywide evangelistic mission of Word and Deed!

African Enterprise does just that. What follow are just a few of the many hundreds of stories stretching over three decades.

In 1978 alone, African Enterprise found itself (stretched to the very limits) with 30 major invitations to fulfil. So the East African AE team and the South African AE team combined for ministry in cities from Cape Town to Cairo and from Monrovia, Liberia to Mombasa, Kenya.

Open Doors that None can Shut

In 1980 Michael Cassidy went on a sabbatical tour and study time to North America and Europe. There he wrestled with himself and about AE in a serious time of reflection and stock-taking.

However, four times, through different people in different places at different times over a few months, the Lord gave him Revelation 3:8 as a word for himself and for AE as a ministry.

Not surprisingly, Michael returned from his study sabbatical with these words ringing in his ears. "I know your deeds. Behold, I have placed before you an open door that no one is able to shut; I know that you have little power/strength, yet you have kept my word and have not denied my name" (Revelation 3:8). Michael knew he was being told that the "doors" to Africa were open. He had only to discern which, and to walk through them in faith.

In August 1981 a combined South African/East African team headed for Zambia, and the Copperbelt mission. Dozens of churches, months of preparation, hundreds of meetings: 4,000 new Christians the result. This large number was both encouraging and a challenge, as the follow-up department in South Africa strove to keep in touch with each inquirer for at least one year from the time of initial commitment.

One millionaire begged the team to return for another mission in 1982, after his wife was healed and brought to faith through the mission. He even offered to pay the travel expenses of the team.

One AE team member from Zimbabwe, Gibson Madombwe, preached in a prison, where one of the prisoners interpreted for him. After he had finished interpreting, the interpreter told Gibson that he, too, wanted to decide for Christ. So the prisoner/interpreter became a Christian. But Madombwe was scheduled to preach elsewhere and of course would continue to need an interpreter. He said to the prison authorities: "Listen, I haven't heard a guy who can interpret this well. We've got meetings throughout the town and I want him to come along and interpret for me."

As the prisoner had committed a major offence, the prison authorities agreed to let him out only if an armed guard could also go along. So off they went immediately to the next meeting: Madombwe, the prisoner – still in his striped prison uniform, and an armed guard.

Later that day, the AE team offered to get their prison interpreter normal trousers and a shirt, but the prisoner refused. "No, this is how the Lord found me, and this is how I am going to stay." So for the remainder of the mission, Madombwe stood up in dozens of meetings to preach, to be interpreted by a man wearing a prison uniform, standing next to a guard who had a rifle trained on him. There was never any danger of Madombwe losing the crowd's attention! Madombwe concluded simply: "Just as he did when he walked the earth, Jesus calls and uses people from all segments of society."

All Pulling Together

A few months after the Copperbelt Mission came "Hope '81", a mission to Windhoek, the capital of Namibia. In this politically divided area, the Christians of 15 denominations and 45 congregations decided it was time to make a stand of Christian unity, and hold a mission. The AE team spoke to nearly 20,000 people, and welcomed 800 who wanted to begin life anew, with Christ. Michael stayed with the theme of factions versus unity, and urged: *"Find each other in Christ. Pray for political leaders in all parties. Repent of all forms of racism."* His challenge rang out across the vast stadium and drew repeated outbursts of spontaneous applause. One evening Michael preached to a predominantly Afrikaans-speaking mixed-race congregation with the help of a good interpreter. However, Michael broke one of his own rules that night: always have a briefing session with your interpreter! In the rush, and due to some late transport, the meeting of preacher and interpreter was too short. Michael told two hilarious stories that night and when he hit the punchlines in English his interpreter roared with laughter and was quite unable to translate the joke to the bewildered and waiting throng. Through much splutter and giggles he finally regained control and managed somehow to convey the joke in Afrikaans, to the delight of the audience.

All round Windhoek at that time were political posters put up by conservative whites opposed to independence for South-

West Africa. They read: "Blankes, Saamtrek" i.e., "Whites pull together." In the closing multi-racial rally in the rugby stadium, Michael surprisingly drew a big cheer, even from the whites there, when he contradicted the poster: "It's not 'Blankes Saamtrek'," he said, "it's 'Almal Saamtrek' i.e., 'Everyone pull together.'"

Mutare for Jesus

July, 1982, and the combined teams of AE arrived in Mutare (formerly Umtali), a picturesque town in Zimbabwe's north-eastern highlands. They were to hold a three-week mission. Umtali's new name, Mutare, meaning border or boundary in Shona, in Latin means "Be thou changed!" – and that is just what happened.

In front of 3,000 people, one former freedom fighter wept bitterly, confessing to awful killings. His mother, who had been praying for him and now witnessed her son's conversion from the back of hall, rushed to the platform, sobbing as she embraced him in front of the cheering and rejoicing throng.

A woman who had hated her husband for thirteen years after he had divorced her, was reconciled to him and to his new wife. The three of them sat together at several meetings, sharing their newfound unity at the foot of the cross.

An American journalist, Ted Olsen, wrote after the final rally and the great procession which preceded it:

A long line of cars, trucks and buses stretched several kilometres through the city. Drivers hooted noisily. "Mutare for Jesus" banners festooned their vehicles. Motorists going the other way wheeled around to join the joyful procession as it snaked its way to the stadium for the final crusade meeting...

That final meeting, addressed by Michael and Steve Mongoma, drew nearly 10,000 to the soccer stadium on that last Sunday in July. At its close, with the skies overcast and a stiff wind whipping the air, hundreds responded to the invitation, bringing to well more than 5,000 those who had signified their desire to commit their lives to Christ since the campaign began.

Dean John Knight of St John's Cathedral in Mutare said: "Though a team of dedicated evangelists spoke dozens of times in two weeks, their efforts were incidental to something far greater. You see, God has for many years prepared Mutare for himself. He has now moved to claim it." Dean Knight, the Mission Chairman and a key promoter of the campaign, admitted:

> Months ago when AE began to look to our local clergy for support in their "Mutare for Jesus" campaign, I was sceptical. I've never been much for mass evangelism of this sort and we were *not* a united group of city churches.
>
> But after those initial meetings with David Richardson and Chris Sewell I could not help being impressed by AE's prayerful, systematic and unrelenting effort to bring about a great happening of the Holy Spirit. And then I heard of the prophecy. I was told that ten years ago in the city of Salisbury, now Harare, a prophetic statement had been made in a meeting: "In ten years from now, a light will go forth from the city of Umtali which will transform this country and nations round about."

With that, this leading Anglican of the city had come out in full support of the AE campaign.

First came a week of "stratified evangelism". AE's evangelists from Kenya, Malawi, Tanzania, Uganda, Zimbabwe and South Africa fanned out across Mutare, preaching in factories, schools, institutions, army camps, police quarters, businessmen's lunches, and in community halls. "We moved right into the fabric of life in the city. We went to the people where they were. For a solid week, our evangelists spoke about 25 or 30 times a day," said a mission report. It was David Richardson's first mission outside South Africa and it had taken the best part of a year to set up. "I read all that Michael and John Tooke had written about stratified evangelism and other missions where AE had tried this 'saturation' approach to reach every sector of the city," he said. "Then I went out on the basis of Revelation 3:8 and tried to put it all together in Mutare. By the time Michael arrived for the main week of preaching, he seemed astounded to discover that we had already held over 600 meetings and that we had set up seven venues around the city for simultaneous mass meetings each evening. This way we could use all the leading evangelists in AE and preach to seven large groups every night."

AE team member Dr Sam Nkulila from Tanzania, a psychiatrist, spoke to 100 workers at a tea factory. When he asked if anyone would like to invite Christ into their life, all 100 responded! This was Africa! This was also Africa's proverbial hunger for the gospel.

At an army camp, 550 ex-freedom fighters asked Christ into their lives. More than 1,000 Bibles provided by the Gideons were snatched up and the next day another battalion requested Bibles.

In all, the pan-African mission to Mutare was an event that would have been beyond the dreams of even the young AE team of many years before. For more than 50,000 people came to the meetings; and 6,000 of these made decisions for Christ.

Six thousand people to follow up! In the aftermath of the mission, all this discipling kept AE's Andrew Mohibidu of South Africa and Chris Sewell of Zimbabwe mightily busy as they helped the new Christians to settle into existing local congregations across the city.

Warm Heart of Africa

Then in 1983 there was "Blantyre for Jesus" in Malawi, known as the "Warm Heart of Africa". It had been a nightmare of a mission to put together, with endless difficulties over organisation, logistics and getting official government and police permission, as well as the reluctance of the CCAP – the main Presbyterian denomination – to participate fully. At times the whole idea of going to Blantyre was nearly abandoned. But finally, in late 1983, African Enterprise swept into the capital of Malawi, holding their breath. Too late to turn back now – make the most of opportunity for the next three weeks, even though several key team members had been knocked out with sickness and one with bereavement.

The 27 members of the team (from South Africa, Kenya, Zimbabwe, the US, UK and Canada) set out to infiltrate the city at every level. They spoke to schoolchildren, students, teachers, miners, accountants, politicians and office workers. They went into homes, schools, churches, factories, sawmills, hotels, businesses, post offices, the museum and the airport.

Leaders' luncheons gave Michael and Steve Lungu and others the chance to share the gospel with some of the most influential people in Malawi – including five politicians and the chairwoman of the Women's League of the ruling Malawi Congress Party.

In the second week, Michael, Steve and other evangelists ran simultaneous open-air rallies at a whopping seven strategic venues each night across the breadth of the city, from Banwe to Chilomoni, spilling over into the nearby city of Limbe. All venues drew wonderful crowds, because AE had circumvented the transport problem by using the seven different regional venues.

The response to all this was thousands of people surging forward to receive Christ. The sheer numbers had the AE evangelists stunned at first. They questioned the sincerity of the people. They did not want "half-baked" commitments. They gave stern and highly demanding altar calls. Still the people came. Incredulously, the evangelists began to accept that they really did "mean business with God". Preaching at a bus stop, Chris Sewell asked the 40 or so passengers waiting for a bus who wanted to take Christ. All 40 put their hands up. Chris wondered if this was for real, and further explicated the cost of discipleship. Again all 40 raised their hands. Determined not to secure cheap responses, Chris asked those genuinely wanting to receive Christ to kneel on the pavement. All 40 spontaneously knelt. As the astonished Chris led them in prayer, the bus arrived. The even more astonished bus driver honked his horn and swished the doors back and forth. No one moved. Goggle-eyed, he then drove off.

"They missed the bus to town and caught the bus to heaven," laughed Chris.

A week later, Chris met a radiant young man who asked if Chris remembered him. Chris stared blankly. "I was at the bus stop," he beamed, "and I found Jee-sas at the bus stop!"

Response Overwhelming

Local church leaders, seeing this hunger and response, were dumbfounded. Several pastors, who'd been thinking of leaving the ministry because they felt so spiritually dry, suddenly discovered the reason: they had not yet been converted themselves, nor ever truly found Christ and been born again! So they sorted that out at once, with tears of joy, as Christ became a living reality to them.

Out of the rallies came stunning testimonies. One young man who had venereal disease and a horrific rash on his body went home after being prayed for – to find that he had been healed.

A tough thug of a man, who was feared locally, was somehow persuaded by his wife to attend a rally. He made a decision for Christ, to the utter astonishment of all who knew him.

The wife of a senior civil servant went to a meeting, became a Christian, and went home to terminate three separate affairs she had been having at the same time behind her husband's back.

A Buddhist woman, shattered by the experience of four miscarriages, came forward for prayer, found Jesus as a living reality, and in him found comfort and solace for the first time.

A woman crippled with arthritis for four years was prayed for. She had no further need of the cripple chair she'd been using.

One lady who became a Christian during the mission soon fell very ill. A few weeks later she died. But she'd been busy in the short time she'd had before going to the Lord. At the funeral relatives said she'd led three people to Christ before her death.

An AE team ventured into a mining company's recruitment camp. It was littered with brothels and nightclubs, and the customers came outside in astonishment when the team of eight evangelists began their impromptu outdoor rally. At the end, about 500 miners tentatively came forward for prayer.

Some Muslims and Hindus came to the rallies out of curiosity, and 20 stayed behind to become Christians. Dave Peters played a key role in discipling them.

Queries came in from factory managers: "Hey, where did all our thieves go?" Petty theft had plummeted, for the first time ever. Monday absenteeism was also down and thus contributed to improved productivity.

Michael Cassidy would write later:

My, my, oh my, what a time we have had in this place! My heart is just simply overflowing with praise and gratitude to God for the exhilarating things we have seen. Some 80,000 people (aggregate) have been in our meetings with an astonishing 8,000 coming to some new commitment to our Lord Jesus.

To prevent any problems of boredom, the team led a whopping 283 meetings in the span of a fortnight. Yet no one felt fatigue! Praise God.

All our hassles and obstacles in getting the thing off the ground can now, from this perspective, be seen as the works of spiritual opposition and darkness. Clearly God had a mighty miracle of harvesting in store.

I think I can say it was possibly the happiest, most joyful, most buoyant and most fruitful mission we have ever done.

On the final day of "Blantyre for Jesus", three columns of thousands of singing people marched through the city and into the upper ground of the Kamuzu Stadium.

The impact on the city was so great that the editor of Blantyre's newspaper, *The Daily Times*, was moved to remark in an editorial that Blantyre was becoming a "born again" city.

Follow-up

Across Blantyre, the churches were delighted to welcome new Christians, some needing extensive counselling. Follow-up meetings, intended to teach converts about their new faith, became popular with people still curious about what had been going on at the mission. "We've been thrilled to find they arrive and want to give their lives to Christ," wrote one church leader. "The Spirit is continuing to work in Malawi, even though the mission is over!"

The follow-up department outdid themselves: eight volunteer workers working eight hours a day managed to post out the 8,000 follow-up letters to people who had indicated some new form of professed commitment to Christ. One of these was a young man named Songe Chibambo, a great preacher and tireless worker. The team were struck by him. Soon he and his wife, Lucy, joined the Malawi team fulltime and Songe later became the Missions' Director of the AE team in South Africa.

Michael concluded:

I have never seen so much joy, praise and laughter amongst the people and the team. But importantly, it has produced a remarkable harvest. It seems that every one of these citywide missions in Africa becomes more fruitful than the one which preceded it. It also alerts us afresh to the fact that this is harvest time in Africa. Our pan-African AE teams must move quickly through the harvest while it is yet day, and while the reaping opportunities are so gloriously numerous.

The Lord is going to use Blantyre as a springboard into other countries. I feel we are on the edge of an explosion into the rest of Africa.

Certainly "Blantyre for Jesus" launched a permanent African Enterprise presence in Malawi. The team became integral to the wider Central African AE ministries into Zimbabwe, Zambia and Mozambique, as well as Malawi.

In March 1984, African Enterprise decided to do an evaluation of the Blantyre mission. At its annual full inter-team conference, pan-African missions were on top of the agenda. Blantyre had been, everyone agreed, a "mountain-top time", when God did a glorious work "of deepening our love, unity and mutual commitment". Now it was up to AE to scrutinise their structures, programme and mission methodologies, so that they would continue to be maximally effective.

More Over the Horizon

But now there were more pan-African missions just over the horizon: Monrovia in Liberia, and Freetown in Sierra Leone. Michael wrote: "Over a period of many years, we have been praying for these different African cities. It is amazing and exciting now to see so many of them beginning to come on line." Freetown, however, never did fire up. In spite of several visits there by David Richardson and Steve Lungu nothing really significant ever developed in Freetown. Maybe one day. Michael still remembers seeing the Prime Minister and Foreign Minister there during his 1961 tour and later standing alone in the pulpit of an empty Anglican church and praying: "Lord, one day I want to preach in this city." May it be.

Gweru Midst Unrest

"Good News to Gweru" was also difficult, but at least it happened. In June 1984 Gweru, the major city of the Midlands of Zimbabwe, was rocked with civil unrest. Government soldiers were shooting at rebel forces in occasional running battles down the streets. Not the ideal conditions for outdoor evangelism!

However, African Enterprise was glad just to be there at all. Gweru had never been an easy place for a mission, and several attempts to organise one there had failed in the previous seven years.

The first stumbling block had been the degree of sheer depression and apathy among the whites of the city. This was easy to understand: there was a mass white exodus going on, plus a severe drought, and these two factors had in turn led to a steep economic downswing. So the whites were unhappy, preoccupied and spiritually apathetic. The blacks were little better: when they considered the problems stacked against them, they also had reason for deep discouragement. This had affected many black pastors, who felt all but hopeless.

However, even in the misery of Gweru there had emerged a core of dedicated black and white pastors committed to evangelism. In long talks with African Enterprise, this group, representing the twelve different denominations of the city, resolved to proceed, come what may.

The result was what Michael would later describe as "an experience of both trauma and triumph".

The African Enterprise team had brought out all its big guns for this push. Michael Cassidy arrived at the head of a powerful 30-member team from nine countries (Zimbabwe, South Africa, Malawi, Uganda, and Kenya, plus guest participants [mission experts] from the US, Norway, England and Australia).

Mission headquarters were soon buzzing. One journalist wrote: "This team is really geared for action, and the mission office is like an army headquarters!"

Then, steadfastly, the AE team advanced to take the city for Christ.

"What joy we experienced when against all odds the mission began with a highly successful opening rally!" Michael later wrote. "Some 6,000 people sat spellbound in a wind-swept stadium to hear the good news about Jesus." That first day 859 people responded to the call after Stephen Lungu of AE Zimbabwe had preached. 643 of these were professing commitment for the first time.

The very next day, vicious riots broke out between two rival political parties, very close to the mission office. The riots spread great fear among the inhabitants of Gweru. This was traumatic for the community and highly problematic for the AE team. It became the pattern of the mission – glorious breakthroughs of the gospel accompanied by alarming political disturbances which seemed to rock the city with fear, tension and a consequent toll of about ten deaths.

Despite the violence all around them, the AE team still had work to do, as they slipped out of the mission office regularly during lulls in the fighting. They went on to do 20 meetings across the city that first day. In many cases, the team members found themselves counselling and praying for those who were traumatised by the riots, and who sought stability and assurance in Jesus Christ.

Over the following two weeks, riots or no riots, the AE evangelists fanned out to visit the schools, businesses, prisons, factories, government offices, women's groups, marketplaces, and virtually every other sphere of Gweru's life. Greenwood Mkandawire, an AE intern from Malawi, even sang in Gweru's nightclubs during the mission – making good use of his experience as a cabaret artist before conversion.

Meanwhile, Stephen Lungu of the Malawi team and David Wakumire from Uganda approached the army camps nearby, and were able to spend several hours speaking to soldiers – a truly miraculous gospel opportunity. A visit to the barracks of the North Korean-trained Fifth Brigade saw 105 of 315 soldiers responding to the call to commitment. Stephen Lungu and David Wakumire also addressed soldiers at Guineafowl Barracks, the Zimbabwe Military Academy and the army maintenance depot.

At the same time, Michael went after the leaders of the city. He addressed a "leaders' lunch", which brought together the Governor of the Midlands province and his wife, the Mayor of the city, the Commanding Officer of the Zimbabwe Military

Academy, the Commanding Officer of Thornhill Airforce Base, a senior representative of Zanu-PF, Zimbabwe's ruling party, the Regional Director of Youth, Sport and Recreation, a Deputy Commander of the Fifth Brigade, and the Commanding Officer of the Zimbabwean Republic Police.

David Peters and Stephen Lungu decided to tackle the Bluehill Probation Camp to speak to 50 boys awaiting trial for crimes. Both David and Stephen were old-time gangsters themselves, so they identified easily with the boys – and led 19 to the Lord.

Chris Sewell, mission co-ordinator and a former member of Rhodesia's CID, had two opportunities to speak to the Gweru police, both the uniform branch and the CID. He shared his own story, and twelve policemen made a commitment to Christ.

At Mtapa Hall, a venue surrounded by beer halls, the evangelists began to despair one night when the time for the meetings came, and not a single person had come into the hall to listen to them. Then they had an idea. They moved the PA system so that one loudspeaker would reach the women's toilet, which had a window overlooking the nearby and very noisy beer hall. Then, turning up the volume as loud as they could, they began to preach! The deafening sound very soon overcame the bleary-eyed drinkers, who came stumbling into the hall to find out what on earth was going on. Who was behind these disembodied voices and this huge noise? More and more arrived, until the hall was filled with about 300 people. There were several dozen conversions that night, plus one very drunk young man who kept sobbing that he was sick of his life, of meaningless drinking and clubbing, but what could he do? The next day he arrived at the mission office in town: sober, prepared and resolute. Then and there he asked the astonished evangelists to introduce him to Jesus. So they did. And with what rejoicings!

During the last week of the mission four venues were booked for the evangelists – one in the city centre and three in the surrounding townships of Mkoba, Mtapa and Senga. One evening Mtapa Hall was suddenly taken over by a political rally. As the politicians and their followers roughly pushed in, the AE evangelists and their followers got out of the way. "We had to move out quickly," David Peters of AE said later, "to avoid a dangerous situation."

So it went for the entire mission. Though the team was struggling daily to hold meetings in a riot-torn, traumatised city in political chaos, there were nonetheless amazing breakthroughs in personal encounters with the people.

Michael said later: "It had been a long time since we conducted a mission under such demanding circumstances. Yet God was faithful and we rejoiced in the professed response of nearly 4,000 people during the mission."

What lay ahead for the new Christians? Michael and the city pastors implored the supporters of AE worldwide to pray for them, as they faced such a difficult time in this convulsed city.

On the practical side, Greenwood Mkandawire and David Hotchkiss, the AE media and radio expert, worked hard to put together a series of radio programmes to help young converts grow in their faith. These were broadcast for three weeks after the final rally. This was the first use AE had really made of radio in follow-up.

Good News

The months sped by. July 1984 arrived, and Missions' Director David Richardson had some good news to share with the teams: a mission to the teeming city of Monrovia was definitely on the books for March 1985.

Liberia, a small country in West Africa, is a fascinating enclave and mix of African and southern American Creole culture, created by the return of black slaves from the United States about 160 years ago. Its capital, Monrovia, is unique: an African city with a distinctly American flavour. The street vendors sell Chiclets (a popular American chewing gum), lollipops, and US cigarettes along with local produce. Yellow taxicabs rush up and down as noisily and as maniacally as they do in New York!

Although Liberia was economically and socially depressed, leading Christians felt it was spiritually ripe for the gospel. At the invitation of the Archbishop of Liberia, the Rt Rev George Browne, the AE Set-up Directors David Richardson and Gershon Mwiti of Kenya had visited the Liberian capital to discuss the possibility of a citywide mission. David travelled on his own for the first visit, flying on Pan Am out of Johannesburg. When the plane touched down at Roberts Field, the former American World War 2-era Air Force base, it was 3 am. All were asleep except the crew and David, who remembered later that:

> I gathered up my luggage and headed for the door. A cabin crew member asked me where I was going. I replied that I was getting off here. "No," she said, "nobody gets off here. It's just a refuelling stop." "Well," I said, "this is where I will be working for the next three weeks." She asked me to wait a minute while she called the senior Purser. I waited at the door looking at the blackness out there with just a few single lights in the distance. I prayed and claimed that "open door".
>
> The purser came with an expression of deep concern on his face. "Sir I understand that you intend to disembark?" "Yes," I replied. "My ticket indicates that Liberia is my final destination." "Do you have a visa for Liberia, sir?" he enquired. "Well, yes I think so. It should be waiting for me with my host, Archbishop George Browne." "You *think* so, sir? Do you realise that Liberia is a military dictatorship and once you leave this aircraft we can no longer be responsible for your well-being, sir?" I swallowed hard and assured him that I would be fine, thanked him for his concern and disembarked. I was met by an armed guard in a slouch hat and a sling of bullets across his chest – just like the Mexican cowboys, I thought. He led me into a dingy room and called an immigration officer. I explained that I was expecting Archbishop George Browne to meet me with a visitor's visa. Clearly the Archbishop was not there. Three hours later he still was not there and I was wondering now how far away that Pan Am jet was. George Browne and his dear wife arrived half an hour later explaining that they had come through three police roadblocks and had been greatly delayed. Documents changed hands and probably some money, although I didn't witness the transaction, and we were on our way – back through the police roadblocks – a two-hour journey into the city as the sun rose above the lush vegetation and squalor of Monrovia.

Gershon Mwiti accompanied David on his next trip. They went in some excitement and trepidation. Monrovia had in the past been over-churched and under-evangelised. All the traditional churches were represented in the city, plus a wide range of evangelical and Pentecostal churches. Yet African Enterprise had heard there was little contact between the various groups of Christians of the city, certainly not between these groups and the mainline churches.

After talks with the Archbishop and with many of the church leaders, it was clear to David and Gershon that the Christians of Monrovia really wanted to join forces, if only temporarily. Getting to that point alone had been a major struggle, "It took nearly a year of fervent prayer and much diplomacy, and Satan certainly exploited the divisions during the early stages," reported David. "But praise God – there has been a reconciliation, and the unity that we need to nurture and protect a mission is now in place. The door has opened wide for us to hold a mission there next year. If we can leave behind a united Christian witness, it will be one of the most significant results of the mission."

The idea of a mission to Monrovia was very special indeed to Michael Cassidy. He felt an attachment with the city stretching back over many years, especially to his student tour of Africa in 1961, when he had first sought God's will for his ministry in Africa. It had been on the beach at Monrovia, walking alongside the beautiful ocean there near Radio ELWA, that Michael had first asked God for 50 years of ministry in Africa. Now, over 20 years later, "Monrovia is opening and I believe other West African cities will follow!"

Yet it was never going to be easy. Preparation for the mission struggled from the start. Monrovia had 250,000 people: one-third Muslim, one-third Christian, and one-third African traditional religions. There was widespread social unrest, and the people faced tough living conditions due to the poor economy. Also, political tensions were rising by the day: 1985 was election year for Liberia – a critical time, with the hope of moving from a military junta to civilian rule. So, trouble everywhere, but "all this only makes Liberia even more ripe for the gospel", according to Archbishop Browne, patron of the mission.

An Arresting Afternoon

David Richardson recalls an afternoon in Monrovia when he was informally "arrested" by an inebriated policeman for supposedly illegally taking a photograph of a street vendor:

The officer ignored the cries from the street vendor and the crowd who were all suggesting sums from one dollar to 20 dollars as my penalty for taking his picture without his consent. However the quite unsober officer had some new ideas of his own. "You mus cum to de stashun to be queshuned," he slurred. Suddenly I was afraid. He was arresting me and wanted to take me to the police station for interrogation. I was in a country ruled by a corrupt military dictatorship and it was not impossible for them to discover that I was a permanent resident in "racist South Africa" even though I travelled on a Canadian passport. This was a serious matter, my life was in danger and I was alone. I prayed for God's help and mercy. Suddenly I said "Officer, we can settle this matter – let's go and phone the Archbishop of Liberia, who is my host, and he will help us resolve this matter and will confirm that I know what photographs I can take." "No," he said, "we go down to da stayshun for dis." A chill ran down my damp back as he took out his large revolver, the crowd stepped back and I knew I needed to get out of this situation fast. I said "Officer, come with me first to my hotel across the street there and we can sort out this matter." I began to walk through the crowd not knowing if I would hear or feel a shot or not.

The crowd closed in around me and we moved in a dwindling group across the empty street. Then it was up the eight flights of stairs and into my fourth-floor room. Once inside, the officer seemed to sober up a bit and he carefully looked around the room. Then in silence he took out a piece of paper and wrote on it $100 and handed it to me. He wanted money for himself. The gun was pointing right at me and I explained that I worked for the church and that I did not have that kind of money. (It was over two months' wages for a Liberian police officer in those days, but the government often did not pay its employees for several months.) The officer was desperate too. He suddenly volunteered that he was a Christian too, a Preshbeteereen! "Well," I said, "Then we are brothers and I am sure we can work out this problem together. I am willing to destroy the film right here in front of you." He pointed to the paper with $100 on it. The gun was still in his hand. I said "Look officer I can't pay that but I am willing to make a donation to your Presbyterian church. I do apologise for any unintentional offence and here is $60 – it is as much as I can give you." He looked at the cash in my hand, took it and left. I locked my door and took a loooooong cool shower as I thanked the Lord for his mercy.

David concluded his yarn, recording that after the mission Michael received from Dr Gary Demarest, a Presbyterian AE USA board member a cheque for $100 to compensate for David's loss of both face and cash! "That should balance the books on behalf of the Presbyterians!" he said.

In fact, the AE pan-African mission to Monrovia was so important that, as Michael Cassidy said, "Screwtape proceeded to attempt everything in his power to sabotage it."

First, Pan Am, the airline the AE evangelists were booked on to fly to Monrovia, suffered a strike. There were not many flights to Monrovia at the best of times, and this caused massive complications in getting there at all. In fact, it necessitated flying to London and then doubling back to West Africa.

An Extraordinary Witness

Then the first group of South Africans finally to set foot on Liberian soil, after flying to Monrovia via London, found themselves flying home hours later, despite assurances from the authorities that they would be granted special permission to be in the country. It involved AE's media team – Mike Odell, David Hotchkiss and Sam Hlatswayo – plus Abiel Thipanyane and ministry associate Barry Wittstock. And it happened like this. They were carrying all of AE's sound and PA equipment, the latter involving $340 excess baggage charge. After the team had passed satisfactorily through immigration, collected all the equipment and weathered customs, they were approached by some officials (although they were not in any uniform) who indicated to them that there was a problem and they could not proceed. They were taken back to the airport building and then a lengthy discussion ensued. It appeared that the Security Police had picked up that they had South African passports and would not allow the AE team to proceed into the country. This meant they were taken back into the transit area. The distraught mission representatives had to get into a car and travel the 36 miles from Robertson Airport into the city of Monrovia. No telephones were operating between the airport and the city and the only communication the officials had was via walkie-talkie radio.

So the five AE men waited in the transit section of the airport until about 3 pm that afternoon when they were informed there was a flight out of Monrovia and that the whites – Mike, David and Barry – would not be allowed to enter Liberia, while Abiel and Sam would be allowed to stay because they were black.

At this point, Abiel indicated calmly that if the authorities were not going to allow the whole group in then he was not prepared to remain behind while the others were deported. "I have spent my whole life in South Africa fighting against this kind of discrimination," said Abiel. "We are brothers in Christ on this team, black and white. And if you refuse my white brothers, I refuse also to enter your country."

It was an extraordinary witness.

While the authorities did a double-take at this astonishing utterance, the AE crew wended their way back into the airport, plus the sound systems, and began the gruelling journey home, via Ethiopia, no less, this time.

Just before leaving for Monrovia himself, Michael was astonished to see his five colleagues walk into his home to tell this tale. "Though it had cost us R50,000 in air tickets, I was never more proud of my guys than at that moment," said Michael later. "They had stood on Christian principle and brought a thunderbolt witness into Liberia, as the story spread when the mission got underway – though without sound systems!"

Michael and minstrel Brian Gibson, who had UK as well as South African passports, got in alright and finally joined the rest of the team (made up of Kenyans, Ugandans, Malawians and Zimbabweans, as well as members of six other "Western" countries) in Monrovia.

As usual, the AE team began the mission by spreading out across the city. This was easier said than done, for there was no public transport and precious little petrol for private use. Soon even getting to the meetings at all became a victory for both AE evangelists and the people of Monrovia. David Richardson found that, for 45 US cents, you could get a taxi to anywhere in Monrovia so he did a deal with two taxi companies to make our office a taxi-rank for the ten days of the mission. It worked like a charm.

However, when evangelists realised they just weren't going to make it, they could not warn anyone: there were no telephones. One afternoon, Michael was so ill with gastric flu he had to be raced to the hospital, but no doctor could be found anywhere for some hours. Hoping to phone the mission office to say he could not preach, he was told there were no phones. "The phones were destroyed five years ago in the revolution and have not been repaired," an orderly informed him as they searched for a doctor. Was this the "possession of difficulties"?

When the evangelists did make it to their meetings and stood up to speak to several hundred or even thousand people, then – ZAP! – a power failure would plunge everyone into the dark, and cut the PA system as well. Preaching teamlets were glad to have a couple of battery systems and a couple of small petrol-driven generators. But having all the city lights go out at once when they were roaring through the city centre in a rusty old taxi was more than a little disconcerting! In one TV interview, Michael and his interviewer suddenly vanished into darkness. No one seemed fazed.

Perhaps that's why Michael and the evangelists christened Monrovia as "one of the most demanding missions in AE's history".

Where's Your Office?

But there were moments of comedy as well. David Richardson remembers how, on his visits, he sought to:

> build the new unity among the church leaders. During each trip I would take an AE colleague with me. Sometimes Steve Lungu or Gershon Mwiti who led our Kenya Team. Almost without fail we would be invited to appear on local TV. There was one programme run by the Council of Churches and one run by Gus Marwieh called "Ministry Of Hope". During preparation for one interview with Gus he suggested that we tell the viewers (90% of the population of Monrovia) where our Mission Head Quarters was situated. Now, Monrovia does not have simple street names with logical numbering – but locals know your address by means of information like "near Mama Jane's Shabeen" or "nearby the tire shop" or "next to the old oil storage tanks". So I told Gus where our nice double-storied house was that had been given to us as

the Monrovia Mission base. He looked surprised, and then a little shocked and then burst out laughing – "Oh, Oh," he chuckled, "You can't say that on TV!" "Why not?" I asked, "Where is the house?" He laughed harder and said in Liberian English "dat's neah da poopoo factry." "What's that?" I asked – "Da poopoo factory," he howled – "da watta woiks – da sewerage farm – what do ya call dis place down south?" "Oh," I said – "the sewerage treatment plant – what do Liberians call it – the poo-poo factory?" "Yes," smiled Gus, "en hey man, you can't sey dat on de TeeVee." "Well," I asked "is there no other way to tell them where we are situated in Monrovia?" "Noooo," said smiling Gus, "everybawdy know dat place across de road frum de poo-poo factory, but I don't know how we gonna tell de people."

Soon, Dave, Steve and Gus were in the TV studio. Recalls Dave:

The opening credits began to roll – actually wound by a studio-crewman turning a large handle that rolled a large blind between two rollers – the signature tune came on and Gus announced with his usual exuberance – "ladies and gentemen, brudders en sistahs, tonigh we have wit us on Ministry-o-hope, two grea bruddes visiting Liberia frum da fantastic mission called African Enterprise. Welcum agin to Monrovia Brudder Daverichesen en brudder Steveloooongoo. Brudders welcum back in owa mid-ist!"

The interview went along fine as we shared the great vision of the Monrovia churches combining to share "good news" with everyone in Monrovia. As we were closing, Gus asked us where people who wanted to join with us in this great citywide event could find our headquarters. The camera swung toward me and my face came into full view on the monitor in front of us. I said, "Well, you will find us in Monrovia right down near – what was that place called Steve?" I said, as the camera swung away from me and Steve's startled expression filled the monitor – "The poo-poo factory!" spluttered Steve, as the sudden question caught him off-guard. There was a stunned moment of silent shock as the word sank in, and then... Gus burst into laughter, the picture on the monitor wobbled wildly as the cameraman broke into howls of laughter and the whole studio roared in surprised mirth. "Oh yes," I said, "the Poo-poo factory. That's where you can find us and we would love to meet many of you there at the double-storied house. We need your help! Please come!"

Pandemonium reigned supreme in the studio, everyone was staggering around, howling with laughter and stamping their feet with mirth... Gus finally recovered and with his ear-to-ear grin he drew the show to a close and the credits again wobbled across the screen as the two laughing men wound up the rollers. After the show they all came up and thanked us for the best bit of fun they had had in a very long time. We left without great assurance that we had got our point across to the watching Monrovians. We were wrong!

The next day people stopped us in the street and giggled, saying "Hey, you de guys wit de office near da Poo-poo factory – man we laaff so muush laas night when you say dat on de TV, en we know right where yo's are," they chortled, as we walked on to be greeted by the next chortling group. From that day we were on the "map" and many did come to help.

No Giving Up

As the mission got properly underway, there were endless, less light-hearted, difficulties. Yet it never crossed anyone's mind to give up. The show went on. Despite everything, hundreds of mission meetings and dozens of rallies ran concurrently in nine major venues throughout the city for 17 days, and led to some heartwarming stories. It was these which made Monrovia one of the most rewarding of missions.

Chris Sewell, AE Zimbabwe team leader, visited the National Police HQ, where he shared his faith with about 80 officers. A vision of a new life entered their hearts, and 50 asked him to pray with them, wanting to commit their lives to Jesus.

Then there was Chazzy, the young married taxi driver who was transporting two evangelists to a school meeting. "I was a very strong Muslim and didn't want to have anything to do with Christianity." But when the AE team members simply asked him what Mohammed had done for him, Chazzy was speechless. "I had no reply. So then I listened to the testimonies of what Jesus was doing for people. He did something for people! So I decided to surrender my life, too, to Jesus and become a Christian."

Danny, who had been studying engineering in New York, was home in Monrovia on holiday. He was in town one night while a major AE mission rally took place in the Tubman Stadium. He needed to get home, but only had 50 cents in his pocket. So Danny climbed into a taxi and told the driver to take him as far as 50 cents would get him. The driver dropped him outside the Tubman Stadium. Wondering what the noise and singing was all about, Danny walked into the stadium. When he realised it was a "religious" gathering, he decided to get out as fast as he could. But suddenly there was a power failure, and all the lights went out. Danny groped around in the dark, but could not find the exit. Then the lights came on – and he bumped into a group of friends. They led him to a seat behind the platform – and there he was stuck! So he decided to listen to the message. By the end of the evening he had decided to become a Christian.

Richard, an associate evangelist from Youth With A Mission, was returning to the mission office after a meeting. He began to get a little desperate when four taxis passed him without stopping. Then a man came by on a bicycle and Richard asked him for a lift. The man agreed and Richard climbed on with his Bible. He started to witness to him and by the time they reached the mission office, the man was ready to make a commitment to Christ.

One woman who went to Michael Cassidy's two-day lay training workshop entitled "How to share your faith" came away inspired and determined to share her faith at the first opportunity. She was walking down the street when she saw a bus driver and a passenger having a fistfight. She took off her glasses, handed them to a bystander and sailed into the fight. She commanded them to "Stop, in the name of Jesus Christ!" Immediately the two men fell back, and the bus driver gasped: "That is such a powerful name." The woman then went on to lead him into a Christian commitment in front of all the passengers and the crowd that had gathered.

Another woman who was very distraught had decided to end her life. She had some outstanding family business to settle, and so decided to drive to the home of a relative before killing herself. She arrived to find a crowded house – AE evangelist Stephen Lungu was there at a home meeting. The woman stayed and was so moved by his testimony that she became a Christian that day, and all plans of suicide were dropped.

At the Ministry of Justice, a meeting was organised for the staff, and the two AE team members assigned to it were surprised to find that within that official building was a chapel! After they spoke, the AE evangelists hesitated: should they risk embarrassing the staff by inviting them to come forward? They decided to do so very politely, and to their amazement, the "platform was flooded" as 25–30 people declared their need for a spiritual dimension to their lives.

Meanwhile, Gershon Mwiti was meeting the press. He held a meeting attended by twelve journalists. He spoke to them about their need for Jesus, and was staggered when five of them responded by making commitments to Christ. Gershon's comment was that previously he had only known one journalist in his entire life who was a Christian!

Steve Lungu was invited by the First Lady, Mrs Doe, to preach to a meeting of important women and wives of MPs at the State House. When Steve arrived, the First Lady moved sedately towards Steve to greet him, but collapsed in uncontrollable giggles when she recognised him from TV and remembered that famous factory near which the mission office was located.

In the midst of all the fun, games and hassles, a gift: the leading media of Monrovia decided they liked the mission. TV and radio reporters, full of goodwill, were suddenly everywhere. The mission was given unprecedented coverage, at least in AE's experience.

Spirited Closing Rally

The closing rally, with 10,000 present, was described by Michael as "probably the most spirited closing rally we ever had". A 1,000-voice choir filled the stadium – drawing thousands of curious spectators. In fact, the music in that mission, and especially from the choir, led by choirmaster Timothy Thomas, often brought the crowd to its feet, roaring with delight, especially with the choir's thundering and dramatic rendition of "He is Lord." Thomas would keep the volume mounting and mounting by twirling his arms and hands faster and faster, like a whirligig or racing windmill, till suddenly he would stop and instantaneously, with electrifying precision, the choir would go silent, then on a fresh signal thunder out the home straight of the song as the crowd rose wildly to its feet cheering and dancing.

"If I could take that choir to London," said Michael at the end of the closing rally, "I could fill Covent Garden Opera House for a month! Never have I more regretted not having our AE media and PA crew to record what we heard tonight."

At the end of the mission, Archbishop Browne presented each AE team member with an unusual present: an embroidered banner saying "The Greatest Crusade Ever in Liberia".

During those eventful two weeks, 8,000 people had responded and professed commitment to Christ. It was a far cry from 24 years before, when a single white South African theological student had walked along a Monrovian beach and dared to dream dreams for the kingdom of God.

Bishop Augustus Marwieh, an old friend of the AE team from way back, summed it all up in one line: "This mission has been the most significant event in the history of the church in Liberia."

In a postscript comment to the Monrovia Mission, Mike Odell later said:

> In reflecting on how some of us had to come back and how a lot had gone wrong, I was asking the Lord what this was all about. We had done all our preparation. We had been marshalling prayer for months. We really thought we had got everything buttoned down and yet somehow we ended up spending an awful lot of money which achieved nothing. I was led to the passage in Matthew 12, where Jesus is talking with the Pharisees over his authority and power over the demonic. What particularly spoke to me was verse 29: "How can one enter a strongman's house and plunder his goods unless he first binds the strongman? And then he may plunder his house."
>
> I can clearly recall David Richardson sharing with us after one of his set-up visits to Monrovia how occult and demonic practices were very prevalent in that city and that we needed to be praying specifically about this. This was a real eye-opener to me and made me realise that we had probably not covered all the bases in terms of spiritual warfare and that, in future missions, we needed to be particularly vigilant regarding the prayer covering for the missions and for everyone involved in them. Of course I rejoice that, in spite of the setbacks we experienced, the mission went ahead and many came to the Lord.

But perhaps Gus Marwieh got it right in the farewell party for the team, when he shouted exultantly in his matchless Liberian Creole accent: "Da Debbil – yes, da Debbil – he got a right to fight – but he ain't got no right to win!"

"Yeah, man. Tell it!" chorused the AE crew.

Chapter 16

The Era of ERA Missions

In the following years the city strategies of AE moved more and more to a holistic approach with the attempt to bring Evangelism, Reconciliation and Action (ERA) together in a single model.

In early 1981 that search was deepening as the South African team ventured into the desperate black township of Elsies River, near Cape Town. Michael and the team had seen poverty often enough before, but they were shaken by the desperate needs they met at every turn.

Staying in the home of Rev Njongonkulu Ndungane, later to become Anglican Archbishop of Cape Town, Michael Cassidy was introduced to the wrenching needs of the community.

Michael tried to describe it later: "It's hard even to verbalise it in meaningful terms without sounding crude or melodramatic. Human brokenness, personal fragmentation, marital heartbreak, incredible social dislocation and community disruption due to Group Areas legislation all stared us in the face with eyes of fire."

The Elsies River Mission had a profound effect on African Enterprise.

Since Elsies River, our burden for the black townships of South Africa has deepened even more. I believe God is wanting to do a special thing in the black townships, not only in winning thousands to Christ by the Holy Spirit, but in getting his people both in the townships and in white urban South Africa to face the phenomenal challenge, the desperate human need and the spiritual openness and opportunity which these townships represent.

For Elsies River *was* spiritually open: the people made African Enterprise and its message more than welcome. Some 26,000 men, women and children came to the meetings, 9,000 to the closing rally alone. 800 people professed new commitment to Christ. John Tooke had worked long and hard to develop material for follow-up use, and used it certainly was. More than 10,000 people wanted to join the nine-week "Who is Jesus?" course.

"To us this evidenced immense spiritual hunger and openness, bearing in mind the massive fear factor for most people about going out at night. As a team, we felt we were setting our eyes on a mighty spiritual harvest which is crying out for reaping."

Michael felt the need with real anguish of heart. "Elsies River has 100,000 warm flesh and blood humans, all profoundly precious to God, and all profoundly committed to bringing in a new social order in this land. They want a New Day. And the pent-up political and emotional energy must be controlled and guided by the Spirit of Christ into peaceful change, or it will run amok with violence!"

So – African Enterprise set about planning a number of caring, holistic ventures into the townships. In the coming months and years these would include: Edendale, Imbali, Guguletu, Elsies River (again), Umlazi, Soweto, Galeshewe, Lamontville and many others.

In most of these situations we found a rich spiritual harvest waiting for us, and a warm and sometimes overwhelmingly appreciative response from the people. However, we also discovered that numbers of young people in these areas are progressively disillusioned with Christianity and the church, and are beginning to explore the Marxist alternative. This underlines to us even more the importance of giving serious attention to the townships.

Possession, Prisons and Politics

In other countries other desperate needs arose. At Luanshya in Zambia, AE team member Abiel Thipanyane began a mission, and came across a staggering amount of occult practice. "I have never before seen so many people involved in witchcraft, even educated people!" he reported back. On one evening alone, Abiel had the challenge of four "possessed" people turning up at one of his meetings. After hours of prayer, each one was delivered from demonic spirits and came through to a radiant peace and a newfound rest in Christ. The local pastors had watched proceedings wide-eyed, and Abiel then spent a good deal of time talking with them, and explaining to them what had happened in spiritual terms. "I was then able to teach the local pastors how to minister themselves in these cases," he said later.

Meanwhile, David Peters of the South African team went to visit a prison near Maritzburg. He shared his own testimony of turning from Hinduism to Christianity, and how Jesus had come to mean more to him than anything else in the world. The men listened in rapt silence, and when he had done, 75 prisoners indicated that they too, wanted this Jesus. David Peters was astonished, but not as much as the station commander. Back in his office, he turned to David. "I just cannot believe what I have just seen. Please, please, can you come back on Monday?"

David did better than that – he began to visit the prisons three times a week, and many men, especially from Hindu or Muslim backgrounds, asked for a chance to talk with him. Many asked him to pray with them. Some of these "prison converts", once released, in turn helped David in the ongoing prison work.

If Jesus Christ could change prisoners' hearts, it seemed he could also stop some people from committing crimes in the first place. A mission in Kampala brought a man with an unusual story out of the crowd in the city square to speak with Bishop Festo. "I must tell you Brother," he said, "until I came by here today, and heard you speak, I was planning to have an enemy of mine killed. I have already made arrangements with the gunman. Now I can forgive my enemy. I will go and tell him this. Please pray that I can also find this gunman, and stop him."

The East African team joined forces with some associates, and about 60 evangelists in all set out to visit 21 Ujamaa villages near Dodoma, Tanzania. "One night our meetings went on until nearly midnight because people were accepting the Lord, standing and testifying. After midnight we stopped the meeting and told them they could meet the Lord wherever they were, but they were still testifying!" More than 10,000 attended the closing rally; 3,000 eagerly accepted this Jesus who brought them such joy.

Healings

In Ndola, Zambia, David Peters had to be a bit careful. The political situation was so tense that there was a lot of shooting in the streets. But, said David:

> If I ever saw God work it was there. People were leaving their canes and walking. Blind people were seeing. The deaf were hearing. It was just like the Book of Acts. A rich man's wife who had severe stomach problems was saved and healed. "There is now not a pain in my body," she said, "and I've been suffering with this for six years."
>
> One man came to our meeting completely paralysed. I called all those ministers who were negative about healing. We prayed, and first his legs, then his hands, started *moving*.

A blind man was brought by his little grandson to David one early morning as he preached from the top of a barrel to a crowd who had come to hear the Word and be prayed for. After the preaching David went to the old man and was deeply moved by both his faith and that of the child.

David prayed fervently for the old man's blind eyes but nothing seemed to happen.

The disconsolate child led the old man away. But when they had gone about 100 yards, something awesome happened. Suddenly there was a cry almost the whole Copperbelt must have heard: "I can see. I can see."

As this miracle of God became evident, David was mobbed and one old lame woman with a stick testified that she had been healed when she touched David.

So amazing were the healings and the gospel response that even healing evangelist Reinhard Bonnke, who was ministering elsewhere in Zambia, sent observers to report on the miracles in Ndola.

The local newspapers also carried both stories and comment. Terence Musuku, in a major full-page article in the daily newspaper of Ndola said: "I was among the uncountable ailing people healed in Ndola's Anglican Cathedral. Stomach ulcers which had been tormenting me since 1966 were cured immediately."

Musuku's extended article in the newspaper recorded endless testimonies of healing including the following:

> During the sessions conducted, Mrs Diana Pandala, a nurse working for a surgery in Ndola, had her high blood pressure cured, to her disbelief. Afflicted by severe high blood pressure, Mrs Pandala had been experiencing heart attacks since last May, but, as from the time she was healed she has become as fit as a fiddle.
>
> Mwansa Makulu, a Form Two student at Chifubu Secondary School has no more leg pains. He had been feeling the pains since he was involved in a road accident six years ago.
>
> Lidia Madi, 20, of 300 Kabushi Township, tormented by stomach pains since she became matured, was among those healed. "To me, life was all hell. I could hardly sleep at night due to stomach pains. I am now so happy."

The healings were so well attested, and the news was so powerful, that one morning soon after this a stranger knocked loudly on the door of one of the local clergy. When the drowsy clergyman stumbled out to see who it was, the stranger announced: "I have heard what is happening at your meetings. I am a witchdoctor, and I've come to see this power that you have!"

Michael Cassidy notes:

> To many Western observers, these healing sorts of stories seem incredible. But in Africa, a theistic continent if ever there was one, people bring a simple, profound faith that God can and will heal. Their minds are uncluttered by secular, humanistic presuppositions that the supernatural can't happen. So often the supernatural does indeed happen as people, many times with little availability of modern medicine, look in simplicity to Christ for healing and receive it. I have seen this and can bear witness to it.

One Zambian MP came to a meeting and afterwards took David to one side. "I'm going to report all this to the government. We want you to come back. Soon. And Mr Peters, just phone us and we will pay your air ticket!"

The Business Sector

May 1984 brought "Good News for Johannesburg", a mission which set its sights on the business community of South Africa's most strategic business and economic centre. The churches of Johannesburg, numerous parachurch organisations, and a number of businesses actively supported the mission. By the time it began, AE estimated that some 9,000 Christians were involved, throughout the city centre.

Set up by the highly capable and irrepressible Dave Meaker and many others, the mission focused on breakfasts and luncheons for homogeneous professional units of doctors, lawyers and judges, industrialists, accountants, bankers, or academics. One senior industrialist, who had recently come to Christ, was asked to host a breakfast at the Carlton Hotel for fellow industrialists. He expressed terror at the thought! "But no one will come," he wailed. Finally he agreed. He decided in advance that to get 40 or 50, he should send out 400 invitations. Imagine his shock and astonishment when some 300 accepted and the largest dining room in the hotel had to be taken. At the breakfast someone observed: "75 per cent of all the wealth of South Africa is generated by those in this room." Next day when some 300 accountants gathered, the same person commented: "These 300 accountants do the accounting for the 75 per cent of South Africa's wealth generated by those who were here yesterday for the industrialists' breakfast!"

With the lawyers and judges, Michael spoke on "You be the Jury", as he presented the evidence for the resurrection! For those in the motor trade the theme was: "How to Fire on All Cylinders". For the bankers it was: "Life's Ultimate Investment".

One waiter serving bacon and eggs was so moved by the testimony of a popular Christian athlete at the sportsmen's breakfast that he was converted during the meal!

In all, Michael Cassidy and the team reached about 5,000 of the city's key leaders. Nearly 400 came to a new spiritual response. But as Michael said, "The full significance of this mission is more in what it has begun in Johannesburg than in what it has thus far achieved."

He also noted that in his view "this category of the business and professional person between say 33 and 55 is among the most open to the gospel, because by then they have pushed all the buttons and tried all the options to find meaning in life. Now, they are ready to come back by a process of elimination to look again at Jesus Christ, having found that nothing else works."

Another leadership mission like this called "Top Level Encounter" took place a few years later in Cape Town. This had far-reaching spiritual consequences in some of the professions and industries of the Mother City. The civil and construction engineering industry has an ongoing ministry to their profession and its workers which began at one of the mission breakfasts. One of those in whose heart a seed was sown was Graham Power, who has been the leading light behind the Transformations Movement in South Africa which fills stadiums for prayer on Human Rights Day, 21 March, each year. The spiritual and social transformation of countries and cities all across Africa is now Graham's vision, dream and prayer.

East African Openness

Both the leadership sector and those at grassroots level have manifested an amazing openness in East Africa as well. James Katarikawe, head of the Ugandan team, led a mission to Mbarara in April 1984. Like many towns in war-torn Uganda, it had been largely destroyed during the war of liberation. It had crumbled buildings, empty spaces, and severely traumatised people. On top of that, a few months before, in late 1983, the people of Rwandan origin were chased out of their homes in Mbarara, and lost everything.

Against a background of such ruin the Bishop of East Ankole diocese invited the AE team to conduct the mission in Mbabara. The town "opened its doors wide" to them. Team members preached in both primary and secondary schools, in the District Commissioners' office, in the banks, prison, police and army barracks, in market places and every corner of Mbabara.

At one prison, 108 prisoners came to the Lord. The hardened criminals were in tears. One of them was still in a dirty shirt stained with blood. "Everyone in my village hates me, and

I've hated them until now. I want to thank Jesus for coming my way."

In the army barracks, soldiers from the Colonel to the Private sat and listened attentively for more than one hour. Seven soldiers were converted.

The Sunday morning final rally at Mbabara drew 10,000 people. The AE team left behind 1,097 professed new Christians, including 19 Muslims.

A mission to Meru, Kenya, in late 1986, illustrated the various struggles the AE teams could face at times. The Meru mission, led by Gershon Mwiti, with a team of 30 evangelists, "looked doomed to failure before it even started".

There was unbelievable muddle, constant confusion and opposition. "It gradually became obvious to us that we were not wrestling just with human forces, but against something spiritual in nature. We sensed demonic forces were at work in all this senseless division we met at every turn." The AE team pressed on in prayer, and shared their reading of the situation with the Christians of Meru.

The insight made people step back and look at how they had been behaving. Suddenly it seemed as if they "woke up", as from a trance. "Then we began all to come together and act as one at last." Suddenly mission sympathisers came from all directions with transport, PA systems, money, accommodation, publicity, unity, and more prayer.

The government officials, politicians and businessmen of Meru, who up till now had attended church in a lukewarm way, suddenly began to get interested in this mission. They began to chip in ideas on venues and invitations and how to meet their colleagues. As a result the gospel was preached everywhere in the town for eight days! The town hall was crowded to overflowing each night. Then several politicians asked the AE team members to come and address their regular "political" meetings. Gershon spoke to one such gathering of 2,000 for about 20 minutes. Then he invited anyone who wanted to commit themselves to Christ to come forward, and 150 responded.

In all, 50,000 of the 80,000 people of Meru heard the gospel in Meru that week. There were 6,000 decisions for Christ. A great throng flocked to the closing rally which was due to end at one, and went on instead until 4 pm.

In August 1988, in Tanga, a coastal town in Tanzania, one Omani Mussa, a Muslim, woke up from a vivid dream that his life was about to be totally changed. So he carefully swept the area under the big mango tree beside his simple home, prepared his tea over a charcoal fire in the marketplace, and then sat and waited for something to happen. A few hours later, as the coastal heat began to take hold, a white Datsun 4WD pulled up near his tree. Several East African AE team members got out, and put battery-powered loudspeakers on top of the car. As children and adults drifted over to listen to what they had to say, Omani found he already had a front-row seat. He was among the five people who came to Christ that morning. "I know God spoke to me last night, and I know he has now changed my life." The team went on to hold another 109 meetings, at which 700 professed commitment to Christ.

In October 1988 a Ugandan team of more than 100 evangelists went to Jinja, an industrial town in northern Uganda, at the head of the Nile. The openness of the people astonished even the optimists. Ugandan team leader Edward Muhima sought to try and understand this incredible spiritual receptiveness. "The people of Uganda have lost faith in their fellow humans. They thought things would be all right after independence. They thought things would be all right when Amin took over, then when he was ousted, then when Obote took over again, then when Okello and then Muzeveni came to power... But it takes more than politicians to put one's life right."

Livingstone Okoti, who worked 22 years as a watchman at the Jinja hospital, accepted the Lord when an AEE team came to his house. So did Ayireni, an older lady who happened to be visiting the house next door. Even some Muslims opened their mosque for discussions. The imam talked with the AE team members for hours, and more than 20 Muslims converted to Christianity during the eight days of the mission.

ERA Mission

In 1988, the political tension in South Africa was near boiling point. This gave African Enterprise a major problem. AE found that in the hugely polarised context of South Africa, it was increasingly difficult to get large numbers of Christians from diverse backgrounds and denominations together for really major missions. Such were the levels of alienation, distance and confusion amongst Christians that if AE were to wait until everyone was on side, it would not get around to doing any more missions at all.

Across South Africa, people were so heavily preoccupied with the deteriorating political situation and with survival and maintenance that the very thought of a major mission involving great expense, huge organisation and great distraction from the urgent and politically immediate was just not acceptable in most communities.

So the South African team needed a new mission model. It decided upon an alternative to its former community or city-wide model. So – the ERA Missions were conceived, formally bringing together the three key aspects of previous missions. ERA stood for Evangelism, Reconciliation and Action. An ERA mission was always of short duration: that was its special distinction – running from a Wednesday or Thursday through to Sunday. This meant they were relatively easy to set up, relatively inexpensive and "we simply ride with the church or churches which are willing to do so, rather than wait until everyone in the place is on side. So the missions are inevitably smaller in magnitude, more modest in structure, more limited in goal, and more manageable."

It also meant that AE could do one or two ERA missions a month, rather than one big one every three or four months.

ERAs were also structured to make AE's approach more holistic, and geared for the ruptured South African context. So as well as evangelism there was reconciliation and building relationships in a context of alienation. At the end of each mission, there was an appeal for those willing to be part of an "ongoing task force" to come forward as volunteers. Evangelists would pray for the group in front of the whole congregation and commit to them the task of taking the threefold work forward (Evangelism, Reconciliation and Action) in that town. This ensured "pretty effective follow-up".

ERA missions proved very popular, and varied in size from one or two congregations to an entire community. When the churches in the small Eastern Cape town of Fort Beaufort modestly decided on an ERA, their enthusiasm soon got the better of them, and they ended by holding 130 meetings in four days – which impacted the town at every level, and exhausted the team!

Pulling Out the Stops

That same year as South Africa was downsizing, the East African team was pulling out all the stops for two major regional missions at Kigali in Rwanda, and the Malawi team was tackling Mzimba in their own country. They spoke to literally tens of thousands of people in a mixture of large public rallies and smaller meetings throughout the cities.

In the late 1980s the Christians of Botswana contacted AE, wanting to stage a citywide mission. The result was the November 1990 "Gaborone for Jesus", when four AE teams from South Africa, Zimbabwe, Malawi and Swaziland converged on Gaborone, capital of Botswana, for a major regional mission.

The team was made up of 17 members from South Africa, eight from Zimbabwe, and four each from Malawi and Swaziland. They faced searing heat and torrential thunderstorms but, undampened in heart, they traversed the city relentlessly. In ten days 21 evangelists, helped by twelve back-up supporters, addressed 311 meetings. This included 167 "stratified evangelistic" meetings in homes, schools, hospitals, colleges, clinics, government offices and factories. Then there were 68 open-air meetings in bus stations, marketplaces, sports fields, and any other open space they came across. Then there were 46 major public meetings in halls, plus 30 church services.

Michael Cassidy addressed the crowds at the large Boipuso Hall in Machel Drive each night, with back-up help from AE members and counsellors. One young woman came forward, was joyfully converted, and then immediately began helping counsellors by writing down the names of other people who'd come forward for commitments. Another woman heard about the big meetings, and invited her estranged husband to go to a meeting with her. She had hardly spoken to him in two years. At the meeting she made a re-commitment, and he was converted as well. And great was the rejoicing.

Bulawayo

Another hive of activity with all stops out was the Bulawayo citywide mission in the autumn of 1991. Some 650 meetings were handled by the team in ten days flat. The team, 70–80 strong (including back-up and support), ministered in this Zimbabwean city's schools, colleges, hospitals, factories, marketplaces, clinics, government offices, and even the Mayor's Parlour. "The spiritual hunger was terrific, and the response most encouraging in most situations," said one. Another found it was "especially good to see the different Christian denominations making new connection with each other".

So how did a typical day pan out? One such day went as follows:

9 am to 10.15 am: AE team members met with the locally trained witnesses, evangelists and pastors for worship, prayer, reports and final planning for the day. Of the twelve venues the evangelists had used the night before, nine had gone well, three had had problems. "We reflected on how best to solve the problems."

Eric Makgoga, of AE South Africa, said he'd ministered to a man who kept saying: "I have killed people, I have killed people." It had been during the Rhodesian bush war. Eric had helped and prayed with him through to the discovery of Christ's forgiveness.

One young Bulawayo lad then told how his mission teamlet had been boarding the early morning buses daily and were riding all over the place sharing Christ with the passengers. People kept saying: "Please don't stop, tell us more. Ride with us further." "Book of Acts stuff, that!" said one team member.

10.15 am. The team scattered to the four corners of the city to begin the 104 meetings scheduled for the day. The day after had 80 meetings scheduled, the day after that, 102.

Late Afternoon: Counselling people.

Evening: Mass rallies.

Boredom was never a problem when African Enterprise held a city mission!

End of the Drought

One interesting incident during the Bulawayo mission related to the dreadful drought which had afflicted the area for a couple of years. Things were desperate. In the opening meeting of welcome with the Mayor and other civic leaders present, Michael told the Mayor and the crowd that he and the team were praying for the drought to break before the end of the mission. Ten days later, as Michael, who had been sitting next to the sceptical Mayor, began his talk in the final open-air rally, the heavens opened and the rain poured down. The Mayor, sitting under a canopy, was riveted and his attention seriously secured while Michael and his sermon notes were soaked and many of the crowd fled for cover.

In his heart Michael wailed: "Come on, Lord, couldn't you have waited half an hour?"

Thankfully the rain eased, the crowd regathered from nearby houses, and the meeting went on. At the end hundreds professed commitment to Christ and 57 came forward on another appeal to offer themselves for fulltime Christian service.

The mightily blessed Mayor was overjoyed. It had rained across the country. God had heard his people. The drought had broken! And Michael still has the soaked and smudged sermon notes as a memento of a prayer-answering God!

Incidentally, a year later, when the team went back for follow-up, all 57 of those offering for fulltime service were there for further counsel.

Harambee '92

Another very special ministry project for African Enterprise was Harambee '92 ("Pulling Together" in Swahili) in 1992 in Pietermaritzburg. It marked the 30th anniversary of African Enterprise's first city mission back in 1962.

Michael Cassidy wrote later to the worldwide AE family:

That week we had a deeper sense than ever before of coming together as a *total* ministry from across the continent and around the world. We felt profoundly re-commissioned to the challenge of reaching out. Political barriers in the past had prevented all the teams from ever before coming together in this way, and it was fitting that this extraordinary experience, with about 45 of our East and Central African AE colleagues, should both close the first major chapter of AE and open the new one.

Harambee celebrations included a spectacular fellowship and dedication supper for about 1,100 people of many racial, national and denominational backgrounds. Throughout there was "a sense of spiritual buoyancy and joyful celebration amid the extraordinary blending of peoples". It brought home to Michael "a vision of what the new South Africa, the African continent and indeed the world, should look like".

When Michael honoured his old mother, Dee Cassidy, for all she had done for him in his life, the crowd rose and applauded spontaneously.

Especially moving for Michael was the opening rally at the City Hall on Sunday 16 August, and the week of ministry that followed it, when the hall was packed every night.

This city hall was where it had all started 30 years before – for Michael the start of his vision to evangelise the towns and cities of Africa. One of the original members of the team, Paul Birch from Canada, who became Chairman of the Canadian Support Office, was able to return for Harambee, and sat himself down once again to play on the same city hall organ on which he had first played for the first mission 30 years before. "That felt special and really wonderful," beamed Paul.

From Africa With Love

AE then crowned its 30 years of mission in style after the week of celebrations and seminars and rallies, as 33 East and Central African colleagues, along with a substantial South African team, set off on a "From Africa With Love" ministry tour around the country. They split into seven teams, in order to minister in 17 cities.

The teams also went to meet and pray for key political figures. Especially memorable were the prayer times with Chief Minister Mangosuthu Buthelezi at Ulundi in Kwa Zulu, then President F.W. de Klerk at Union Buildings in Pretoria, then the

Conservative Party leader, the notoriously right-wing Dr Andries Treurnicht. From there the teamlets met with the leadership of the Afrikaner Volks Unie (AVU – a group advocating a separate Afrikaner homeland) and then went on to meet with Mr Oliver Tambo and most of the Executive of the African National Congress at Shell House in Johannesburg. The team handed out gospel books which were warmly received. Oliver Tambo, suffering from the effects of a stroke, was deeply moved when the team prayed for the Lord to touch his body. One ANC leader said to Michael a week later: "Most people who come to Shell House to see us come to talk politics or money. But you and your team came to minister and care for us."

After the ANC visit, the day ended with a visit to the leadership of the PAC (Pan-Africanist Congress) whose slogan was "One Settler One Bullet". Edward Muhima had a strong word here when he stressed that in Uganda they had learned that violence breeds violence and has its own laws of continuity. "Amin killed 400,000 people and Obote, coming to liberate Uganda from Amin, killed another 450,000! Once violence is in the system you can't get it out."

Edward had had an equally direct word for President de Klerk in the team's moving private time alone with him in his office in Union Buildings. "Mr President," he said, "we salute you for what you have done thus far to bring a new situation in your country. But for Moses truly to bring the new day for his people he had to forsake the courts of Pharaoh." Bishop Gresford Chitemo, East African team leader, obviously moved De Klerk as he spoke gracious words of repentance for the hatred Tanzania as "a front-line state" had come to feel for all white South Africans. "We should have hated just the sin, not the sinner."

The team was impressed, before praying for De Klerk, when he said: "Our answers here will only come through the Cross of Christ."

In the Eastern Cape Emmanuel Kopwe for his part visited the insecure homeland leaders of the Ciskei, who knew their days of homeland rule and power were very numbered.

Harambee '92 was to have some very significant spin-offs for South Africa. As the team found so many of the leaders in different parties expressing similar visions for the new South

Africa, the sense developed that there could be some significant value in trying to gather senior leaders from all sectors for some deep experiences of dialogue and personal encounter. This gave birth to the vision of the Kolobe Lodge Dialogue Weekends, which so significantly impacted the first democratic South African elections in April 1994. But that is another story for another chapter.

Evangelism, Reconciliation and Action – it was all coming together.

For AE all these developments and linkages and areas of impact were a far cry from those four young dreamers fresh out of seminary 30 years before.

Chapter 17

The Doors Keep Opening

God had promised AE "open doors" in Africa. Said Revelation 3:8 – "I have set before you an open door which no one is able to shut." That proved true as door after door to major African cities kept opening. Some key doors in the mid-1980s opened in Swaziland, Malawi and Zambia.

The "Good News for Harare Mission" in November 1985 broke new ground. For the first time African Enterprise mounted an outreach to the whole *city centre community* of a large city in independent black Africa. Harare is a very large city, and it was felt by the churches that a citywide outreach was just too great a task. So African Enterprise set out to share the good news with all those who worked just within a ten-kilometre radius of the city centre. This covered the "heart" of the city's government, judiciary, finance, business and commercial sectors, as well as Harare's wealthy central suburbs.

Even this was an enormous task: 108 churches were deeply involved. The mission targeted Harare's leaders: in business, in commerce, in government. It was built around breakfasts and dinners designed to present the gospel to thinking enquirers. Bankers, business professionals, engineers, architects, teachers, lawyers and those from the media and advertising, all were the targets. The lawyers' breakfast alone boasted a cabinet minister, the country's Chief Justice and eight judges.

Through a series of lunches, 800 city-centre professionals were reached by Michael Cassidy and by the Rev John Wilson of AE's Uganda team. With his background as a senior business executive in Caltex Uganda, John could identify with his audience, while his current ministry of reconciliation in Uganda and the Middle East enabled him to relate to the problems of Harare, and spice his talks with vivid and poignant anecdotes.

Four evening rallies were also held in the new International Conference Centre, a breathtaking venue built alongside the new Sheraton Hotel. These rallies were led by Michael and Stephen Mung'oma of the Kenya team. Stephen, with his natural dramatic ability and sense of humour, was a big hit with the crowds, as was Michael's clear and compelling presentation of the gospel. In all, "We praise God for some 13,000 people from the central suburbs of Harare who have come to our meetings. Last night alone we had a full house of 5,000," said one report.

There was one slight hitch: on the first evening the woman in charge of security, taking her job seriously, barred a stranger from entering a backstage door to the hall. The stranger turned out to be Michael Cassidy, who urgently needed to get in – he was due to preach. Later that night the security lady opened the door of her own heart to Christ. "Thus did eternal security triumph over temporal security," records Michael's journal!

Kampala and the Death of John Wilson

For the next pan-African mission, African Enterprise decided it was time to return to one of its "own" countries. Uganda was shakily getting back on its feet after the fall of Obote, and needed all the encouragement it could get. So a mission to the war-torn and ravaged city of Kampala was warmly welcomed.

The Greater Kampala Mission was a whopper. It came naturally under Bishop Festo's wing, and would run for an entire year, with key AE evangelists coming and going, working alongside the still shell-shocked Ugandans. In all, 47 city church leaders representing hundreds of churches from 30 denominations and 28 parachurch organisations wanted to be involved.

Bishop Misaeri Kauma, spokesman for the Anglican Archbishop of Uganda, grew more and more excited as the months went by. The Greater Kampala Mission was shaping up to be an historical first for Uganda. For the first time in its history the Christians of nearly all denominations were coming together for one purpose: evangelism.

There was a lot of Episcopal purple about as both Anglican and Catholic bishops were deeply involved, as was His Eminence Cardinal Emmanuel Nsubuga.

Things were going full steam ahead, preparations were well in hand, and churches throughout Uganda were watching eagerly from the sidelines, eager one day to follow Kampala's lead.

Then suddenly, a devastating tragedy struck.

The Rev John Wilson, deputy team leader of the East Africa team, was in Kampala one afternoon when he was accosted by gunmen. They surrounded him quickly, ignoring his wife Mary's cries of protest. They forced him to hand over the keys of his car, and then shot him four times. Thirty minutes later, John had bled to death with the shattered Mary looking on. His whole family would feel forever bereft by this, but most especially his beautiful and dynamic daughter, Victoria. She would come in due course to feel a deep, compelling challenge to take far and wide her father's message of love, forgiveness, reconciliation and deep Christian discipleship. "Perhaps no other woman in the world is as greatly indebted to her father as I am," she said. "I recognise the great gift God gave me in my father, and how I wish every little girl, every young lady, every woman in the world would experience such a relationship with their fathers. How I wish every man who has a daughter would realise how important it is that they put on, and leave on, the light for them!"

Victoria adds:

And there is no light brighter than the one that is lit from within. A father's primary function on this earth is to be a reflection of our heavenly Father. He is to love and nurture his family. He must be there for them, provide for them, protect them, and guide them in the ways of righteousness. By being a reflection of God to his children, a man gives his children the greatest gift of all, a love for God that is natural, exciting and revolutionary. He lights a beautiful fire within each child. A light that never burns out. A light that keeps on shining even after he's gone and the world around seems dark and bleak. A light that gives them the courage to stand alone even as the world around them rewards immorality and selfish ambitions.

Bishop Festo and Michael Cassidy, close personal friends of John, were completely devastated, as was the whole AE family throughout the world.

John had been "ambassador-at-large" for African Enterprise, as well as assisting Bishop Festo in preaching and teaching in East Africa. His great diplomatic skills were put to good use in the role he played in co-ordinating the historic Pan-African Christian Leadership Assembly in 1976, attended by 800 Christian leaders from 48 African countries, including a delegation of 80 South Africans (who then helped to give birth to SACLA, the South African Christian Leadership Assembly a few years later in 1979).

At the time of his death in March 1986, John had also been deeply involved in some precarious negotiations of bringing together Christian leaders of the Middle East churches, as well as in preparing for the Greater Kampala Mission, due to begin in June. The Middle East work had brought together on the Island of Aegena a secret consultation of Israeli and Arab believers, the latter coming from fourteen Arab countries. AE never publicised this. But it had been an extraordinary event which Michael, Festo, John and AE's Keith Hershey, who had done a lot of the admin, never forgot. But John was the one who primarily brokered it all.

However it was always Uganda which was John's primary love and over-riding concern. He had been one of the very first refugees to return to Uganda after Idi Amin was deposed to help rebuild that shattered country.

Michael flew to Kampala to preach alongside Bishop Festo for the funeral. What could he possibly say? What sense could be made of anything? Then, still heartbroken, Michael wrote: "I began to realise that Screwtape had over-reached himself in killing this man, and that God was going to use John's death in the most glorious, redeeming way."

Michael also began to perceive that out of John's shining life and shocking death came some very painful but perhaps timely reminders for the African Enterprise teams, especially the South Africans, in their tumultuous political situation.

The first was the *tremendous urgency of the hour*. In evangelising Africa, African Enterprise was working against time. "Each of us has to 'work while it is still day, because the night comes when no man can work.' We must work while there is still divine opportunity, because none of us knows 'when for us personally the night will come'." And the team spoke directly to the churches of Africa when they pleaded: "Please grasp this! Whatever we are going to do we must do *now*."

The second was equally serious: *evangelism is never a neutral activity*. You have to be aware of whose toes you are stepping on when you lead someone to Christ. "We wrestle not against flesh and blood, but against principalities and powers." It was powerfully impressed upon Festo and Michael in those days after John's death that "we so often go into ministry not fully aware of all we are up against. It was certainly a demonic work to have a man like John gunned down. The whole area of spiritual warfare and prayer is something we as evangelists must take very seriously."

This became further underlined when ahead of the mission Festo became seriously ill and couldn't leave the UK, where he had been ministering, and Stephen Mung'oma, one of AE's other key evangelists, was stabbed in Nairobi. While other evangelists had managed to get into Uganda, Michael feared that with the hatred of South Africa, he might be denied access, even if he used his British passport, what with having to declare South Africa as both birthplace and place of domicile. He and minstrel Brian Gibson arrived late one evening at Entebbe Airport, praying much God would grant entry. As they approached the immigration office's desk all the lights in the airport building went out. The official, wanting to keep the passport processing going, stamped both Michael's and Brian's passports and immigration forms in the dark. As Michael and Brian moved away from his desk, all the lights came on again!

"Well, Lord," said Michael, "while you normally sponsor light, we see you can also if it suits your purposes sponsor darkness!"

The Greater Kampala Mission went ahead, and though in deep bereavement and mourning at the loss of John Wilson, the AE evangelists knew that John of all people would have urged them on to proclaim the gospel from every rooftop of the city. They did their best, and were delighted to welcome 3,500 newly committed Christians at the end of the mission.

Lilongwe

In May 1987, while the farmers of Malawi gathered in their maize, a 37-member AE team harvested the people of Lilongwe. After a year's thorough preparation, and countless hours in prayer for Lilongwe, the team found on arrival that thousands of people were ripe and ready to respond to the gospel. All they needed was to be gathered into the kingdom of God. This African Enterprise did, during two weeks of intensive preaching and radio broadcasts.

"Lilongwe for Jesus" was a major pan-African effort: the 37 evangelists came from the AE teams in Uganda, Kenya, Tanzania, Zimbabwe, South Africa and Malawi. Associate evangelists from Botswana, Germany and Australia pitched in to help.

The Rev Yeremiah Chienda, a Malawi team member, had received a promise from God in the form of a prophecy that promised "good spiritual rain" for the period in late May of 1987, and the forecast came true for Malawi's capital city. "Lilongwe for Jesus" was an immediate success.

Every day the evangelists scattered throughout the city to the open-air markets where hundreds of people gathered to buy and sell. Setting up portable loudspeakers they would begin to preach. Soon a huge crowd would gather around, listening intently. Some of the meetings carried on for up to two hours, as they spoke and counselled.

Schools were closed for the last week of the mission as Malawians went to the election polls to vote for members of parliament, so every meeting was full of children. One child sat through a rally and then ran home to wake up her sleeping mother. "You must come and listen," she insisted. The mother came, and committed her life to Christ that night.

Home meetings turned into mini open-airs as friends and neighbours packed into houses and spilled over into gardens to hear the evangelists. Many meetings had to be moved outdoors for lack of space. People passing in the street would stop to listen in. Two such women, who had been friends for many years, but who had become enemies, were reconciled. Their husbands had been in a car crash several years earlier, and only one survived. The widow had blamed the couple for her husband's death.

Public rallies were held in six different venues throughout the city every night. Some of the loud-speaking equipment was so effective that people heard the gospel clear across the neighbouring suburb! People also poured out of bars to listen in the streets.

Stories to Tell

Every meeting, big or small, public or in a home, produced results. Every evangelist had a story to tell of changed lives after speaking out the good news of Jesus Christ. "We have given such a simple and clear message, and the people have reacted in the most amazing way," said one team member. "Everywhere we go there are serious seekers."

One businessman said that after giving his life to Christ, he had slept "a full night for the first time in years".

Grace Bayona (now Kalambo) from Tanzania, "Amazing Grace" as the team love to call her, and later leader of that team, was speaking at one rally, when a drunk man joined the crowd and began to make trouble. Two policemen failed to catch him, so several in the crowd ran to help. They chased the man all over the field, finally caught him and led him away. Silence then resumed as they let Grace have her say in peace.

One woman, ill in bed, listened to the message being preached in Biwi. When one night Stephen Mung'oma prayed for those who needed healing, she asked God to heal her. The next night she arrived at the rally to tell everyone: "Here I am. Jesus healed me."

An army captain conspired to bring a notorious prostitute to one of the rallies. Finding her at a local hotel he lured her into his car with the promise of buying her a drink. But once she was safely in the car, he drove her to a public rally. She was "dumbfounded" on hearing the testimonies of those who had already come to Christ, and listened carefully as team member David Wakumire explained the gospel to her. In the car going home she prayed a prayer of commitment to Christ with one of the Malawian interpreters.

Jack Garratt was preaching at a labour exchange where about 300 men had gathered to seek work. They all drew around him to listen, but when a man appeared shouting that there was work available, Jack's congregation disappeared! Jack waited patiently for a while, and most of them drifted back. Then he resumed his talk. At the end, "There was a sea of hands of those who wanted to become Christians," Jack related. "So I explained three times the cost of commitment to them, and then said that those who still wanted to become Christians should follow me to a nearby field, which would mean that they would be missing opportunities for jobs." Some 175 men followed Jack.

Ministry to the diplomats of Lilongwe also reaped results. Michael Cassidy spoke to one meeting arranged for the diplomatic community which was so well attended, and so enjoyed, that they requested another meeting. Afterwards the Zambian High Commissioner met with the Mozambican Ambassador to fill him in and encourage him to receive the message of the mission.

At the end of two weeks, Stephen Mung'oma said: "We have been to every residential area, every market and every factory in this city. Almost every one you meet in the street has heard of Lilongwe for Jesus. I think we reached at least half the population of the city."

The mission chairman, an exhausted but happy man, added: "Everything we planned has succeeded. Our dreams have come true. We have saturated nearly every corner of this city with the gospel. Now we must make sure that the efforts of the mission are not lost."

When the reckoning was done, it was found that approximately 4,000 people had responded and professed commitment to Christ, including 51 Muslims.

Manzini

Manzini, the colourful, bustling major city of Swaziland, was the venue for a particularly responsive pan-African AE mission of 1988.

An urgent Macedonian call to "come over and help us" had been received from the Swaziland Conference of Churches, the Council of Swaziland Churches, and the League of Churches.

On the surface, Swaziland was already a Christian country. Of its 700,000 population, 77 per cent would have ticked

"Christian" under religion. Yet the churches of Swaziland were still determined to hold a major mission, for they felt their nation to be in deep need.

Neil Pagard, one of AE South Africa's major set-up directors, had been sent to Manzini to investigate. Neil's parents had been American missionaries in Swaziland and he had grown up there, returned to the USA for college and seminary education and come back to Southern Africa with Campus Crusade. Neil spoke fluent Siswati, the native language that is closely related to Zulu and Xhosa in South Africa. He had also taught high school there and knew most of the main politicians and business professionals as well as many of the royal family. Neil reported: "Swaziland has seen a great deal of missionary activity, but most of it has been 'surface' evangelism, with little depth of teaching. The church leaders' main complaint is that they have been overrun with hit-and-run evangelists who blitz Swaziland, and then disappear, leaving only very short-term results."

On 6 August 1988, Swaziland was to celebrate 20 years of independence. It was a time when the people of Swaziland were taking stock of themselves. The churches wanted to make a contribution to this, to encourage people to take *spiritual* stock. So for the first time ever, they had banded together to invite AE to hold a major mission to Manzini.

"Manzini for Jesus" would run from 31 July to 14 August, encompassing "Independence Day". "It seemed fitting for the Church in Swaziland to have a major spiritual thrust that would coincide closely with the celebration of independence," Neil said.

As in all preparation, there were long talks between the AE team and the key Swazi church leaders. AE wanted their insight into the current culture and context of the country, the spiritual needs of the people, and the conditions of the churches there. AE also asked its worldwide supporters for regular prayer back-up.

This prayer support was acutely needed when weeks before the mission Mission Director Neil Pagard and his lovely wife, Billie, were involved in a very serious car accident. Billie was to suffer very serious brain damage from which she was never to recover. Said Michael once: "Neil Pagard is one of Christendom's ultimate and special inspirations as to what marital commitment and vows are all about as he has stuck so lovingly and caringly to Billie 'for better, for worse' and ministered to her, 'in sickness and in health'. Neil is one of life's princes."

As July 1988 arrived, a team of 40 AE evangelists from seven countries moved into Manzini. Their team leader was the Rev Stephen Mung'oma from Uganda.

The mission began in style: the Queen Mother of Swaziland graciously invited the 40 evangelists to come to the royal residence for an opening meeting. The Queen Mother herself presided.

Next day, the 40 evangelists were off and running. Almost literally. They had a punishing daily schedule which over two weeks would take them to most nooks and crannies of Manzini. At 7 each morning the team would leave the mission office and spread out to lead assemblies in each of Manzini's schools. Then it was on to literally dozens of meetings throughout the rest of the day. These were held wherever the people of Manzini were: in hospitals, factories, prisons, the army headquarters, the police headquarters, offices of every kind, the university, various training institutions, and the open marketplaces.

Such "stratified evangelism" penetrated deep into the secular life of the city, while "missionettes" were held in several local churches each night to help the already committed Christians to think through their faith again.

All Sorts Hear the Gospel

The Manzini market became a favoured place with the AE team members. It is a bustling place, full of farmers with their fresh vegetables piled high in their vans, women with paraffin cans of maize for sale, little stores with sewing machines buzzing busily inside, and mats spread everywhere with hundreds of baskets of every design and colour.

Every day just before lunchtime an evangelist, often Orpheus Hove of the Zimbabwe team, and a helper or two, would descend on this marketplace and begin to sing. Africans love music, and the response was immediate: men would begin to sway, and women began a foot-stomping dance. Once their attention was thoroughly gained, Orpheus would step forward to preach the gospel.

People setting up their goods stopped and just stood there, vegetables still in their hands, while they listened to the clear and challenging words.

Other AE evangelists would set up their simple PA systems near parks or bus terminals, or wherever people congregated with time on their hands. All the evangelists then had to do was make enough noise to attract attention. Always crowds gathered, curious and willing to listen.

David Peters and Stephen Lungu visited a women's prison, and were allowed in to talk to the pregnant women and mothers with little babies. Wardens stood around watchfully. As everyone listened to the two preachers, an Indian and a Malawian, a woman crept in from the side and cast anxious glances over the crowded area, searching for a particular person. But her attention was caught by the message. When the men ended, she could not contain herself, and neither could the person she was hunting for. Mother and daughter both went forward in response to the message, and unexpectedly met again in front of the evangelists. They both broke down in floods of astonished tears, and were reconciled right there. Then as the other prisoners and even wardens were moved to tears, they told their story. The daughter – a freedom fighter – had been caught transporting weapons through the country, and jailed. The mother had searched and searched for her, fearing she must be dead. Finally she tracked her to this prison, hoping against hope to find her, and never expecting to find Jesus waiting for her as well.

Another day, two drunken women stumbled across an open-air meeting by accident, and stopped to listen. At the end, they came forward. The evangelist, Vasco Seleoane, doubted they meant business, and asked them to go away and think about it. The next night the two women, now sober, were back, with a friend, who also wanted to know more about Jesus. The following week the three women decided they could find a good venue for evangelism. So they came and found Vasco, and dragged him to the spot they'd found. He approved immediately of their choice: "What could be better than the spot between the Kentucky Fried Chicken and the bottle store?" Vasco Seleoane said later. "Here we could catch those who were both hungry and thirsty!"

Meanwhile, AE evangelist Songe Chibambo ventured out into a far-flung rural community, looking for an old lady who had been sending all sorts of messages to the mission office, pleading for an evangelist to come. When Songe and his interpreter finally found the village, they had no trouble finding the old lady. She had been busy putting up a mission marquee! She had erected a small tent under a tree, and even lit it with a candle. Songe was inexpressibly moved.

The old lady also turned out to be a dab hand at publicity. She'd spread news of the mission far and wide, and a few hours later people began arriving, much to Songe's astonishment.

He was temporarily speechless when a counsellor for the king of Swaziland, who lived in the area, solemnly turned up for the meeting, along with his wives.

By now the crowd would have filled the little tent many times over, so Songe used the tent as a backdrop, and simply preached his heart out to the people who gathered around him among the trees. Among those who turned and found Christ to be real that night were the king's counsellor and his wives. History does not relate how he reconciled the polygamous ways and culture of Swaziland with his Christian conversion!

In another outlying area, Lozitha, near the royal residence, Chris Daza of the Malawi team found his congregation consisted almost entirely of the wives and children of the royal family. The old King Sobhuza had over 100 wives and a Sunday outing with his family necessitated a couple of buses! The first night a prince's wife came forward for prayer for her ear. She was healed. The next day she came back with a full costume of Swazi traditional dress for Chris.

Back in Manzini itself, and far from royalty, other team members were visiting the local fruit and jam factory at midnight. Midnight was "lunchtime" to these nightshift workers, who slept during the day. The workers were at first astonished when the evangelists arrived among them at such an unsocial hour, and were then deeply touched that anyone should bother with them. Some 2,400 of them listened willingly, and so warm was their response that this midnight meeting with them became a regular fixture of the mission. One night the workers stood stoically in the dripping rain for an hour, urging the evangelists to continue whenever they showed signs of flagging.

The local church leaders were amazed by the support given by local non-Christians. When a minister had placed an order with a butcher for meat to feed the team throughout the mission, the butcher announced he was giving them the meat for free.

One old lady who had been blind for five years heard about the mission, a day's bus ride away for her. She was absolutely determined to go. So her friends got her on the bus, and other passengers helped get her to the rally. Once at the rally, people offered her accommodation. The old lady attended the mission meetings every day, and as the days went by, her eyes began to clear. First, she was able to make out shapes. Then, wonder of wonders, she woke up early one morning and was awestruck to watch her first sunrise for five years. The old lady stood up and testified to the whole assembly that night. "God has revealed himself to me at Manzini. My heart could see him before. I knew that if I came here, my eyes would be healed. I believed in him completely. And now I can see. Praise God for his goodness to me!"

After testimonies like this, little wonder that the AE team felt thoroughly blessed by the Manzini mission, and more thankful than ever for Neil Pagard and his endeavours, all carried out amidst fearful grief over Billie. The fact was that there had been open doors everywhere they went: to government, civic leaders, the royal family, and a great swathe of the general population. In all, 463 stratified evangelism meetings were taken. Several thousand people professed commitment to Christ. There was a jubilant closing rally at the National Church, attended by the king's representative, members of Parliament, and thousands of ordinary people from Manzini and Mbabane, Swaziland's sprawling capital city.

AE had to leave then, but were glad to hear a few weeks later that a comprehensive follow-up scheme was underway, "with much greater effectiveness and thoroughness than anything we have seen in follow-up for quite a while".

Zambia this Time

Dr Kenneth Kaunda, the president of Zambia, graciously agreed to be Patron of the next pan-African mission, "Lusaka Back to

God" in May/June of 1989. He welcomed African Enterprise's visit to his capital city.

While the mission was still at the planning stage, under set-up directors David Richardson and Gershon Mwiti, it became evident that this mission could have far-reaching repercussions. "We sensed that Lusaka was a strategic city for this time – a critical meeting place of the ideological, racial and political pressures that are building up in Southern Africa," said Michael. By this time Gresford Chitemo, the gracious and godly Tanzanian Anglican bishop, had taken over the overall leadership for the four East African teams after Festo, stricken with leukaemia, had gone to be with the Lord in 1988. "One of the saintliest Christians and soldiers of the Lord it has ever been my privilege to work with," Michael said of Gresford Chitemo. "Also often a wise counsellor, friend and many times father confessor for me."

In Lusaka together and co-leading the mission, Gresford and Michael felt that the mission needed to be backed by "more serious spiritual warfare and intercession than anything we've done in years".

"It would be sheer folly to imagine we could go into a major city like that and seek to capture it for Christ without there being a tremendous spiritual battle against thrones, principalities, powers and strongholds which can only be stormed by weapons that are not carnal but mighty through God" (2 Corinthians 10:4).

In the days that would follow, "what a joy it was to see the Lord prove himself greater than communication or organisational difficulties, illness, accident, and even transport!" One great kindness: the president, Kenneth Kaunda, graciously granted blanket visa approval for all South Africans who would be taking part. Any others needing visas were helped by the ANC (Mandela's African National Congress) protocol officers at the airport, who had offered to assist AE after David and Michael had met with several ANC executives – among them an impressive man called Thabo Mbeki who was to succeed Nelson Mandela as President of South Africa.

In all, 50 or so AE team members from across Africa, as well as associate evangelists from further afield, joined forces. Team Leaders Michael Cassidy and Gresford Chitemo rejoiced in the "tremendous spirit of camaraderie. Everyone just closed ranks, put their shoulders to the wheel and applied themselves to the huge challenge of penetrating that great city for Christ."

Soon David Richardson and his advance team returned from Lusaka to give their final preparation reports. They were full of fizz and excitement: "We had 200 pastors come to the three courses! There will be dozens of opportunities for you all!" But they had detected a "seize the moment" attitude in the Zambian approach, and felt it only fair to warn the team: "You need to go to Lusaka having made yourselves available to the Lord and literally ready for anything. Allow the Lord to prepare in your heart and on paper the kind of messages you will need in virtually every situation you can think of. You'll need to be *absolutely flexible!*"

On paper, the mission plan fell neatly in two: the first week would be Christian outreach to the leadership circles of Zambia, and the second week would concentrate on all other sectors of the city.

Then the AE evangelists spread out. Day after day they visited and spoke to staff in the Prime Minister's office, many other government offices, several of the banks of Zambia, insurance companies, Rotary Clubs, and various embassies. Then it was on to the primary schools, high schools, universities, colleges, marketplaces, soccer fields, stadiums, street corners, shops and women's meetings in homes. 10,000 packs of follow-up literature were given out.

Bishop Gresford Chitemo preached in one Anglican church in the presence of the local bishop. The latter was shocked out of his mind when Gresford gave an appeal for commitment to Christ and most of the congregation came forward! He was even more startled when several people began to manifest demonic spirits and then watched as Gresford exorcised and cast out the spirits and the people were left "sane" and in their right mind.

TV and Radio Too

The mission was publicised at least twice daily on Zambian radio and TV. Team members were even invited to do morning and evening devotions and epilogues on both radio and TV, "a marvellous opportunity". One morning at 6 am, Michael and minstrel Brian Gibson were to appear for 20 minutes on the TV show "Good Morning Zambia". But other interviewees due to appear in the next two hours failed to appear. So Michael and Brian had two hours up till the 8 o'clock news to preach to the nation. Brian interspersed the spoken word with gospel songs and even did a couple of his famous aerial somersaults on camera. This certainly helped to wake up Zambia more thoroughly than in years!

Television also came into its own again when the service from the Anglican Cathedral was televised nationwide. People on the streets began looking out for, recognising and even hailing the "Back to Lusaka" team members.

One day Michael Cassidy and Gresford Chitemo visited a soccer stadium. Inside, two squads of the national soccer team were practising. A horde of hero-worshipping youngsters watched eagerly from the stands. The AE evangelists then invited the soccer team to join them in the covered stand. Most of the team came. Bishop Chitemo gave an address, and Michael followed, but when he gave the call for those who wanted to give their lives to Christ, no one quite expected what happened next. They all streamed down, including the whole soccer team. And there, kneeling on the concrete, they prayed the prayer of commitment.

Another day AE evangelist Stephen Mung'oma found he had no electrical power for the public address system at an outdoor meeting where he was to speak. He stopped a passing taxi, asking him for the loan of his battery. The driver was naturally reluctant. After all, without a battery he could not run his car. And without his car, he could not earn a living. But without his battery Stephen couldn't preach! Stephen asked him how much he would earn in an hour. The driver told him 300 kwacha (US$4). Stephen paid the driver 300 kwacha to borrow the battery for one hour. He used it for his PA system, and led 53 people to a new life in Christ, including the temporarily stranded taxi driver.

David Peters went to speak in a prison, where, as a former gang member himself, he led 305 of the 336 prisoners into a profession of faith in Christ. He was asked to return daily for the rest of the mission.

The final rally was televised on national TV across Zambia,

as was the closing Presidential Prayer Breakfast with President Kaunda and his entire cabinet. At the latter after Michael and Gresford had shared, most of the cabinet professed commitment and received follow-up material for weeks afterwards.

By the end of the mission, the team took some 500 meetings in twelve days, resulting in 6,000 commitment inquiries. These were then followed up by local churches working with AE.

In nearly every meeting, AE evangelists had noticed an extraordinary number of young people under 30. Michael took note of this and rejoiced. "The mission to Lusaka left behind a new foundation for the future of Zambia – through the youth who had made decisions for Christ."

To protect and nurture these most vulnerable young Christians, AE was delighted to learn that about 45 per cent of the churches in Lusaka were taking part in follow-up. Several weeks after the mission, a Christian lady there wrote to AE to say that one church she'd visited had already held three baptismal services for new converts. "And this is a church which requires a number of classes before baptism!"

Michael and Gresford closed the Lusaka chapter as they had begun: by asking for solid, unremitting prayer. "Nothing we have been able to achieve in Lusaka has been possible without the enormous prayer support we have had from all quarters: from our support offices and friends overseas, from the home-towns of all our team members, and from Lusaka itself," they said.

"Now we need a blanket of prayer over Lusaka, asking that the Lord will raise up many committed local helpers to follow up the work of the Holy Spirit. They need wisdom as they counsel, support and love those who have only just come to know the Lord Jesus Christ as their Saviour."

Swaziland Again

In early 1990 it was back to Swaziland, this time to the city of Mbabane. The mission began with a Leadership Breakfast for the prime minister (who was ill and didn't make it) and for members of his cabinet and other key leaders (who did make it). Then about 50 evangelists (from South Africa, Zimbabwe, Uganda, Kenya and Malawi) and AE support workers set forth to try to win that key city for Christ in a new way.

AE teams, working with the churches in Mbabane, held about 500 meetings, visited markets, government departments, hospitals, hotels, parliament, bus stations and community halls to share the gospel. As always, the AE team wanted to touch every stratum of human life in Mbabane, from the top downwards.

Their success is best summed up in two "snapshots" of the mission:

The first scene is of a poorly dressed, barefoot woman who crept forward during an evangelistic address in a dusty marketplace to lay a few bananas at the feet of the evangelist preaching.

The second scene is of Michael Cassidy and Edward Muhima sharing the gospel at the royal kraal at Ludzidzini, graced by the Queen Mother and about 20 members of the royal household with the team all having to sit on the ground so that they were not "taller" than the Queen!

To be sure this was one of the most unusual doors of opportunity.

Dar Back to God

In 1991 came the Door to Dar – this was Dar es Salaam, lovely capital of Tanzania.

In many ways the door had been partially prized open in 1985 with an earlier mission set up by the energetic Emmanuel Kopwe, then team leader of AE Tanzania.

Many in that great city to this day remember the tremendous march or procession for Jesus Christ in the 1985 mission. Says Grace Bayona: "History will record that in the nearly 25 years of independence, Dar es Salaam had never seen a procession or a march in the Name of Jesus and the Christian faith." This was the time when Tanzania was under a strong anti-Christian government.

> However, AE managed to organise this great Christian procession from three major areas of our city. And being something new, even non-Christians joined the procession in their thousands and in consequence many were reached with the gospel.
>
> In fact as our evangelists took the gospel to people wherever

they were in schools, markets, bus stops, hospitals and so on, we were birthing for our team and the church of the country the regular use of stratified evangelism, now so widely used here.

So memorable was this outreach for the church of Dar es Salaam that almost immediately plans began for a second and greater thrust, which finally came to fruition in the "Dar Back to God" Mission of 1991.

Again Emmanuel Kopwe was very much in the driving seat. But "the possession of difficulties was still as real as ever as Tanzania's policy makers were shifting from communism and socialism to Islam and Muslim rights following the election of a Muslim president after Nyerere had retired".

Many in the church were fearful of being active in matters of faith and AE Tanzania was determined to lift up the cross.

Remembers Grace: "The devil seemed to keep up a constant attack on us. The battle included the break up of our interdenominational committee, unconfirmed participation of expected evangelists, the arrival of preachers we never invited and never knew, and a sudden 600% increase in rent which landed us before the Rent Tribunal – all at once!"

She adds: "In our meetings at schools, markets, bus stops and other venues, curses from Muslim fundamentalists were thrown at us and they even jeopardised some of our venues with insults and mockery. The public sensed that 'our long preserved peace' was being endangered by these 'awakening Christians'!"

However, when Steve Lungu, Bishop Chitemo and Edward Muhima came to minister in the final rally on 4 August 1991, the ground was packed with 12,000 adults led by the cabinet minister for Home Affairs.

Among those who accepted Christ that day was a Muslim gentleman. He was afterwards discipled properly through careful follow-up. Today he is a pastor with the African Inland Church Tanzania (AICT), and has a standing testimony to Muslims for the power of Christ.

During the mission, two significant leaders came representing the government: the Minister for Home Affairs and the Dar es Salaam Regional Commissioner.

The two leaders called on AE to extend the gospel through

deed – actions. Both challenged the team to respond to the needs of street kids and disabled people of the city so as to avoid this development of a "factory of evil" among the city's citizens.

The process began with all the mission evangelists fasting for a day, and then giving the proceeds to a woman who was caring for 90 street kids.

The theme of the mission had been: "Return, O Israel, (Dar es Salaam) to the Lord your God, for you have stumbled because of your iniquity" (Hosea 14:1, RSV).

For the 600 who professed commitment, they seemed really to have returned to the Lord their God.

Yes, the Door to Dar really seemed to have opened. No wonder Emmanuel, Grace, Enoch and others on the team rejoiced.

A Wide Door and Effective

In fact whether it was Kampala, or Lilongwe, Manzini or Lusaka, Mbabane or Dar es Salaam, it could be said of each one "a wide door for effective work has opened... but there are many adversaries" (1 Corinthians 16:9). Yes, "the possession of difficulties" was still there. But "the God who is greater" (1 John 3:20) was also still there to help the team prevail.

And, yes, as other doors began opening, it seemed clear that they were indeed doors that "no one was able to shut" (Revelation 3:8).

Chapter 18

From Cape
to Caíro

After the departure of the Canadian David Richardson to head
AE's office in Canada, Michael in 1995 appointed Ernie Smith as
AE's new pan-African Missions Director. Like David before him,
Ernie quickly proved himself a determined, rugged trooper for
the gospel who would slug it out in city after city across the con-
tinent, with his faithful lieutenant Udo Krueger alongside him.

The Ernie–Udo Roadshow

The "Ernie–Udo" roadshow of mission set-up in AE has become
almost a legendary operation.

In fact with the range of their set-up endeavours embracing
everything from the very effective and freewheeling mission in
Sea Point, Cape Town in 1992 to the two pan-African missions
in Egypt (1999 and 2001), one could certainly say now that the
AE team was not only operating from east to west across Africa
but from Cape to Cairo.

One of the missions where the Ernie–Udo roadshow was
seen in classic form was the major "Harare for Jesus" citywide
mission in 1994. Ernie and Udo's shoe-leather advance work
had produced a staggering 996 meetings to be tackled in ten
days – in other words almost 100 a day. Udo's prodigious computer skills got every single meeting listed on a daily computer
printout for each team member recording their particular
meeting venues, language to be used, translator assignments,
time, place, means of transport, what to be fetched, when to be
returned, type of literature – and if need be dress-code!
Nothing, but nothing, was left to chance.

Ernie's heart for follow-up was also deep and true. Of Ernie
Michael once said, as Paul did of Timothy: "I have no one like

him who will be genuinely anxious for your welfare" (Philippians 2:20).

Like his wife Colleen, Michael's secretary for so many years, Ernie had the true spirit of the servant and would soldier in to the most impossible and desperate situations and pull them round to readiness for a mission. Udo's spirit was similar and the light in his little mission office would regularly burn into the small hours of the morning.

Amongst the many memories of Harare for Jesus was a Presidential Prayer Breakfast for President Robert Mugabe and his cabinet and some 200 other leaders. Feeling very unwell before the meeting, Mugabe told Michael he had called for a doctor and nurse. The team decided to pray for and lay hands on the president. When the doctor and nurse arrived a few minutes into the breakfast, Robert Mugabe despatched them expeditiously saying: "I am feeling fine now."

After Michael's address the president started his speech, which was meant to be 20 minutes or so and had been "speech-written" for him by someone on the mission team. After a few minutes he abandoned the prepared text and began to reminisce and reflect on his early life in a mission school, his spiritual search for meaning which had led him to abandon Christianity and seek answers in Marxism-socialism. But nothing had meant anything. The rambling odyssey which manifestly astonished his staff and all present, took an hour and a half to share, at the end of which he said maybe he should come back to look again at Christianity.

Asked by Michael if AE Zimbabwe could set up an annual prayer breakfast like this, he said he'd love that. But later efforts by the AE team to do this seemed to get blocked at bureaucratic level by protective lieutenants of the president.

Had they succeeded, one wonders how they might have impacted the seemingly spiritually receptive president and affected the later course of things in Zimbabwe.

Post-Genocide Rwanda

One of the more complex missions the set-up team was involved in, this time under the direction of AE's Rwanda Team Leader Antoine Rutayisire, was in Kigali, Rwanda, some 15 months after the cataclysmic genocide of April 1994 when nearly a million people died.

Upon arrival in Kigali, some of the AE team met with Bishop Onesphore Rwaje, Chairman of the AE Rwanda board, and Antoine Rutayisire, who mentioned that many people in the country were feeling that it was not peaceful enough for a mission. "How can you have a mission when the country is gearing up to have another war?" they asked. Antoine related the dilemma of many of those who had left the country in the wake of the genocide, a good number of whom would have been implicated in killings: they could return to Rwanda to face justice, remain in exile and resign themselves to dying there, or they could re-enter the country to fight on a win-or-die basis. Sadly, many were thought to be gearing up for the third option.

Even among those who remained in the country, Antoine asked, "How do you ask people whose neighbours killed their children now to live happily with those same neighbours alongside them? Justice does need to be done, but how do you do it?"

The brokenness of so many of the Rwandan people the AE team encountered was earth shattering. Stephen Lungu prayed for a man who had lost all of his relatives and only survived by lying motionless and remaining undetected in a mass grave among dead bodies until the killers departed. David Peters prayed for a large group of women, 85 per cent of whom had lost their husbands. David, who had recently lost his dear wife Edna to cancer, was able in some measure to relate to their distress. Antoine shared how so many were not only suffering the loss of loved ones and relatives, but of their whole circle of friends. Almost all his friends had been wiped out and he was thus in a new city of strangers and surrounded by people he did not know. Going over a list of scores of interpreters he had used in the AE mission in Kigali in 1989, Antoine found only two who weren't dead or in exile.

Into this cauldron of pain and anguish, the AE evangelists, along with the invited help of Archbishop Desmond Tutu and Ugandan First Lady Janet Museveni, sought to bring the gospel of hope, healing and forgiveness in Jesus Christ in scores of daily meetings all across the city, including a private luncheon for the president, vice president and prime minister, and then a gathering for the National Assembly (Parliament) and ambassadorial corps which Archbishop Tutu addressed.

Weeping also overtook the team when they were taken to a rural church at Ntarama where the human remains of people slaughtered during a service were still strewn across the floor and their skulls piled outside. Tutu cried a great deal as well.

Michael's journal for Monday 31 July captured the scene:

The whole thing was unspeakable as we looked into the church, saw the dreadful stenching remains, the clothes decaying and rotting, pieces of limbs here and there, skulls, either on the floor or on the altar, and others all gathered together on a shaded platform just outside the church.

Again there were press and TV cameras all round, as is Desmond's lot in life. As we got to the church itself Desmond paused and then broke down. At one point I thought he was going to faint. David Peters seized him and held him up, as did John Allen, his personal assistant. David began to pray out loud for Desmond and all of us reached out our hands to lay on him. It was a sacred and special moment in spite of TV cameras closing in. Many around were in tears as well. I found myself somewhat appalled at my own sense of emotional control. Perhaps I was just benumbed and dumb-struck.

I sort of froze within as the appalling enormity of it all bore in on me.

As we peered into the church, and then moved around it a heavy and ponderous silence overtook all of us, with nobody having words and everyone staring at the ground or into the heavens somehow or other locked in our own private thoughts, secret wonderings and poignant questions.

Prisons

One place where forgiveness and hope were most desperately needed was in the prisons, which were overcrowded beyond anyone's worst nightmare.

The team had two visits to the major prison, the first with Archbishop Tutu to see the situation and the second (after Tutu had left) for preaching and ministry. The wretched and massively overcrowded conditions appalled the team and the next day this was conveyed by the visitors to the top leadership of the country.

Michael's journal again captures the details:

Our time with the President, Vice-President and Prime Minister was fruitful, Desmond again making the point that the over-crowding in the prison was quite unacceptable. The three leaders conveyed to us the difficulties they were facing in trying to extri-cate the really serious criminal, genocidal and "crimes against humanity" criminals among the exiles, from those who were led astray and manipulated into committing atrocities. The issues of amnesty, forgiveness and justice, and how to meet the demands of each, were exercising them greatly. Desmond was clear on the importance of justice, but that it should be tempered with mercy. Whenever Desmond made that point I felt it rang right. The three Rwandan leaders recognised that obviously they could not put 200,000 or more people on trial but how to distinguish the dif-ferent levels of crimes in which people had become involved and get to the hard core of the matter was almost as difficult. Perhaps some kind of international tribunal could help and they indicated their need and desire for the UN or the Organisation of African Unity or the rest of the international community to do something more to help them in their plight.

We later heard from the Red Cross that if all the accused in Rwanda were processed by British law it would take 40 years, and by American law, 140 to 200 years. Imagine several hundred thou-sand OJ Simpsons!

Desmond and I sought to interact with their struggles and make a number of suggestions. We ended with a good word of prayer for these brethren. The President reminded me that he also, along with the Prime Minister and others, had been in the meeting I had at US Ambassador David Rawson's home in February 1994, just weeks before things blew up. Just imagine if we could really have got all the leaders of all those different par-ties meaningfully communicating at that time, say in a dialogue weekend. They had been open – but the urgent as always overtook the important.

Michael remembered that:

none of us in all our days had been prepared for seeing human congestion of that sort with thousands and thousands of people crowded into minuscule space and open courtyards or in cells, some of them quite big, which gave off from the courtyards. As we came into each section or open area and squeezed our way through the sardine-like crush of humanity, the men cheered, danced, shouted, smiled and waved, some even waving Bibles at us, others reaching out pathetically to touch us and, behind every face, a different story of crime, horror, guilt, innocence, hope, despair, laughter, tears or whatever. If only one could have seen what lay behind each of the thousands of faces before us.

The women's section with a couple of hundred women, some with babies hanging on limp breasts, was pitiful beyond the telling and also crowded beyond the imagining. The desire of all these young women to be prayed for or blessed, or even just to touch the outstretched hands of the AE evangelists, kept tears welling up in everyone's eyes.

A Reconciliation Picture

After Antoine and Gershon Mwiti of Kenya had preached from a rickety table in a pitifully congested courtyard, something unusual happened. Says Michael's journal:

> As Gershon was finishing his prayer, a very strong sense came to me from the Spirit that we needed to present "a picture" to them to convey the importance of not just vertical reconciliation with God, but horizontal reconciliation and forgiveness with one another. While Gershon and Antoine had been on the table preaching and translating respectively, Steve Lungu was standing with me while Paul Bahati of AE Rwanda was on the bench alongside the table. I rather unceremoniously seized Dave Peters and asked him to stand between Steve and myself as I equally unceremoniously pulled Chinese Chye Ann to stand up on the bench next to Paul Bahati.
>
> Then grabbing the microphone from Antoine as he and Gershon finished, I handed it to Paul. So here we all were, standing in a line on the bench with all eyes riveted upon us, a black Malawian, a brown South African Indian, an old whitey colonialist, a black Rwandese, and a yellow Chinaman! We then all put our arms round one another to demonstrate our fraternal bonding in Christ. I then cried out to one and all (some 10,000 people in that prison with maybe 3,000 or 4,000 able to hear us), that here in Steve was a black man who had hated and wanted to kill whites, but now in Christ had the capacity to forgive and love me as a representative white. Then there was David who likewise as

an Indian had hated white people and had been caught up once in violent Indian politics. I added that in South Africa many blacks hated Indians even more than they hated white people. But here we are before you all, as brothers in Christ and each of us is bonded here to a black Rwandese in Paul Bahati, and finally to Soh Chye Ann, the yellow man from the Far East. This is what the Gospel is all about. So too here in Rwanda it requires the power of Jesus for Hutu to bond themselves to Tutsi and Tutsi to Hutu and both of them to the Twa and the Twa to both of them.

The Spirit was moving. The place was riveted. For a throng of humanity such as we had it was a gospel marvel that you could have heard a pin drop. The Spirit seemed to take the point home with almost tangible impact all round us.

Said evangelist David Peters of the experience later:

Michael took us by surprise, and as we linked our shoulders together, the eyes of those in the prison just opened up wide. They could not believe the sight. For them it was something they had never seen before. Especially the different colours all together. They just stared. I for my part was dumbfounded because it was all so unexpected. How I wished there could have been a camera there to catch that moment, with the prisoners' eyes suddenly all lit up; but cameras were forbidden. Maybe in the hearts of those prisoners they were picturing a future for Rwanda.

Soh Chye Ann, an Anglican AE evangelist from Singapore, and later to head the Asia Desk of the Church Missionary Society in London, expressed his thoughts afterwards this way:

It is very difficult to describe one's feelings when we looked at those thousands upon thousands of prisoners without hope or dignity. But when the five of us of different colours stood there, and Michael used us as a powerful visual aid of what Jesus can do as he brings people of different races, backgrounds and ethnic groups together, I was praying that this point would truly get through so that they might have a desire to reconcile with one another even as we have learned to love one another, and live together in harmony.

Light Relief

Amidst all the trauma and tragedy of Kigali there was nothing comic or light-hearted to relieve the sense of sadness for the team, aside from one episode. In one of the evening services, evangelist Orpheus Hove had to excuse himself rather urgently, just before addressing the crowd, to answer a call of nature. The only facility was an effectively doorless and minuscule two-by-two corrugated iron structure perched precariously on a bank. Once enthroned, Orpheus was suddenly faced in the moonlit night by a moon of another sort: one of Rwanda's more substantial ladies was backing menacingly into the convenience towards him like a cement mixer gearing for action! Realising that entering the tiny structure and turning round inside was impossible, she had accordingly prepared herself outside in the dark and was now reversing "blind" into the facility and before you could say "Jack Robinson" or ring 911 she had just about deposited herself on the paralysed lap of the shocked and momentarily speechless evangelist. The dual shrieks of the competing incumbents probably caused a temporary halt in the evangelistic service close by. But history offers no more details. The modestly unsettled evangelist somehow recovered his composure enough to preach effectively just moments later!

Four Not Three

The closing rally, with the country's president and most of his cabinet present, brought together some 11,000 people to hear Michael and Archbishop Tutu minister the gospel. Before the president addressed the throng, Michael, somewhat to the astonishment of the crowd, laid his hands on the president and prayed for him. Said one observer later: "That's when we knew a new day was coming in Rwanda."

Before Michael gave the main evangelistic address, Archbishop Tutu gave a riveting sermon from Daniel 3 about Shadrack, Meshack and Abednego in the fiery furnace. But then, amazement, amazement, astonishment for King Nebuchadnezzar – how many does he see and count? Certainly not three, now there are four. And who is the fourth? Desmond dramatised this with genius, amusement and power as he elucidated the incredible implications of the fourth person present in the fiery furnace with the three young men in their hour of trial and need. He acted out Nebuchadnezzar counting one, two, three, then blinking his eyes as he saw a fourth, and then starting to count again in unbelief. One, two three – surely not, but yes, my goodness – there are four! The Son of God was there. The Lord of Heaven and Earth had come to his children in their fiery ordeal and was with them. Said Michael: "Desmond applied this to believers in Rwanda and it was powerful, powerful indeed."

Thus did many Rwandans, not least Antoine Rutayisire and the panting AE team, come to register and rejoice afresh that in the midst of their epic tragedy and traumas, Jesus was with them.

Addis Ababa

Later that year (1994) another extraordinary opportunity presented itself as the door opened for a really major thrust in Addis Ababa, capital of Ethiopia.

Over 2,000 church leaders, pastors, evangelists, young people and women's groups were mobilised to make this great occasion. AE and its national partners took almost two years' prayer coverage all over the city and in others as they geared up to see the great hand of God moving on the famous capital.

The mission was started in ten centres of the city using auditoriums, theatre halls, and churches. The city was covered with that great theme of "The Eleventh Hour". It was a week of puzzle for thousands of people. The day came for the puzzle to be explained as people flooded to halls and auditoriums all over the city, with multitudes lining up for several kilometres to get into the theatre halls to hear the gospel. The city had not seen such an evangelistic mission in Ethiopia for 35 or 40 years. The ten centre meetings began on Monday and ended on Friday evening. Said Team Leader Berhanu Deresse: "As people responded in their hundreds, so we knew there was rejoicing in heaven. We felt we overheard the great singing of the Angels in Heaven."

At the same time there were over 1,000 young people moving right across the city handing out invitations along with tracts that spoke of the saving power of Christ. That great army of God worked day and night. At night street girls were also confronted with the gospel of our Lord Jesus Christ. The most neglected street boys sleeping outside in the corner of the streets were ministered to by mission workers. The Lord honoured their efforts and as a result 5,000 people came to God through the witness of those committed young people.

"We saw miracle after miracle," exulted Berhanu afterwards, "as sick and demon possessed people were prayed for and healed. This brought such great excitement to the young people."

Race Track

Berhanu's post-mission report vividly recorded the amazing event: "The great army of 2,000 mission workers moved on the final Saturday to the largest horse race field. This place takes approximately 1,000,000 people. The people began to come from all corners of the city. In hundreds and thousands we saw people flooding into the field. By 8 am we had about 150,000 and by 9 am there were over 300,000 people. This was a miracle of God."

The 1,000-voice choir of young people with different costumes representing all tribes of Ethiopia was very colourful. Their first song was "Our gospel will yet reach the end of Ethiopia and extend to the end of the world. His saving power will reach our nation..." Berhanu went on:

After their song, evangelist Stephen Lungu, our Team Leader in Malawi, preached his first message and gave his testimony. There were a few young people who had come to make trouble but when they heard Steve's testimony and identified it with theirs, they were quiet as midnight. Steve preached over 30 minutes and you could have heard a pin drop in the midst of those 300,000. A time of miracle happened when Steve invited people to the Lord. He told them to run to the Lord to be saved and people literally flooded to the front in hundreds, most of them crying and many feeling very hopeless. There were over 1,000 who came to the front. We were fortunate to have around 500 trained counsellors and then added more to help. AE's evangelists with some of the church leaders hugged each other and cried because of that great joy of the Lord. It was a time of refreshing. We could feel and hear the Spirit of God moving in the midst of that great crowd. The choir was singing "Jesus my Saviour Changes Lives".

Historic Happening

The AE team, especially those from outside Ethiopia, were also astonished to find so many demon-possessed people manifesting demonic responses. As this happened they were prayed for on the side by a great team of prayer warriors and intercessors skilled in this kind of ministry.

One of the historic dimensions of this mission was that the government was willing to put a great police force at the disposal of the mission meeting to ensure law, order and protection. For many of the Ethiopian believers this was very significant because the previous communist regime had seen the church as a threat and had therefore carried out much persecution of Christians. One of the young policemen even came up to an AE evangelist to ask spiritual questions and found himself being led to the Lord while in the course of his police duties! All in all over 10,000 people came to a professed new commitment to Christ during the Addis mission.

And the after-effects of the mission have continued since then, with significant church growth in many congregations. Recently a young man came up to Berhanu to tell him of an incident which happened during the Addis mission. He had been witnessing to somebody near the Saudi Arabian embassy. All of a sudden a group of radical Muslims who were regular pilgrims to Mecca got hold of him and started beating him. They said they did not want him to talk about Jesus in that particular area. At that point another young man came up and spoke to those who were inflicting violence on the young preacher and this resulted in his being freed. However, the miracle was that the young man who brought the help accepted Christ not long after that and became an evangelist in his church. He is now a pastor.

In Malawi Stephen Lungu even met an Ethiopian woman who had come to Christ in the Addis mission and had travelled far, still telling her story.

Commented Berhanu Deresse recently: "We have so many

stories of this kind which we hear all over the place and even outside Ethiopia. God is writing a lot of stories and bits of Heavenly history through these missions in Ethiopia."

Going for Gold in Ghana

Another very happy and memorable mission took place in Accra, the capital of Ghana, in February 1997. Team leader Dr Nii Amoo Darku and his colleagues and mission committee had done a great job of set-up.

The visiting AE evangelists were shown round Accra the day before the mission began in order to get a feel for the place and a sense of its dynamics. They were fascinated and amused at the many signs around the city that the gospel of Christ had made quite an impact on the culture. These were seen in the names of all kinds of shops and business enterprises. Thus there was for example, one which read "It is the Lord Bus Service". Others which caught the team's attention were "The Mount Zion Bus Shop", "The God Our Provider Metal Shop", "The God's Way Beauty Saloon", "The God's Obey Transport", "God Will Make a Way Fashion". What particularly struck Michael's fancy was one which called itself "The Exodus 14:14 Hair Salon"! "What on earth could that refer to?" wondered Michael. Back at the mission base he opened his Bible and read the scripture: "The Lord will fight for you: you have only to sit still." So here was a new scripture for all husbands to give their wives as they headed off to the hairdresser – Exodus 14:14: "The Lord will fight for you: you have only to sit still!"

As usual there were the many different kinds of stratified evangelism meetings, and many little interesting human happenings. Thus when Stephen Lungu, Ralph Jarvis and Alex Theophilus, AE's sound system man, went to speak at a police station, they waited an hour for the station commander, who had seemingly forgotten them or not announced it. Anyway, while waiting for some of the police officers to gather, a young man came into the police station and asked what the AE men were there for. He then asked that they pray for him and they had the privilege of leading him to the Lord there and then. Steve Lungu said they left him "beaming with joy" and they were beaming too, even though the main meeting never took place.

Antoine Rutayisire of Rwanda told how in one hospital he went to the outpatient area to minister and found one woman screaming with pain and writhing all over the place. Antoine prayed for her and in a matter of moments she had normalised and was seemingly out of pain. Said Antoine: "I don't really know if she was healed, and I would not want to take my hope for the reality, but even so it appeared something had happened to remove the pain."

Another interesting opportunity was laid on for Michael to address the so-called "Traditional Chiefs and Queen Mothers". "The room," said Michael, "was jam packed, with some staggeringly impressive men and women dressed in multi-coloured and startlingly beautiful traditional dresses and garbs." The team learned to their amazement that there in Ghana one of the chiefs had led the way in forming an "Association of Christian Chiefs". Before Michael was asked to address the group a talk was given by a prominent lay woman, Mrs Joyce Wereko-Brobby. She focused her talk on the sacrifice of Jesus and how his shed blood necessitated no other kind of sacrifice, whether animal, bird or even human. Team members were staggered to hear that in certain remote parts of Ghana human sacrifice still took place. Joyce warned against any kind of involvement in Satanist rituals, or the occult, or involvement with witchdoctors.

Steve Lungu preached at the Living Waters Church in a long, extended and exhausting service. He said that at one point the minister had the people praying on their feet for a solid hour. When Steve finally came to preach, he imagined nobody would have any energy left to listen. But in fact he had a good time and some 20 young men responded to his appeal, seven of whom had never been in a church before.

Grace Kalambo, AE's team leader in Tanzania, spoke in an engineering workshop to some 70 or so workers, all of whom indicated a great eagerness to respond to Jesus. She then went on to address 15 or 20 young women trainees in a dressmaking shop. Not having an interpreter, her driver stepped in to do the honours and seven or eight young women professed commitment.

Grace also joined Antoine Rutayisire in a police station followed by a prison with some 70 prisoners, both male and female, most of whom indicated a desire to receive Christ and were prayed for.

Gottfried Osei-Mensah, at that time an assistant to Michael for International Affairs in AE, but now AE's International Chairman, spoke in a seminar of 120 theological students from three different theological colleges or Bible schools. Gottfried's amazing skills in Bible teaching produced a deep impact in these colleges, as in other places where he ministered to young theological trainees and ordinands.

Geoffrey Rwubusisi of AE Uganda had one fine experience in ministering in a district police headquarters with all the police officers and commandos present. He spoke on "The Crisis of Leadership in Africa". The traffic chief, the CID chief and the police commander were all present. At the end of the meeting the police commander asked all junior officers to stay behind, and shared about the personal impact which Geoffrey's message had made on him in terms of the challenge to follow Christ and forsake all forms of corruption. He added: "Ghana has not really been free or ministered justice properly to people because we have not been really free or just ourselves."

In another situation David Peters and Alex Theophilus went to the central prison. The organiser for the meeting was nowhere to be seen, but the chief inspector ushered David and Alex into a foul-smelling cell housing 16 men and two women. David and Alex preached their hearts out with deep feeling for these people. It transpired that the chief inspector was a Christian and he spoke encouraging words to the prisoners. The team felt, however, that it really needed to challenge the authorities about the conditions in some of these prisons. Not surprisingly, there was a 100 per cent response to the gospel from those who heard the Word. The team was concerned about follow-through, but hoped that the chief inspector, having announced his intention to shape up in his Christian life, would reform the conditions in his prison.

AE Chairman Gottfried Osei-Mensah preached in one church whose missionary zeal was so immense that they had planted no fewer than 60 new congregations in seven years.

Medical Ministries

One of the interesting features of this mission was a strategic alliance the AE team made with the Christian Mission Resource Foundation headed by a medical doctor and former Ghana Airforce commander, Dr Sam Annankra. AE had raised some funds for medical work in Ghana and these were passed to Dr Sam's medical foundation, now set to operate during the course of the mission in close collaboration with AE. Thus it was that Dr Sam and his fleet of medical workers were all wearing T-shirts emblazoned with "The Church in Mission with African Enterprise" on the back and John 17:21 on the front with "United in Christ". An assortment of tents had been rigged up in some of the town squares where masses of people were seeking to eke out a living selling goods. In one tent they could listen to the presentation of the gospel. In another they could receive personal and individual counselling. In a third they could receive medical attention and examination, whether it was for eye, ear, stomach or gynaecological problems. Hundreds and hundreds of people were involved in these three processes of seeking help. Towards the end of the day, next to the clinics, the Jesus film would be shown, sometimes watched by up to 1,100 people. There was a great sense of deed and Word coming together in these contexts.

As the mission headed into its home straight, the indefatigable and ever-capable Udo gave the team the statistics. The total number of meetings a few days before the end of the mission stood at 487, with 154 of these being what Udo called "pure stratified evangelism", i.e., not main meetings, leadership meetings or services. The total number of people reached at that point was estimated at close to 126,000. The average attendance at all the stratified evangelism meetings had come out at about 60.

One big mistake was holding the closing rally on Saturday morning rather than the team's normal Sunday afternoon. Saturday morning, as a number of the team had feared, turned out to be shopping time or family time and hopeless for a closing rally. The team was shattered when a mere 150 or so people turned up. But everyone gave it their best shot and it was gratifying to see how local musicians, preachers, people leading in prayer or making announcements did it as if there were 100,000 present!

However the mission ended on a high with a wonderful dinner evening for parliamentarians. The only hitch was that the caterers got trapped in a traffic jam and the food was only served at 9.30 pm for a meeting that had started at 7 pm! However the ministry went wonderfully and many parliamentarians and their wives came forward at the end to be prayed for by the team that the Lord would help them and give them his wisdom as they sought to conduct their parliamentary business and govern the country.

Flying home the next day Michael's journal had this entry: "As I dictate this, there is a BBC film crew on the aeroplane and a rather large camera is staring straight at me, the cameraman obviously having an eye for the best-looking fellow on board! Actually, Ralph Jarvis said to me when I woke up and came to after the Accra/Luanda leg of the flight when I had slept: 'You have no idea how horrible you look when you have just woken up. How does Carol cope?!' With friends like that, who needs enemies!"

Rough Ride

Not all missions, however, are a joyride with great responses and celebrations everywhere afterwards. Sometimes a mission can feel very much a failing experience.

Such was the case in 1998 with Luanda in war-stricken Angola. The Ernie–Udo roadshow, strengthened in this instance as in numbers of others by the late Sheckie Masika of Zimbabwe, almost tumbled off the road. Discouragement and depression tugged at the team's spirits almost every day. Said Ernie:

> When the mission structures were first put in place 367 people signed up to be on one or other of the committees. We had never ever had such a response in my experience. We had the mission manual translated into Portuguese and each member had a copy for their respective committee. From this great start things started to go wrong. The structures began to disintegrate. It would appear that many signed up thinking this was going to be

a paid job, and when they found this was not so they became disillusioned and left. There was also a gap in the leadership. The mission chairman apparently neglected to get alongside these committees, especially in the early stages, and further crumbling resulted because of this lack of guidance.

At this early stage Ernie, Udo and Sheckie seriously considered pulling the plug. All the locals pleaded with them not to, saying that given the threat of ongoing war, if ever a city needed a mission Luanda did. There were other problems. Firstly, the prayer committee collapsed. "This was probably the major disaster," said Ernie. Initially everything looked good with the prayer team headed by Rev Moousaqui, President of the Association of Presbyterian Churches. He had a big team and did much creative work disseminating the prayer needs round the city. In fact, prayer groups met every Saturday to pray for the mission and a prayer rally, attended by a whopping 7,000 people, was held in May 1998. But then not long thereafter Rev Moousaqui suffered a severe stroke which took him out of action. The person who took over was never able to bring the same vision and leadership to this committee and the attendance at the prayer meetings began to drop off until there was hardly anyone coming. Another problem for Ernie and Udo was that they found that everyone wanted to be compensated for their services, including the Christians. Music groups wouldn't sing unless paid $100 per event for the instruments and $50 for the vocals. In addition, transport was very expensive and interpreters and evangelists were few. Most churches lacked a strong evangelical or evangelistic tradition. The "amanha" (do it tomorrow) syndrome proved lethal. The fact that inflation was raging unabated at more than 1,000% and corruption was rife at every level did not help either.

Then a number of very odd, even extraordinary, things happened:

- The mission chairman's brother died three weeks before the mission's starting date. Being the eldest the chairman had to take charge and was gone for the week at such a crucial stage.

- The wife of one of the pastors, on the publicity committee, was killed in a hit-and-run accident. On the day of the funeral his nephew was also killed, and the nephew of the mission chairman also died. This happened nine days before the mission.
- The Wednesday before the mission was due to start, the chairman was summoned to meet the government Director of Religious Affairs. He was objecting to certain non-member churches participating in the mission. To be a member is a mere formality, but written application has to be made and this takes a long time. Ultimatum – drop their names from the mission letterhead or permission to proceed with the mission will be withdrawn. This brought much drama, five days from lift-off.
- In the same enquiry AE's participation was questioned. The mission chairman said he had heard that AE was suspected of recruiting mercenaries to fight against the government. Result, said Ernie: "I had to write a letter explaining who we are, give our history, our involvement in Luanda etc."
- Adding to the permission workload and the above distractions was the drama of the visas for those coming from East Africa. "This took much of our precious time. One of us spent an average of three hours per day for about seven days. Having to re-route the flights cost an additional $2,900."
- During the mission week one of the mission vehicles had an altercation with some soldiers. The vehicle pulled out of a parking bay just as an army truck was passing, causing the army truck to stop suddenly to avoid a collision. "The soldiers didn't like this so they shot at the vehicle, beat the driver on the head with a rifle butt, and when one of the pastors intervened he also got smacked around with the rifle butt. Not serious but shaking for anyone."
- The owner of the team base had a young man of about 18 looking after the place at night.

We don't know all the details but on Saturday night, eve of the final day and closing rally, a friend visited him and for whatever reason he shot and killed this friend. We had planned our celebration lunch with the pastors and workers to be at the base. Because of this the ladies who came to cook for the lunch were unhappy to be operating there after this tragedy. Eventually they were persuaded. However, while we were all at the rally and the ladies were alone at the base, a gang of about 20 youngsters, friends of the deceased, set upon the base, blaming us for the tragedy. They threatened to beat up the ladies. They forced them off the base and made them sit on the sidewalk. Fortunately one of our pastors happened to drive by and called the police to intervene. He had to pay the police a bribe of $160 before they would take action.

Welcome to evangelism in Africa, folks! "But given all of this and the enormous difficulties," said Ernie afterwards, "we have to believe that the fact that we even had a mission at all should be seen as a miracle."

God's Mercy

However, God's mercy is wonderful and in spite of all of this some amazing things happened. There was a splendid and well-attended business forum. The daily Reconciliation Seminars led by Emmanuel Kopwe were, as Ernie put it, "an outstanding success". In fact, Ernie, Udo and Sheckie Masika felt this should have happened two or three months earlier. If people could have come into deep reconciliation in the post-war context much sooner it would have made all the difference. Said Ernie: "It was incredible after the Reconciliation Seminars to see the expressions, the huggings and the offering and receiving of forgiveness. If only we had got this all in place sooner!" Emmanuel Kopwe also had some very fruitful meetings with members of parliament. This was perhaps the cherry on the top of an otherwise very difficult, frustrating and seemingly failing mission.

The closing rally, at which Emmanuel preached, drew a small crowd of about 1,000 people, but Emmanuel preached his heart out and some 150 folk responded.

Said Ernie afterwards:

One of the things which distressed me in this mission was the range of problems, plus the tragedy at the base of the death of that young man, plus very inadequate accommodation and food caused numbers of the team to become downcast. This was uncharacteristic of the AE team. But things just finally got to them and I too became despondent. However, I must single out Emmanuel Kopwe and Orpheus Hove, both of whom were great pillars of support in this mission, and they really helped us through. Particularly Emmanuel, given the heavy load on his shoulders in terms of the ministry demands which were upon him as well. I believe he was God's man for this moment in this mission.

Into the Land of the Pharaohs

One of the more exotic and fascinating doors open to the AE team as the old century ended was the call and opportunity to minister in Egypt, land of the Pharaohs.

In reality, the open door in AD 1999 was not the first time AE had been into Egypt. Michael and Festo had done missions there with a big team back in 1978, focusing on Cairo, Assuit in Upper Egypt and Alexandria. That was the time an Egyptian came up to Michael and Festo after they had preached a combination and duo-type sermon together in Cairo. Seeing the two African brethren, one black and one white, preaching together, the Egyptian said: "Michael, you are the milk of the gospel and Festo is the chocolate!" A milk-chocolate gospel; yes, that was what the AE teams all across Africa sought to present as personalising, incarnating and epitomising the gospel of reconciliation.

Ever since the ministry to Egypt in 1978 the team has sought to maintain strong links and relationships in Egypt, with a view to developing a team there. David Richardson and AE's International Chairman Gottfried Osei-Mensah have been the ones who spearheaded these linkages.

Then, imagine the excitement of the team when an invitation came from the Protestant churches of Egypt to go and conduct major campaigns of outreach there in 1999.

The mission covered nine cities simultaneously, namely Alexandria, Benha, Minouf, Tanta, Port Said, Zagazig, Fayoum, Beni Suef and Cairo, where most of the action took place. In order to cope with the 55 venues each night the team partnered with 20 local evangelists and seven expatriates, plus the 30 or so from AE. During the build-up AE was involved in training lay people each month over many months, all of this covering a host of evangelism-related topics. This was something new for many of the Egyptian pastors in so far as they had never seen this kind of thorough build-up to a mission before. In partnership with Campus for Christ, Ernie and his crew also trained some 500 people in door-to-door visitation. During the proclamation week these folk visited in excess of 6,000 homes.

It was a memorable and wonderful time and everyone came back on a high. In the aftermath of the mission there was a manifestly new level of co-operation between the different church groups. Eight new branches of the ECEC (Egyptian Combined Evangelism Committee) were formed in eight other cities besides Cairo, which had previously hosted the only one. The team was thrilled that the Egyptian churches decided to continue the programme of house to house visiting.

However, even before the team left, the calls and cries for another mission were already loud and clear.

Back Again Two Years Later

The wonderfully happy and successful thrust of 1999 served only to whet the appetite of both the Egyptian pastors and the AE team. Accordingly, a further formal invitation came to go back in 2001 and build on the foundation of the initial endeavours.

This effort was a bit more ambitious and in addition to the nine cities tackled in 1999 a number of others were added, namely Bush, Suez, El Minya and Assuit. The team tackled this endeavour in two bites over two weeks. They were in seven of the cities in the first week and six in the second week, but with the main focus on Cairo.

The large AE team of 40 or more fanned out across Egypt into these various communities. Because proclamation in public places is impossible, all the ministry had to be carried out from the base of various local churches.

Focusing on Cairo

One of the things anyone coming into Cairo has to get used to quickly is the driving style of all and sundry, which certainly keeps evangelists living very prayerfully and most of the time just on the edge of eternity. Terrifying as this was for the AE visitors, Michael nevertheless could record in his journal:

I have realised here that while the driving seems incredibly dangerous and risky, with the cars all rocketing down these roads with literally inches on either side of them, actually the driving is very skilled. People get raised on that sort of driving, as with mother's milk, and learn the ropes. I've also realised that it is quite a normal procedure where you have what is obviously meant to be a two-lane road used for three lanes of traffic! All the car in the middle has to do is just straddle the line down the middle of the road and cars will pass on either side with anything from 10–18 inches to spare and often going fast. But drivers use their mirrors, their wits, their lights, their horns and it all seems to come out in the wash at the end of the day.

As to pedestrians, they will step out across six lanes of traffic in what looks like a totally suicidal enterprise to cross the road. But they sway this way and that, they walk or edge up the little channel between vehicles, then slip across while someone touches their brakes or sways their steering wheel, or the pedestrian pulls in his backside or jumps forward or sways backward and one way and another crosses miraculously to the other side. The kind of thing I would never in a million moons consider doing myself, seriously. It would seem to the uninitiated to be completely reckless with one's life. But everyone does it. Even oldies, also young couples carrying children. Literally as one watches, one feels this will end in a fatal accident but with cars speeding by on either side, the pedestrians somehow know which way to look, which leg to pull in, which arm to stick out, which part of the anatomy to sway forward or backward, or how to use their legs to dodge. And so they make it across. One is left breathless just watching this spectacle.

Fanning Out All Over

With team members fanning out in ministry morning, noon and night, it was always exhilarating to gather at the mission base at the Anglican Cathedral mid-morning each day for a team meeting for prayer, praise, report-back, planning and strategising.

Each day had its cluster of fascinating, moving or entertaining tales. Edward Muhima, team leader of Uganda, thus shared about a fine service he had been in with over 300 people and some 30 or more responding at the altar call. He noted that local people draw a distinction between "Christians" and "believers". A Christian is someone who is in the Christian church and is only visibly and nominally within the Christian community. But a believer is someone who has truly committed his life to Christ, found him as Lord and Saviour and been born again of the Spirit. Mere "Christians" by this definition are discouraged from taking Holy Communion.

Mbulelo Hina from AE South Africa shared about a man he had prayed for in one of his services. The man had a heart problem. However the man had then given his spiritual heart to the Lord and testified that now he had a new peace in his spiritual heart and could entrust the healing of his physical heart to Christ. Indeed, he said: "Even if the Lord does not heal my physical heart, I am happy and rejoicing because my spiritual heart has been given to Christ and I know that He is taking me to heaven when I die." Mbulelo also shared the interesting experience of the master of ceremonies who had been co-ordinating the service giving his life to Christ at the end of the service. "The brother realised," said Mbulelo "during the service that he had not understood the gospel or surrendered his life to Christ. Although he had been co-ordinating and leading everything, now he knew that he himself needed to become a committed believer and true Christian. And he did so."

Stephen Lungu reported that in one church where he had preached the number outside was greater than the number inside. He said one man began crying out: "Lord, have mercy, I am a sinner, I am a sinner." Steve went right to him and led him to the Lord there and then.

Mike Odell, leader of AE South Africa, told of his preaching experience in one church. He recalled how a man came up who had been on drugs and who expressed an eagerness to come to Christ and who did so. There were a number of first-time commitments, and especially exciting and most especially encouraging were young people making commitments for the first time. Mike expressed the kind of inadequacy all team members feel when a five-year-old paralysed child was brought forward for prayer. "But I know," he said, "that as we pray for these different situations we can be fully convinced that prayer does make a difference. You never quite know what that difference will be or what the Lord has done. One may not see a dramatic New Testament-type healing in front of one's eyes, but something always happens, whether in the body or the mind of the needy person or in the family around them." All the AE team would go along with that.

In another situation one woman Michael had prayed for said her husband wanted to leave her, become a Muslim and take their child. She was anguished beyond measure but in the middle of praying for people after the service, she went back to Michael and said she and her husband wanted to invite him for dinner right after the service. The pastor agreed with this and accompanied Michael for this meal. As usual, after all the services, the meals provided for the team would begin about 10.30 or 11 pm or later, and often go on until 1.00 or 1.30 am. Anyway, this was quite an extraordinary time for this family as the husband promised Michael he would not leave his wife and that he wanted to commit his life to Christ. His brother, an engineer, also said he wanted to commit himself to the Lord. Says Michael's journal: "So in the early hours of the morning, with the last vestiges of strength and energy I could muster, I prayed a prayer of commitment sentence by sentence with the pastor translating it into Arabic, and then these two gentlemen saying it out loud in Arabic phrase by phrase. It was a very special moment. At the end of it the husband said in his broken English: 'My heart is changed. I feel different.'"

The Magic of Molokhea

Incidentally, talking of meals and hospitality, the team was always chuckling and commenting on the sumptuous fare and the delicacies with which they were served. One particular such delicacy is a sort of soup which looks rather like spinach soup but is made from some other kind of leaf and is called "molokhea". The team found that to get any crowd of people on side, they only had to say that what they really liked was their "molokhea"!

The team were all highly amused when they heard how their colleague Steve Lungu a few weeks previously had gone to the Egyptian embassy in Harare on a Friday afternoon, a couple of hours before they close, seeking an Egyptian visa. They told him he couldn't possibly have one there and then and would have to come back on Monday. But Steve was unable to wait over in Harare for several days, as he had to get back to Malawi. So instead of creating a scene, Steve just told the immigration officials at the embassy that all he wanted to do was get back to Egypt so that he could have some more molokhea. This produced side-splitting hilarity amongst the officials, who went inside to the ambassador and reported: "Here is a fellow who wants to get a visa quickly so he can get back to Egypt and have some more molokhea!" This seemingly collapsed the ambassador as well and in about 20 minutes Steve had his visa!

Testimonies

Paul Bahati from AE Rwanda shared about one situation when he expressed his dismay about the low physical wall in the church separating men and women. It was explained to Paul that in Egypt the Muslim men and women are kept very much apart. Therefore in some churches they follow the tradition of the general culture. Paul queried this procedure from a gospel perspective and the minister said they would think about what he had said.

Enock Kagya from AE Tanzania described a number of testimonies given in a service where he was preaching. He had been much struck by one woman who said she had come forward for special prayer two days previously for very high blood pressure and chronic sickness. The way she had got to the church in the first place was really remarkable. She said that she had been asleep and that the Lord had woken her up and said: "Go to the church." There she had been prayed for by Enock, and was now reporting a completely normal blood pressure. She testified about this healing with tears of gratitude.

Shiferaw Feyissa, from AE Ethiopia, told of being in one congregation which had been overflowing with many people coming for prayer relating to sickness. Shiferaw commented on the insistence of people to be prayed for and shared how one huge man was constantly saying: "I won't let you go until you have prayed for me!" After Shiferaw had prayed for him, he said he was "very happy"! Shiferaw reported on another meeting which he had reached by an extended train journey. It was a tiny church with only 30 people, but four of them professed to be coming to Christ for the very first time.

One precious young teenager came to Michael and his assistant Jamie Morrison and said: "I love, love, love Jesus. You see, when I was six he appeared to me and I saw him." Thus had she found her Lord.

It was interesting that many Egyptian believers testified to the team that they had found the Lord through "Jesus or an Angel appearing to them in vision or in their bedrooms". One young man, an ardent lay evangelist for his Lord, was asked how he had found Christ. "One night Jesus appeared to me and stood at the end of my bed," was his simple reply.

The team were much touched by all the expressions of gratitude and the lavish gifts given them in the farewell service and celebration held for them in the Anglican Cathedral. Dr Frank Mdlalose, the South African Ambassador to Egypt and previously the Premier of KwaZulu-Natal, was also there with his wife Eunice. Michael and the team had been much involved with Mdlalose in the run-up to the 1994 South African elections.

In one of the final report-back team meetings, Ernie Smith indicated that for the last mission in Egypt two years previously the team had spoken to an aggregate of about 86,000 people. He said that he felt the numbers in this mission would be similar with some 600 meetings having been conducted. Some 43 people had been trained as trainers of trainers and during the monthly sessions in evangelism, witness and house-to-house visitation, a further 625 had attended the training sessions over the last eight months in the run-up to Egypt 2001. In the previous mission about 6,200 homes had been visited through the 500 people trained as visitors, and Ernie anticipated again that in Egypt 2001 the figures would be similar. All the team were thankful indeed for the training Ernie and Udo provided to all these lay people as it had paved the way for ongoing evangelism after the team left.

Commented Ernie afterward: "There were many difficulties and inconveniences to put up with, but everyone hung in there and made the best of it. Result – they all had a ball!"

By the end of the mission, Udo's guesstimate was that 64,000 people had sat under the team's ministry and the number of first-time commitments was 4,000. Stephen Mbogo, AE's Kenya team leader, would return some months later to do follow-up with these new believers.

Most of the team flew out of Egypt in the early hours of 11 September, their hearts rejoicing at so many newfound friends and their new understanding of life and realities in the Islamic world. They were not to know that a few hours later, as they all began to arrive back home, so the world would change forever, as militant Islamist hijackers in the United States crashed planes into the World Trade Center and the Pentagon.

A new day and age had opened.

The team wondered what this would all mean for future ministry in Egypt and in the Islamic world.

In fact, for ministry anywhere in Africa.

More to Come

As this book goes to press the indefatigable Ernie and Udo are working on pan-African missions to Port Elizabeth in South Africa, Abidjan in Côte d'Ivoire, Kinshasa in Congo, and others. They know "there remains very much land to be possessed" (Joshua 13:1).

Ernie retires at the end of 2002 and will be succeeded by AE's Ghana team leader, Dr Nii Amoo Darku.

Nii Amoo knows, one would guess, that he is stepping into shoes that will be hard to fill. But he will. Because "the doors" will open for him just as they did for his erstwhile predecessor. Thanks be to God.

Chapter 19

By All Means to Save Some

AE evangelists seem to be creative people. So they are always coming up with ingenious and fresh ideas for outreach. If the Apostle Paul could say that he was ready to try "by all means to save some" (1 Corinthians 9:22), then why should AE not follow suit?

An assortment of significant methodologies thus emerged and have proven effective. Space allows the mention of just a few.

Operation Foxfire

This was the name that the Zimbabwe AE team gave to a new venture it launched in June 1980 under the leadership of AE team member, the late Sheckie Masika, who died tragically in a car crash while on assignment for AE.

The name was borrowed from the Old Testament story of Samson's devastation of the Philistine harvest. He'd sent out 300 foxes, two by two, each pair with a flaming torch. By this ingenious means the fields were set alight (Judges 15:3–5).

Sheckie Masika liked the idea of setting Zimbabwe alight with the gospel and spoiling the territory of the spiritual opposition, and so he determined to send out pairs of his own "foxes". These would be young Bible college graduates seeking ministerial experience. Once chosen they were sent out in pairs to teach, pray for the sick and preach across rural Zimbabwe. These young pairs of evangelists, or "foxes", were sent under the covering of AE, but with modest provisions, and little money, much as Jesus had sent his disciples. Their basic aim was to evangelise and help people see the value of reaching God through Jesus rather than their ancestors. They travelled mainly by bicycle. They were asked to keep a journal and record things which happened, some of which were almost straight from the book of Acts.

A necessary component was Operation Esther – hundreds of women in Harare who committed themselves to pray by name for the young people and the villages to which they went. This was vital "prayer covering" for Operation Foxfire.

Ten Foxfire teams set out to permeate 50 of Zimbabwe's so-called Tribal Trust Lands, areas set aside under the old colonial regime for black farmers and residents only. By October 1980, Foxfire had twelve pairs of lay witness teams throughout Zimbabwe. Although this rural work somewhat contradicted AE's urban focus, with so many urban and other people displaced by the war, the crying needs of the moment were in these stricken areas, so the Zimbabwe team felt AE needed a presence and a witness there. Besides, many of these people had urban links and others would soon be moving to the cities in search of work. Moreover, in places where churches had closed and pastors had fled, who would venture but youngsters who were totally intrepid and fired with the grace of Christ?

In the early years after the liberation bush war, these Foxfires showed remarkable courage as they went to preach and re-open churches in many remote areas where churches had been forcibly closed during the war and the pastors forced to flee. In one situation, two AE Foxfires were apprehended by a radical and embittered band of former freedom fighters. These men demanded that the AE youngsters deny Christ, which they refused to do. Finally they forced them to dig a large hole cum grave and made them stand on the edge of it.

"If you don't deny this Christ of yours, we will shoot you, and you will fall backwards into your own grave," said the guerrillas, with guns aimed at the kids.

The youngsters replied: "Shoot us if you will, but we will never renounce Jesus."

As one of the soldiers raised his rifle, the senior commander suddenly called out: "No, let them go. They are brave!"

Dream

In late 1981 Operation Foxfire was featured in one of Zimbabwe's daily newspapers. The reporter wrote: "These rural missions aim to set Zimbabwe on fire for Christ, but at the same time the young foxes are proving to be of enormous benefit to the communities with whom they live and work for two-month periods during the year."

By mid-1982, when Foxfire was only two years old, its dream of taking the gospel into remote rural areas and establishing churches of new converts was coming true. After months of hard work in identifying and establishing leaders from the new little fledgling churches, training them in how to disciple others, and in constant prayer and Bible study with them, Foxfire could report that as well as many little groupings, two sizeable congregations had sprung up out of their labours – one with 200 and the other with 400 members, no less. "This is astonishing! There was *nothing* there before," commented Orpheus Hove of AE Zimbabwe.

Soon Chris Sewell, then the AE team leader for Zimbabwe, reported that: "Demons are being cast out and people are getting healed, so that the local witchdoctors are complaining they are losing customers... The church elders decided we should withdraw from the areas until they have had discussions with the people... Sounds familiar? Look in Acts 19!"

In late 1984, Foxfire teams ventured up to the Mozambican refugees on the north-eastern border, and this proved to be the most difficult and challenging ministry so far. There was real physical hardship as they lived with the refugees in tents in unbearably hot, dry and squalid conditions. "Pray for these committed young men as they minister faithfully in this needy but much neglected field," said one newsletter.

Three years later, and Foxfire was still there. "Our Foxes are now ministering to 8,500 refugees in two large camps for Mozambican refugees just inside the Zimbabwe border. Foxfire teams help the refugees with cooking and clinic duties, and this participation gives them a platform to share their faith."

By early 1988, Foxfire had grown to eight more young men, all Bible college graduates. Trained, commissioned and sent, they fanned out across the Zimbabwean countryside to

Bindura, Masvingo, Nkai and Filabusi, to reach the unreached peoples across Zimbabwe. Their reports home were enthusiastic. "What a wonder it is to be here to see Acts 16:31 being fulfilled in front of our eyes! As one man gets saved, he is followed by his entire family! We have even been witnessing to a professional Nyau dancer (a witchcraft dancer)."

Another new church sprang up among the workers on the Rundudzi estate, near Guruve. Many there had been heavily involved in witchcraft. Now 65 people were converted, baptised and formed the core of the new church on the compound. They met each week for Sunday worship in the estate's beer hall – and then would leave before the regulars arrived to drink.

In 1992 Operation Foxfire, now becoming more urban and in line with AE's mission statement, launched a ministry to the people living in the notorious Mbare hostels of Harare. Sheckie had long felt a burden for these Mbare hostels, where 200,000 people lived, up to 20 to a small room, in a cesspool of crime, violence, drugs, prostitution and human decadence.

No one in their right mind would want to go anywhere near the Mbare hostels, but the Foxfires visited all the same. They decided to arrive amid a splash of publicity. They launched their arrival by showing a film on a huge outdoor screen. People were hanging out of the windows in the nearby barracks to see the screen, erected on the dusty ground between the barrack buildings. Some 3,000–4,000 people watched the two-hour Jesus film, based on the gospel of Luke. It was so successful that the Foxes decided to run it again – and again. In all, throughout the three night-time showings at the Mbare hostels in Harare, some 10,000 people saw the film.

It was a start. The newspapers liked what they saw. The Harare *Sunday Mail* said: "As the authorities are still scratching their heads pondering on how to improve conditions in the Mbare hostels, a Christian organisation, African Enterprise, has moved in to ease the suffering of the hostel dwellers." Soon Foxfire found some allies, and began working alongside a small Presbyterian church, many of whose people came from the hostels.

Foxfires in South Africa Too

Inspired by the example of the Zimbabwe Foxfires, the AE South Africa team decided in 1994 to adapt the primarily rural model that Zimbabwe had employed for the urban centres and schools of South Africa. Mike Odell, AE's Media Director at the time, headed up a successful pilot South Africa Foxfire programme, with Songe Chibambo assisting.

With the programme a success in 1994 and 1995, the South African team took a two-year break to seek further funding and find a fulltime Foxfire director, as Mike was being occupied more fully as acting South Africa team leader. In 1998, Greg Smerdon, a bright, dynamic young man who had committed himself to fulltime Christian service years before under Michael Cassidy's ministry, came on as Foxfire director and took the ministry to new heights.

Greg's vision and aim with the programme is to recruit young people from different denominations and diverse racial backgrounds with a vision to fulfil four fundamental objectives. (1) To empower the youth with essential skills such as trauma and stress counselling, conflict resolution, lifeskills, designing ministry events, bridge building skills, sports evangelism and many others. (2) To equip them with basic methodologies that will enhance their ability to evangelise and witness effectively. (3) To provide them the opportunity to empower other young people with the skills they have acquired. (4) To return to their local churches and multiply the skills, knowledge and experience they have acquired in the one or two years on the programme.

The Foxfires now began to venture into cities all over South Africa, primarily in schools ministry where principals, whether Christian or not, were overjoyed to avail their students of the helpful input the Foxfires brought in terms of teaching lifeskills and empowerment, talking with students during breaks and leading school assemblies. Depending on each school situation, the Foxfires would either overtly or not-so-overtly share the gospel with the students.

Then pulsating music, clever and sometimes hilarious skits, gospel dramas, personal stories and dynamic preaching rocked almost every school they ministered in. "There's a buzz in our school because of you," one school head said, echoing what other heads felt about the Foxfires. At Thalana High School in Dundee, in northern KwaZulu-Natal, where a student had previously been stabbed to death and a teacher's tyres had recently been slashed, Grade 11 pupil Temban Stuurman said that students used to swear at preachers and tease them: "I don't know what happened in these last few days though because the pupils showed you Foxfires respect, so I thank God for you... I can even see a difference in some of the teachers."

One of the difficulties in the inter-faith culture in South African schools is being direct about Christ. Director Greg Smerdon recalls that "I was lying on my bed one night and suddenly I saw a book about Gandhi. Then it struck me – if I talked about Gandhi and other great leaders, then I could talk about Jesus. Maybe this is the way to go in the new South Africa. Talk about others in order to have a platform to mention Jesus. After all His is the name above all names and using that name the Lord can work wonderful things."

Aids

One big plus of the Foxfire ministry and its access to schools is that it has enabled the team during its LifeSkills course to address the cataclysmic HIV/Aids issue, South Africa having the highest number of HIV positive people in the world. The Foxfires, rather than preaching "safe sex" and a condom culture, have stressed the importance of sexual behavioural change in the young.

"You need to embrace the Bible's way on this matter," they will say in school after school, "and that means sexual abstinence before marriage and faithfulness within marriage. This is the only way for so-called safe sex, and the only way to curtail the HIV pandemic."

During the session on sex before marriage and promoting abstinence, one of the girls, Lindiwe, kept very quiet. She stayed behind afterwards and shook her head as she said: "It's too late." Lindiwe's group leader, Nosandi Mzilikazi, comforted her and explained that it's never too late to change your ways. Nosandi explained later that she listened carefully and was really challenged by the big moral and behavioural choice she now had to make.

In one of the other groups another learner said: "I wish someone had told me all of this before. Then I wouldn't have made the mistakes I've made." She was eight months pregnant. Maybe she was HIV positive as well.

For Any Who Will Listen

While the Foxfires did a lot of school ministry, they would also seek to share the gospel with people in shopping centres, markets and central squares, as well as ministering encouragement to groups in churches. While their focus has been on young people, they seek to reach out to anyone who will listen or who has a need.

In Chatsworth, near Durban, Greg Smerdon noticed a man, wearing a Muslim koufia, who had moved towards the group of Foxfires after they finished performing a skit. Greg greeted him and introduced himself. The man responded by saying: "My name is Ahmed and I'm a very religious man." He pointed out the building where he had just been praying and then told Greg he was suffering from a brain tumour behind his right eye. This was impairing his sight. "I serve Jesus, who can heal you right here, right now," Greg responded with confident faith. Ahmed backed away when Greg offered to pray for him, fearing other Muslims would see this and thus reject him. "God isn't limited by whether you close your eyes or not," Greg insisted. Ahmed agreed and, as Greg prayed, Ahmed said "I felt three pricks behind my eye and I felt light inside." Ahmed was given some tracts and a copy of John's gospel and invited back the next day to meet with the Foxfires. He did return, greatly appreciative of his new faith and his new ability to see "crystal clear".

Radio Outreach

Foxfire teams generally travelled on bike or foot, but another AE ministry was airborne, via the talents of Abiel Thipanyane and the radio waves of planet Earth.

Though many AE evangelists have broadcasted extensively over the years, Abiel's radio ministry was the longest-running and most consistent. Abiel was a "natural" on radio, and put his talent to good use. When in March 1976 he was offered the chance to do a weekly radio broadcast on Radio Lesotho to the Sesotho-speaking people of South Africa, he snapped it up.

The radio producer's hunch had been right: soon Abiel's weekly slot on Radio Lesotho was drawing thousands of Basotho listeners each week. Letters and questions from all over Lesotho and indeed from all over South Africa poured into the studio. Abiel was thorough and conscientious: he answered each letter personally, prayed for the person, and sent them helpful Christian booklets. One listener, so taken with Abiel's voice and presentation, decided Abiel must be a cardinal or a bishop, or even the founding father of a new denomination. He wrote to ask if he could come and join Abiel's church. No such luck!

Other radio ministries also developed from the AE studios. One magazine programme called "New Life" has been produced for years by the talented David Hotchkiss. This is broadcast by shortwave through Trans World Radio and others, and it is heard across the continent as far afield as Ethiopia. Michael also began a weekly programme called "Daywatch", diligently researched by Amy Morrison. This is broadcast on nine South African stations. The programme takes its subject matter from the daily newspaper and the issues and happenings raised there, and then seeks to address them from a Christian perspective and a biblical world view.

"In many ways radio is the medium for Africa," says Dave Hotchkiss, as everyone has a radio set whereas relatively few have TV sets.

Letters from listeners to the radio programmes are often either poignant or encouraging or both. For example, a pastor from Swaziland wrote: "Every Sunday I carry a heavy load of work for my church. Thus at the end of the day I become so exhausted. Your programme refreshes me very much."

In similar vein another pastor, this time from Zambia: "I have been listening to Michael Cassidy's teachings with keen interest for a number of years on the radio."

Said one listener: "Please would you send me the notes on depression which you spoke about a few weeks ago on Radio Pulpit... I myself am suffering from depression and am on treatment." Often a programme will strike home to the exact needs of a particular listener: "Dear Mr Michael Cassidy: Thank you so much for the talk on pornography this morning. It was what I desperately needed to hear and I need to get it for my son-in-law... God in all His love gave this message to me at a very crucial and painful time in my life. Many thanks for your wonderful programmes on Radio Pulpit."

For another woman the problem was very different: "Please send me a copy of your talk on the lottery that was on Radio 7... it was very interesting to hear the facts how it was robbing us of our income. I have now not played it for weeks."

One listener from Uganda wrote in: "I am an ardent listener to your programmes on Trans World Radio. The varied programmes have helped my understanding of the Holy Scriptures and are gradually changing my life in accordance with the Word."

In Congo, AE's first team leader, Pastor Babaka, had a daily radio programme and another weekly one. This reached far and wide but especially impacted Kinshasa. In early 1998 Pastor Babaka, a Belgian-trained lawyer as well as a trained minister, took part in a project with his radio station, calling people together in a stadium to pray for this stricken country. With no other publicity than the radio, 120,000 people turned out. New team leader Nico Nteme and his team continue the radio ministry there.

In Africa, radio reaches where few other media can go. Michael Cassidy realised this in the summer of 1961 when he and Ed Gregory began their trip round Africa. The first night in Tripoli, Libya, they saw scores of people, young and old, sitting around radio sets on the waterfront. "Ed," said Michael, "radio must become integral to AE's ministry." Well, praise God, it has!

Audio-Visuals

Abiel Thipanyane, that versatile evangelist, also put his talent with the spoken word to many good uses. He helped pioneer an extensive AE tape ministry that runs countrywide today in South Africa, and even further afield. He broadcast extensively via Trans World Radio. He also helped pioneer the development of African Enterprise's early audio-visual unit.

Of course, the work of an evangelist is not always plain sailing. St Paul discovered this on his missionary journeys around the Mediterranean. But even Paul never ended up on an audio-visual oxcart! Abiel was doing ministry in mountainous Lesotho with AE's audio-visual mobile unit, which at that time was a one and a half ton truck, a caravan and an impressive assortment of sophisticated audio-visual equipment. He would then be able to move around the region, showing films and preaching to the people for about a week in villages or towns. This simple scheme worked wonderfully and many came to Christ in consequence.

However, roads in Lesotho can be perilous and at one especially deep crossing, even the 4 x 4 was defeated. Abiel, however, was not. Calmly he loaded on to his head and shoulders what he could carry, waded the river, scaled the shoulders of a low mountain, waded through another river, and then climbed the mountain slopes up to the village he was to speak at.

When he arrived, the people fell on him in a frenzy. "What kept you?! We need that equipment tonight!" It seemed the Christians had been advertising a big meeting for that evening.

Abiel explained about the impassable roads, the truck sliding off the road, and the unfordable river. Then they all rushed back to the stranded 4 x 4, someone found an oxcart, and the other equipment was hurriedly carried across the rivers and dumped on the cart and tugged up the mountainous path.

That is how the highly sophisticated AE audio-visual unit, complete with a 16 mm projector and generator, arrived on the splendour of an oxcart. And none too soon! The Anglican church there was packed to capacity. A quarter of the people had never seen a film in their lives, and the Jesus film made a great impact. Abiel showed the film again the following morning, and the church was so packed that many were standing outside.

Hospitals

Another "means of saving some" has been that of going directly to where the sick and needy are in hospitals, rather than waiting for someone to bring them to evangelistic meetings. Again, Abiel Thipanyane led the way here. It grew out of his AE role as director of Sesotho ministries. In the mid-1970s, Abiel travelled about Lesotho in the van that was his mobile mission and audio-unit. Whenever he arrived in a town, the local hospital was always on the "must visit" list of places to visit. These visits so flourished that soon invitations came in "to stay longer, even for a week".

Abiel's first mission to a hospital was in March 1975, when he visited Morija and pulled up in front of the Scott Hospital – Lesotho's oldest mission hospital. Scott Hospital had been the first base of the earliest Swiss and French missionaries when they arrived in Lesotho in 1833. So it was fitting that AE's Sesotho hospital ministry should be launched from the same site.

Abiel's programme for evangelising hospitals was ambitious and thorough. He'd organise and hold five or six meetings every day for up to a week, and by the time he'd finished, he'd have spoken to domestic staff, groundsmen, outpatients, inpatients, dispensary workers, clerical staff, nurses, senior staff, doctors, doctors' wives and pharmacists. People who were in distress were counselled at midday, between his meetings. Evenings were for large open-air meetings on the grass outside the hospital (attended by up to 400 people) before he'd go back in and do an epilogue for the whole hospital over its intercom late at night.

The response was always encouraging, and sometimes overwhelming.

In one hospital in the Transkei, directed by the great missionary doctor, Gerrit Ter Haar, a close friend of the AE work, the team had a difficult two days. Suddenly, the senior matron of nurses and the assistant matron were converted, and the floodgates broke. Abiel and Ebenezer then found, to their dismay, that as interest in the mission grew, a succession of nurses, paramedics, clerks, and school students came to the team with exceedingly complex personal problems. Very aware they were evangelists, and certainly not experts in counselling, the team prayed desperately: "Lord *you* have the answer, give *us* guidance!" At such times there was a strong sense that the Pauline gift of "the utterance of wisdom" (1 Corinthians 12:8) was being bestowed on the team.

Other Needs

Other needs invariably came to light. They ranged from family matters and sexual issues to fear of demons and coping with "the demands of ancestors".

One senior student nurse had for four years suffered severe headaches which doctors were unable to treat. Other nurses were frightened of her and avoided her because of her bad temper. She despaired, and privately feared she would go mad or die. After hearing about Jesus, she prayed, and asked forgiveness for the sins of her life. To her amazement, she found not only forgiveness, but also experienced a wonderful healing – the pain was gone and the headaches stopped. Incredulously and shyly, she was received into the loving family of God in the hospital, and at the end of the mission she was making friends with her nursing colleagues for the first time ever.

At the Cenzibe Mission Hospital the team talked with workers who admitted they struggled to give up ancestor worship. "They wanted to be Christian and follow Jesus, but at the same time, they did not dare neglect their ancestors. It seems there are many people who are Christians, but who still feel that the power of Jesus is not enough to protect them from witchcraft," said the mission report. The team sought strongly to minister to this need.

Over the years, hospitals became an important part of AE ministry. Like the missions to private schools, hospitals provided a ready-made structure both for the organisation of a mission, and the aftercare of converts. This made the effort involved well worth while, because proper follow-up and nurture could be counted on.

Lay Witness Missions

Lay witness missions, originally conceived in the United States, were another low-key, locally focused ministry which AE incorporated into its armoury, tried out, and was delighted to see proved successful in a multitude of local churches. The ministry came into AE through Zimbabwe, via a ministry called New Life For All, whose modus operandi was lay witness mission. This was an ingenious way to work with a single congregation so that the inner core of members would be renewed and refreshed and the outer fringes of the congregation would be evangelised. It was all done by trained laypeople who shared their personal testimonies and led small groups in a local church from a Friday evening through Saturday, then ending with the Sunday morning service. Chris Sewell of the Zimbabwe team, having experienced about 45 such missions, said: "I have never failed to have been touched by the love of God poured out as we saw so many people reached by this means of training lay people to share their faith and then took them into a mission situation to do it, rather than using a professional evangelist."

By 1981, AE South Africa, with the help of AE Zimbabwe, had more than 100 lay witnesses, who conducted ten to twelve missions a year all over Natal. David Richardson had joined the lay witness team in 1978 and was chairman of the organisation when AE took over its administration in 1980. David directed this new AE ministry for several years before Denys and Margaret Davis, a couple of deep piety and astonishing gifting and energy, took over the leadership. They have run scores if not hundreds of these missions which regularly have the effect of reviving and galvanising local congregations and bringing hundreds to Christ.

Over the years, Denys and Margaret have systematically trained literally thousands of lay witnesses, and conducted such missions all over Natal and beyond. Commitment was so high one dear lady even gave up defending her bowls championship in order to go on a lay witness mission!

For Denys and Margaret there was invariably a special thrill in these weekend lay witness missions when ordinary lay people were trained to share their personal testimony in a church and then given opportunity to do so. Generally they would take in a team of lay people who would share their faith in the simplest way possible in a local church which had been prepared for the mission, and then watch the impact. Somehow the uncontrived testimony of a layperson, not a professional minister or evangelist, always got through very powerfully. More than that, the impact on the probably terrified lay witnesses themselves after seeing God bless their testimony was often profound: "Amazing. The Lord can use even me."

And they would move on, transformed.

Getting to the Oldies

Early in 1998, a letter arrived at AE from a ministers' fraternal in Margate, one of the most popular holiday resorts on the south-eastern KwaZulu-Natal coast. The letter asked if AE would be prepared to undertake a mission exclusively to a retirement complex. The letter was directed immediately to Ralph Jarvis, AE's Communications Director, who had been led into a powerful ministry to seniors in local churches and old people's homes ever since he came to Christ in Port Elizabeth in 1983.

"Can we do it?" was the only question put to Ralph. It was hardly asked when it was answered, and Ralph was off to Margate, about 220 km away from AE, to start talking to the ministers working in the large Village of Happiness, with its almost 800 residents.

Ralph plunged into the deep end, not knowing how to swim in this particular pool but prepared to leave it to the Holy Spirit to show the way.

It was the start of AE's formal Seniors' Ministry, which Ralph based very firmly on Leviticus 19:32 – "Stand in the presence of the aged, show respect for the elderly and revere your God."

"As far as we were concerned that wasn't a suggestion – it was the eleventh Commandment," Ralph said. "We have stood in the presence of the elderly, we *have* shown respect in everything we've done, and, in being obedient in these two elements of this Scripture, we have revered our God. Every one of our team members brought to the ministry an extraordinary heart for the elderly and their own gifts. That made it alive and vibrant and joyful. I really believe it was the joy of Jesus that was seen in us by so many of the seniors who needed it so desperately that made the difference."

In the first four years, Ralph took teams of people from AE and ministry associates into 19 retirement complexes in South Africa, from old people's homes to upmarket villages, touching and changing lives through the simple system of love and respect linked to fun and the ability to listen and hold hands with those who, in many cases, have been rejected by their own families, dumped and forgotten.

On a Saturday about three weeks before the start of a mission, Ralph visits the town or city to train representatives of local churches in how to minister to seniors. Many of those at the training will form the mission team, or will simply use the knowledge gained to move into ministry through their individual churches.

Each mission day starts with devotions with team and residents and, where possible, staff. Tea is taken with the residents – teas and lunches are always a great, non-threatening fellowship time – and from there the team moves into gentle and sensitive one-on-one ministry. The afternoons are spent continuing to build relationships, as well as the team presenting the always-popular singalong on the Monday and a wonderful programme of stories, read by Ralph, from Tuesday to Friday. By Friday, many of the residents have committed or recommitted their lives to Christ.

It is a simple recipe for assuring the elderly of God's love and their future with him. And the oldies love it!

One old man said: "I was overwhelmed by everything the team brought to the complex. This is the first time I have attended talks like these. Ralph's team has been sent from God, who has let us know that He is alive and that we can be alive with him."

Another observed: "The whole atmosphere in this home has changed. There is now an atmosphere of love and hope. There are smiles on people's faces and light in their eyes. People aren't glaring at each other anymore!"

One woman, who was given a hug and told she was loved and respected, said: "Oh, you have no idea what it's like to hear that..."

"You're a dear person to worry about my soul," smiled one old woman to Ralph.

"I feel I have been given a fresh start," said another.

It was wonderfully gratifying when one old lady said: "I wasn't ready to meet the Lord, but after today, I am ready. Praise the Lord."

A chaplain to one old people's home said: "The complex was saturated with the love of the Lord. Extensive and deep ministry took place and people were brought into God's kingdom, others strengthened and yet others brought closer to a decision."

Says Michael:

I am so thrilled with this relatively new ministry in AE to oldies. My dear old Mum was in an old-age home for eight years, and when visiting her I was always so challenged and moved (except once when one old dear called my Mum and said, "Your *brother's* come to visit you!!") by the sight of all these old folk sitting and staring both into space and into eternity, so many of them not knowing the Lord. This new outreach in time to people on the edge of eternity is surely one of the more strategic we could be doing. My prayer is that Ralph's great work will be duplicated throughout all our teams.

The Block Buster Experiment

In 1995, when AE South Africa experimented with some decentralisation processes and sought to begin teamlets to do local ministry in major cities around the country, two of the places where this really flourished were Port Elizabeth and Pietermaritzburg. In the former, AE's core teamlet of Wellington Jansen and Shan Fox became major catalysts for gathering the church of the city together for prayer, renewal, evangelism and outreach. The Eastern Cape area had suffered much in the apartheid era and there was a great need for the churches to come together in new fellowship and relatedness in order to minister to the pain and fragmentation of this area. Anglican Bishop Eric Pike, and his successor, Bishop Bethlehem Nopece, have commented with some regularity on the amazing ability of AE's little teamlet to be catalysts in drawing the church together, the consequence of having secured a deep level of trust and confidence from pastors and clergy around the city.

As the fortieth anniversary of AE's first citywide mission in South Africa in August 1962 approached, so the idea of doing a major pan-African outreach in Port Elizabeth was put on the table and quickly secured warm affirmation. If we are thinking of the principle of "by all means saving some", then the so-called Block Buster scheme of Wellington and Shan, though developed in Argentina, is novel for AE.

By this scheme the entire city is broken down, according to the city map, into blocks one kilometre square. Research is then done into what churches and Christian resources are located in each block and then an attempt is made to connect these to the special needs of people, homes, factories, schools, or whatever exists in that block. As the Christian resources of that block are linked to the need and as the believers in that one kilometre square block come together, so they are challenged to make their own particular block the target and focus of their own witness and outreach during the citywide endeavour.

Clearly the potential is here to mobilise the church very widely and secure knowledge of the real prayer needs plus grassroots witness and evangelism on a massively decentralised basis and covering every square kilometre of the city. This is the Block Buster approach being experimented with at this time. If the model could be used so successfully in Latin America and especially Argentina, then why not in Africa?

Inner-city Counselling Centre

As indicated, the other city where decentralised AE teamlets have flourished has been Pietermaritzburg, where a significant and highly effective outreach has been developed through AE's longstanding and indefatigable Indian evangelist, David Peters. He and a largely volunteer group of seven other workers in 1995 set up an office and counselling centre right in the middle of a shopping arcade in downtown Pietermaritzburg. They called it the Lord's Counselling Room. Being right there in a shopping arcade, people are naturally attracted to the big sign. In consequence, many who are in need or trauma or even perhaps just filled with curiosity will make their way into the Lord's Counselling Room.

The extraordinary thing is that it is frequented by the most astonishing range of people, from schoolchildren, business people and city leaders, through to labourers and even witchdoctors. As a by-line, unemployed people are taught to sew and learn various handcrafts so that they can earn some money. The broken and fractured come and receive extended counselling, ministry and prayer. Even demonised people have sought the help of David and his colleagues and been delivered of demonic spirits.

From the Lord's Counselling Room, David and his crew spring forth to daily ministries around the city and business houses, in the police stations, in the hospitals, clinics, and most especially on a weekly basis, with the mayor and many of the city councillors. In early 2002 Deputy Mayor Ms Zanele Hlatswayo asked David to bring to her the leading pastors of the city to hear what they were doing and to seek counsel from them. Ministers from some 47 churches and para-church organisations met with her. This resulted in a letter from her to each councillor in the 37 wards of the city to inform them of the AE PMB team's availability to pray for them regularly as they carry out their civic duties. Meetings with the mayor in his parlour or with the city council as a whole have happened regularly. Said Ed Silvoso of Harvest Evangelism to Michael: "If you want to win a city go first for its mayor and council, even before its pastors!" This has been key in David's strategy.

Following this, another government department, that of Home Affairs, asked David and the team to come and hold weekly devotions for their staff.

To crown these endeavours and to move from the powerful to the frequently powerless, David and the team hold a weekly open-air rally down in the city centre near the Anglican Cathedral. Many people every week profess commitment to Christ after these open-air meetings.

Comments Michael:

David and his late wife Edna have been amongst the most extraordinary workers in our ministry anywhere. David's ability to operate in the power of the charismatic gifts which the Apostle Paul speaks about means that he is able to impact all kinds and conditions of people from the highest to the lowest. His gifts of healing have become legendary and when he operates in the gifts of wisdom and knowledge, by which he is able to understand supernaturally what people's problems are, it is awesome. I have seen this gift at work many times myself and been stunned. In one instance he asked a troubled woman where her mother lived. She said "Johannesburg". "Has she got a statue of a Buddha in her lounge?" asked David, "because that is what in the Spirit I see." The woman began to shake and acknowledged this to be the case. David told her that once this was removed, both she and the family's troubles would cease. And thus it was.

Yes, certainly the Lord's Counselling Room in the city centre of Pietermaritzburg has been one of the more unusual, inventive and effective vehicles of outreach which AE has produced anywhere in its many ministries.

Helping the Shepherds and Shepherdesses

Though the idea of helping in the ongoing training of ministers and pastors is not novel, no account of AE's diversified methodologies would be complete without alluding to this dimension of its work.

African Enterprise was not long into its ministry before it came up against this question. It was wonderful and inspiring to "harvest" souls for the kingdom of God, but where could you put them once you had them? No one at AE wanted to see young Christians dumped in old barns of spiritually dry churches where their tender young faith would simply dry up and wither away.

These thousands of young Christians needed teaching in healthy churches that would nurture them.

That led on to a second question: what made for healthy churches?

Well, one vital ingredient was to have clergy who were not only well-intentioned and godly, but also motivated, trained, and able to teach others. The clergy of Africa are by and large very sincere and dedicated, but many are less than highly trained and most are un-resourced, un-encouraged, and often incredibly isolated. So from the earliest years, AE team members made time in their busy schedules to help the clergy of the various regions in which they ministered. This has been done for many years throughout South Africa, where "church growth" seminars laid on by AE are now part of the landscape, largely pioneered by AE's John Tooke out of his studies at Fuller Seminary's School of World Mission Institute for Church Growth.

But pastoring the pastors has gone far beyond South African borders.

Abiel Thipanyane and his colleague Samuel Makhetha pioneered a significant ministry to the hundreds of local clergy throughout Lesotho. They began with a training seminar in 1974, and over the years Abiel held dozens more. The clergy travelled for miles to reach these conferences, always eager for further encouragement and training. It enabled them to make the most of their ministry to their far-flung congregations.

In Zimbabwe, John Tooke and David Peters led one of the

country's earliest regional pastors' seminars in June 1980. More seminars followed for local Christian leaders in Gweru, Bulawayo, Mutare and Harare, to name but a few.

The team was taken slightly aback at one conference when 50 to 60 clergymen suddenly announced that they themselves had never truly come to a personal knowledge of Christ. One admitted: "I feel I am not converted. I have been a long-time pastor, but I need Jesus myself!"

But it was perhaps in East Africa that the need for helping the clergy was most urgent. Idi Amin's eight years of terror had blown Ugandan society apart. Clergy were inundated with people whose lives had been fractured if not destroyed. The pastors had lived through the years of terror, too. They were fraught and badly strained. They needed help if they were in turn to build up their people.

So African Enterprise East Africa launched a series of diocesan clergy conferences across Uganda from 1980 onwards. At the urgent invitation of the various bishops, AE teams visited most of the dioceses in the next few years. Hundreds of clergymen and their wives came along. Such was the support for these conferences, that the provincial secretary for the Church of Uganda had been known to siphon fuel from his own car and give it to the team to get them to a pastors' conference in Kabale. Able teachers such as Edward Muhima, John Senyonyi and Geoffrey Rwubusisi, later made a bishop, spearheaded these endeavours, backed up by the multi-gifted Ephraim Gensi.

AE even staged one National Clergy Conference attended by 1,500 pastors from right across Uganda. The meeting raised their morale greatly, and as Canon James Katarikawe reported: "They caught a vision of preaching Christ to suffering Uganda."

As early as 1981, invitations were flowing in from Kenya and Tanzania from bishops wanting similar seminars and help for their far-flung, often discouraged clergy. The East African team's diary filled quickly. In fact in Kenya, at the archbishop's invitation, Bishop Festo had addressed over 1,000 pastors at Kenya's National Pastors' Conference in Nairobi. Other seminars filled up quickly in Nairobi, Nyeri and Nakuru, and hundreds of pastors came to conferences in dioceses such as Mombasa and Mount Kenya East.

In Tanzania, the bishops also opened their dioceses to

African Enterprise, including Morogoro Diocese and Dodoma Diocese. When AE team evangelist Matt Nyagwaswa, of the famously wide smile, was consecrated a bishop in the African Inland Church in 1985, more than 40,000 Christians from all over Tanzania, Kenya and Uganda came to the service to recognise him and his great gospel labours. Even the President of Tanzania, Julius Nyerere, attended.

In due time in the late 1980s and 1990s Berhanu Deresse of Ethiopia developed a training ministry for pastors from all across East Africa by which extensive input would be made into their lives, renewal of spirit achieved and encouragement given to go back into what is often a back-breaking and generally lonely task. Many came to the AE training centre in Karen, Nairobi. Many others were reached and helped when the energetic Berhanu and his colleagues took the training courses as an extension programme out to where pastors lived and worked. This took the team all round East Africa, Sudan and Ethiopia.

Later Berhanu, as AE's Ethiopian team leader, with the massive backing of the whole Evangelical Fellowship of Ethiopia, would have endless training opportunities with pastors and clergy. Indeed this would prove to be the key to AE's incredibly fruitful city campaigns in for example Debrezeit, Nazaret, Jimma, Asmara, and especially Addis Ababa where the closing rally drew 300,000 people. Always the key was the astonishing teaching and training ministries Berhanu had undertaken with the pastors and clergy.

Commented Michael: "Berhanu's set-up skills for missions were prodigious. But most important of all was the meticulous and extended training input he always undertook for months ahead of time with the ministers. This ensured some of the most effective follow-up of converts which we ever saw in the work."

In Malawi the demand for clergy conferences was also enormous. For one such conference in September of 1981, most of the clergy of the country turned out. Michael Cassidy rejoiced: "It constitutes an extraordinary opportunity to impact an entire country in just a week or so!"

In Tanzania, after an AE visit, the dean of a large church in Mwakaleli mused: "You know, for years I have tried to solve the church problems by committees. Now I see that reconciliation is much simpler!"

Zaire/Congo

Zaire was another example of a church over-stretched and under-resourced. Since 1972, when it had become a diocese, the Anglican Church in Zaire had grown from 30,000 to 200,000 in just 13 years. So the clergy caring for all these extra tens of thousands of people were stretched to the limit. With its vast distances and poor transport, isolation and lack of teaching, this was a special problem and challenge. So AE was delighted to be able to hold a refresher course for three weeks for 47 senior clergy in the spring of 1985.

AE East Africa also offered the facilities of its newly established Christian Leadership Training Centre in Nairobi for 20 of the top church leaders in Zaire to meet. Four bishops and eight archdeacons from widely spread out areas of Congo came all the way to Kenya – and were delighted just to meet one another for the first time. In classes by day they concentrated on learning the latest skills on church leadership and management, and reflected deeply on the personal life of the Christian leader. By evening, they had spent hours talking together, discussing the challenges facing them back home in Zaire.

In 2002, South Africa's Vice Chairperson, Esmé Bowers, went to Congo to visit and encourage the AE team under Nico Nteme and to help bring some extra training for women focusing on women's ministries.

Esmé had an astonishing and overwhelming time as hundreds of women turned out for her training seminars. Esmé's journal for her final day in Kinshasa records:

> This is my last big meeting and I arrive at 9.30 with the humidity higher than the previous days. Move over David Livingstone. I am sure you never had such large meetings in Africa, (2,000 women today) nor did you take these anti-malaria tablets which make one feel so queasy! The first training session is a major struggle. As I retire for refreshments I quietly take time for intercession, knowing that there is going to be a birthing of something in the Spirit. So I need to fine-tune my spiritual ear to the voice of my Master.
>
> The women are beginning to understand the implications of taking their city for God through prayer. Our final concert of prayer continued for about an hour increasing and decreasing in

decibels. We needed to end the day so I moved to the podium to draw the prayer to a close and as I stood there before these praying women God gave me a vision:

> There was a blazing fire sweeping through the city burning up all the rubbish in the city, as I looked beyond the wall of flames I saw the burnt black soil and immediately green leaves, plants, flowers and fruit began to grow so quickly I was taken aback. God showed me that He would sweep through the city of Kinshasa and would destroy the bad and restore new life to the city. The spiritual revival will bring economic renewal and peace to the city.

As I shared with the women what I saw in the vision, a holy shout went up from those assembled (I still get goose bumps when I think of this) and prayer continued in greater earnestness for the city. What a way to end three days of partnership with the Women's Desks of the Church of Christ in Congo!

Concludes Esmé: "In my spirit I sense that the city is ready for mass evangelism and the churches have confidence in AE and will partner with them in a mission. Getting the crowds and co-operation of the church leaders will be no problem."

The Challenge Continues

Over the last 40 years, literally thousands upon thousands of clergy across the vastness of Africa have been encouraged and trained through these various seminars and conferences, mostly in their own locality, and sometimes, when feasible, at the AE training centres in Nairobi in Pietermaritzburg. In all of this, AE team members had one simple aim: to help these many clergymen to "catch a new vision of Christ and the ministry".

When this happened, there was always great renewal and rejoicing.

One pastor summed it up: "I am going back to my church a new person. I am ready once again to take up the challenge of being a worker in the Harvest for our Lord Jesus Christ." And he too, no doubt, and following the Pauline preacher, would be trying in new ways "by all means to save some".

PART THREE

Word and Deed:
Striving for Holism

Chapter 20

The Deed Part of It

For I was hungry and you gave me food, I was thirsty and you gave me drink, I was a stranger and you welcomed me, I was naked and you clothed me, I was sick and you visited me, I was in prison and you came to me... (Matthew 25:35–36, RSV)

African Enterprise's reason for being is evangelism and reconciliation. There are plenty of aid and relief agencies in Africa, many of which have efficient, extensive networks, staffed by professionals and experts in relief aid.

However, there have been times in the last 40 years when such urgent needs and such desperate wants have so stared AE in the face that the teams have felt that even though relief work steps out of their primary line of expertise, something simply had to be done in Jesus' name to help relieve the suffering.

Michael Cassidy notes with approval the words of Martin Luther King, "Any religion that professes to be concerned with the souls of men and is not concerned with the slums that doom them, the economic conditions that strangle them, the social conditions that cripple them, is dry as dust religion." Michael adds: "We can go further. We can say it is false religion. Deeds are demanded of us. Words and deeds belong together – the words interpreting the deeds and the deeds embodying the words of Christian compassion."

So, over 40 years, AE has been involved in a great number of practical care projects, which express the "deed" side of things. Apart from anything else, the Mission Statement of AE commits the work to biblical holism when it says that the ministry exists to "evangelise the cities of Africa through Word AND DEED in partnership with the church." Here are just a few examples of how this has played out on the ground.

Uganda

The Idi Amin years of 1971 to 1979 were a very dark chapter in Uganda's history.

In 1971, when Idi Amin had just come to power, the Ugandan team of African Enterprise was in its infancy. Throughout the early 1970s, the East African AE team had done what it could to minister to an increasingly troubled, then terrorised society. But Uganda slowly fell apart under the government's total mismanagement.

By January 1977 the situation was critical. Thousands of innocent people were being tortured and killed. The House of Bishops gathered in Kampala to protest publicly against the mass killings. They presented a plea to President Idi Amin to respect human rights.

On 16 February Archbishop Janani Luwum was arrested, and the next day he was killed. It then became known that Bishop Festo was next on the list. Festo and his wife Mera had to flee at once, the very next day in fact. As thousands of people were dying the two Kivengeres made their way to Rwanda, then to AE Nairobi, and thence to the USA to meet the AE board there, and then equally rapidly back to the UK to confer with AE UK. There were thousands of Ugandan refugees in desperate need, and Bishop Festo was determined that African Enterprise should do something to help them.

The US and UK AE boards, along with AE Australia, began to contact people they thought might be able to help. By April 1977, African Enterprise discovered it had a new ministry on its hands: RETURN, or the "Rehabilitation, Education and Training for Ugandan Refugees Now".

RETURN was to be based in the Nairobi office of African Enterprise. John and Mary Wilson had already succoured many Ugandans coming through, but as the floodgates opened and destitute refugees poured into Kenya, they needed help. The Rev Daniel Serwanga, a gifted administrator and John Wilson's right-hand man in several large projects, had joined the AE office in Nairobi after the first PACLA Conference (Pan-African Christian Leadership Assembly) of December 1976. Dan was badly needed. As well as helping scores of bewildered Ugandan refugees, AE still had its regular work to do, and major commitment to meet that year in extensive missions in Cairo and Nairobi.

Easter 1977 was approaching. Since his flight from Uganda a few months before, Bishop Festo had travelled many thousands of miles and spoken to dozens of people in his efforts to set up RETURN. But now reaction was setting in. Although his public stance was always of Christian love and forgiveness, he also felt deep anger and bitterness taking hold within him. His beloved Uganda was ravaged, his Archbishop murdered, his home closed to him, his daughters still in Uganda and in daily danger of arrest and death. He was tired, heartsick. Friends asked him how they should pray. "Just say," he began once, "*Oh God, Uganda...*," and he trailed off helplessly.

Moment of Truth

On Good Friday Bishop Festo was alone. He walked up London's teeming Regent Street to the "BBC Church", All Souls, Langham Place, an old favourite of his. He quietly joined the congregation for the three-hour service of meditation on the crucifixion. It was the first time in weeks that he had had the opportunity of attending worship as a private Christian. Gradually his thoughts settled and he began to wait on God in prayer.

Then came a mighty moment of truth when Bishop Festo felt God facing him with his bitterness and anger. In what he would always afterwards consider the high point of his spiritual pilgrimage, Bishop Festo struggled and found the grace that could grant him charity for even Idi Amin. When peace finally came, it was "fresh air for my tired soul. I knew I had seen the Lord and been released; love filled my heart."

For the next few months Bishop Festo flew from one country to another, meeting hundreds of refugees, and referring them on to AE offices in Nairobi, Pasadena, London and Sydney.

The AE international boards soon came to realise just how big the task was going to be. They were deeply concerned as to whether they could cope. Still, the AE boards felt for Festo in his pain, and determined to do the best that they could. They sent out urgent and ongoing SOS's to their supporters.

By February 1978 African Enterprise was financing, placing and maintaining around 1,000 refugee students on university campuses the world over. (And it would do so for the next four years.)

Then the orphans began arriving: people carrying small Ugandan children turned up at AE in Nairobi to say their parents had been killed or lost. The small AE office was no place for dozens of destitute children. After frantic negotiations, Dan Serwanga found a local Kenyan orphanage that agreed to have them. This was a lifesaver, as in the following months nearly 200 children were brought to the AE office.

Support from Thousands

As time went by, the African Enterprise boards felt deep sorrow and sympathy for the Ugandans, but also considerable alarm. AE was an evangelistic association, run on an administrative shoestring. It was neither staffed nor equipped nor qualified to turn overnight into an international relief agency. Urgent top-level meetings were held between the heads of the international boards, the directors running the international offices, and Michael Cassidy and Chief Administrator, Malcolm Graham. Fortunately, other powerful Christians were willing to come alongside. By May 1978 the Billy Graham Association and the Archbishop of Sydney and Primate of All Australia, Sir Marcus Loane, were lending support to RETURN.

Bishop Festo certainly did all he could to bring in aid. On a visit to Australia that spring, he grabbed the opportunity of media interest in him as an exiled Uganda bishop. Warwick Olsen, head of AE in Australia, estimated that by the time Festo left Australia, some seven million people may have heard him talking about RETURN. It was a great boost to the AE work, which had by now received hundreds of thousands of dollars from thousands of donors.

After a time of private prayer and fellowship together early that summer, Festo and Michael summed it all up in a spectacularly understated way. "We are rather astonished at the way the work seems to be developing."

At the 1978 Lambeth Conference for Anglican bishops worldwide, Bishop Festo met up with his fellow bishops from Uganda, and heard yet more stories of misery and terror.

By now the writing was on the wall for Idi Amin, however.

That autumn, faced with increasing internal threats to his regime, including disaffection in the army, Amin tried to divert attention by attacking Tanzania. In October 1978, he sent Ugandan troops and aircraft across the border into Tanzania. After that events moved quickly. The invasion floundered, and by early 1979 things were falling apart. Thousands of Amin's troops deserted him, leaving behind such a vast array of weapons that the Tanzanians had trouble carting them all away. Other Ugandans slipped away from Amin, across the border, to join up with the exiled Uganda National Liberation Army.

Within weeks, Amin's army had been thoroughly routed. Then an indignant President Julius Nyerere of Tanzania in his turn decided to invade and liberate Uganda. For the next several weeks, the tension for all Ugandans was almost unbearable. Festo, in Nairobi for the annual AE inter-team meeting, hastily urged that they launch yet a further appeal. Whatever happened now, Uganda would be needing aid desperately. (Another £140,000 would be raised that spring alone.)

In mid-March, Nyerere, whom Bishop Festo was to describe as "the most unusual and unselfish leader on the African continent", decided that he would have to install an interim government until Uganda got the chance to hold free elections. To organise this, the Moshi Unity Conference was held in late March, and Bishop Festo, along with other leading exiled Ugandans, flew to Dar es Salaam to discuss Uganda's future and select its new leader. He was among those who approved the choice of Yusufu Lule, an elderly Muganda and former Makerere University lecturer. Lule, a Muslim convert to Christianity, had worked closely with Festo on RETURN. Bishop Festo himself was approached, with offers of high government office. Some even wanted to push him into the presidency but he smilingly refused. He was, he said, a minister of the gospel.

On Monday 9 April 1978 Amin fled Kampala with the help of Libyan friends.

On Tuesday 10 April Tanzanian troops took Kampala. It was more of a victory parade than a foreign occupation: the "occupied" Ugandans cheered, beat drums and whooped it up in the streets. Amin's regime was over; the country was now under the Uganda National Liberation Front (UNLF). International and internal support were immediate, and Lule was sworn in as the new interim president.

Returning Home

With the fall of Amin, Bishop Festo dropped everything and prepared to return to Uganda. (To the exasperation of a number of English churches, which had spent months preparing a mission with him as the guest evangelist. Congregations from Birmingham to Cambridge, London to Mersey, lost thousands of pounds in cancellation fees for big venues, but Festo for once was oblivious to all calls for evangelism: he was going *home*.)

But what a home to go to! Idi Amin had reduced Uganda, once "the pearl of Africa", to a broken, bleeding country. The people were physically, mentally and spiritually bankrupt. Fear, cruelty, corruption, betrayals, greed and violence, were everywhere.

The biggest phase of Bishop Festo's ministry was about to begin. It would absorb him for the rest of his life. If a man can be said to have his "hour" in life, Bishop Festo's hour had certainly come. For at President Lule's invitation, Festo led the call to all Uganda for national reconciliation. With his access to international aid through AE, he was asked by President Lule to be the first Chairman of Uganda's and the Church of Uganda's National Committee on Relief and Rehabilitation. In the years to come, Bishop Festo would help attract millions of pounds of aid into the country from a wide variety of sources, for the physical relief of the impoverished citizens – saving hundreds of thousands of lives. He would also point the way towards the moral rehabilitation of Uganda as he urged the reconciliation of warring factions within the country.

AE Pasadena sent its first relief shipment to Uganda only 24 hours after Amin's regime fell. Within days, a regular supply of relief was flowing into Uganda, from numerous international relief organisations, including AE.

Bishop Festo, his wife Mera and several other Ugandan bishops landed at Entebbe Airport in a gentle drizzle of rain on Friday 11 May 1979. An international welcoming committee was waiting to greet them, including President Lule, the Archbishop of Uganda, Rwanda, Burundi and Boga-Zaire,

John Stott – always a great encourager to Michael and Festo. Here during a significant ministry tour round South Africa under AE auspices. (August 1988)

Nelson Mandela and Michael Cassidy in jovial mood. Michael had just presented Mandela with a gift copy of Billy Graham's *Peace With God*, as requested and personally signed by the evangelist. (Pietermaritzburg 1992).

During Harambee '92 tour of South Africa by Pan-African AE teams, a visit was made to then President F.W. de Klerk. Here he addresses the press following the encounter with AE team.

AE South Africa team gathers to celebrate election-miracle announcement, April 19th 1994. Lois Stephenson leads worship at this miraculous and never-to-be-forgotten moment.

Muchakos Mission, Kenya. 300 missioners engage in "Operation Clean Up" and sweep streets just before the mission.

Irrepressible AE evangelist, comedian and youth worker, Jack Garratt, here as The Right Irreverend Thrutchpump, always kept thousands of youngsters (and adults) in hysterics – then won them for Christ!

Some cheerful AE Chairmen. (Left-right) Emmanuel Kibira (Tanzania), Harry Mkombe (Zimbabwe), Bishop Onesphore Rwaje (Rwanda), and Dr George Wanjau (Kenya) – 1993.

Ghana Team Leader, Dr Nii Amoo Darku challenges business leaders at the Accra Mission in 1997.

Grace Bayona Kalambo - "Amazing Grace" – in full flight! (1997)

300,000 pack in! Part of the largest crowd ever in the AE ministry - Addis Ababa Mission set up by Ethiopian Leader Berhanu Deresse – 1994.

Dr Calvin Cook, friend extraordinary to the AE ministry, opened up the first mission to Pietermaritzburg in 1962 and still serves on the South Africa board.

Team leaders gather in 2001. (Left-right) In front Antoine Rutayisire (Rwanda), Mike Odell (South Africa), Simukayi Mutumangira (Zimbabwe), Stephen Lungu (Malawi), Edward Muhima (Uganda), Berhanu Deresse (Ethiopia). At back Stephen Mbogo (Kenya), Wellington Jansen (Port Elizabeth teamlet), Nii Amoo Darku (Ghana), Michael Cassidy (International). Grace Kalambo and Nico Nteme missing.

A place where many good things happen - the AE Centre in Pietermaritzburg, South Africa.

Servants extraordinary of the ministry, Malcolm and Bertha Graham. During International Partnership Board (IPB) meetings in Dar es Salaam, Zanzibar is also explored for a mission! (1999)

Mark Manley, new South African Team Leader - 2002.

The American "Father of the Work". Bruce Bare, first Chairman of AE USA and International Chairman Emeritus, has visited Africa an amazing 57 times at his own expense. Here pictured with his wife Adaline who let him do it, plus Carol and Michael. (1999)

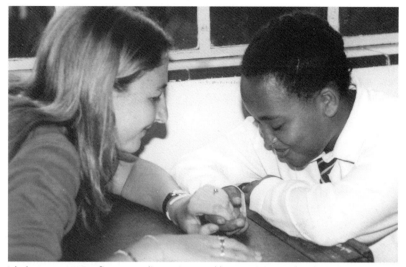

A holy moment. Foxfire evangelist Karien Jonckheere ministers deeply to a young South African scholar.

Rev Nico Nteme, Team Leader of AE Congo.

Michael's International/Pan-African Admin and Set-up Teamlet. (Left-right) Udo Krueger, Jamie and Amy Morrison, Michael Cassidy, Colleen and Ernie Smith, Brenda Harrison.

Silvanus Wani; John Wilson, and other AE team members, along with reporters from *Time*, *Newsweek*, CBS, and various film crews.

With a large umbrella over him, and a large microphone in front of him, Festo choked back his tears. "It is a great, great joy to feel the fresh air of liberty... We have... very deep wounds, deep sufferings, but Uganda is not destroyed... It is a new day!" What was needed now was the "wonderful healing love of Jesus". It was the "only antidote to the poison" of the Amin regime. And we "can't reconstruct without reconciliation"!

Reconciliation. Relief. Reconstruction. In the years to come, Bishop Festo would call them "the three Rs of AE" for Uganda.

Soon emergency relief aid from numerous governments, agencies and individuals worldwide was flooding into Uganda: medicines, food, clothing and blankets. Plane after plane landed at Entebbe each day. The planes were met by relief trucks, which then set off across the country.

But sadly, events in Uganda spiralled out of control again later in 1979. Lule was ousted, and once again complete civil chaos threatened. As if this was not bad enough, a three-year drought that affected a great swathe of Africa at this time had finally brought the north of Uganda, especially the Karamoja region, to the brink of famine. More than half of the total population of 350,000 faced imminent starvation. On average, 200 people were dying every day.

In 1980 Kevin Lyne, an Australian AE board member and office director of AE Kampala at the time, ventured north to see for himself. He came back badly shaken. "We saw people, particularly children, with their eyes set back in their heads, extended bellies, and arms and legs like matches. It was very shocking."

The famine hit world headlines: this was the worst natural horror that East Africa had ever seen.

New Priorities

African Enterprise did not step into the breach so much as plunge in, head first. With the American office behind him, Festo's cry for help was heard far and wide.

Feeding starving children was now a new and first priority. African Enterprise negotiated with the Ministry of

Education, and it was agreed that to begin with, AE would provide the children of nine schools in Karamoja and Soroti with a noonday meal for a minimum of 18 months. So AE began its Northern Uganda School Feeding Programme with 3,000 children a day.

Soon the AE School Feeding Programme had grown to 4,000 malnourished children a day.

In May 1979 Milton Obote returned from Tanzania, and the Ugandan people turned hopeful eyes to him for some leadership. But the famine continued. 1980 passed uneasily, as it was soon evident that Obote was also corrupt. AE redoubled its efforts, and soon it was feeding 9,767 children a day, in 35 schools across Karamoja. AE's Kevin Lyne and Willi Stegmaier reported that: "Instead of only two counties, as originally planned, we are supporting all boarding schools in all seven counties of the districts of Moroto and Kotido."

Truckload after truckload carried in tons of maize meal, baby food, sugar, oats, powdered milk, soybeans, cooking pots, ladles and clothing to the destitute people of Karamoja.

Meanwhile, at least there was some good news. By now most RETURN students had completed their courses in foreign universities and colleges and were returning to help Uganda, many by taking up government posts. Bishop Festo was enormously proud of them all, calling them "Uganda's most valuable natural resource". Senior Ugandan government officials later said that the African Enterprise RETURN programme had been one of the few means of preventing Uganda from being completely smashed.

By April 1981 AE had, incredibly, doubled its feeding programme yet again: "Now we are reaching 20,000 children in 75 schools a day. After just four weeks on just one meal a day, the change in them is unbelievable!"

May 1981, and African Enterprise launched a Baby Immunisation Project in Kampala.

July 1981, and sadly, Uganda was on the slide once more. Civil chaos was almost complete: little or no infrastructure, spiralling inflation, widespread violence, no rain, and cattle rustlers sweeping the country.

September 1981, and by now African Enterprise was feeding 29,500 children in over 80 schools throughout northern

Uganda each day. "Many classrooms are again bustling with activity!" But there was no end to the famine in sight, as the drought continued unabated. Bishop Festo said: "We'll need emergency relief at least into 1982 – or Karamoja will lose a whole generation."

The drought was killing people throughout Uganda and Kenya, and that year AE also distributed 200 tons of milk powder to some of the worst drought-hit areas, including the Masai, Mount Kenya, and the Nairobi slums.

By December 1981 the AE Kampala Baby Feeding Project was well underway, and gradually increasing. AE staff were also providing milk and baby food to all city council clinics.

Putting out the Blaze

Michael Cassidy wrote to African Enterprise's worldwide family, explaining what was going on:

"Any Christian organisation working in Africa will come up against the stark physical needs of people. This has happened to African Enterprise, and the crisis has temporarily diverted us from our expertise and main purpose of evangelism over to relief care, even though the bigger agencies are also at work. But sometimes, when the house is on fire, putting out the blaze comes first for everyone."

But this particular fire just raged and raged. What to do with all the orphans? African Enterprise friends in West Germany lovingly supported hundreds of them at the St Moses orphanage in Jinja. Other AE friends supported two orphanages in Kampala – Toro Babies Home and Kitgum Children's Home. AE provided hundreds more children with the opportunity of attending day care centres throughout Kampala and surrounding areas.

But it was no easy task. AE staff were by and large evangelists, not trained relief administrators. AE took on many more secretarial and admin staff in its Nairobi headquarters, and laboured under enormous strain. Staff were working feverishly trying to administer vast relief projects as well as carry on AE's main ministry of evangelism. "It all nearly blew us out of the water," said one senior AE staff member in later years.

People like Kevin and Lola Lyne were the reason why the

whole thing did not dissolve into chaos. Kevin had been a senior insurance executive and a foundation director of the Australian board of AE. In 1979 he had gone to serve as Office Director of AE's Uganda office, and he was later made the First Director of AE's Aid and Development Secretariat in East Africa. It was Kevin Lyne's administrative skills that made possible all the relief and development projects which AE undertook in Uganda and Kenya during these years.

1982 arrived, and with it, more trouble. Idi Amin had virtually demolished Uganda's once model healthcare system, and so diseases that had not previously caused problems now spread to epidemic proportions. Measles, polio and TB swept the country.

The Ugandan government turned again to African Enterprise for help. At the time, in all of Uganda there were only 420 healthcare facilities and 550 doctors for a nation of 15.2 million people. This worked out at roughly one doctor for every 27,636 people.

The Great Shoot-Out

After consultations, African Enterprise took a deep breath and at Bishop Festo's ceaseless urging, decided to try and organise an immunisation campaign. This was an extensive effort, which would involve Western medical teams treating tens of thousands of children.

The result was "The Great Shoot-Out". AE appealed urgently for help around the world, and more than 270 Christian medical doctors and nurses responded. Within months, they had inoculated thousands of children against measles and other diseases.

Rocketing inflation took a heavy toll on everyone. Kevin Lyne wrote of his heartbreak at seeing the number of babies and small children whose mothers could not even afford the local green banana, matoke. (At this time, a bunch of matoke cost more than a week's wages.) So AE managed to set up some relief aid for Kampala, and was soon feeding 6,500 helpless people a day, in addition to the more than 35,000 children a day that AE was feeding in schools across Uganda.

Archbishop Silvanus Wani, the new Archbishop of Uganda, would later write:

> African Enterprise was the first Christian organisation to bring relief goods into Uganda immediately after the war of liberation in 1979. Since then, through AE, many dioceses have received food, milk powder, medicine, second hand clothing, farming implements and seeds, so that we may start all over again. We in the Church of Uganda have welcomed the ministry of African Enterprise, not only in its relief work but also in the spiritual rehabilitation of our people.

"The Great Shoot-out" spread slowly across the country through the use of mobile clinics. By March 1982, AE doctors and nurses had reached 49 of the 100 schools targeted by the Aid and Development Office. At Mengo Hospital in Kampala, AE provided the refrigerators and cool boxes needed for properly storing the polio, measles, diphtheria, and other vaccines. By July 1982, AE's Dr Tom Weisenburger and his wife Diane had immunised 25,000 children against measles in Kigezi diocese alone. In the end, more than half a million children would be inoculated.

AE sent dozens of mattresses to Soroti Hospital, in the northwest of Uganda. When cattle raiders plundered and killed in the area, the hospital was filled with patients, and at least AE had the comfort of knowing that its mattresses were being put to immediate good use.

Overseeing the relief work was highly dangerous. AE staff worker Willi Stegmaier persisted in regular visits to the more than 50 schools throughout Karamoja where AE had feeding programmes, despite the fact that the lawlessness of the area had driven every other major international relief organisation out.

And so it went on throughout 1983 and on into 1984. AE medical teams often risked their lives to take immunisation and basic medical care throughout Uganda. AE even managed to build eight new windmills for Karamoja, to provide water for eight large populated areas. They also dug twelve shallow wells to serve villages of 500–1,000 people.

In December 1984 the Canadian government donated some of its surplus milk to AE for use in drought-stricken Kenya.

There was enough to provide five cups a day for 4,500 people for three months.

1985, and Uganda was still in torment. In the Luwero Triangle, north of Kampala, about 300,000 people were massacred in 1985 to 1986 for helping the then guerrilla leader, Yoweri Museveni, and his troops, in their struggle to free Uganda from Obote. Finally, on 27 July 1985, Uganda had another military coup. Obote fled the country after a short period of confused military rule and on 29 January 1986 Yoweri Museveni became president.

Restoration of Peace

Bishop Festo warmly welcomed Museveni, and applauded his platform: the restoration of peace, the removal of tribalism as a basis for government, and the establishment of a broad-based representative government. Bishop Festo believed that in Museveni Uganda at last had a leader who cared about the country.

An era had ended: Uganda's agony was over. As Uganda began to calm down under Museveni's sensible policies, Bishop Festo and African Enterprise's help would be needed less and less. With some sort of civil order being rapidly restored, many international aid agencies were only too happy to move back into Uganda and bring their professional expertise to helping rebuild that unhappy country. And indeed, the end of an AE era was approaching in another way as well.

In April 1986, Bishop Festo fell ill, and in May he had a tumour removed from his brain. He got well, but fell ill again at the end of 1987 with leukaemia. In March 1988 Michael went up to Nairobi to see his friend and be with him for one last time. The two men had deep times of sharing and reflection. Mera Kivengere said: "Michael, the Lord has given us Psalm 100:3: 'I know that the Lord is God! It is He that made us, and we are His; we are His people and the sheep of His pasture.' So we never forget that the Lord is God. We are in His hands and He knows what He is doing. We are His sheep and He is our Shepherd."

As Michael and Festo linked hands, as they had so often done before, and prayed, both were struggling with their emotions. They had travelled a 20-year journey together. They had

had differences at times, but their friendship was deep and their love for one another profound. They had also traversed both Africa and the world in gospel proclamation and spiritual adventure. Now their paths, they sensed, were diverging. Words were not easy, nor many. But with Mera they knew that the Lord was God, that it was he who had made them, called them and enfolded them as "the sheep of His pasture". Michael was not to be with Festo again until he preached at his great colleague's memorial service in Namirembe Cathedral in Kampala in May 1988, Festo having died on the 18th of that month in Nairobi Hospital.

Many thousands of people around the world mourned Bishop Festo, and many hundreds of thousands within Uganda. The Christians there believed he and African Enterprise had been called by God to step into the breach in the worst moment of Ugandan history and to help save the country from utter ruin.

With Bishop Festo's death, an utterly exhausted African Enterprise began to cut back on its relief work in Uganda. It handed many of its projects over to the "big boys" in relief aid, like World Vision, who were superbly equipped to do the work. The AE team felt like a little car that had been rocketing around at Formula One speeds, and was about to fall apart at the seams. The last ten years had been an exhilarating ride, answering Uganda's emergency call, but one for which, in the long term, the AE vehicle was simply not adequately built. AE had its own roads to travel, and its own urgent God-given business to which it must attend.

The Word and Deed commitment however remains, though carried out in more modest and manageable categories.

Bonginkosi

A good example of a more modest and manageable category of "word-deed" ministry was that of Bonginkosi in South Africa at the other end of the continent.

It had taken a small crust of discarded bread, tossed away into the fine red dust at a lower primary school for black South African children in Edendale, a township near Pietermaritzburg, to launch Bonginkosi.

If Bishop Festo had spearheaded the "deed" side of things in East Africa, it was two women, Daphne Tshabalela and Barbara Davies who gave the major impetus in the south. In due course Barbara became an AE team member and Daphne a board member.

It was August, 1972, and Daphne Tshabalala, the head-mistress of Nichols Primary School, was having her sandwich lunch. "Just as I was finishing, I thought suddenly of an errand that had to be done. So, still holding a crust of bread in my hand, I left my office in search of a child to send." A little boy was lying in front of her office, under a tree. Next to the child was a dog. "I threw the crust of bread to the dog, but to my greatest horror, the child jumped up, faster than the dog, to rescue that crust and eat it himself."

Daphne never got over the shock of that moment. "Like a flash of lightning, very big words stood before my eyes telling me: *There are really hungry children in this school.*"

When she learned that the child had had nothing to eat for two days, Daphne was horrified. She felt she had to do something to help. And what about the other children? Were there many others this hungry in her school? All night Daphne agonised over the incident. She had no financial resources. There was no one to whom she could appeal for help. She had only God. So next day she and some of her staff prayed. "God, perform a miracle," they pleaded. "Feed our children..."

The miracle began in a suburb of nearby Pietermaritzburg. Barbara Davies, a white housewife, was just finishing knitting the second of two sweaters for her housekeeper's children. As it happened, they were also pupils at Nichols School at that time. The sweaters created quite a stir, and one of the teachers timidly sent a simple message to Barbara: would she be willing to help other children with their needs? Barbara had been seeking guidance about what God wanted her to do, and went to see Daphne and the school.

"I was horrified, the first thing I saw was a classroom with open, gaping holes for windows, and the children, many without even a jersey, were huddled around a fire trying to keep warm." Then, to realise that many were also severely under-nourished, was almost unbearable to Barbara. "I knew God had spoken. I couldn't return to my comfortable home in Maritzburg, have a hot cup of tea, and say, 'Shame, what a pity children are starving in Edendale,' without doing something about it."

Barbara knew this task was from God: she was to help these desperately needy children.

So the feeding programme was launched. Through the support of Christians at Barbara's white church, a slice of bread plus a cup of enriched soup was given each day to the 30 neediest children. (On the first day, one little girl would only drink the soup; she hid the bread under her dress to take home to her little brother, who was also starving.)

Within a week, Daphne saw these children, who had been so sluggish and apathetic, suddenly wake up. They were revitalised, energetic and at last, eager to learn.

"What shall we call ourselves?" Barbara wondered. "Bonginkosi!" said Daphne. "It is Zulu for 'Praise the Lord'. After all, isn't that what we say every time we see a child fed and happy!"

In the years that followed, Bonginkosi grew rapidly, until it was feeding several hundred children a day. Costs were kept to a minimum because all the work of preparing the lunches was done by volunteers. For years Barbara Davies co-ordinated the women, black and white, who did the daily work.

Always a Need

The need was always there. With the high unemployment rate among black people in the urban areas (about 50 per cent) there were well over 32,000 children dying in South Africa each year from malnutrition-related diseases. One-third of children under fourteen were underweight for their age. For some children, a Bonginkosi lunch was the only meal they received all day. As one teacher observed: "Without Bonginkosi many of these children would have been in their graves instead of in these classrooms."

Instead, through this child enrichment programme, many young children in the black townships had a chance to progress in their studies, despite their impoverished backgrounds.

For the first five years of its existence, Bonginkosi was run by Daphne and Barbara and friendly volunteers. Then in 1977, when Barbara had joined AE as a team member, Bonginkosi came to the attention of the team. Michael Cassidy had been feeling that God wanted AE to reflect in its own ministry the dimension of Christian love expressed in action, and was pondering what to do. To take on the burden of Bonginkosi was John Tooke's idea. "Why doesn't African Enterprise share the vision of Bonginkosi with other congregations and schools, which could be encouraged to start their own Bonginkosi programmes?"

Team member Ebenezer Sikakane, who himself lived in Edendale, agreed. He pointed out that as long as Bonginkosi remained only at Nichols School, the people of Edendale would think Barbara and Daphne were doing it just out of friendship. If strangers like African Enterprise took it on, the Christian aspect to their motivation would be more obvious and doors would also open for gospel proclamation.

So it was that Bonginkosi became the caring-action dimension to African Enterprise's ministry. Daphne and Barbara were delighted. AE could offer them such resources! Administrative support, financial support, and publicity. Through AE contacts, invitations to come and talk about Bonginkosi spread far and wide.

Soon, because of AE involvement, there were Bonginkosi feeding programmes elsewhere in Edendale, as well as at Rietvlei, Imbali, Ashdown and Eshowe, as more churches joined the scheme.

Bonginkosi continued to run itself by linking willing churches of any race or denomination with needy schools. Churches thus sponsored specific feeding schemes. One happy spin-off of these "pairings" was that deep and lasting bonds were forged between whites and blacks who were "neighbours", but who otherwise would never have even met.

By August 1978 Bonginkosi was feeding nearly 1,000 children a day. By the beginning of 1980, numbers had grown to 3,000 children a day. That year the numbers tripled, so that by the end of 1980, Bonginkosi had over 40 workers, feeding 8,000 children a day locally and another 1,000 in rural areas of Natal. Also, by now four schools had a basic weekly healthcare service staffed by voluntary nurses, both black and white.

Wider Partnership

The Bonginkosi partnership did not stop in South Africa. Fellowships of Christians who heard about the programme through AE, and who wanted to support it through prayer and giving, sprang up in England, Germany, Switzerland, Canada, the USA and Australia. One woman in England got married and asked that instead of wedding presents any donations be sent instead to Bonginkosi.

In time, three "branches" of Bonginkosi developed: a small resource centre (of teaching materials), some healthcare and education in the community, and the Bonginkosi Home for abandoned children and orphans.

Then a Bonginkosi worker saved the lives of two children when she found them with their mother by the banks of a river with nothing but a packet of mouldy bread and bits from trash bins. It only strengthened Daphne and Barbara's determination to establish a community centre for destitute women and children, where they could find food, clothing and at least temporary housing.

So in April 1982 the two women set off for the United States to share their plan for the Thuthuka Centre with churches from Tennessee to Washington, Massachusetts to California.

By now, Bonginkosi was daily feeding 13,000 children in dozens of schools in black South Africa. There were also various first aid clinics and self-help groups springing up. A Bonginkosi pre-school was even set up, to care for toddlers whose mothers worked as labourers in the fields of the local farms.

Tragically, Daphne died suddenly of lung disease in 1983, before the Thuthuka Centre was fully running. Barbara was heartbroken to lose her dear friend, but knew that the Bonginkosi project must carry on. They had built something very precious in Bonginkosi.

As Daphne had said, "In a country like South Africa, where black and white are standing apart, the Lord wanted a way, a practical way, that he could use to make it possible for us to cross the barrier. So he gave Barbara and me Bonginkosi, to do together..." Barbara in her turn had come to see the depth of hurt suffered by the blacks. "Bonginkosi hadn't the power to change the laws which separated us, but we each had the power to change the *attitudes* which separate us. God had called us to work together and to reach each other's hearts."

Bonginkosi gave enormous benefits to the giving churches and receiving schools, never mind the children. These black/white adult partnerships provided avenues for reconciliation. Under the banner of Bonginkosi, churches and concerned Christians linked hands with needy black schools, teachers, parents and children. As these congregations gave food, clothing and medical assistance, they began to build relationships. White Christians visited a school in Mamelodi to ask the principal what he needed to help the children of his school. "Our hearts were touched when we saw tears come to his eye as he realised that his prayers for the children were being answered."

Also giving herself day and night to this work for years was Lesley Richardson, wife of the intrepid David, AE's mission set-up director, who threw herself into this venture and shared its needs far and wide. When Barbara stepped down as director in early 1985, Leslie took over and together with Patrick Zulu and Dorcas Mkhize pressed the vision forwards, at the same time establishing a companion children's project called TREE (Training and Resources for Early Childhood Education). TREE operated initially under Bonginkosi and then was released to fly on its own. Lesley built up a staff and trained over 200 pre-school teachers and eight teacher-trainers before she and David left for Canada at the end of 1991.

The Church of the Ascension in Hilton, Natal, Michael's home church, also made contact nearby in the impoverished valley of Sweetwaters with unemployed mothers and grandmothers of the children in the schools where they were providing soup. Sarah Dottridge and Carol Cassidy still do this work along with other volunteer helpers from round about. Together they work to provide a means of income for these women. The mothers and grandmothers have been taught how to crochet blankets and also make hats from plastic bags, which are then sold locally. The extra income helps many to find some relief from their extreme poverty. Likewise, Pat Caldwell, also an initiator of this programme, now teaches other women to make candles as a self-help project .

From Small Seed to Large Tree

By 1990, the small seed planted by Daphne and Barbara in 1972 with 30 children had grown into a large tree, like the parable of the mustard seed. An impressive 10,500 children a day in 51 schools throughout South Africa were receiving a cup of protein-enriched soup and a thick slice of wheat bread as a result of the Bonginkosi ministry. Weekly medical clinics treated injuries, scabies and malnutrition. Helpers visited homes to teach health education and deliver clothing, blankets and emergency rations. Home-making skills were taught at sewing clubs, while gardening, soccer and choir clubs kept the boys busy. Wherever possible the gospel was also shared and a spiritual message presented.

In August 1992 Bonginkosi celebrated its 20th anniversary, and who better to do it with than Dumisani Majozi, who'd been a little boy at the school when it all began. Twenty years before, in 1972, Dumisani Majozi, from a wattle and daub hut, was sleepy and dull in school – failing everything from sheer lethargy born of hunger. Then Bonginkosi began, and within six months he had gone to the top of his class. He worked hard, kept going, and ended with a Masters degree in Counselling Psychology. Twenty years on from Bonginkosi, and Dumisani was personnel manager of a large company in Durban. Without Bonginkosi he would have ended up on the streets, destitute, or dead.

Bonginkosi flourished in this manner right until the South African elections of 1994, when the government took over the feeding of its schoolchildren from charitable organisations. However Bonginkosi is being revived in AE South Africa as the "Bonginkosi Support Programme for Children at Risk" to focus now on the desperate needs arising from the Aids pandemic ravaging South Africa, and especially KwaZulu-Natal, possibly the most severely affected area in the world. With 750,000 South African children already orphaned, and the figure set to climb to three million in the years ahead, the Bonginkosi contribution, via a networking of partnerships, could be truly significant.

The Deed Stuff Goes On

We have highlighted two major stories in two major arenas of the ministry, but what Bishop Festo, Daphne Tshabalala and Barbara Davies, as AE's "deed pioneers" planted in those early years has by philosophical and theological commitment, by intention, and by compassionate necessity, continued and spread throughout all the sectors of the ministry.

Indeed, all kinds of other projects expressing this commitment have continued under AE's Aid and Development Department, much of it in the last seven or eight years directed out of AE's Australia office by Mike Woodall and Ethiopian refugee Mehretab Tekie. One of their most impressive endeavours has been the Kwimba Reforestation Project carried out in conjunction with the AE team in Tanzania. This project, largely financed by AUSAID, the Australian government aid agency, has focused on Kwimba, an area in north-west Tanzania, east of Lake Victoria, which was in the process of turning into a desert. With their crops, livestock and livelihood gone, the people were desperate and were moving into towns where there was no work, and thus aggravating the urban problem.

The AE Tanzania team made a cry for help and Mike Woodall, Mehretab Tekie and others responded. This resulted in a reforestation project in which some eight or nine million trees were planted over a number of years. This brought about a total transformation of the area. As people came back they were also evangelised. How chuffed then were the Tanzanian team, Mike Woodall and Mehretab when the Australian government declared AE's Kwimba Project one of the best and most professionally handled reforestation projects they had seen anywhere in the world. This was certainly a feather in the cap of the Directors, Brian Polkinghorn and Anthony Muyengi. Muyengi is the new director for the "Magu Food Security Project", another reforestation scheme to help threatened people sell wood to buy food.

Just north of Tanzania in Kenya a very different kind of venture was embarked on in the slum city of Mathare Valley on the edge of Nairobi. There destitute women and children are taken off the streets and taught crafts of sewing and crochet work and at the same time are brought to Christ and discipled.

Next door to Kenya in Uganda, the team there has kept up Bishop Festo's great tradition with a whole catalogue of projects ranging from Aids awareness and helping Aids orphans through to the great Nile Vocational Institute established near Jinja near the source of the Nile. Here young men and women are trained in the practical skills of carpentry, electrics, bricklaying, building, sewing and many others.

Just an hour's plane ride from Entebbe in Uganda is the Rwanda team with its great projects of caring for some 2,700 orphans and 900 widows.

Jumping across the continent from east to west, we find the Ghana team caught up similarly in a tremendous scheme for street kids. Some 200 street kids are financed over some three years by AE as boys learn a trade and the girls take a three-year course in hairdressing or sewing. When the girls graduate from the sewing class, they are given a fine sewing machine which enables them to go out and earn an honest living, many of them having come off the streets or from totally destitute families.

When Michael Cassidy visited the Ghana team in 1997 and was shown these projects, one of the recently graduated hairdressers, and now an instructor, gave him a fancy haircut while an amused team leader Dr Nii Amoo Darku took a photograph to prove that it was for real! Following the citywide mission to Kumasi, when some 40 prostitutes were converted and brought to Christ, AE got one of its most worthwhile endeavours underway in a three-year discipling, rehabilitation and training project for these young women.

Says Clement Somuah, Chairman of the Ghana board, "These are amongst the most useful and creative projects which our team has undertaken and they are much appreciated by the wider community."

Moving south, similar "deed ventures" have been undertaken in both Malawi and Zimbabwe while in South Africa a three-year diploma course in Social Empowerment and Community Development, developed by Dr Marilee James and Marit Garratt, and now run by Mbulelo Hina of AE South Africa has proved not only incredibly popular but highly effective. Students come several times a year over a three-year period to do short-term intensives of academic input before going back to their communities to work out that input practically in a wide assortment of projects. The annual graduation ceremony at the AE centre is always a proud moment for these folk, their families, and especially for Mbulelo.

Future

As the AE ministry moves into the future, albeit primarily as an evangelistic endeavour, nevertheless it remains cognisant of the Lord's celebrated challenge in Matthew 25:37–40 when he speaks of that Final Day of Judgement with the righteous asking: "Lord, when did we see Thee hungry and feed Thee, or thirsty and give Thee drink? And when did we see Thee a stranger and welcome Thee, or naked and clothe Thee? And when did we see Thee sick or in prison and visit Thee? And the King will answer them, 'Truly I say to you, as you did it to one of the least of these my brethren, you did it to me'" (RSV).

"Pray for us," says Michael Cassidy, as he speaks to AE friends around the world. "Pray that we will not fail our Lord by being so heavenly minded that we are of no earthly use, but also that as we carry out the deed side of our gospel, we may not ever fail faithfully to be bringing people spiritually to a personal knowledge of Jesus Christ as Lord and Saviour. Keeping the balances – that's the challenge!"

Chapter *21*   # Gather My Saints
Together Unto Me

One of the scriptures which has always meant much to African Enterprise is Psalm 50:5, where the Lord speaks to the Psalmist saying: "Gather my saints together unto me."

For African Enterprise, this Old Testament injunction reflects the heart and desire of God in a special way. He wants his people together. In the New Testament this is reflected in Jesus' High Priestly prayer that his disciples "may all be one... so that the world may believe that thou hast sent me" (John 17:21, KJV).

For this reason, Michael Cassidy and the AE team made inter-church co-operative evangelism their basic style and philosophy of outreach. "We wanted even our evangelistic endeavours to be catalysts in drawing the Body of Christ together."

All down the years, one of African Enterprise's major contributions has been its ability to gather the church on probably the widest basis it has ever been gathered in Africa. In reality AE's ecumenical conferences have drawn from left, right and centre in the church and this has been significant and often without precedent. Rev Tom Houston, then Director of the British and Foreign Bible Society, said in 1979 after SACLA (the South African Christian Leadership Assembly) that "in terms of representation, the conference was a far more ecumenically advanced experience than anything I have seen before in the UK or USA".

Said Tom: "You people got together the fundamental, the sacramental and the sentimental, and that's quite an achievement!"

The need for drawing the Body of Christ together had been brought home to AE quite forcibly during Mission '70 in Johannesburg. Although some 300 churches throughout the great metropolis had participated, and a staff of 40 fulltime workers had come together to tackle the city, Johannesburg still nearly lived up to its nickname as "the graveyard of evangelists".

Certainly AE found it tough going. Michael would later write (*Prisoners of Hope*, page 23):

> For although many things went splendidly... yet there was failure too. The meetings in the great African townships of Alexandra and Soweto were poorly attended. Mission '70, we were told, had started in a white man's world and could not therefore succeed amongst Africans... Above all, we saw evangelism torpedoed time and again by the inertia of the local parish. Ministers gave the impression of being tired, bogged down and trapped in the web of ecclesiastical machinery. Some had despaired of moving and motivating their laity to active witness... others admitted having lost their message. Here and there clergy spoke of leaving the ministry... many felt alone and isolated. On top of everything was the overwhelming complexity of the race problem. Should one be protesting about injustices? Or was it enough to restrict oneself entirely to presenting a personal gospel?... Our hearts went out to clergy and we became committed to them as never before...

After Mission '70 in Johannesburg, Michael and the team prayed about what the next big step should be for AE. They felt strongly impressed from God to branch out on a new venture: "The Word came through to us so clearly to try and call together the whole Church of South Africa to speak to the nation."

It was an enormous task. One of the first people Michael Cassidy shared it with was John Rees, chairman of Mission '70. John Rees was a deeply committed Christian layman with a passionate social concern. When a few months later John Rees was appointed General Secretary of the South African Council of Churches, it became the first vital step towards realising a church congress. For now the two men most deeply concerned for the congress were leaders of two organisations of the churches of South Africa. The South African Council of Churches' constituency comprised the mainline denominations and their official leadership. African Enterprise's constituency by and large took in the more evangelical and Pentecostal elements within the South African church, but had the confidence and trust of most of the mainliners as well. This made it possible to mount this first major congress under the combined sponsorship of the two organisations. Rees became Chairman and Michael his Programme Director. A cross-denominational committee took on the task of steering it all.

The South African Congress on Mission and Evangelism

The South African Congress on Mission and Evangelism was set for 13–22 March 1973 in Durban. In the lead-up to it, just about everything that could go wrong *did* go wrong. It was hardly a mystery as to why: in wanting to hold the first ever residential inter-racial meeting of Christians on South African soil, AE was driving a cart and horses through the maze of legislation the South African government had in place to protect "the South African way of life" (for whites)!

Because of governmental non-cooperation and even opposition right up to cabinet level, everything was a struggle. No venue could be found where the congress could meet and be housed inter-racially. Hotel after hotel refused. Then all overseas speakers to the congress (including Billy Graham, Leighton Ford and Michael Green) were barred from entering South Africa.

Michael Cassidy wrote to Dr Ted Engstrom, then chairman of AE's increasingly anxious USA board:

1. The Congress goes forward regardless. Nothing whatever will prevent its taking place.
2. There is no need for panic from anyone. We are working on the "powers that be", and things are in hand... If necessary we will make other plans, even if these are less than ideal.
3. No one must withdraw or waver at this stage. We have our hand on one of history's levers and we have no intention of letting go. Nor must anyone else. South Africa could be at a crossroads and with faith, courage and an iron-will, we could under God, press the country down the road to life rather than destruction. Pray with us that our efforts will avail. (*Prisoners of Hope*, page 36)

In anguish of spirit at the barring of all overseas speakers, congress leaders turned to God in prayer. Michael was given the verse: "No weapon that is fashioned against you shall prosper and you shall confute every tongue that rises against you in judgement" (Isaiah 54:17, NRSV). So he, John Rees, John Tooke, David Bosch and the congress team pressed on, and strongly petitioned the prime minister, among others. They simply refused to take no for an answer.

Slowly all the government resistance and red tape stretched and finally broke. Written permission was given for non-racial accommodation in a Durban hotel, permission was given for inter-racial bussing, and all overseas speakers were finally allowed into South Africa. After months of grief, Michael Cassidy and John Tooke spent the first morning of the congress in a state of delighted disbelief and thankfulness to God that it really was happening all around them, after all.

The congress took place as scheduled from 13–22 March 1973. Eight hundred delegates from most South African denominations came together, though Dutch Reformed involvement fell through at the last minute, and the Pentecostals were not strongly represented.

The major aims of the congress were, firstly, to *hear together* the proclamation of the gospel. The top evangelists in the world shared their understanding of the gospel from their hearts, with moving results. Secondly, the South African Christian leaders would explore together the relevance of the gospel and the meaning of mission and evangelism *in present-day South Africa*.

Seminal Experience

The congress was a profound happening and what many would afterwards call "a seminal experience". Michael wrote later: "By a myriad miracles of grace, there were no incidents, and even the huge Billy Graham rally with some 50,000 people present in Kings Park went off without a hitch. One of the municipal bus drivers was so intoxicated with the joy of the inter-racial bussing that he gave his heart to Christ and put up a sign outside his bus: 'If you want to praise the Lord, ride my bus!'" There were many similar heartwarming stories of how black and white Christians found fellowship together for the first time ever, not without tears, anger, confrontation and brutal honesty, but with Christian love as well. At first there was no real dialogue, just intersecting monologues. Said one black delegate: "We all came along with our own eggs. Tentatively we put them into one basket. But we did not get an omelette." But that changed as the nine days went by.

"This conference is taking the South African church by the shoulders and shaking it into the future!" wrote one news reporter about the congress.

For the church in South Africa, the Durban congress was a major milestone. For the first time ever, the bulk of South Africa's spectrum of Christians had come together. The Durban congress drew the so-called evangelicals and the so-called ecumenicals together with everything in between: the pietists and activists, verticalists and horizontalists! Michael wrote: "They met together, prayed together, wept together, agonised together, and not surprisingly, grew together. Each learned from the other and to my mind gave birth in those days to a new Gospel *holism*, which has to greater or lesser degrees in different sections been a mark of the South African church ever since."

Church historian Dr John de Gruchy of Cape Town University wrote afterwards:

> Five years as an ecumenical globe-trotter has provided me with a reasonably wide experience, but I have never experienced or imagined possible what occurred in Durban from March 13th–22nd, 1973. Eight hundred people of virtually every racial, theological and ecclesiastical variety found in Southern Africa, together with visitors from East Africa, Europe and North America, confronted each other and ended up by discovering one another as members of the one Body called into fellowship for the sake of the gospel in the life of the world. This does not mean that all is now well and that the kingdom has finally arrived in our midst. It does not mean that everybody ended up in agreement, that tensions are no more, that theological differences have been overcome and rendered obsolete. No. It means that the Body of Christ is greater than any one of its constituent parts, and that the healing power of the gospel is more potent for personal and social change than any one of our own unavoidably partial interpretations of it.

No Cheap Victories

De Gruchy went on to stress that he did not believe:

> that any cheap victories were won at the Congress for I believe that the experience of living together, praying together, and wrestling with the issues together, was an intensely demanding exercise. The triumph is that it was not an exercise in futility but in repentance, forgiveness and conversion in totally unexpected ways. Without drafting, debating or passing one resolution (surely a record in itself), I have seldom experienced the sense of resolution that was present during the final few days. Conservative evangelicals spoke of socio-political issues with a deep-felt concern such as I have rarely heard: socially-concerned ecumenicals spoke about personal evangelism as though it were the most obvious priority in the life of the church today; Pentecostals seldom mentioned Pentecostal experience but spoke profoundly on forgiveness. And that was all right because charismatic Anglicans and Catholics took over where they left off!

Dr Gruchy concluded his reflection:

> And what about blacks and whites? The fellowship was there, the confrontation was there, conversion was there, possibilities were there. No evaluation dare be made at this moment for reality is here and now. All I know is that some black brother has offered me his eyes and ears so that I might see and hear things to which I have hitherto been blind and deaf (*Prisoners of Hope*, pp. 160–161).

My Brothers, I Need You

Many felt the same. For some, it all came to a head as John Gatu of Kenya spoke near the end of the congress: "I want you now," he said, "to turn to the neighbour on your left and right and say: 'My brother, my sister, I need you.'" With profound emotion congress delegates began to move amongst one another, usually seeking out their "problem" person and saying "My brother, my sister, I need you."

Here at last were Christians of all racial shades and stripes and all denominational shapes seeing themselves as complementary parts of the Body of Christ. Here were genuine children of God beginning to experience their glorious liberty.

No wonder this was a seminal moment for the South African church.

The Rhodesian Congress

At the Durban Congress in March 1973, there were as indicated, Christian leaders from other countries and quarters of Africa and beyond.

Thus, for example, there were participants from Rhodesia (now Zimbabwe) and from Kenya. Out of the involvement of Gary Strong (then director of a lay training movement called New Life for All) and Phineas Dube from Rhodesia came a similar congress in Bulawayo in May 1976, with AE helping and facilitating.

The Rhodesia Congress hoped to provide an eleventh-hour opportunity for the Rhodesian church to find its role in the sociopolitical crisis then gripping the country. All trust between black and white political leaders had broken down. Blacks were turning to violence and whites to intransigence.

Christians in Rhodesia were themselves deeply divided over the political issues. And so, as the African Enterprise teamlet of Michael Cassidy, John Tooke and Ebenezer Sikakane set off to take part in the congress, they asked for special prayers. "The Rhodesian Church must put its own house in order..." believed Michael. "Christians must become catalysts par excellence in the on-going process of bridge-building. Never forsaking the way of love, they must also stand for justice, human dignity, peaceful change and everything that love demands."

Called "The Rhodesian Congress on Evangelism in Context", the gathering aimed to look at the complexities of carrying out realistic evangelism in an atmosphere of a developing guerrilla war and a confused population. Discerning Christians were concerned to see that evangelism still be carried out in a context of bitter conflict and uncertainty. Prominent local church leaders presented papers on a variety of subjects relating to the nation and its spiritual and social needs. The issues of political involvement by the church was very much on the front burner and a source of tension and considerable debate.

As the congress had such strong political overtones, we will have cause to return to its method and message in the chapter relating to AE's involvement in the political process.

But suffice it for the moment to register that the seminal and consequential outflow from Durban was not just local, but international as well.

Thus was born in similar fashion yet another mighty congress and coming together of the Body of Christ, this time in Kenya and involving the church right across the continent of Africa.

PACLA (Pan-African Christian Leadership Assembly)

Amongst those who came from East Africa to the Durban Congress in 1973 were Dr David Barratt, the famous Christian missiologist and statistician then resident in Nairobi, and also the Rev Dr John Gatu, the senior Presbyterian leader in East Africa. It was Gatu who had challenged the South African congress members to move to one another and say: "My brother, my sister, I need you." Up in Kenya, Michael went with John Gatu to share the South African experience with John Mpaayei, Director of the Bible Society of East Africa. Mpaayei got excited as Gatu and Cassidy shared the vision of gathering the church from all over Africa and from all sectors. Clearly the Durban experience had been one of tremendous learning and mutual discovery for different sectors of the Body of Christ. This was critical for South Africa at that moment. But how much more critical for the wider continent as a whole. So what would happen if Christian leaders from all across Africa came together for the first time ever to share their perspectives, to seek reconciliation, and have time for reflection and evangelistic strategising? It was a heady dream.

Festo Kivengere also warmed greatly to the idea. He and Michael decided to share it with the wider AE team soon to meet in Glion, Switzerland, just prior to the great Lausanne Congress on World Evangelisation of July 1974.

It was an excellent opportunity to discuss the vision of a pan-African gathering as AE teams from South and East met for a week of team reflection and planning. When all greeted the idea warmly, Festo and Michael went on to present the notion to a specially convened meeting of all the other African delegates at the Lausanne Congress itself. It was certainly a time for dreaming big dreams: 3,700 Christians from 150 countries had met to consider the challenge of *world mission*. "The thought of a Pan African gathering commended itself as from the Lord, and we all went to work," recorded Michael's journal.

The PACLA (Pan-African Christian Leadership Assembly) committee which convened later that year in Nairobi included internationally known African church leaders such as the Rev John Mpaayei, the Rev John Gatu, the Rev Gottfried Osei-Mansah (Chairman), Dr Don Smith, Dr Ken Tracey, Rev Eliazaro Ouma, Rev John Tsuma, the Rev Daniel Serwanga, the Rev David Gitari, Graham Carr, Bishop Festo Kivengere and Michael Cassidy (as chairman of the programme committee). The Rev John Wilson of the East African AE team, fresh from his Anglican ordination and Masters degree in Missions from Fuller Seminary, was made the co-ordinator of PACLA.

Obstacles to the approved vision of PACLA were not so much political, as in South Africa and old Rhodesia, as theological. From the start, getting PACLA off the ground was a nightmare. Its first aim of simply gathering "Africa's rising Christian leadership from all walks of life" nearly died right there. Never mind meeting in order to "renew, revive, inspire, and challenge" themselves – simply meeting *at all* had Christians in many sectors across Africa crying out in alarm.

Michael would later describe it thus:

> "People to the left and right of the theological spectrum hit panic stations about a centrist gathering, even though its theological base was 'an open evangelicalism'." Michael's file of letters on PACLA preparation, he recorded afterwards, "will one day be worth a few thousand dollars to some rash or weak-minded PhD student wanting to do a thesis on African ecumenics in the mid-20th century! In fact, the depressing file will show how necessary PACLA was!" (*Together in One Place*, page 26)

"Too radical!" cried some. "Too conservative!" cried others. "Too evangelical!" "Too ecumenical!" "Too Pentecostal!" "Too liberal!" ("Too *hysterical!*" was AE's exasperated conclusion.)

For weeks many invited participants held back from giving a verdict on their participation. Financial support was also blocked as misunderstandings, misinterpretations and misconceptions abounded. On just one of many trips, co-ordinator John Wilson travelled throughout Central and West Africa trying to communicate the vision of PACLA. From Senegal to Dakar, from Guinea Bissau to Gambia to Niger and Upper Volta he went, talking, reassuring, answering endless suspicious questions. With his gracious spirit and diplomatic skills he was just the man for the job. Also his deep knowledge of both the ecumenical and the evangelical postures across Africa stood him in good stead.

Sabre rattling from church leaders on all sides, however, continued. But slowly, surely, "over it all was the glorious sense that God was in PACLA. He was overcoming the obstacles... He was helping all of us with our pride and prejudices... Meanwhile, from all over Africa, leaders from the evangelical side and from the ecumenical side were finally preparing to come to PACLA!" (*Together in One Place*, page 32)

Getting nearly 800 people from 49 countries together in one place was in itself a task of daunting proportions.

First there were immense communication difficulties. Letters were posted and never seen again. Even cables went astray. Speakers whom the PACLA committee thought had been firmly booked for months did not even know they had been *invited* up to four weeks before the actual event itself.

Travel, too, was a nightmare. Whole airliners had to be chartered. Would the planes be filled or fly empty? Block bookings of air tickets also needed to be made on regular airlines, all of which cost tens of thousands of dollars, on behalf of people whose travel arrangements remained obscure or even completely unknown. Finally Titus Lwebandiza of AE Tanzania set off on a major safari round Central and West Africa to tie up loose ends – and loose ends there were! Airline? What airline? Tickets? What tickets?! Titus had a major job on his hands.

Financial headaches set in daily. Some $400,000 was needed to run PACLA, with $150,000 coming from Africa itself. In spite of many generous donations, the congress committee was still short of $130,000 right up to two weeks before PACLA began. Urgent last minute fundraising and prayers solved that one.

Michael Cassidy and Chris Smith worked 18 hours a day for weeks on the programme trying to finalise speakers, brief them and tie up a thousand loose ends.

Finding accommodation for the participants, as well as enough rooms for plenary sessions and smaller meetings, was also a challenge. Here Dan Serwanga, office manager of PACLA and soon to join AE, came into his own, along with prodigious help from South Africa's Bertha Graham, Malcolm's wife. Dan's administration skills and capacity for sheer hard grind when it came to chasing venues became legendary. Only occasionally did he snap: such as when one caterer announced he would want his staff to lay several hundred tables in the plenary hall *during* the plenary session before lunch!

Visas for 80 South Africans were a particular nightmare and were only granted at the very last minute, when all the South Africans were actually waiting at Johannesburg Airport to board their flight. This had come about through the zero-hour intervention of Kenya's Attorney General, Mr Charles Njonjo.

Intense Excitement

By Thursday 9 December 1976 the moment had come. For the staff, who had been working 17 and 18 hours a day for weeks to make it all happen, excitement was intense. Planeload after planeload arrived from every corner of the great African continent. And this despite numerous horror stories of incomplete documentation, lost passports and flights changed, cancelled, or altogether vanished.

In the end the biggest relief of all for congress organisers was that the chartered planes were all full, though few passengers had confirmed their flight places! Organisers also found that most of the stewards, stewardesses and air crews had been "evangelised" by excited Assembly delegates by the time they all arrived in Nairobi!

As well as 800 delegates, some 140 programme participants and speakers made their way to the spectacular Kenyatta Conference Centre in Nairobi that evening.

From the start, it was as Billy Graham had predicted. He had never feared that PACLA might end as it had begun: in conflict, tension and disagreements. "God will overrule. This is one of the most prayed-for conferences I have ever come to. The place will be bathed in love." And so it was at many levels, though there were to be problems. In any event, for ten days Christian leaders from 49 out of Africa's 51 countries rubbed shoulders with each other and interacted on the wide range of challenges facing the church and problems facing the continent. The mix was extraordinary – archbishops, bishops, leading Free Church members, professors of theology, evangelists, youth ministry experts, pastors, church growth specialists, long-time missionaries, business leaders and even some politicians, plus Christian leaders from around the world. Noted Billy Graham again: "I can see PACLA is set to be even more important than I had already anticipated. I believe this is the most significant Christian conference this continent has ever seen."

PACLA began with the chairman, Gottfried Osei-Mensah of Ghana, paying generous tribute to the sacrificial work of the early missionaries. They had, after all, been the first to scatter the seed of the gospel across Africa and so sowed the beginnings of the modern African church. There had been mistakes, but the task now was "not to condemn, but rather to discover where Christianity stands in Africa today, and what specific contributions our Lord is calling *us* to make... "

Thus Osei-Mensah challenged PACLA to relate the Christian gospel to modern Africa, with all its "strengths and weaknesses, its perplexing social and ideological cross-currents, its dark corners, its bright spots... "

A crucial starting point, as Michael, Festo and John Wilson saw it, was to "help Christian leaders throughout Africa, and thereby their followers, to grasp that regardless of their differences of tradition, denomination, nationality, race, language, culture, perspective, priority, theological association, political philosophy and so on, they were nevertheless all *already* one in Christ".

Throughout the ten days of intensive talks and study and prayer times that followed, this became increasingly real in the experience of the delegates. Jesus Christ was the only one capable of drawing them all together. The Christian church, not the Organisation of African Unity (OAU), gave Africa the only inner coherence it had.

The South African Connection

Perhaps the spiritual turning point of the conference came through an unusual vehicle in an Afrikaans professor and missiologist called David Bosch. It was the climax of a bumpy build-up brought about by the controversial South African presence in the congress.

Apart from all the tension relating to securing visas for the 80 South Africans, and then the extensive press publicity surrounding their arrival, there was general anxiety in the congress about delegates coming, especially white ones, and even more so Afrikaans ones, from the politically explosive context of apartheid South Africa.

"There are some shakings in our delegation about the presence of the South Africans," said a church leader from Chad to Michael. And shakings on this score there were throughout PACLA.

Perhaps the greatest shakings of all were in the South African group itself.

John Tooke remembers that "even as the jumbo jet took off from Johannesburg, some of the young black participants began to notice the presence of a number of Afrikaner dominees (ministers) on board the aircraft. The erstwhile suspicions ever present in all cross-racial South African contact asserted themselves. 'These guys are BOSS (Bureau of State Security) personnel,' they began to tell one another. They would inform the press in Kenya, they vowed."

In fact, before the plane had even crossed the Limpopo, all the alienations and animosities of South Africa were brewing. Then in the assembly itself the alienations intensified.

Eventually, as the group struggled desperately to achieve some sort of togetherness for its daily meeting, it was John Wilson of AE Uganda, that great reconciler and diplomat, who managed to get everyone to agree even to sit together for a couple of hours in the same room. Then it took the rest of the time on day one to elect a chairman. Dr Frank Mdlalose, a Zulu politician later to be Premier of KwaZulu-Natal and then South Africa's Ambassador to Egypt, was finally put into the chair. No sooner had he begun officially to get the meeting underway than the time was up. Frustrations and hostility were up too.

Wait and See

As struggling efforts were made amongst the South Africans to connect in their group over the next few days, so these tensions spilled out into the wider conference. Imagine then how the conference felt mid-way when an Afrikaans Dutch Reformed professor took the rostrum to speak on "The Recovery of Christian Community in Africa Today". A number of delegates had come to Michael Cassidy as programme chairman and asked him to remove this prominent Afrikaner from the programme.

"No way," replied Michael emphatically. "Just you wait and see what will come forth from this brother."

Few in that wider gathering knew of Bosch's powerfully courageous and prophetic stand in his own country, but their hearts began to melt as he spoke. "We have failed," he said, "to create that new community in Africa, that really different community, which should be an alternative to all other communities on earth. Have we really understood what it means to be the church in the world? Have we really understood what Jesus came to do on earth and how his community and his teachings differed from all other existing communities and teachings? Have we not, in reality, domesticated our faith and adapted it to this world to such an extent that it literally says exactly the opposite of what it was supposed to mean?"

As David humbly and agonisingly shared his own struggles as an Afrikaner to find reconciliation with blacks, many in that auditorium began to be deeply moved and also sensed that they too had their own arenas of alienation or distance in their own countries, cultures or churches. The problem of alienation was not just a South African one. Nor could it be solved easily anywhere.

Said David Bosch:

Reconciliation is no cheap matter. It does not come about by simply papering over deep-seated differences. Reconciliation presupposes confrontation. Without that we do not get reconciliation, but merely a temporary glossing over of differences. The running sores of society cannot be healed with the use of sticking plaster. Reconciliation presupposes an operation, a cut into the very bone, without anaesthetic. The infection is not just on the surface. The abscess of hate and mistrust and fear, between black and white, between nation and nation, between rich and poor, has to be slashed open.

The Dutch Reformed professor finally concluded by sharing a deep and moving personal testimony:

> One evening, about a year ago, my wife and I had a visit from some black members of our church. Our discussion inevitably was on what it means to be Christians in South Africa today. The attitude of the blacks was: "In spite of everything you two whites say tonight, you still belong to the group of oppressors. You benefit from the system, we don't. You are privileged, we are not. You remain white and we black, your feet remain on our necks." We talked until the early morning hours and it seemed as though we would never be able really to find one another. We were not people, but blacks and whites. We were not people, but categories. Eventually when the blacks were preparing to leave, my wife broke down and wept, pleading for understanding and acceptance.

PACLA at Calvary

In his book on PACLA entitled *Together in One Place*, Michael Cassidy described the moment:

> Almost choking with emotion, and struggling to hold back his tears, the professor reached out an unsteady hand to sip from the glass of water. The atmosphere was charged. The sense of the Spirit's presence, overwhelming. Conviction, brokenness and the spirit of repentance swept across the auditorium. Everywhere people were struggling with their emotions.
>
> The Dutch Reformed leader continued: "And so these black brothers left. But the next day one of them returned, on behalf of the others. He said: 'Your wife's tears made all the difference. If it can still happen in South Africa that a white woman weeps because of a desire for real, human fellowship with black people, then this is something that cannot be explained logically, it must be of God.'"
>
> PACLA was now at Calvary. All were at the foot of the Cross, because here was a man at the foot of the Cross. Something of immense importance for Africa was taking place. Healing and reconciliation were happening. Fractured and divided members of the Body of Christ were coming together. The cost of ministering truly to Africa's wounds was now being glimpsed. For there

was Bosch – the in-between person – and the symbol of so many of Africa's in-between people – crushed.

Small wonder then that all felt with penetrating power the force of Bosch's conclusion: "Reconciliation takes place when two opposing forces clash and somebody gets crushed in-between. This is what happened to Jesus. This is what the cross is all about. There is, also for us, no escape from the Cross. We either stand with the one crucified on it, or we stand with the crucifiers. There is no middle way."

Bosch's powerful words of testimony and challenge went home to a thousand hearts like darts driving into a tender target:

> Are we prepared to follow the way of the Cross for the sake of real Christian community in Africa: We, who are today gathered here from all over our continent? It is such a temptation to reply with a show of bravado: "Of course, I will follow where he leads me, even to the Cross." I myself am less confident. I know myself and my repeated failures too well. And I know my fears and prejudices. But I also know our Lord Jesus Christ, and I know, from the testimony of his word and his Spirit, what he expects from us in the form of real community. I know him as the Lord of compassion. I know he will also have compassion on me. And upon you. Kyrie Eleison. Lord, have mercy upon us!

As PACLA came that night to the Cross so, in the view of many, did the African church begin to move to a new place in terms of its task of mission and evangelism across the continent. "If we could find our way to one another, we can find our way out to the continent in effective mission and evangelism," people said.

Truly Pan-African

PACLA was probably the most truly pan-African event ever. Michael would later write that it was:

> Togetherness across normally impossible or complicated divides. East was meeting West, North was clasping South, English was embracing French. The Sahara Desert had been spanned. The Zambesi River had been crossed. Diplomatic barriers had fallen.

The paper war had been won and impossible visas from impossible places had been granted to impossible people. And we had come together in one place.

The question now was how to remain together. Not organisationally, because that never interested us. But spiritually, functionally, relationally. It was the PACLA spirit, not the PACLA organisation, we were concerned to perpetuate. How else could we justify the PACLA experience, the expense involved or the entire massive expenditure of energy and effort?

The answer was seen in encouraging the PACLA leaders to have ongoing contact, continual cross-fertilisation, to keep talking. "In Jesus the bridge is already built, but we must keep crossing the Bridge!" (*Together in One Place*, pp. 273–275)

Overall, PACLA provided God's people across Africa with a tremendous opportunity to see what God was doing elsewhere on the continent. It was also a time of deep spiritual renewal for the delegates. Hundreds recommitted their hearts to the Lord, and thus refreshed, then gathered to pray and plan with a vengeance for the evangelisation of Africa.

On 19 December 1976, 800 delegates reluctantly packed their suitcases and prepared to depart on the long, chaotic journeys home. Many knew that for them, this would be a once-in-a-lifetime experience, that never again perhaps would they have the chance to meet their brothers and sisters in Christ from right across Africa. But at least they now knew that they themselves were part of a very real, if invisible, network of Christians stretching across that vast continent. For many leaders, PACLA started off valuable relationships that would give them mutual encouragement and help in the years to come.

Certainly PACLA stirred Africa widely and set off a chain reaction of positive Christian initiatives from Cape to Cairo.

In time they would come forth. For AE it meant they were on the continental map of Africa as never before.

NACLA

The chain reaction directly involving AE's ability to mount ecumenical conferences now revealed itself again in Rhodesia. PACLA spawned in Rhodesia both another Christian Leadership

Consultation, as well as NACLA, the National Christian Leadership Assembly (the Rhodesians at that time being unable to decide whether it should be ROCLA or ZICLA in view of the country's imminent name change!). In 1978 NACLA drew together 600 delegates from 53 denominations and gave them highly valuable help in ministering in a war situation. AE, while deeply involved in NACLA set-up, became even more involved in NACLA follow-up, which was officially entrusted to African Enterprise by the NACLA committee.

SACLA

But SACLA in South Africa was to be the "biggie". To be sure, PACLA had set African Enterprise thinking yet again. A startling degree of consensus and fellowship had finally emerged among the South African contingent at PACLA. It was centred on the charismatic figure of David Bosch, whom God had used in such a signal way in Nairobi. With his inspiration and encouragement, AE was soon planning for the South African Christian Leadership Assembly (SACLA).

For Michael the journey to the SACLA vision had come via depression, discouragement and despondency. Writing the story of SACLA, Michael's sister, Olave Snelling, put it this way:

> Michael noted in his prayer diary how cast down he was by the contrast of the PACLA experience in all its light, freedom and exhilarating breakthrough with the South African situation in all its bleakness and hardness. It was a very strange sensation. In his depression over South Africa, he was taking his cue from the newspapers and allowing his reactions to be determined by them.
>
> Realising how much his perspective on the situation was the human one, he began to reread the Old Testament and as he read he began to get that sense of the sovereignty of God in history. Numbers 13 tells the familiar story of Moses sending twelve spies into the land across the Jordan and how they returned having seen the large and fortified cities and the huge human beings beside whom they felt like grasshoppers! The majority report on the situation indicated that it was completely hopeless to contemplate any action against such a powerful adversary. But Caleb and Joshua looked at the situation in a completely different way. They looked at the situation with the eyes of faith and, with the

God-factor in mind, they were confident that the Lord could and would prevail.

Michael recalls the divine challenge. "Are you with the ten or are you with the two?" He felt like a grasshopper in the South African situation. Very quickly he had to move from being with the ten to the two. On 2nd February 1977, he prayed, "Give me, O God, the spirit and the faith of Caleb and Joshua." The mood of black depression gave way. With the thought of the South African nation before him, he found he could think afresh with new faith and a renewed perception of God at work in history. (*One People* by Olave Snelling, page 8)

Yes, what about now gathering the South African church on a wider and more extensive basis then ever before? What about a South African Christian Leadership Assembly?

Similar things were happening in the heart of David Bosch: "As I have travelled around South Africa since PACLA," he wrote to AE, "I have also found people saying, 'Well, if it could happen in Nairobi, why not in South Africa?'" Thus was born the resolution to bring together the group of South Africans who had been at PACLA. They met. Not surprisingly, it was decided to proceed with the idea of SACLA. A council of 200 was formed and then a small executive under the chairmanship of David Bosch. Michael Cassidy again would direct the programme.

Key Contributions

Incredible backing came from all quarters. Especially notable were the contributions of people like Vusi Khanyile and Caesar Molebatsi.

Remembers John Tooke: "Vusi Khanysile combined a passion for black liberation with capacities for accepting and listening to whites while Caesar Molebatsi revealed and propagated his legendary spirit of forgiveness after having his leg amputated through the witless behaviour of a white drunken driver. It was this great spirit of black striving for freedom combined with a spirit of forgiveness that created the great arena for reconciliation which SACLA represented."

Notes Olave Snelling in her SACLA chronicle:

Mr Vusi Khanyile, at that time working for the Anglo-American Corporation but seconded to SACLA as Motivation Director, summed up the feelings of the SACLA Executive when he said: "This Conference brings to mind the period that the disciples of Christ spent together with other believers in the upper room of a house in Jerusalem waiting in prayer before going out to live and work as a new community of believers. If at SACLA we give the Holy Spirit a chance to act in our lives, something will happen to the heterogeneous mass of people assembled. If we keep still enough, we can hear our Father in heaven challenging us, admonishing us, and encouraging us. However, we cannot forever remain in the 'upper room'. We live in the world. Our mission is in the world and not in the upper room."

He then added: "We face, at a number of levels, moral issues which contribute to a way of life in South Africa that has produced economic discrepancies, injustices, the loss of dignity and a host of aching needs. Our previous failure truly to meet with one another has meant that many of these South African agonies have been obscured. They must not be in the future." The Executive set itself assiduously to the task of meeting head on the challenges of those words. (*One People*, pp. 8–11)

Fierce Opposition Too

But opposition was fierce – from the government, the security police, conservative denominations and radical white right-wingers. Michael's journal on 16 April 1979 described trying to deal with "an incredible concatenation of falsehoods, distortions, gross misrepresentation and chronic mischief making. All calculated in hell to pull SACLA to the ground. Anyway, Lord, I stand prayerfully on your ability to control and undertake and vindicate. 'But thou, O Lord, be not far off! O thou, my help, hasten to my aid' (Psalm 22:19)."

A Pentecostal security policeman in Port Elizabeth, unable in conscience to cope with the security police's decision "to pull SACLA to the ground" went conscience-stricken to his minister to share his anguish. The minister conveyed what was happening to Michael, who phoned David Bosch at once. The two men remembered that "right after this all hell popped with fresh efforts to destroy the Assembly".

As people all over the place now mysteriously refused to

sign up for the conference, David Bosch said to the executive: "This vision is unsellable." With only weeks to go till the conference opening, registration was pitiful; 400 people a day would need to sign up if the target of 6,000 was to be reached. It seemed an absurd expectation. Yet by God's mysterious ways, by deep prayer in many places and by some incredible labours from a few, the assembly was finally on track.

In fact, SACLA was later seen as one of those special divine triumphs over human intransigence. Castigated as political by right-wing whites and as irrelevant by militant blacks, SACLA organisers rode out a roller-coaster, harum-scarum buffeting from the time the vision took shape post-PACLA, until the day the gathering opened against the backdrop of hammer and sickle slogans painted by protestors on its logo at the Pretoria Show Grounds!

SACLA ran from 5 to 15 July 1979. It drew 6,000 South African Christian leaders from every racial background and from umpteen denominations to Pretoria.

Michael wrote later: "Screwtape, with his normal lack of discretion, had over-played his hand with white right-wing hysteria, as this finally brought the blacks in in a big way. So SACLA opened as the most representative racial and denominational Christian gathering in South African church history."

Together at Last

While Durban 1973 had lacked Pentecostal and Dutch Reformed support, SACLA had such support in considerable measure. More than 500 DRC leaders were involved, while hundreds of Pentecostals and Charismatics praised and hugged and loved everyone else out of their normal restraints and inhibitions. But it did not stop there. "Amid the euphoria of togetherness, agonising issues of polarisation and hurt were faced. SACLA spoke fairly and squarely to the issues of a divided land," wrote Michael. "A magnificent reconciling address by then Bishop Tutu on the opening night set the tone."

Then there was the fact that inter-racial housing in homes and hostels in Pretoria could further develop the black/white relational aspect of SACLA. One young man from an Indian family in Pietermaritzburg arrived late for the conference and it seemed that there was nowhere for him and his friend to stay. They had to spend a freezing winter night on the floor of their Combi van. During that night they prayed, "Oh Lord, is there *nowhere* else where we can stay for the rest of the conference?" Reporting his plight to the reception desk the next day, the lad was told there was indeed a home where he would be most welcome. Would they like to go and stay with the Oppenheimers? (This was Nicholas Oppenheimer, son of Harry Oppenheimer of Anglo-American Corporation fame.) The two boys had a fabulous, almost royal, time! When the young man got back to his humble home, he said to his father, "Gee, Dad, we're really back in Bethlehem's manger now!"

The press, especially the Afrikaans press, after being initially very hostile, were also now intrigued, and began to spread news of SACLA and its daily happenings and messages to the far corners of South Africa.

While the ten-day assembly began and ended each day in plenary, during the day five smaller sub-conferences ran for five groupings: (1) pastors and their leading laity; (2) church youth group leaders; (3) civic, political and business leaders; (4) university student Christian leaders; (5) high school Christian leaders.

Before supper each day the assembly also broke into dialogue groups of twelve or so with representatives drawn from all the sub-conferences. Massive confrontation, then deep healing and finally real change happened in these groups. A specialist researcher in Human Change from Harvard University said later: "I have never seen such deep change happen in so many people in such a short time."

Chairman David Bosch described the very fact that SACLA had happened as "a miracle". To all the delegates, God's presence was mightily evident in the astonishing unity which developed out of almost bewildering diversity. "SACLA has enabled me once again to have hope for South Africa," said one youth leader. "SACLA was a baptism into the unity of the Body of Christ," affirmed Dr Calvin Cook, then of Rhodes University.

Rev Joe Masango of Sharpeville said: "SACLA is opening the church to find its real unity: it's also going to further the message to Afrikaners and blacks to resolve their problems through dialogue."

Fear to Fellowship

George Singh, an Indian schoolteacher, and his wife, Betty, were to be put up in an Afrikaans home in Pretoria. They were terrified at this prospect and so were the host and hostess! But by the end of their time in this lovely home George and Betty had friends for life. When they phoned their Afrikaans friends on their return home, the couple said: "We are lost without you."

A young African girl from Soweto said: "I have two homes now. One in Soweto and one with my Afrikaner friends in Pretoria." And again she had been so nervous about going to an Afrikaans home. This experience was multiplied thousands of times over.

A senior South African politician said: "SACLA is the watershed we have been waiting for." It had become a symbol of hope to many and to many a challenge to trust God in looking at the future with his eyes, not man's. The way forward was to be a way of faith, fellowship and obedience. SACLA had been a rebuke to negativism and an onslaught against the destructive attitudes in the church. It had shown the country in microcosm what it ought to be in macrocosm.

A visitor from England had been talking to an African Methodist minister from the Transkei, one of South Africa's so-called Bantustans, or independent homelands. "Do you know," said the Transkeian, "I sent a telegram to my son and told him to get to SACLA even if it means spending his last cent? There *is* a way out of the South African dilemma without violence!" Till then both he and his son had, out of sheer desperation, been dedicated to a violent solution to the South African problem.

An English-speaking South African spoke of SACLA in the language of the book of Genesis saying: "Up until SACLA ended, the Afrikaner was to me the Egyptian governor in the story of the people of Israel in Egypt. In SACLA the scales have fallen from my eyes and in the Afrikaner I have now seen Joseph, my brother." (*One People*, pp. 21–22)

A Vision in Heaven

For African Enterprise,

> SACLA was a vision from heaven of how the church in South Africa could and should work all the time. Here were the people of God together – gracious Afrikaner academics, lively charismatics, cautious politicians and businessmen, irrepressible black teenagers, sensitive white students, patriarchal Xhosa pastors, attractive young housewives and mothers, dignified Episcopal clerics, plus eager-beaver pressmen and journalists from everywhere. We even had church leaders from 10 or 15 other African countries present, plus observer delegations from around the world.

And it all happened in Pretoria. "If *there*, then *anywhere*," mused some in astonished wonder.

Assessing the impact of SACLA afterwards, Michael would write: "SACLA was, of course, a foundational, seminal and therefore non-repeatable event. But it showed that God's people can indeed be gathered together and in their togetherness they can help the world really to believe that the Father did indeed send the Son. And that, after all, is what evangelism and the whole church of Christ are all about."

Other Gatherings

Following SACLA in 1979, AE's next major effort to gather church leadership was the National Initiative for Reconciliation (NIR) in October 1985 when the political heat in the country was red hot. This is discussed in Chapter 23, along with the Rustenberg Conference convened in 1990 not long after the release of Nelson Mandela and the unbanning of the liberation movements.

As far as AE was concerned, the conferences catalogued in this chapter constituted the Himalayan peaks of their endeavours. But there were others, less exalted and less impactful, such as a second PACLA Conference in Nairobi in 1994 and a second Rustenberg Conference in 1998 with some of the same parties involved as in Rustenberg one.

Conclusion

As for Michael Cassidy, he was thankful to be able to look back over the years and feel that there had been at least some meaningful attempt to respond to that great scriptural challenge of Psalm 50:5: "Gather my saints together unto me."

In attempting to obey that word, AE as a whole and in its different teams in different parts of the continent had felt that one of the gifts or charisma put into the ministry by the Lord was to fulfil this precious yet demanding task of seeking to bring the Body of Christ together to face the challenges of mission and evangelism on the African continent. AE had not pulled off these ventures alone. There had been many others involved with them from different sectors of the church. But what they did know was that togetherness in the Body of Christ was something very precious to the heart of their Lord and that it had been a great privilege to participate in this sacred calling reflected in the prayer of Jesus when he cried out on the night before his Crucifixion: "I pray... that they may all be one, even as Thou, Father, art in me, and I in Thee, that they also may be in us, so that the world may believe that Thou hast sent me."

Of the early church, the book of Acts could record: "All who believed were together" (Acts 2:44). That was their secret.

For AE this was both a goal to aim for and a dream to embrace. And gathering the saints together will always be a primary goal and a key step in the fulfilment of that dream.

Chapter 22

Making Disciples of All Nations

Jesus' final word in Matthew 28:19 was: "Go therefore and make disciples of all nations... teaching them to observe all I have commanded you." Our Lord wanted not just converts, but disciples.

This mandate argued in the AE mind for a deep commitment to training and discipling. Yes, this could and should be done out there where missions were happening, but as the team could not and should not travel 52 weeks of the year (100 days a year away from home was the agreed and accepted limit), this called for a home-based training ministry.

Yes, Home Sweet Home. A place all your own. There's nothing like it.

For 16 years the South African AE team had been in rented accommodation in various office blocks around Pietermaritzburg. From one small room in 1964, to a few small rooms, sometimes near noisy pipes, sometimes up dark side streets. As the work grew, so did the longings of various team members one day to have a base and a training centre that they could call home.

Over and above that, Michael Cassidy and the early team had seen in the United States and Canada the very powerful spiritual consequences of conference-centre ministries where converts could be built up in the faith, ministers refreshed, encouraged and helped with their preaching, lay people trained in witnessing, evangelism, church growth, worship and cross-cultural relating. Also in a racially divided context people could meet and find each other. Consultations and think-tanks on issues could be run and papers put out with their findings.

In short, as the years went by, AE team members saw there was so much more they could be doing, if only they had the space and place in which to do it. To train clergy and laity in mission, to encourage them in discipleship, to encourage the fractured communities of South Africa to meet for talks of reconciliation. "Yes, but *where* do we meet them?" "*Where* shall we take them this time?" became a tiring refrain.

The search for a centre was on from as early as 1965. But all possibilities seemed endlessly blocked.

Finally, in the late 1970s, the African Enterprise team and board in South Africa decided that both for the sake of its ministry and administration, it was imperative that AE should buy its own premises. So – the search began in earnest. Estate agents came up with a variety of properties: some wonderful but too expensive, some cheap, but totally unsuitable.

And then, one day in the early summer of 1979, a 20-acre plot of land was discovered that was ideal for the purpose. It lay about 10 km from the Pietermaritzburg City Hall, up a lovely wooded valley. The property itself was rich in character, with an abundance of natural vegetation, and bounded by two sparkling rivulets. On one side lay the Natal Parks' Board property, with its well-placed picnic sites, and on the other side were the cool depths of natural forest and plantations, perfect for an afternoon's stroll.

It was so peaceful and isolated that only one little road off Town Bush Road led to it, called "Nonsuch". For years this road had been so obscure that even locals had debated its existence: "There's *none such* road as that..." Except that there was. So Nonsuch Road it became.

The property consisted of a magnificent sprawling white house, built in a gracious Cape Dutch style. It was more than 120 years old. Beside it stood domestic quarters and a garage.

The 20 acres it came with would enable AE to build the buildings it needed, and even better, there was an option of buying considerably more land at a later date. (AE would eventually buy an additional and adjacent 135 acres.)

It cost just R84,000 (by the mid-1980s it would be worth more than R1.25 million). Just before AE took ownership, the owner of the property was approached by a property developer and offered much more than AE could put down.

The owner paused, reflected and then said: "No! Somehow I feel this place is meant to go to this Christian group. So I am not interested in another and better deal."

The team rejoiced.

Lights Blink Green

All this happened just after SACLA in July 1979, when the team was brought to the moment of decision. "Shall we go ahead?" they asked themselves. "Yes," was the answer. The lights all seemed to be blinking green.

But they needed the funds.

So AE put the matter before its supporters worldwide. It also discussed the issue carefully within the team. AE wanted to get its priorities and reasons for the centre right, from the start.

Bishop Alphaeus Zulu, then chairman of the AE board of South Africa, set out AE's line of reasoning to the AE family worldwide:

It has become evident over the years that the work of proclamation of the gospel requires extended premises. Our teams have gone out on missions in our own country, in Zimbabwe, in Zambia and Malawi. They have found deep hunger for the gospel. Ministers and other Christian leaders have desired broader and deeper training in the follow-up work which evangelisation demands for lasting fruit to be reaped.

People have wanted to come to a base to share life with our teams, as well as receive instruction. The churches also, in our immediate environment, are keen to make greater use of the talents and skills we, by the grace of God, possess and can offer. Furthermore, our proximity to the city gives scope for us to provide spiritual refreshment to many ordinary Christian people who suffer the strains of modern life.

South Africa is bedevilled by the mistaken belief of many people that God wants *separation* from one another, even within the Christian family. Because AE is non-denominational and non-racial, it is especially through a centre that AE can most effectively fulfil its ministry of reconciliation and remind all Christians that the advent of the kingdom consists primarily in the breaking down of walls of partition.

Finally a centre is necessary to enable us to serve the churches better. Because AE has no desire to become a church, it is a most fitting instrument to serve the whole church. I am satisfied that it cannot be right that the work of "equipping the people of God for the work of ministry" should be restricted solely by lack of physical facilities.

It was significant that Professor David Bosch, as a leading missiologist in the South African church scene, a good friend of AE and a board member, should also support the centre idea. Its training facilities were "desperately needed in our torn and agonising South African society. It can equip Christians for their role as agents of reconciliation in a context increasingly characterised by fear, bitterness, hatred and alienation. I believe that AE, because of its unique composition and ministry, can fulfil a crucial role in this regard."

The AE family worldwide understood this, and funds came in. One English solicitor, in particular, who wanted to remain anonymous, donated a significant sum out of his inheritance. So the centre was purchased in December 1979. After 16 years of "wandering around like Abraham without roots" AE was coming home.

They couldn't move in all at once: there wasn't room in the stately old colonial homestead. But a few of the AE staff made a beginning, and on Friday, 15 February 1980, Dr Bruce Bare, a "founding father" of AE since that first 1961 board in Pasadena, and now Chairman of the AE International Council, formally opened and dedicated the Southern Africa HQ and Christian Leadership Training Centre for training Mission and Evangelism.

The Fun Begins

Then the fun really began. What exactly was AE going to *do* with the buildings and all this land? There were architects to meet, city council officials to woo for planning permission. Big dreams were dreamed, and modified by actual costings. A budget was worked out, builders brought in, and soon the work began.

The whole team moved quickly out of Chancery Lane, but some of them used their homes for offices until they all finally reunited at the centre in October 1980. Michael told AE friends in the *Update* publication that "the hectic pace of AE's operation has been slowed by the beauty of the surrounding lawns and the orchards bounded on two sides by pure rivulets. Team meetings are now held under willow trees and not in close proximity to the cooling plant of a nearby department store as before!"

Who was going to run the centre? That was easy – John Tooke. He had had a major role in the training and back-up side of AE ministry for many years: so directing the work of the centre would be the fulfilment of his dreams.

Who was going to administer it? That also was easy: Malcolm Graham, AE's administrative genius who kept the good ship African Enterprise in immaculate order, upright and steadily afloat in the water.

Who would teach? Team members such as Abiel Thipanyane, David Peters, Vasco Seleoane, David Richardson plus John Tooke and Michael themselves were all naturals. Others could be drawn in.

Who was going to staff the site? A housekeeper was found, Rene Richards, and a gardener, Petros Ndlovu, who took one look at the 20 verdant acres, and said "Help!" Assistance came in the form of many volunteers, including gardeners Brian and Lorna Christian, who volunteered to do the initial landscaping of the gardens. (John Tooke and Michael Cassidy were touched when Brian once shared that every morning he woke up and said: "Lord, what do you want me to do in that garden today?")

Memos from this period are full of all sorts of issues, including "what shall we name the various buildings? After famous missionaries, evangelists? Or... ?" One unit took John Wilson's name, and another Festo Kivengere's, another Nicholas Bhengu's (the great Pentecostal Zulu preacher), and yet another took Michael Cassidy's Sesotho name Mojalefa. Many years later when John Tooke finally left AE, the major training wing was named after him. "Not a good idea," said John, "to name things after living believers in case they blow it!" But the training wing stands as a symbol of gratitude for years of dedicated work by this gifted evangelist, writer and teacher.

Early projects run from the centre included the AE media department and tape library, the Ambassador Youth Programme, the Unreached Peoples' Project under one-time intern David Bliss of Wits University boxing fame (to bring to the attention of the church the people within Africa unreached by the gospel), the Church Growth and Discipleship Department, and the Lay Witness Mission Training Programme for laity and clergy.

By August 1981 things were buzzing. "The architect is working full speed on the plans, and the money is now in hand to start the first dormitory cabin. It is very exciting, we are dreaming of all the possibilities!"

Early Bridge-building Encounters

In late 1980, following the difficult Kimberley Mission, the first group of black youngsters from a township (Galeshewe on the edge of Kimberley) came for a time of encounter and fellowship. This was when Luthando Charlie (whose tale was told earlier in this book) became a committed Christian, just weeks before being imprisoned by the South African security police.

Then in September 1981, AE invited 55 black youth leaders from one of South Africa's most explosive trouble-spots, Elsies River near Cape Town, for a ten-day stay at the AE Centre. The aim was to help provide Christian insight into issues ranging from politics and forgiveness to marriage. The young people came all the way by bus from Cape Town, a journey of 1,600 km. One youth leader said: "It is tremendous to see the attitude of the whites here toward us blacks. We sense that they have really accepted us. It's my prayer that we'll go back to Elsies River and really practise the things we have learned here." The harmony of AE's multi-racial team had made a deep impact upon the young people.

Michael was very encouraged by these early forays into reconciliation from the centre. "These young leaders will multiply their learning in youth groups, high schools and community projects. There will be real spiritual community uplift in what is a very depressed and shattered area."

Throughout 1982 the frenetic activity continued, until the AE training centre resembled an anthill, as the staff and builders busily came and went every day, labouring away under the watchful eye of John Tooke. Early every morning, very early, a cavalcade of cars and vans would wind their way down Nonsuch Road: evangelists, administrators, secretaries, gardeners, housekeepers, builders, electricians, plumbers and various labourers. Soon the monkeys would retreat from the grass to chatter indignantly in the trees at the builders and their noisy machinery. Meanwhile, inside the buildings, the staff set to work. Missions were planned, training courses written, lectures prepared and plans for seminars and conferences etched out.

A Busy Place

AE was a busy place. Just one example from a spring morning in 1982: within an hour had come phone calls from Mutare in Zimbabwe (AE's David Peters), Australia (AE board member), Durban (AE's David Richardson), Israel (AE evangelist), a local girls' college in Pietermaritzberg (AE evangelist), the Bonginskosi ladies Daphne and Barbara ringing in from Canada, and AE evangelist Steven Mung'oma ringing in from the India Keswick Convention. Each phone call meant checking diary engagements, and spawned letters and notes to other staff. Any secretary that joined the AE staff soon had a good grasp of where cities were worldwide, and if she could also type letters, make phone calls, photocopy, file and perform administrative juggling acts while all about her other phones rang, typewriters clacked, clamouring evangelists came and went, and photocopiers hummed away against a background noise of whirring cement mixers, hammering, sawing and drilling, then she was definitely the right person for the job!

By early 1982 the centre smelled of fresh paint and more of the place was open for business. The administration staff had a few offices up and running, and the courses began. That year two cabins were completed, and three chalets made nearly ready. Although it would not be until early 1984 that the centre was fully operational, already modest-sized courses were underway.

In June 1983 a number of South African Christian leaders met together at the AE Centre for the first two of six consultations on controversial issues facing the church in South Africa. The participating delegates said afterwards how extremely valuable it had been to be able to meet on neutral ground (non-racial, non-denominational) within South Africa. Barriers of misunderstanding and division had been crossed in the calm, non-threatening, atmosphere.

"YES!" said the African Enterprise team. They were delighted with all that was developing.

March 1984, and the first proper training programme at AE's South Africa Training Centre began. Michael Cassidy stood up in a conference room of his own centre and taught 40 people the rudiments of "lay evangelism". It was a very happy morning – the fulfilment of years of dreaming and hard work. Michael set to with great enthusiasm, covering the subjects so dear to his own heart: the personal spiritual life of the believer, how to bridge the gap and win the person, gearing the church for evangelism, tools for evangelism, apologetics and the work of the Holy Spirit.

After that, the programme did not so much unfold as take off: seminars on evangelism, worship in mission, principles and practice of effective prayer, Bible study and cell group leadership, conference for church youth leaders, care for the ill, labour/management consultation. The Ambassador programme for young aspiring evangelists was launched under the eager Nico Kleynhans. The team were amazed: "In only ten days of programmes, we have had more than 350 visitors!"

This delighted the team, but none more than John Tooke, who'd spent two years planning for these courses. "They have surpassed all our expectations. I am wonderfully excited and full of gratitude to God for the dream of the AE teaching and training centre which has now come true."

Early comments from black clergy were especially heartwarming. "To think I have only eight years of ministry left! But I'm going to use them for evangelism as never before in my life," said one at the close of one course. Another added: "I have had four years of theological training, but I never understood what evangelism was really all about until these last few days."

Development

Future development would include a variety of evangelism training courses for laity and clergy of all races; courses specifically designed to help people prepare to hold missions; Ministers' Refreshment Programmes; Businessmen's Retreats (to help strengthen the witness of Christians in industry and commerce); and Leadership Retreats (to help bring South

Africa's decision-makers together in a ministry of reconciliation). Finally, Discipleship Training was offered – tools that could be used in congregations. (Training was offered in teaching confirmation, leading Bible studies, releasing the gifts within congregational life, mobilising congregations for mission and other practical aspects of ecclesiology.)

One aspect of the work especially cherished by the team was the Youth Discipleship Camps. Since the township of Soweto had erupted in violence in 1976, AE had worked closely with various young people to try and heal the gaping wounds of distrust, anger and conflict. The Youth Discipleship Camps were enormously satisfying: AE now regularly brought in 50–60 black teenagers from the townships to the AE Centre for two weeks of direct, honest and healing communication with their white peers. Inevitably, to Michael and John's prayerful delight, during these two weeks the tensions of the South African "pressure cooker" gradually cooled into a time of relationship healing. The young people, black and white, began to discover their unity in Christ.

The centre was a great help to African Enterprise's many other individual ministries, such as that of Abiel Thipanyane, whose radio ministry went from strength to strength. Since 1978 he had been broadcasting a programme on Radio Lesotho. "Tebisa Maikutlo" (literally "go deeper in your thoughts") went out on Sunday morning. It was pre-recorded in the media unit at the centre, with teachings of a gospel thrust. Abiel had built up a wide audience over the years, and received a great deal of mail from listeners, many of whom had made commitments to Christ as a result of hearing the progammes. Now with a simple studio all his own, some quiet space and technical backup, there was no stopping him.

Of course, all this cost money. During 1983 the AE offices worldwide had worked long and hard to supply the funds needed, and had met every deadline. But by mid-1984, finances had temporarily dried up. The situation became so bad that Michael Cassidy, John Tooke and Malcolm Graham were forced to sign off the builders, put an embargo on any new staff, and cut back in a thousand other ways. There was a painful period of retrenchment before funds starting flowing again.

By spring 1985 the intern programme, now under the capable Dennis Bailey, had an official name: AE Project TIM (Training in Mission). The interns were known as Tims or "Timothys" and they were challenged to follow their namesake from St Paul's letter: "You too must be tough, courageous, dedicated, aiming to please the One who has enlisted you in His service." The first batch of six young AE interns to complete the year's training course were: Tsietsi Seleoane of Soweto, Mark Staney of Australia, Heinz Kusel of Natal, Chris de Bruyn of Natal, Cameron Barker of Grahamstown and Greenwood Mkandawire of Malawi.

By now the centre could accommodate up to 70 people. It could handle day parties (picnics and retreats) of up to 150 people. It was a facility available for anyone to use – either to attend AE-generated programmes, or various groups wanting to hold their own meetings. There was even a "clergy cottage" on offer, a special facility set aside for church leaders who need extended periods of rest, refreshment and retreat. All this took a staff of five permanent members, approximately ten volunteers, (with a great need for more on a free-board-and-lodge-and-pocket-money basis!), five part-time labourers and voluntary gardeners.

A Typical Day

All in all, the centre had become such a hive of activity that it was hard to imagine how AE had ever survived without it. In June of 1985 Michael described a "typical day", in order to share with the worldwide AE family just what was involved in "all the agonies and ecstasies of Christian ministry"!

> I wake up at 4 am, agitated about my preparation for Top Level Encounter in Cape Town next week. It's an outreach to leaders, so the messages must be up to scratch. I know I mustn't be anxious, but I am. I find Carol awake too, also with Cape Town on brain and heart! At 6 am we read the Word together and pray.
>
> 7.55 am: I arrive at the centre for team and staff devotions and am greeted by Shaun and Margot Islip, just out from England. We have waited four years for Shaun – a marvellous minstrel from David Watson's team. He'll work with us and also a church nearby, to oversee our music and worship ministries.
>
> 8.00 am: Devotions: led by Bill Winter and Isaac April. Today we focus on the Cross. Open prayer follows. It comes in English,

Zulu and Afrikaans. This feels good as we are in South Africa. Andrew Mohibidu, head of follow-up, takes us into Romans 8 – the flesh life and the Spirit life.

And I feel the Lord is doing a new thing in AE. He is not static but dynamic, is leading us on, and dealing with us in terms of deepened spirituality, renewal of our structures, and better financial stewardship.

Spiritually, 1985, has been a period in which we sense the Lord slowing us down, refocusing us on himself, stripping us of self-satisfaction and putting in us new yearnings to relate to him more faithfully, to repent more truly of our sin and shortcomings, to deepen our love for each other, and to know more exactly his plans for us in the ever-more traumatised South Africa of today.

9.00 am: Devotions over, we hear reports and prayer requests.

Bill Winter is going to King William's Town to speak at its 150th anniversary.

Top Level Encounter in Cape Town is in high gear. Pray for effectiveness and fruitfulness.

Port Elizabeth – great news! Missions' Director David Richardson reports that the trip he and I had down there a week ago to discern whether to cancel the mission (owing to political turmoil and unrest) has helped clarify the way forward. Things are finally firing on all cylinders.

Administrative Director Malcolm Graham now gets up for his weekly financial report and prayer request. We plummet from the heights to the depths. The atmosphere is deeply serious. We are in trouble. We are falling short R10,000 each month on budget and the deficit is heading up to R50,000. Funding initiatives are shared. Further drastic cost-cutting measures are explained and for the first time ever we hear the dread words of possible staff retrenchments. It is painful talk. But Malcolm reminds us of "the great cloud of witnesses" (Hebrews 12:1). We mustn't faint. God is faithful. We go to prayer in groups. We thank God for each of our donors. They have been more than faithful. Help us also Lord to see how to cut back, and find fresh funding resources.

10.00 am: Now to introduce Shaun to the work. First to the mailing room, and then to the accounts office. Staff know as of this morning that not a single item of expenditure is to be made without Malcolm's personal approval. At the centre's cabins we see cleaning up after our conference last week on "Spirituality in Mission". In another chalet we catch Songe Chibambo of Malawi on his knees. In my heart I praise God for such prayerful young people.

We walk on, the beauty of the place enveloping us. I introduce people. Steve Bollaert – moved from set-up to be Malcolm's personal assistant. Jenny Cahill – doing follow-up mailings. Dennis Bailey – doing TIMS and Michaelhouse set-up, plus a mini mission programme. Derek Bruce – making sure 40,000 "Updates" are mailed this week. John Tooke and Charles Pitchers – gearing up for opening tomorrow's centre course on evangelism. I have lectures to get ready for that! The pressures with the privilege! Anthea and Brenda tell me I must write *Update* today. They have deadlines to meet.

We go on to meet more staff and secretaries – all colleagues and friends. I am proud of them as I introduce them and thankful for the diversity of gifts in this team. Later Bill will take our new colleagues to see our media office, tape library (R2,000 sales per month, praise be!) the homemade radio studio where Abiel Thipanyane's AE programmes for Lesotho and Transkei are recorded. David Bliss' Unreached Peoples' Project is next door and they are buzzing in preparation for a conference.

11.00 am: The day proceeds. Letters, phone calls, planning discussion etc.

5.30 pm: Well, time is up. I must hurry home. Tonight, Nellis du Preez, my administrative assistant comes at 8.00 pm and we will work late into the night on the evangelist's course, Cape Town preparation and letters. Praise God we don't have to do this too often! – it will have been a long day.

Formal and Informal Courses

Finally, in 1986, after a two-year wait for planning permission, the last of the buildings in the administration block and offices were completed. For the first time in the history of AE's ministry, *all* the staff had suitable accommodation. There was much rejoicing as typewriters, telephones, computers and desks were shifted into the new administration block.

Also, funds had been received to build the Training Wing, which would virtually complete the first major phase of the building project.

In 1987 the Christian Leadership Training Centre launched its two formal training programmes – the Certificate in Mission and Ministry and the Diploma in Missiology.

By spring of 1991 the first course in the Diploma in Social Empowerment and Development was completed by eight students, ranging from a doctor of medicine to a Standard 7 pupil.

By June 1992 the AE Centre was offering everything from formal programmes like the Diploma in Missiology and the Certificate in Mission to informal programmes such as weekend conferences on a variety of subjects applicable to the church (evangelism, worship, prayer), and Youth Discipleship Camps; to non-formal programmes for interns coming to spend up to ten months with AE, and other apprentices or volunteers who come for shorter periods.

In the nineties, in spite of the political convulsions of the first half of the decade and the huge transitional adjustments of the second half, the AE team attempted to keep its varied programmes at the centre on the go. Especially important were the Bridge-Building Encounters run by Charles Pitchers and Themba Sibeko. In these programmes ten or 20 young people from each of the racial groups would come to the centre for a week or so. They would start out as a fellowship of strangers, tense, anxious and fearful of real encounter with one another. But by the end of the week, through the facilitation of Charles and Themba, and as the Spirit of God worked, the barriers would come down, stereotypes would be broken, false mythologies exploded, and fears would vanish like the morning mist while true, deep and accepting relationships would be born. As the young people parted at the end of their BBE, there would be hugs and tears and the exchanging of addresses, phone numbers and e-mails.

With Steve Bollaert, Colleen Hurd and later Pieter and Bessie van der Merwe handling the direction, management and hostessing of the centre respectively, the place progressed and occupancy of the facility was, one way or another, up to about 95 per cent of the weekends of the year. And still today church retreats, educational seminars, youth weekends and women's conferences all find a happy venue as the AE Centre comes into its own.

New South African team leader, Mark Manley is, however, deeply resistant to mere maintenance operations. His far-seeing and proactive vision is to see the centre used much more extensively for both informal and formal training. He not only wants to see the Africa Leadership Development Institute (ALDI), started in the late 1990s by the visionary Phineas Dube of Zimbabwe, develop and grow in extent, numbers and depth, but he also wishes to see even formal university degree courses offered at the centre by virtue of extension associations developed with both overseas and local seminaries and universities. A degree course in Christian Leadership is one of the central pillars in Mark's vision.

"Knowing the proactive visionary and activist that Mark is, he will almost certainly pull this off," comments Michael, thinking back in some amazement and wonder at the tiny seedling vision for the centre when it began back in 1979.

East Africa

Less well developed because of meagre local financial resources is the AE Training Centre in East Africa at Karen, just outside Nairobi.

Not surprisingly, in East Africa as well as South Africa, the frustration at not having a home had been growing throughout the 1970s. But the East African team was catapulted into setting up a headquarters by the crisis situation in the late 1970s in Uganda.

It all began with PACLA, the Pan-African Christian Leadership Assembly held in Nairobi in 1976. PACLA needed administering, and a new team was born of this, for it brought together the two men who had been key in the administration of the Assembly: the Rev John Wilson and the Rev Dan Serwanga. John and Dan needed an office to administer PACLA – and so it came into being. After PACLA, AE decided to keep the office going with funds given by the churches in Nairobi.

Then in 1977, as we have narrated, the Archbishop of Uganda was murdered, and refugees poured out of Uganda. Children and women, students and teachers, doctors and lawyers, priests and bishops flocked to Kenya. The PACLA/AE office became the focal point for these refugees. AE would not have dreamed of turning them away. "We were challenged to translate our theoretical speeches during PACLA on Christian leadership and fellowship into practical leadership and Christian service," said Bishop Festo.

The range and volume of administration this involved meant the AE office would have to be a permanent fixture, and the AE regional chairman of the time, the Rev John Mpaayei, pressed hard to have AE legally registered in Kenya. Nairobi was perfect: its metropolitan nature made it a natural co-ordinating centre for the East African team of African Enterprise.

But rising costs of renting office space meant that for the sake of good stewardship, AE needed to purchase property while it was still reasonable. This it had funds to do, and so a roomy property in Karen, a suburb just outside Nairobi, was found and bought. Administrative staff moved in, but that was not all. The East African team also wanted to establish some sort of training facility to help pastors and laity have a chance to learn more about their Christian faith. And so the AE team decided to appoint a "principal" for their centre.

The Rev Dr Michael Senyimba was chosen. He went on to draw up a number of training programmes, from practical evangelism, to pastoral counselling, to leadership training. The aim was not to mimic the year-long Bible college courses, but to offer accessible short-term courses to laity and clergy to help them minister in their local churches.

In the years that followed, a principal's home, dormitory block, kitchen block, lecture rooms and other facilities would be added.

Here too, rather as in South Africa, extensive courses were run as funding became available. Sadly, the shortage of funds often prevented programmes at that centre from developing the way the team would have liked.

When Michael Senyimba left to take up a senior church post in Uganda, Berhanu Deresse of Ethiopia picked up the baton and began to run with it. However, he found in due time that many of the courses he wanted to run were most cost-effective when taken out to the different regions or countries from where the calls were coming.

However, the Karen Centre remains a place where Christian leadership training modules can still be effectively mounted and these ventures continue apace, especially now with the Kenya team adding some further conference facilities as a part of its own headquarters now located on a section of the Karen property.

The East African project is still in many ways embryonic but it is up and running and the potential is immense.

Chapter 23

**The Precarious Mix
– Faith, Politics
and the Kingdom**

The matter of how the Christian faith intersects with and relates to politics has always been a vexed one.

But for Michael Cassidy, Festo Kivengere and AE the matter ended up becoming relatively simple. It was simply a question of applying the love ethic of Jesus to the issues of society. It was a question of "seeking to do to others what you would have them do to you". As Michael once put it to a member of President P.W. Botha's cabinet: "Not one of you in your cabinet would want to be on the receiving end of apartheid." That reality alone, (i.e. "the do-unto-others law"), should have alerted apartheid's proponents to the fact that there was something wrong and immoral about it.

There was also the fact for Michael and Festo, as had been impressed upon them in the Nairobi 1969 mission by the great missionary statesman, E. Stanley Jones, that Jesus was the cosmic Christ, the author of creation and therefore the universe and humans and society only "worked" when they followed the Jesus way. As Jones joined the team for part of their mission he always stressed that the laws of Jesus, including the laws of love, justice and morality, are written into the fabric of creation. Creation thus only "works" the Jesus way. This includes politics.

This truth gripped the team. Michael later explained it more fully in *The Passing Summer*:

> Because Jesus is the agent in creation, seeing that "without him was not anything made that was made" (John 1:3, RSV), all reality and all the cosmos, has his stamp upon it. What Christians

believe, therefore, is not that Jesus imposed a morality on man, but rather that he exposed more fully and completely an intrinsic morality in the universe itself. A good and moral action will therefore have not only Jesus and scripture behind it but the universe and the cosmos as well. Conversely, a bad or evil action will therefore stand not only under the judgement of God and scripture, but also under the judgement of life and the cosmos.

Christian ethics are therefore always on the side of fullness, happiness, true fun, completeness, peace, health, political stability, justice, social harmony, and so on.

Laws cannot, therefore, be "broken", but one can be broken by them. No one breaks a law; he can only illustrate it in operation. To jump off the Empire State Building is not to break the law of gravity – only to illustrate it!

Morality and Reality

Michael went on to note:

> To be moral, therefore, for the Christian, whether in personal, family or political ethics, is not to be narrow, prudish or politically obtuse, but simply to co-operate with the moral and spiritual structure of reality. Moral obedience is not obedience to an arbitrary decree, but to the way things are.
>
> The moral law is the law of nature, and the law of nature is the law of life. In other words the laws of God's world all interlock – and when man is called to be sexually or financially or politically moral, he is simply being called to play the game of life according to the rules of the game established by the author of the game for our happiness and well-being.

Implications

Clearly the implications of this principle were shattering for places like Uganda and South Africa. Noted Michael: "This means that the way we are made to work is also the way God wants us to work. Creation thus works his way or else works its own ruin. We are free to choose in politics as in life, but we are not free to choose the consequences. A law, which operates regardless, will always have the last word."

"All this meant," said the South African team leader of AE, "that the fundamental issue facing us in South Africa is whether we live in a moral universe or not. If we do not, then we can discriminate and get away with it. But if we do live in a moral universe, we can't and won't get away with it. And the judgements of life, of history and of the universe will become the judgements of God, because he has made one sort of universe and not another – a universe in which we reap what we sow (Proverbs 22:8)."

Having explained all this in a letter on 24 June 1980 to Dr Piet Koornhof, then a cabinet minister in P.W. Botha's government, Michael concluded:

> Exactly how all this is to be worked out within the realities of the South African situation is for those of you who are Christian politicians and statesmen to decide. But of this I am sure – anything that breaks with Christian principle will not work. It will only produce the kind of mounting fury which is now threatening to engulf our whole society – if not right now, then within a few years. It is self-deceiving to see all this as the work of a few agitators. It is not. It is a reflex in the machine, as it were, to what happens when the rules are broken. It is the cogs in a watch grinding to a halt because of sand which should not be there.
>
> Put differently, it is life and the universe in *reaction*. So my challenge is to encourage subordination of policy to principle, bearing in mind that it is better in the eyes of both time and eternity to lose in the short term with what must ultimately win, rather than to win in the short term with that which will ultimately lose. (See *The Passing Summer*, pp. 218–223.)

So for AE it was a matter pure and simple of seeking justice for all and understanding, as Michael often put it, that "justice is simply love built into structures". That's what it was all about. Not complicated really. This understanding made Paul's hymn of love in 1 Corinthians 13 one of the most political of chapters because it calls on every Christian to work the love ethic into every aspect of life – and that has to include the political. Michael once preached on that chapter and its implications for society in a conservative white church in his home town. It was 25 years before he was invited back!

Festo Kivengere and Idi Amin

For Festo Kivengere this love ethic coming from the Cosmic Christ of Creation not only required that its implications be worked out in political and social structures, but it required that the Christian show love, even to political enemies. One might not like what they did, or the political sins they committed, but one still had to love the sinner while hating the sin.

It was this kind of posture which Festo, Archbishop Janani Luwum, the AE team and the Ugandan church had to try and manifest as the Ugandan political crisis heated up.

With Idi Amin's regime becoming more brutal, oppressive and murderous by the day, the Ugandan church generally and Festo specifically were struggling to know how to respond. What, for example, were they to do about the fear, anxiety, torture and death which was coming to many? In February a girl from Kenya who had been studying at Makerere University, having been warned that she was in peril, sought to escape. But at the airport she was arrested and then disappeared or "was disappeared", as Ugandans often said. In March that year, a Makerere University student was shot at the gate of the university and the entire student body was overcome with grief. Their student leader gave a very hard-hitting speech against Amin's regime. Then he fled the country. The year moved along with these kinds of atrocities, killings, lootings and executions proliferating. At the end of the year (1976) came PACLA, attended by Archbishop Janani Luwum, Bishop Festo and many other Ugandan Christian leaders.

Festo's Challenge

In late January 1977 some 30,000 Christians gathered at Bweranyangi for the consecration of a new bishop. Festo was asked to give the sermon. With rows of military men, policemen, government administrators, bishops, clergy, Muslim sheikhs, Roman Catholic dignitaries, intelligence officers and representatives of President Amin present, Festo preached from Acts 20:22–28, as part of the designated reading in the church calendar for that day. There they found the words from the Apostle Paul: "I am not scared of these dangers, for my life is no longer of any value to me except that I may fulfil the ministry I have received to witness to the grace of God."

Festo stressed how Christ's mission had reached its climax when he was hanging on the cross. There before him were his enemies: jealous religious leaders, mocking soldiers, Roman authorities ignoring justice, and the mob shouting, "Crucify Him." "Our suffering Lord," said Festo, "loved them all with unquenchable love and He bled to death for them, forgiving them all in advance!"

Describing the occasion and the message, Festo later wrote in his little book *I Love Idi Amin* (pp. 44–45):

> I gave two challenges. The first was to the bishops: "Therefore, under God, watch over, plead for the church which he bought. It is the preciousness of the soul that makes the minister valuable."
>
> After that I challenged the government authorities, because every authority has been given by God to use for his precious people whom he bought with his blood. I said: "Many of you have misused your authority, taking things by force, using too much force. Jesus Christ uses authority to save men and women – how are you using your authority? If you misuse the authority God gave you, God is going to judge you, because he is the one who gave it to you."

At the end a Muslim provincial governor said: "Thank you for your speech!" However, Festo's friends were terrified, fearing that he would be whisked away that day.

But the die had been cast. Everybody knew that the state had been confronted with its brutal injustices and abuses of human rights by a fearless bishop.

As a model of how Christians ought to operate in politically traumatised contexts, the archbishop, Bishop Festo, and other bishops now sought with all vigour to confront President Amin face to face. But the president refused. Said Festo: "He was surrounded by people who feared that our influence on the president might make him change some of his policies that benefited them, and so they advised him against us."

Document for the President

The decision was taken therefore to put their position and concerns in a document for the president. Wrote Festo later:

> In our document we expressed to the president our concern for the church and for "the people we serve under your care". We mentioned the danger that not only bishops are in, but also ordinary Christians, as illustrated by the presence of many widows and orphans in our churches due to killings by government agents.
>
> We listed other strains and iniquities that we are concerned about. We closed by mentioning that we are part of a worldwide community which is deeply concerned for us, as all other religious bodies, and that we care, lest the good image of our country be damaged. This was expressed with all due honour and respect for his position, and was personally signed by the archbishop and 15 other bishops who were able to be present. (*I Love Idi Amin*, pp. 49-50)

Authorities and Religious Leaders Meet

In mid-February 1977, the government authorities said that they wanted to meet with all religious leaders. Says Festo: "We arrived at the spacious grounds of the Nile Mansion Hotel outside the conference centre to find almost the entire army there and large groups of governors, administrators, heads of departments and all the religious leaders."

The archbishop and others were accused of plotting against the state, at which the soldiers shouted "Kill them! Kill them now!" Festo said it reminded him of the day of crucifixion.

There were many other accusations tossed at the church leaders, to which they responded as appropriate.

Finally the gathering was dismissed, with everyone allowed to leave except the archbishop. He was told to stay behind to see the president. Festo and others who wanted to stay with the archbishop were shooed off at gunpoint.

In reality at this time the archbishop was being pressed to sign a confession document, which he refused to do. At which he was shot in cold blood. Recorded Festo: "We were told later that he was praying aloud for his captives when he died. We have talked with eye witnesses who claim they saw him shot and with others who saw the bodies in the morgue with bullet wounds."

Government newspapers next day said that the archbishop had died in a tragic car accident. Festo and others knew better.

The moment had arrived for Bishop Festo and his wife Mera to flee; they were next on President Amin's death list.

They also knew that AE team member James Katarikawe, his wife Muriel and family had had a very close shave. Amin's soldiers had come for them in the middle of the night and they had escaped out the back door of their house to hide themselves in a mosquito-infested swamp at the back of their dwelling. Through the night they all lay motionless, eaten alive by mosquitoes while Amin's soldiers ransacked their home, like attacking piranha fish, leaving it totally cleaned out. All James and Muriel found in the morning was their battered Bible tossed into the middle of their front lawn. But they were alive, praise God, though it had been a close thing.

However, being much more prominent as a church leader, Festo knew for his part that he and his wife had to get out. And quickly. James bravely stayed on to man the office and lead the team.

Of Festo and Mera's flight we have already written.

Challenge

But the challenge now for both Bishop Festo and the church in Uganda was how to respond both spiritually and politically to what was happening. One thing they knew was that they could not forsake the love ethic and imperative of Jesus.

For Festo, as we have indicated, this even included President Idi Amin, who had killed his archbishop. In so doing Amin had also killed the chairman of AE. Amin now had Festo *number one* on his hit list. That was a political thing. How Festo would respond was also at one level a political question, albeit rooted in spiritual conviction. The question was whether love and forgiveness were relevant in the political arena. We have told how Festo fled into exile, just escaping with his life, and then found himself at All Souls' Church in London on Good Friday and feeling very bitter and twisted. The sermon was on

"Father, forgive them, for they know not what they do." Said Festo: "I had to face my own attitude towards President Amin and his agents. The Holy Spirit showed me that I was getting hard in my spirit, and that my hardness and bitterness toward those who were persecuting us could only bring spiritual loss. This would take away my ability to communicate the love of God, which is the essence of my ministry and testimony."

It would also constitute the essence of his political response.

> So I had to ask for forgiveness from the Lord, and for grace to love President Amin more, because these events had shaken my loving relationship with all those people. The Lord gave assurance of forgiveness on that Good Friday, when I was one of the congregation that sat for three hours meditating on the redeeming love of Jesus Christ. Right there the Lord healed me, and I hurried to tell Mera, my wife, about it. This was fresh air for my tired soul. I knew I had seen the Lord and been released: love filled my heart.
>
> This was the spirit in which brother Janani met his death, and this is the release of spirit to be found in the Lord's people in Uganda.
>
> We look back with great love to our country. We love President Idi Amin. We owe him the debt of love, for he is one of those for whom Christ shed his precious blood. As long as he is still alive, he is still redeemable. Pray for him, that in the end he may see a new way of life, rather than a way of death. (*I Love Idi Amin*, pp. 62–63)

This did not mean that Festo and his fellow bishops and his AE team would not politically resist and oppose Amin, because they did this fiercely. But the methodology would be peaceful and rooted in Christian love rather than violence.

A reporter asked Festo: "If you were in a room with Idi Amin and he handed you a revolver, what would you do?" Replied Festo: "I would hand the gun back to Amin and say – 'Mr President, this is your weapon, not mine. Mine is the weapon of love.'"

Justice

A corollary of this love ethic principle for the AE team was that injustice had to be opposed – most especially the kind of rank and cruel injustice epitomised in Idi Amin's atrocities or in the policies of apartheid and racial discrimination as formally inflicted on South Africa by the National Party from 1948 onwards. This had to be resisted. Michael, for his part, could never understand why his many conservative Christian critics labelled him as "political" for opposing apartheid but did not see themselves as "political" for implicitly or explicitly supporting it.

In reality the very notion of politics for AE has always been basically a matter of seeking to apply the kingdom values and principles of the gospel to all of life and to the way people live in society. Seeking to bring all life, including the social and political, under the kingship of Christ and within the effective control of the Spirit of God, meant that no arena of life was exempt from Christian concern. Preaching and living the kingdom of God could not but include facing the political happenings of life. Had not the great Dutch theologian Abraham Kuyper (1837–1920) said: "There is no inch of the created universe over which Jesus does not say 'Mine!'"

The understanding of "politics" AE embraced was therefore broad and with a big "P" rather than a little "p". The team was not on about party politics but political principles drawn from scripture and the sociopolitical implications of scripture. The church does not get into the matter of party politics but presents politicians, statespersons and government leaders with the Judaeo-Christian moral and ethical principles that should guide, shape and be enshrined in political policies. The church's basic concern is to see society operate under the kingship of Christ.

John Stott, always a good friend to Michael and Festo and a great encourager of AE, including its sociopolitical stance, once put it this way:

> The words "politics" and "political" may be given either a broad or a narrow definition. *Broadly speaking*, "politics" denotes the life of the city (*polis*) and the responsibilities of the citizen (*polites*). It is concerned therefore with the whole of our life in human soci-

ety. Politics is the art of living together in a community. According to its *narrow definition*, however, politics is the science of government. It is concerned with the development and adoption of specific policies with a view to their being enshrined in legislation. It is about gaining power for social change.

Once this distinction is clear, we may ask whether Jesus was involved in politics. In the latter and narrower sense, he clearly was not. He never formed a political party, adopted a political programme or organised a political protest. He took no steps to influence the policies of Caesar, Pilate or Herod. On the contrary, he renounced a political career. In the other and broader sense of the word, however, his whole ministry was political. For he had himself come into the world, in order to share in the life of the human community, and he sent his followers into the world to do the same. Moreover, the kingdom of God he proclaimed and inaugurated was a radically new and different social organisation, whose values and standards challenged those of the old and fallen community. In this way his teaching had "political" implications. It offered an alternative to the *status quo*. His kingship, moreover, was perceived as a challenge to Caesar's, and he was therefore accused of sedition. (*Issues Facing Christians Today*, John Stott, page 11)

Although this understanding, as the one owned and embraced by AE, seems simple and straightforward enough, it was not reached in a moment. There was inevitably a journey behind it, especially for Michael Cassidy.

Early Influences

For Michael, perhaps the first key influence relating to justice was his father, the Senior Mechanical and Electrical Engineer in Basutoland, who was imbued with a deep sense of what was right or wrong, proper or improper, just or unjust.

The experience of Michael's grandparents in the Boer War was also formative in so far as they helped bring the young lad to the conviction that people and relationships mattered, that somehow or other this principle was massively violated politically by Britain in the Boer War and that it had had wretched political consequences for South Africa down through the years.

Key also in the formation of Michael's political understanding was his friendship, referred to earlier in this story, with his childhood hero, Patrick Duncan, who lived next door to the Cassidys and who later founded the South African Liberal Party with Alan Paton, Peter Brown and others. Pat Duncan's political commitment to justice was passionate; life was all about ensuring that everybody had a fair shake. He abominated apartheid and all of its ways and he equally abominated anything to do with violence, hence his making Mahatma Gandhi and his philosophy of Satyagraha a guiding star in his political thinking. Michael was impressed and influenced. He came to see that discrimination was wrong and justice was right. Pat Duncan said apartheid would doom South Africa and in 1948 when the Nationalists came to power, Pat walked Michael across a mountain behind the Duncan home and declared to him that this was a political tragedy from which the country would take generations to recover. Said Pat Duncan: "Mark my words, apartheid is a word that is destined to mobilise the world."

Then at prep (junior high) school, Michael's headmaster Douglas McJanet smoked a pipe engraved with the face of Dr D.F. Malan, the great exponent of apartheid and leader of the National Party. McJanet said wryly that "This seems to please both sides." But in reality the pipe symbolised lighting a fire under Malan! Then at high school, Michael's first house master, Jim Chutter, was a passionate politico in addition to being a hilarious school master, and for several years was more preoccupied with the opposition movement known as the Torch Commando than with house mastering.

By the time Michael went away to Cambridge University, aged 18, he viewed the political process as the only way radical change would finally be brought about in South Africa. Even so, he often asked himself: if love and mutual acceptance between the races was what was really required, then how was it that human beings, as frail creatures of dust, could find the capacity to love and accept each other? Was not the spirit of racial intolerance or antipathy too deeply ingrained in human nature to be uprooted by the political process alone?

From Conviction to Conversion to Confusion

When Michael's dramatic, almost Damascus Road-type conversion took place at Cambridge, he immediately recoiled from politics as the answer to South Africa's problems and became convinced that the only way was through Christian conversion. Only if people came to Christ could they become capable of loving one another across the racial barriers. So the conviction that Pat Duncan, Michaelhouse, and Michael's family background had put into his heart that politics was the answer was now replaced by a contrary view that Christian conversion was the answer.

But then rather abruptly and early in the piece he was brought to realise that there were many so-called converted, evangelical, Bible-believing people in South Africa who were either explicit or implicit supporters of apartheid and racial discrimination. In addition to his friend Michael Nuttall, one of those who brought this home to him was Father Trevor Huddleston, who came to lecture at Cambridge not long after the publication of his famous and controversial book *Naught for Your Comfort*. As the book was being launched, Michael went along with his student friends Michael Nuttall and Alasdair Macaulay to listen to the famous Community of the Resurrection priest who had smuggled the manuscript of his book out of South Africa for publication in the UK just before he himself was forced to flee the country. Michael remembers an intense and deep discussion with Trevor Huddleston over an early-morning breakfast, along with Michael Nuttall, John Reeves, son of the late Bishop of Johannesburg, Ambrose Reeves, and Arthur Jenkins, a South African research scholar at Kings College, Cambridge. Huddleston was passionately persuaded and indeed persuasive that political processes rooted in Christian principle and conviction had to be brought powerfully to bear upon South Africa so as to remove the National Party and save the nation from political cataclysm.

Michael was confused. Was South Africa's need either conversion or politics, or both or neither, or something else quite different? This was the issue facing the young student.

Bringing Things Together

Perhaps Trevor Huddleston and Michael Nuttall were right. One had to try and bring these things together. And so Michael and Alasdair Macaulay, his digs-mate, also seeking to work through a newfound and developing faith, were happy to join Michael Nuttall in May 1956 in sending to *The Times* a letter which was almost entirely the handiwork of Nuttall.

The point was that there were some people in England, even in quite high circles, who affirmed that if there were 36 million Africans in Great Britain, then it was likely that white Englishmen would desire a colour bar as much as white South Africans. So they should not be so hard on the South African government. However, the South African trio at Cambridge noted that "the *Tu Quoque* (you also) argument, so appealing to the apostle of self-deception, does not exonerate or excuse the white South African in any way. It merely shows that the Englishman is likely to be as evil as he!"

Earlier on the letter had noted that "nothing is more rooted, it seems to us, in the average white South African mind than the capacity for self deception. It is sometimes deliberate enough to amount to sheer, blatant dishonesty. We deceive ourselves into thinking that apartheid will work even though we know deep down that to work it will require large land grants to the African, and that the European farmer upon whose vote we depend, will not give up his land." Other examples of self deception were given, and then this observation: "The cancer of dishonest self deception is one of our greatest diseases, and we sincerely believe this to be no exaggeration or distortion of the facts."

The long letter concluded: "We love our country. There is a great work to do there. We would urge, in humility, that well-meaning sympathy be not confused with honest thinking about fundamentals. It is tragic that the conscience should be stilled when it ought to be stirred."

Press Reactions

The letter made the little trio quite famous for a while around England, with all sorts of comments in the British press and in academic circles. Comments even surfaced in the South African press in the *Cape Times* on Friday 18 May 1956: "In a letter published on this page, three South African students in England, their eyes freshened by distance, expressed alarm at the rooted capacity for self deception of their white fellow countrymen." The editorial picked up on the line of the three students and reflected on white South Africans generally saying: "Are their powers of self deception really so rooted that they will suffer no feeling of moral crime? If so the outlook is grim indeed. For, truly, deceiving others, bad as it is, is far less dangerous than self deception."

Ongoing Struggle

Michael's struggles to bring the spiritual and the sociopolitical together were further challenged the following year (December 1956) when 156 South African men and women from all walks of life and all racial groups were arrested and charged with high treason. Though the 156 were later acquitted with the charges proving unfounded, the moment of their arrests seemed to call for a response. South Africans at Cambridge decided that a march from Cambridge to London was called for, culminating in a picketing of South Africa House in Trafalgar Square. Michael decided that a march from Cambridge to London was not for him, and he would go by train instead. He did not relish, either, the thought of picketing South Africa House and carrying a black armband and wearing or carrying a cross.

However, having sought to struggle the issue through with Michael Nuttall and Alasdair Macaulay, Michael decided he would do it. On the morning of the picket, in his devotional reading, he read James 2:9: "But if you show partiality (between people) you commit sin." This was a clear biblical word reiterating that the discriminatory ways of apartheid were wrong. That was that. Firm stands had to be taken. Michael would go for it and be part of the picket. In the middle of the day, however, he was suddenly challenged whether this was the way to go when his former English master from Michaelhouse, part of the huge gawking crowd in Trafalgar Square, spotted him, trundled up nonchalantly and said: "And what, Cassidy, pray, are you doing here?"

"I muttered something pretty incongruous," said Michael later, "and probably pretty cheeky, at which the master betook himself back into the throng, shaking his head and wondering what his former pupils would be up to next!"

An official from inside South Africa House came out and said: "I can understand the protest. But why the cross?"

Ah, Yes, indeed! Why the cross?

New York

The summer of 1957, when Michael went to New York to visit relatives, brought things finally and clearly into perspective. Night after night he went to Madison Square Garden to hear Billy Graham as he preached the personal gospel of salvation, new birth and conversion. But then on the television screens at the same time through that summer, Martin Luther King was preaching in the streets of Montgomery, Alabama, and elsewhere in the south, the sociopolitical gospel of social justice. Governor Faubus was trying forcibly to prevent black students entering southern universities and President Eisenhower was sending troops into Little Rock, Arkansas, to enforce student integration, while many so-called Bible believers screamed in protest.

"Yes," said Michael to himself, "both these things are right. Billy Graham is right as he preaches a personal gospel of salvation and Martin Luther King is surely right as he preaches the social gospel of justice and racial integration. And Eisenhower, a strongly professing Christian, was politically right to be enforcing it. They are both flip sides of the same coin of the full-orbed message of Jesus Christ and his kingdom principles." After all, while the Lord's Prayer was on about Heaven and our Father in Heaven, did not Jesus urge his disciples to pray "Thy kingdom come, Thy will be done ON EARTH as it is in Heaven." What happened on Earth, not just in Heaven, was important for the Christian.

And as Michael later went through Fuller Seminary in the four years from 1959 to 1963, this balanced conviction took hold. Then as the African Enterprise team finally returned to South Africa in 1964, it was with this posture clearly and fully in place that they took up their work.

Immediate Opposition

Not long after getting back to South Africa, various little straws in the wind alerted the AE team to the fact that they had caught the attention of the South African security police. One manifest example was a visit to Michael's parents by a "very probing gentleman", said Michael's mother, while Michael was away at the Berlin Congress on Evangelism in 1966. A hundred and one politically pointed questions were put to Michael's parents by this man, who professed to be a radio interviewer intending to interview Michael for a programme on his return from Berlin. Michael's parents twigged and, without letting on to the questioner, went along in seeking to give as honest and full answers as they could about their son and the fact that his basic mission and ministry in life was a Christian one and not aimed at subverting the state or doing anything illegal.

Returning from overseas, Michael heard about the visit to his parents, went to see the man concerned in Durban, and pretending to be totally naïve and coveting a radio interview, poured out the real facts about what AE was, what its aims and intentions were, and how it was actually financed. One of the points specially at issue was that of where AE got its funding. The so-called interviewer, who not surprisingly had no intention of making any radio programme on Michael, indicated that in his view African Enterprise was financed by the CIA. Later check-ups on the man confirmed him to be an informer.

Political Heat Intensifying

As AE South Africa was taking its political stand against apartheid, the political heat was intensifying across the country. Thus in 1970 when the team was in Johannesburg for a year-long citywide mission, it became very evident as they laboured to do evangelism in Soweto that the place was becoming a political powderkeg. The team sought to get a political message indicating their concerns to Prime Minister John Vorster and also to Connie Mulder, then Minister of so-called Native or Plural Affairs. The word came back that things were fine in Soweto and any perils should not be exaggerated.

Six years later, on 16 June 1976, Soweto was to blow. On

that day Michael was conducting a mission to Rosebank Union Church in Johannesburg and he changed his sermon in order to speak generally to white South Africans on the text first of Matthew 23:37 "Oh Jerusalem, Jerusalem, (Oh South Africa, South Africa!), how often would I have gathered you... and you would not", and then Luke 13:34 when Jesus weeps over Jerusalem saying: "Would that even now you knew the things that make for peace."

Personal and Social and the South African Church

However, in 1970 that was still six years away. For Michael and the team the issue with which they had struggled earlier of bringing together the personal gospel and the social gospel seemed to be crying out for integration and acceptance into the life of the South African church as a whole. We have told how Michael decided to approach John Rees, then working in civic affairs in Soweto, and shortly to be General Secretary of the South African Council of Churches, himself a passionate opponent of apartheid, and put to him the idea of gathering the whole church of South Africa to look into the issue of bringing together the vertical and the horizontal dimensions of the gospel.

While this vision related to the church's witness, message and life in spiritual terms, the whole exercise at another level was profoundly political, because the gospel lifestyle of non-discriminatory togetherness and honouring human dignity and value struck at the very root of the divisive and discriminatory lifestyle imposed on the country by the apartheid ideology.

Rees, with his spiritual instincts and commitments to political justice, was an instant convert to the idea and before Mission '70 ended the notion was born of the South African Congress on Mission and Evangelism.

But tracking the political thread, we note that the political authorities, well aware of the political implications of the venture, tossed the book at it and decided to be maximally obstructionist. They would not allow the 25 prominent overseas speakers, including Billy Graham, to enter the country for the congress. They would not allow integrated hotel accommodation. They would not allow integrating riding on the buses to and fro from the congress venue. However, following a powerful showdown which Michael, John Rees and David Bosch had with Dr Connie Mulder, the cabinet reversed its decision and decided to allow all the overseas speakers, including Billy Graham and Dr Hans Ruedi Weber from the World Council of Churches, entry into the country.

Both law and convention were defied as the congress went ahead and booked a brave hotel to handle non-racial accommodation. The team and the Congress Committee also found a bus company willing to risk non-racial bussing to and from the congress venue. It had been a powerful and pretty brutal political interface between church and state. And the state had blinked.

Contributing to the power of the process were two huge multi-racial Billy Graham rallies, the first in Kings Park Stadium during the congress with 50,000 people present, and the second held just after the congress at Wanderers Stadium in Johannesburg with 60,000 present. The rallies created such a sensation that newspaper banners screamed from lamp posts: "Apartheid Doomed". It was not to happen for 20 years, but the writing, even then, was on the wall and Christians from all sectors of the church were playing their part in new ways to bring it about. The vertical and the horizontal components of the gospel were coming together in the South African church in new ways and in the amalgam proving their awesome power.

Rhodesia/Zimbabwe

But South Africa was not the only country in which the sociopolitical concerns of the AE team were finding expression and focus. Rhodesia was another.

Michael, for his part, had long been interested in Rhodesia. That was the country to which his father had first come in the early 1930s as a young British engineer. The struggle to find the way through for a strongly multi-racial community had been long and arduous. In September 1953 the then Southern Rhodesia, Nyasaland, and Northern Rhodesia became a Federation with Sir Godfrey Huggins as its first prime minister. He was succeeded in 1965 by Sir Roy Welensky, a one-time engine-driver, but now prominent politician. The experiment had seemed to have some logic as the three countries formed a natural economic grouping. But the seeds of the Federation's own destruction were within it from the start, the full backing of the African majority population and political groupings not having been effectively secured. The Federation came to an end in December 1963, amidst multiple political convulsions.

Tension and Upheaval

Michael's first visit to Rhodesia took place four years before the end of Federation in 1959. The day he arrived there he found the country in a state of huge tension and upheaval with the prime minister, Sir Edgar Whitehead, having declared a state of emergency. Michael at the time was driving a car from Cape Town to Mazabuka in Northern Rhodesia (now Zambia) for the family of Jack and Ruth Holmes, whom he had met on board ship while returning to South Africa. Ruth had encouraged Michael a great deal by showing him an article which had the effect of urging him to take up his calling in South Africa.

Michael was intrigued by the fact that Whitehead had sought, in his 1961 constitution, to introduce the beginnings of some real non-racialism in Rhodesia with a non-racial franchise arrangement based on certain educational and property qualifications. It was not universal adult suffrage but it seemed to be a step in the right direction. After all the whites of Rhodesia had accepted by a two to one majority a new constitution that would make inevitable in due time an African majority in their legislature. For African nationalists, however, as history would record, the only adequate franchise arrangement was that of full adult suffrage, not a qualified franchise. And that of course would mean the rapid end of white minority rule.

When Michael and the AE team began their work in Southern Africa, this reality was something they had grasped. Knowing that Rhodesia was, in a sense, the pacesetter and political dry-run for South Africa, the team watched with alarm the build-up of political tension as whites became more conservative and extreme and black nationalists for their part drew further away with their cries for full independence, political freedom and majority rule now. The path to crisis and collision had been embarked upon, culminating on 11 November 1965 when Ian Smith declared his Unilateral Declaration of

Independence (UDI) from Great Britain. The dice from both black and white sides had been cast.

AE's Posture

AE's basic posture was always that the Christian church had a unique responsibility and indeed capacity to be a peacemaker and catalyst for peaceful political change in these convulsive racial contexts. The fact was that the Christian church was the only grouping with members in all the different political sectors and should therefore, theoretically at least, be able to propagate Christian values and principles and reconciliation within every political grouping as a means of pulling people together and helping them forwards towards peace.

However, for any Christian contribution to be made it required understanding different contexts as fully as possible. AE always believed that. With that in mind, Michael went to Rhodesia in late 1966 while en route to the Berlin Congress on Evangelism. He took over 100 pages of notes in a few days as he met with an assortment of church leaders, political analysts, lawyers, some black MPs, including Chad Chipunza, and the embittered former prime minister of the Federation, Sir Roy Welensky. Sir Roy told Michael that he viewed Ian Smith's UDI as a politically suicidal and totally retrogressive move. "I may be an engine driver," said Welensky, "but I am not a damn fool like Ian Smith!"

All the straws in the wind indicated escalating political crisis, confrontation and finally convulsion.

Though Michael did not meet Prime Minister Ian Smith then, he did on a couple of occasions a few years later. On one of these, Smith was in a blistering mood having just received a letter from Idi Amin announcing that he was coming down with an army from Uganda to liberate Rhodesia! Smith was apoplectic! Once he had calmed down, he seemed ready to receive Michael's testimony about Christ, whom everybody needed in their hearts, including politicians!

Hearing Michael's testimony, Smith commented: "You sound just like my son, Alec, who keeps saying these kinds of things to me as well."

As it happened, Michael had also got to know Alec Smith

and his friend Arthur Kanodereka, who together brought a powerful Christian testimony to Ian Smith of "a better way". Tragically Kanodereka, soon after coming with Alec Smith to visit Michael in his home, was blown up by a guerrilla bomb planted in his car.

AE Team

Michael never felt he made much of an impression on Prime Minister Smith, being "undoubtedly just one of dozens of people trying to see him and dissuade him from the course of action on which he seemed to be embarked". However, while the AE South Africa team hoped that sooner or later there would be a Rhodesian AE team which could at least make a modest contribution from within, they were gratified that many church leaders from all sides seemed to be involved. So was Moral Rearmament (MRA). So of course was Alec Smith, who laboured day and night behind the scenes to bring opposing sides together for dialogue and negotiation.

In due time (November 1977), in the good providence of God, an AE team was launched in the then Rhodesia under the leadership of Rev Gary Strong, an ardent and fiery evangelist with a very strong sociopolitical sense and a powerful witness to almost all the internal political leaders and figures of all races and on all sides. Many others, like Robert Mugabe and Joshua Nkomo, of course were in exile. Gary Strong would be succeeded in AE leadership in due course over the years by Chris Sewell, John Smythe, Luke Klemo, Orpheus Hove and in 2001, Rev Simukayi Mutamangira, former Dean of the Anglican Cathedral in Harare.

But in the 1970s AE also connected with people like the businessman Ken McKenzie and Rev Ross Main of the Washington Fellowship, who were likewise working behind the scenes from a Christian perspective to try and bring the differing internal leaders together. Michael and Ross even developed code names for all the key players so they could discuss the situation over the phone unbothered by security eavesdroppers. Though Mugabe was outside the country, nevertheless fruitful linkages were on the go with Ndabaningi Sithole, Elliot Gabellah and others. Michael particularly remembers a fruitful and extended conversation and time of prayer with Bishop Abel Muzorewa, later to succeed Ian Smith as prime minister for a short while before full independence under Robert Mugabe in 1980.

Another fruitful visit, along with team member Josiah Mutumba, took place to the deputy president, Mr John Wrathall. Things were incredibly tense and traumatic by that time and the deputy president took a handkerchief from his pocket to wipe away his tears as Josiah prayed for him saying: "Dear Lord, we ask you to bless the deputy president, because we know that you are behind him with your power and ahead of him with your plans." Almost certainly both Josiah and the deputy president knew that those plans included the imminent end of white rule in Rhodesia.

The Rhodesian Congress on Evangelism in Context (Bulawayo)

Of course these various attempts at meaningful linkage behind the scenes with different players in the equation could probably not in the nature of things be very immediately powerful or consequential. Michael was never unrealistic about this. "I don't think we cut much ice with all those endeavours. But on the other hand we believed that if we sought with everyone else, and especially all concerned believers, to do our bit, it could in fact add up to something. And of course one never knows what God may choose to use."

However what could be very powerful and consequential was for the Rhodesian church to rise up and really make a statement about political justice, reconciliation and a new political order, not to mention mission and evangelism.

We have spoken of how Gary Strong, later to lead AE in Zimbabwe, along with Phineas Dube and AE South Africa, put a congress together for August/September 1977.

But coming at the height of the civil war in that country, the political atmosphere was charged and the necessity of facing the political context inescapable.

One hundred and forty delegates from most of the major racial groups and denominations of Rhodesia met. Some 70 per cent were black. They tackled the thorny problem of how the church should advance the gospel amid such national tensions, and address the anguished political context at the same time. Heartbreaking stories from delegates whose own sons were turning to violence emerged. There were many very difficult sessions, when white insensitivity met black militancy head on.

Among the participants was a father who had a son in the guerrilla army and another father with a son in the national security forces. The anguish of the two as they met, with their sons out there trying to kill each other, was awesome and deeply moving.

At one point the conference was nearly brought to an end when a person from an all-white singing group prayed "Lord, we pray that the demon spirit in evil terrorists may be destroyed." The conference erupted and nearly disbanded. It took a day to get it back on track. Of course for whites the black fighters were terrorists, for blacks they were freedom fighters. For whites Rhodesian army troops were defenders of law and order; for blacks they were brutal oppressors.

People with deep hurts from all sides of the political spectrum stood up in quick succession and brought conflicting emotions to the forefront. Tensions ran high. Two men took the lead in bringing the conference back to a sound Christian track. They were Phineas Dube, the black leader of Scripture Union and Gary Strong, the white leader of New Life For All. Because of their influence the conference was able to complete its significant work.

Consensus Around a Call

Gradually a consensus emerged, and found its focus in the document *Call to the Churches and Nations of South Africa*. Michael Cassidy and the AE delegation helped draft it, and it was sent to national, political and church leaders in most of the countries of the sub-continent and was widely quoted in Europe. The document, among other things, pleaded on the one hand for the Rhodesian peace talks to start up again, and on the other, for the task of evangelism to go ahead with all vigour.

The document was seen by many as a model theological and political statement addressing both warring sides in a conflict with the church as the agent trying to bring them together in reconciliation.

Whether in the final analysis the congress would make any real difference to Rhodesia was beyond anyone's guess. The organisers had done their best. The Christian community of Rhodesia had made history in being heard for once to speak as one. They were content to leave the results to God.

Certainly some early results were very encouraging. The "Call" was considered by a reporter of the *Rhodesia Herald* in Salisbury as "a blueprint for a new peace-seeking initiative in the Rhodesian constitutional deadlock".

Prime Minister Ian Smith, when presented with the "Call", said it was "a laudable attempt which needed to be made".

A member of the South African Parliament wrote to Michael Cassidy, saying: "Congratulations on the *Call to The Churches and Nations of Southern Africa*. At last we have a sensible statement which is genuinely Christian and brings a proper appreciation of the spectrum and complexity of the Southern African situation."

He went on:

> I think that you and AE must be congratulated on the way in which you move into situations which are often polarised, or where people have bracketed each other and thus dismissed each other, and in that situation, because of your acceptance and love of the person who may not be fully attuned to a biblical way of thinking, you are able to put in an evangelical emphasis. I think this applies not only in terms of this particular Call, but also in terms of your evangelism.

Said Gary Strong in retrospect: "The conference and its statement were able to speak to people of opposing opinions in an atmosphere of Christian fellowship and courage and urge them to face the future with a deeper sense of God as active at the human level. This way we were able to show that where there was conflict and confrontational situations Christ could still be the answer."

Bridge Over Troubled Waters

From the late 1970s through to the early 1990s the AE teams across Africa, but most especially in Uganda and South Africa, found that politics and the political dimension of life were so pervasive, so "in your face" daily, that there was no escaping them. All of life was endlessly affected. Grief was also most people's daily companion.

Michael remembers the pain and outrage of being forced to sit at different ends of a train when travelling with his colleague, Abiel Thipanyane, to Johannesburg. He remembers going fishing with Andrew Mohibidu at Lake Midmar near his home, and battling to find a place where they could fish together without breaking the law. He remembers a hotelier putting Indian David Peters out of the hotel lounge where the team stopped en route from the Eastern Cape for a bite and briefly to watch a TV rugby game, and how David impacted the silly man with his gracious response before the rest of the team left the hotel.

But in spite of all this, the team held firmly onto the notion that in all these things Jesus could still be the "Bridge over Troubled Waters".

So they all remember well, for example, how the gospel worked through David Peters on another occasion some years later when he was preaching in the Eastern Cape and a rabid white Afrikaner right-winger came into the service. He was away from his wife and kids, living on drink, porn and promiscuity and with a heart filled with hatred for black and brown people. But at least he was in the church and listening to this Indian evangelist who looked a bit like the then president, F.W. de Klerk.

The prodigal husband and father suddenly found himself

being deeply moved. At the end of the service, to his own amazement, he went forward to give his life to Christ. The change in him in subsequent weeks was amazing as he returned to his wife and children, ended his drinking, promiscuity and orgies of porn-viewing and left his right-wing political party. Soon he was out testifying and preaching with blacks at the weekends.

"Now that's real conversion," commented David Peters.

Later this man wrote to AE: "You have no idea what a miracle this all was. You see, I had two pet-hates – Indians, and F.W. de Klerk, who I felt had sold the whites down the river. Now here comes this Indian who looks like F.W. de Klerk and he preaches to me, and I get converted. Amazing! Praise God!"

However, the downside side of this kind of event revealed to Michael and the team again and again over the next few years that even in the Christian church many, especially whites, were still miles away from reaching for serious political reconciliation and a new day in the land.

Lost Opportunities

And this, amazingly, in spite of the fact that SACLA had happened in mid-1979.

However, *kairos* moments of opportunity are so often lost. Although the church's witness went forward from strength to strength, a political polarisation was clearly still underway. Frightened and conservative whites were getting more frightened and more conservative. Militant and angry blacks were getting more militant and more angry. For every step the government took forwards it seemed to take two backwards. But consciences were stirring and the 500 Dutch Reformed leaders who had been at SACLA started a creative disturbance within their church. Indeed, said some, the theological monolith undergirding apartheid was cracked at SACLA and would not be put together again. Processes seemed to be underway by which the Dutch Reformed Church would move slowly and relentlessly, especially under the leadership of Professor Johan Heyns, a strong SACLA participant, to declare in 1986 that "apartheid is a sin". This would put the skids under the process by which theological legitimacy had been given to apartheid. Some Afrikaner theologians and thinkers indicated that in their view this was the beginning of the end for the system. It was also the beginning of the end for Heyns himself, who would in due course be assassinated with a bullet through the back of the head as he read stories to his grandchildren. This was almost certainly the work of right-wingers protesting against his new theological posture relating to the apartheid system.

However, while many positive post-SACLA processes were underway, the gap between whites and blacks seemed to widen. For AE, it seemed as if they were watching the nation and its polarised groups moving like two alienated people in a crumbling marriage towards "irretrievable breakdown". For Michael and AE the only thing which might bring any hope would be a fresh and costly reconciling initiative from Christian people.

To this end, the AE team in late 1985 called some 70 people together at the AE Centre to reflect on the extreme urgency of the situation and take some immediate and creative initiatives. The outcome was the calling together at three weeks notice of some 400 top church and parachurch leaders from 48 denominations for what would be called "The National Initiative for Reconciliation". The NIR, as it was known, convened in Pietermaritzburg in September 1985 with a wide range of invitees, including bishops, archbishops, moderators, black and white, young and old, left and right, radical and conservative. At the far end of the spectrum from one side was an angry group of AZAPO (Azanian People's Organisation) young people and then on the other side there was an anxious but open and tender 56-person contingent from the Dutch Reformed Church.

Desmond Tutu

After an opening Scripture had been read by South African author and thinker Alan Paton, Archbishop Desmond Tutu presented a very powerful challenge on forgiveness and reconciliation.

To the blacks he said: "In spite of everything, we are nevertheless called to the business of forgiveness and reconciliation." To whites he said: "How can you ask forgiveness from someone when you still have your foot firmly planted on his neck?"

He concluded: "True reconciliation, my brothers and sisters, is costly. It involves confrontation because the Cross was confrontation with evil. The Cross showed the evil of evil. Are we ready even to die? Are we ready to die physically, to die to our popularity, to die to our security? Are we ready to be made fools for the sake of Christ?"

Other powerful addresses in the conference followed from David Bosch, Frank Chikane, Khosa Mgojo, Michael Cassidy, Professor Bonganjalo Goba and Professor Klaus Nurnberger, a lecturer at the University of South Africa.

People also registered the point deeply when the ever-vocal and courageous Democratic Member of Parliament, Graham McIntosh, impishly told the NIR delegates: "You don't have to be a politician to know majority rule must finally come. You just have to be a mathematician!"

At the end of the five-day conference the NIR drew up a strong statement of spiritual affirmation, on the primacy of gospel witness and evangelism, prayer, worship and fellowship across racial barriers. It then made a twofold call, firstly for a national Day of Prayer (a Pray Away) on 9 October 1985 – with every one staying home on that normal working day – and secondly for an NIR delegation to go to State President Botha to request him to:

(i)   End the state of emergency.
(ii)   Remove the SADF and the emergency police forces from the townships.
(iii) Release all detainees and political prisoners, withdraw charges against the treason trialists and allow exiles to return home.
(iv)   Begin talks immediately with authentic leadership of the various population groups with a view toward equitable power sharing in South Africa.
(v)   Begin the process of introducing a common system of education.
(vi)   Take the necessary steps towards the elimination of all forms of legislated discrimination.

Encounter with President Botha

To pave the way for the wider NIR delegation to the president, Michael went on 8 October 1985 to meet President Botha in his office in Union Buildings, Pretoria. This was the day before the proposed "Pray Away" which the NIR had called for. He had gone hopefully and prayerfully, trusting for a positive reception.

In the event it was a brutal encounter, with the president, now incensed about the nationwide "Pray Away" due for the next day, resisting what the NIR was asking for, and declining to receive the wider delegation. The president, knowing that Michael as NIR chairman was to be on national television that night in an interview related to the "Pray Away", then insisted he denounce on TV the so-called "Kairos Document" and its drafters. This document, unlike the NIR resolution, was powerfully confrontational and seemed to the president to reflect Latin American Liberation Theology.

"I will be watching tonight, and if you do not denounce the *kairos* people and this document, I will fix you personally."

"Mr President," said Michael, "I cannot do that. I don't agree with all the theology of the document, but it represents a deep cry from the black world which the government and all whites must hear."

Botha was beside himself as the interview ended in distance and alienation.

When Michael told his wife Carol an hour or so later of the presidential threat and how he might have "anything happen" to him the next day, and get "fixed by the president", Carol replied: "Darling, do not on any account be intimidated. Just be obedient to the Lord and trust him."

Pray Away – 9 October 1985

President Botha on 8 October had promised Michael the "Pray Away" the next day would be a flop. In the event he was wrong. Most of South Africa, except for some mineworkers, stayed home on 9 October to pray either at home or in churches.

A photograph in the Johannesburg *Star* on 10 October of South Africa's busiest road (that from Soweto into Johannesburg) revealed a single, lone cyclist. The church of South Africa had in a sense flexed its muscles and called on God to flex his! The state and its president must surely have taken note. But if they had, there was not much evidence of it as the church's reconciliation endeavours just met with more repression.

Many years later in 2000 Michael would visit former President P.W. Botha at his retirement home in George, debrief over the confrontation of long ago and find reconciliation with the now friendly and reflective man.

"But I didn't fix you, did I?" chuckled Botha when Michael reminded him of that grim threat!

It was good in warm, shared prayer to close out the reconciliation experience with the former president.

Many years later in a theological journal, John Tooke noted how the 1985 Kairos Document had rejected the reconciliation route, and added:

> In an attempt to find common ground on the subject of reconciliation and to verify its own integrity, the NIR soldiered on in two areas. The first was to prepare a definition and theology of reconciliation and to publish theological guidelines on such matters as violence, democracy and economics.
>
> ... The second area was to encourage bridge-crossing and relationship-building in such a way that positive understanding of and identification with the black struggle could be effected. This was achieved through cross-cultural teamlets and Christian Encounters in black townships. (*Missionalia*, August 1993)

Encounters

In the so-called Encounters, such as the Mamelodi one, co-sponsored by Professor Nico Smith's Koinonia and by AE, whites would enter black townships and stay in black homes throughout the three-day duration of the Encounter Conference. Deep friendships and deepened understanding of different racial perspectives always flowed from these rich and very meaningful experiences.

Teamlets

The teamlet exercise was also invaluable. One of these took Michael Cassidy and a cross-racial, cross-denominational NIR teamlet into Port Elizabeth and New Brighton township on its borders. During the morning, while looking over Port Elizabeth's own "Soweto" township, the NIR group was tracked by the security police, then arrested and interrogated for three hours by four or five security policemen before being forbidden to preach that night in New Brighton.

Michael replied to his chief interrogator: "Sir, we did not get our mandate to preach and do the Lord's work from you or any man. So you cannot block us and we will be preaching and ministering in New Brighton tonight."

The officer stared at the preacher, turned on his heels and left. What now?

As the NIR group entered New Brighton that night, three Caspir armoured cars, their guns trained on the unwelcome intruders, and loaded with troops, their own AK47's also at the ready, followed the NIR teamlet into the township. When the teamlet disembarked at a local church for the service, Dutch Reformed Professor Adrio Konig went up to one Caspir and quizzed its commander: "Why all these guns and this show of force for a few preachers just with their Bibles?"

"You see, we are frightened, Dominee," said the young man.

Not long thereafter Michael was invited as NIR chairman to be one of many speakers at an ANC rally in the Dan QeQe Stadium. There were 42,000 people present, of whom Michael and Neil Pagard from AE were two of only fourteen or fifteen whites. Apart from calling for the release of Nelson Mandela from prison, Michael was able at the end of the meeting to bring a spiritual message. He noted the endless cries of "Amandla a wethu" (Power to the People), but stressed that that power, uncontrolled by the power of Jesus, would not be adequate. At which he launched into a well-known Zulu chorus (*Unamandl' 'u Jesu wami* – "our Jesus has the power") – in which the vast throng spontaneously joined as in a mighty acknowledgement of the living God.

For Michael and AE this was their style – to try and be relevantly in the political process but constantly call it to operate under the lordship of Christ and in his Spirit.

State of Emergency

The following year as townships burned, violence escalated and political temperatures rose, white fear, insecurity and intransigence were to find further expression as President P. W. Botha declared a state of emergency on 12 June 1986. It was the strictest and most stringent state of emergency in South Africa's history.

AE and the NIR fellowship, however, continued to believe that labouring for dialogue, reconciliation and peaceful change was still the best way. "Let's hold firmly," they said, "to Jesus as the Bridge over Troubled Waters. And let's grasp that with him as the Bridge, we don't have to be bridge-builders, just bridge-crossers."

This even included trying when possible to meet and minister to ANC or other political exiles. In Lusaka on one such occasion, Michael and David Richardson spent meaningful times of interaction with ANC exiles such as Steve Tshwete, Pallo Jordan, Alfred Nzo, Ruth Mompati and others, most of whom, unbeknown to them at the time, would in due time have cabinet positions in the ANC government when it finally came to power in 1994. David Richardson and Michael spent one very memorable and meaningful afternoon with the brilliant Thabo Mbeki in his Lusaka home, little imagining that they were talking to the future president of South Africa.

These sorts of activities and concerns led inevitably to further security police suspicion of AE, with Michael's children even getting phoned at school by police, a call mercifully intercepted by Carol who was teaching there. Then Michael's assistant, Lois Stephenson, was approached by security police and offered twice her salary if she would "inform" on Michael. "Ever loyal and belovèd Loey sure made short shrift of that guy and then 'informed *me*'," chuckled Michael.

AE also had a black informer planted in its youth programme but he was cleverly unmasked by the resourceful Intern Director, Dennis Bailey, and fled. Shortly thereafter, the ever-outspoken Dennis had the brakes of his car sabotaged by the local "Dirty Tricks Brigade", as they were familiarly known.

Dialogue

The Zambian experiences continued regardless for several senior AE leaders, including numerous encounters with then President Kenneth Kaunda, who had a strong spirit of mediation. These were part of an exercise that many other concerned leaders, whether political, business or ecclesiastical, were engaged in to try and keep open the channels of communication between whites and blacks, between opponents of the South African government and the government itself. So the AE crew doing this kind of thing were not alone.

For Michael and AE, along with AE's chairman at the time, Methodist Bishop Dr Mmutlanyane Stanley Mogoba, himself a famous ex-Robben Island prisoner, the Lusaka visits were usually followed immediately by visits to several senior government leaders or MPs in Cape Town to convey sentiments, messages (for example from Kaunda) and political concerns which might facilitate understanding and some more creative response from the South African government to the rising revolutionary tide in the country.

Some of these processes and stories are more elaborately narrated in two of Michael's political books – *The Passing Summer* (1989) and *The Politics of Love* (1991).

Overseas Too – and Sanctions

However, AE South Africa felt that helping people outside the country to understand what was happening and respond appropriately was also important. Endless open doors and invitations came for various team members, especially Michael, to explicate South Africa abroad.

Interpretational opportunities came with British MPs, USA State Department officials, German MPs and Australian policymakers in the Department of Foreign Affairs in Canberra. Opportunities to address prayer breakfasts or lunches in both the Victorian and New South Wales parliaments followed. A perennial issue was whether sanctions should be imposed on South Africa.

Michael's line in the first instance was that South Africa deserved sanctions and had brought them on itself by unbelievable political perversity over a very long time.

However, although believing some economic pressure was appropriate, Michael felt there were also some other factors to consider. (See *The Passing Summer*, pp. 416–422.)

1. Full sanctions would drive the Afrikaner back into the laager, just when he was coming out of it. Would not more carrot and less stick be better?
2. The sanctions drive would involve a miscalculation of the Afrikaner psyche because Afrikaners were not prone to intimidation and would just dig in their heels and become more intransigent.
3. Full sanctions and comprehensive disinvestment would seriously aggravate unemployment, which even without sanctions was already very serious.
4. Full sanctions would seriously affect South Africa's ability to feed itself. If the economic humpty dumpty were smashed, who would put it together again?
5. As hunger and unemployment increased, the propensity for violence and rampant crime among those affected, both black and white, would increase.
6. Capital disinvested from South Africa would not very readily come back. This would result in the country post liberation being unable to finance what change would require in terms of equalising education, medical services, housing etc., etc. The economic weakening of the country would have the effect, especially through escalated unemployment, of long-term destabilisation of the whole region so that although political liberation would arrive, economic liberation would be perilously or even indefinitely deferred.

That Tape

On one of these ministry and briefing tours to Australia and en route to Sydney, Michael disembarked in Perth, in order to hole up in a little hotel for some 48 hours to do his thinking, praying and preparation in seclusion. South Africa was burning and breaking. To talk about it all meaningfully needed wisdom, insight and grace.

One evening while working on his briefing talk for Australian clergy in Sydney, he found "a great weeping" coming over his spirit. "It was an extraordinary and almost perplexing experience. I wept and prayed for South Africa for nearly two hours in possibly the deepest anguish of spirit I had ever known in prayer. Part of the problem was that one's efforts seemed so weak, inadequate and futile. And getting any kind of effective hearing in any of the corridors of power seemed so problematic." All of that and more Michael lifted to the Lord in profound anguish of soul.

Anyway, Michael flew on to Sydney and Melbourne and a couple of days later delivered his briefing lectures on South Africa to packed gatherings of clergy.

However, unbeknown to Michael, still anguished by the powerlessness and often seeming futility of his endeavours, a tape recording of the Sydney lecture was sent by one of the Anglican ministers through to Dr Don Page, then one of the foreign policy advisors to the Canadian foreign minister and cabinet. The Commonwealth Heads of State Conference was soon to be held and Page and his colleagues in the Canadian Department of Foreign Affairs were preparing. Into their hands then came this taped lecture by Michael. Page, a deeply committed Christian himself, was intrigued to learn about what Christians were doing in South Africa and how considerable reconciliation initiatives were underway and how counter-productive, in Michael's view, could be the imposition of full-blown, mandatory and punitive sanctions. He accordingly had a transcript made of Michael's tape and sent to the Canadian minister of foreign affairs but no immediate action was taken thereon by the minister's staff. At a pre-conference meeting in Ottawa, Page next shared the transcript with the foreign policy advisor to the Australian prime minister and together they recommended a more conciliatory policy be adopted at the forthcoming Commonwealth meeting.

Said Don Page later:

When the heads of government met in Vancouver they could not agree on what policy to adopt regarding sanctions being applied to South Africa so the foreign ministers were sent off to find a solution. They produced the Okanagan Declaration with the message of "reaching into South Africa with the message of reconciliation and forgiveness", and this decision can be directly attributed to Michael's speech.

Because this Declaration was subsequently adopted by the Heads of Commonwealth Governments, hundreds of thousands of

Canadian dollars were quietly channelled into reconciliation movements in South Africa.

The sanctions policies still stood, but at least this was not to be the only way of the Commonwealth countries dealing with South Africa.

Perhaps then the tape and the message born in Michael's tears of weakness and anguish in Perth had been heard by God on high and unbeknown to the evangelist at the time, led on to powerful consequences of which he could never have dreamed.

Books to Parliamentarians

Michael's line on this and other matters relating to Christian faith and politics was also conveyed both to South Africa and to all its parliamentarians by his two books, *The Passing Summer* (1989) and *The Politics of Love* (1991). Generous overseas donors covered the costs of sending these books free to all members of Parliament. *The Passing Summer* seemingly even reached Nelson Mandela, then still in prison where Michael sent it to him. Mandela later thanked Michael, for "thinking of me in prison". At the end of 1989, as senior figures were asked in end-of-year Christmas interviews about their "significant reading for that year", two politicians at different ends of the political spectrum, Pik Botha (Foreign Minister) and Archie Gumede, President of the United Democratic Front (UDF), both spoke of *The Passing Summer*. The AE team was gratified by this – feeling that every little bit of Christian input, however modest, could count.

Charlie's Choices

In 1988 AE South Africa had another poignant issue on its hands. It related to helping Charlie Bester, Michael's nephew, then an intern at AE, to work through whether or not to be a conscientious objector and refuse to serve, as summoned, in the South African Defence Force (SADF). Michael and others at AE listened to Charlie for many hours as he struggled with his tender conscience.

Finally he decided he would obey his conscience, even

though it would almost certainly mean a six-year prison sentence.

Said Charlie: "Evil is manifesting itself in a political system and the government of the day is using the army and people of my age to uphold and defend that system." In his pre-trial statement he had written:

> I want to break down the barriers which divide us and I reject violence as a means to do so. If I were to serve in an institution such as the SADF which I see as perpetuating these divisions and defending an unjust system, it would be contrary to all I believe. I see it as incredible arrogance that eighteen-year-old boys, most of whom have never previously been to a township, let alone been involved in its life, are ordered to enter, armed, on the back of a military vehicle to impose law and order on a community they neither know, nor identify with.
>
> I am fully aware that I am breaking the law of the land, and have no guilt in doing so. After studying Christ's commandments and seeking God's calling in prayer, I personally cannot be obedient to this law and to God's calling. I shall submit to the authority of the state and stand trial. I believe that in order for me to follow a path that will best demonstrate my love for God, my country and my fellow South Africans, I must pursue the way of reconciliation and non-violence. I will therefore refuse to serve in the SADF, and take the consequences. (See *Politics of Love*, pp. 59–60.)

The consequences were indeed six years in prison. Michael, representing not only Charlie and his family, but AE as well, seeing Charlie was an AE intern, testified at the trial. Michael remembers well the moment of sentencing:

> The court was recessed for four minutes while the magistrate deliberated on the day. During this recess, Ivan Thoms, another Christian conscientious objector, stood and asked me to say a prayer right there in the courtroom. First Robin Briggs (Anglican Dean of Pretoria) and then I prayed. We prayed for the judge, the prosecutor, the state, the government, Charles, the situation and for the healing of South Africa. This was a moving moment that touched us all. Even some police and soldiers present wept. My sister Judy looked up and saw tears streaming from beneath the cap of one bowed young white policeman.
>
> On his return the magistrate took about forty-five seconds to

pass the merciless sentence and close the case. He said, "Six years is your sentence." It was the only moment in the trial when he appeared to have the initiative. (*The Politics of Love*, page 59)

Charlie served 20 months before being released by a ruling of both President de Klerk and the Appellate Division of the South African Supreme Court.

Mandela Moment

So it was from Kroonstad Prison that Charlie saw on TV the release of Nelson Mandela on Sunday 11 February 1990.

Everything in South Africa now changed gear, of course. The magic moment had finally arrived. Nelson Rolihlala Mandela was out of prison and a free man. The liberation movements, including the South African Communist Party, were unbanned. Political life was normalising. The next few years were to be for the nation, the church, AE and everyone else, the best of times and the worst of times. The big excitement was that the country was passing into the leadership of the world's most famous prisoner and democrat, Nelson Mandela. The downside was that South Africa was becoming a political powderkeg. It was a time for every person of goodwill to do their bit. This included AE.

It was also time for the church to try and speak yet again to the country with a united voice.

Rustenburg Conference

In December 1989, President Frederik Willem de Klerk, in his Christmas address to the nation, appealed to the church in South Africa to formulate a strategy "conducive to negotiation, reconciliation and change". Many, including Michael Cassidy, believed Mr de Klerk's request came from sincere Christian convictions; others saw it as a highly astute political move; still others as a way of appeasing the international community. In any event, the church's influence in South Africa could not be underestimated: its overall membership, nominally at least, represented about three-quarters of the total population.

Observed Michael:

In Durban '73, SACLA '79, NIR '85, we had seen people drawn together from left, right and centre, but never from both extreme left and extreme right. Now we had everything from ultra pietists to radical liberationists. Rustenburg seemed to push out the boundaries of attempted Christian unity to impossible extremes. But it came off, somehow. God's grace, I guess! Also Frank Chikane, Louw Alberts, Desmond Tutu and others were terrific. Beyond that, the confession, apology and seeking forgiveness from blacks for apartheid from Dr Willie Jonker of the Dutch Reformed Church paved the way for a great spirit of humility from everyone to everyone else. Especially when Archbishop Tutu, responding so graciously and movingly for the black side, received the confession and extended the forgiveness.

Out of the struggles of that gathering co-chaired by the unlikely pairing of Dr Frank Chikane, General Secretary of the South African Council of Churches, and Dr Louw Alberts, National Chairman of Youth for Christ, came a church declaration of unusual weight. Chaired by Michael, ably assisted by John Allen, Desmond Tutu's personal assistant, a drafting committee assembled a comprehensive, four-page statement of repentance and sociopolitical intent and called on all political leaders on all sides to work in new ways for a new day in South Africa. The Rustenburg Declaration also made a full and detailed apology to the victims of apartheid.

The Rustenburg Conference presented its Declaration to President de Klerk as well as the leaders of all other political parties, introducing it as "an attempt, within the limited time span of four-and-a-half days, at addressing the results of apartheid and providing guidelines for ongoing action towards a just dispensation for all South Africans".

For the first time ever South African church leaders, this time truly from right across the board, had come together to attempt to provide for South Africa God-centred solutions to the problems. (See *The Road to Rustenburg* edited by Dr Louw Alberts and the Rev Dr Frank Chikane, Struik Christian Books, Cape Town 1991.)

It was a fitting end to an historic year for South Africa – the year of President F.W. de Klerk and the newly released Nelson Mandela.

The Church Had Contributed

While politicians on all sides, and most especially the black liberation movements, had borne the burden of the struggle and had done mighty and formidable things to bring about an end to apartheid, it could also be said that the church in South Africa, in its various experiences of togetherness and utterance, had contributed something truly significant to the process.

In fact from early 1991 onwards, while Michael was away on sabbatical in Australia, and coming out of Rustenburg, people like Dr Frank Chikane, Dr Louw Alberts, Archbishop Tutu, Dominee Johan Heyns and Rev Ray McCauley, together laboured backstage with John Hall, Val Pauquet and others to facilitate the coming together of a broad-based National Peace Committee. This resulted in all sides in the polarised context finally signing a National Peace Accord (September 1991) with signatures from 26 political parties and trade unions plus financial, philanthropic and religious organisations. AE was one among many. (This full story is told in Michael Cassidy's *A Witness For Ever*. See especially chapter 6, pp. 88–105.) Out of all these endeavours, along with those of the South African business world, as focused in the Consultative Business Movement, the political parties finally came together at the extended round-table Constitutional Talks at Kempton Park in Johannesburg through most of 1993 and early 1994, where the new nation's preliminary constitution would be drawn up.

Michael's one big disappointment was that the words "in humble submission to Almighty God, we the people of South Africa..." which he, Ron Steele and Gerald Govender had got in to the preamble to the New Draft Constitution, after extensive consultation with Advocate Albie Sachs, were finally withdrawn from the final constitution. "In my view a serious mistake," said Michael, "as it then implies that the state is autonomous – which it is not. It exists to serve under God."

Kolobe Lodge Dialogue Weekends

For AE, in those transition years from 1991 to 1994, there were three or four significant offerings.

Firstly, the call in April 1993 for a two-year chain of intercessory prayer to go non-stop day and night for two years. As that began to operate with vast participation, and with other prayer initiatives, South Africa's political leaders on all sides of the equation became the most prayed for political leaders on Planet Earth. The AE team believed you can do many things after you've prayed, but very few until you've prayed.

Then from AE's side, with many others on all fronts making their own contributions, came the "From Africa With Love" tour in 1992, when teamlets went and visited the major political groupings and leaders to pray with them and seek to pastor them.

Thirdly, out of the 1992 tour came the Kolobe Lodge Dialogue weekends.

The basic agenda of these weekends, which included relaxation and fun, was to share three things.

1. One's life story and autobiography.
2. One's vision for the new South Africa.
3. One's notion of the steps to be taken to achieve that new South Africa.

The plan was to invite an assortment of politicians from far left, even over to the Communist Party, to far right, some of whom were calling for a separate Afrikaner homeland or Volkstaat, while others even further over were calling for a million guns to solve the "black" problem once and for all. An upmarket game lodge at a place called Kolobe north of Pretoria was selected. AE, as host, raised the money overseas for these ventures and picked up the tab. Michael's assistant at the time, Rev Peter Kerton-Johnson, laboured day and night to organise these weekends.

Between the end of 1992 and the end of 1993, some 96 politicians from all sectors of the political spectrum went through six dialogue weekends, promoted by AE as "A Weekend of a Lifetime". For many people it was exactly that.

Mythologies Explode

The amazing thing about this informal autobiographical sharing was that as it happened stereotypes broke, mythologies were exploded and understanding dawned as to why or how other individuals had reached their political, religious or philosophical conclusions. It did not mean people agreed with one another's postures, but they did reach understanding as to how they got there. Most exciting of all was to see people who had been deep political enemies become real personal friends. This was particularly wonderful considering the level of suspicion which had made some MPs and cabinet ministers and even black party leaders come with armed bodyguards, while one member of a conservative political party had a big revolver holstered to his belt. A couple of black leaders from the Azanian People's Organisation (AZAPO) came with AK 47s in the back of their car.

Contributing to the developing of friendships were the leisure activities the participants enjoyed. These included swimming in the pool together, walking, talking or running in the early mornings, and going on game drives in the afternoons with a picnic thrown in.

One very gratifying spinoff was the way different participants would go back to the "principals" in their respective parties and share what they had experienced. Several extreme conservatives on the Afrikaner side thus went back to General Constand Viljoen, the leader of an Afrikaner "Conservative Front" of parties, many of whom were conteplating violence as the way through. Their word after these weekends would always be "There is another way". National Party Cabinet Minister Danie Schutte, Minister of the Interior and the one in charge of the upcoming first non-racial South African elections for April 1994, said later: "The influence of the Kolobe Lodge weekends on the Afrikaner right wing is not to be underestimated." Addie van Rensburg, a senior leader in the "Afrikaner Volksunie", a group advocating a separate Afrikaner homeland, went to General Viljoen after each of the weekends attended to share his experience. Said Addie later: "No one will ever know how significant and important were the newly discovered postures and outlooks emanating from Kolobe Lodge as we shared these with General Viljoen and others."

Poignant Story

Particularly poignant was the story of Philip Mlambo, deputy leader of the PAC, whose slogan was "One Settler One Bullet".

He had been on Robben Island for a couple of decades with Nelson Mandela and others and had lost an eye there. He had also once been forced by white warders to dig a six-foot hole, climb inside it, have the sand filled up around him until only his head was sticking out, and then be urinated on by the warders. When white people at Kolobe heard this story, many scales fell from their eyes and they almost certainly felt that if that had happened to them, they too might have been saying: "One Settler One Bullet". However, so deep was the impact of the Kolobe experience on Mlambo that a few years later Michael and AE met up with him at a Christian conference in Coventry Cathedral, England, called "Reconciliation '98", where he shared his story and testimony. He was a changed man.

Enter Washington Okumu

In spite of all the wonderful new relationships now in place all over the country, South Africa was profoundly anguished as the year 1994 opened, with the country seemingly becoming more and more polarised as a war atmosphere developed in KwaZulu-Natal between Inkhata Freedom Party (IFP) support-ers and African National Congress (ANC) supporters.

So serious was the situation that President de Klerk, Nelson Mandela and Mangosutho Buthelezi put out a call for a team of international mediators, led by Henry Kissinger and Lord Carrington, former British Foreign Secretary, to come to South Africa to help.

However, in the couple of weeks before this happened, Michael felt constrained, along with his personal assistant Rev Peter Kerton-Johnson, who had helped so much in the set-up of the Kolobe Lodge weekends, to try and draw into the equation someone Michael had met quite a few times in the previous few years in the person of Dr Washington Okumu, a Kenyan econo-mist, diplomat and political scientist. These encounters had happened in England through the Jubilee Initiative organised by Dr Michael Schluter of Cambridge as a fine Christian contri-bution to the South African conundrum and deadlock.

Okumu was a Christian. He also knew Mandela and had on occasion met President de Klerk. In fact, his links to South Africa and working backstage for the cause of South African political change went right back to the days when John Vorster had been prime minister of the country.

Okumu agreed to come to South Africa at Michael's invitation and in the days of 27– 31 March was whisked round the country, especially KwaZulu-Natal, to meet with all political groupings and particularly pick up and inherit some of the relationships built at Kolobe Lodge. A second such backstage trip followed shortly thereafter (6–7 April), just three weeks before the country's first non-racial democratic elections. Key linkages on these trips were to Chief Minister Buthelezi, Nelson Mandela, Danie Schutte, the cabinet minister responsible for the election, to Jacob Zuma, then the ANC leader in KwaZulu-Natal, and later deputy president of South Africa and to Roger Burrows of the Democratic Party. Also to Dr Frank Mdlalose, a right-hand person to Buthelezi, and after 1994 to be the first premier of KwaZulu-Natal. There were many others.

Michael had hoped Okumu would be invited to be one of the international mediators in Kissinger's group, especially as he had studied under Kissinger at Harvard many years before. However, something even better emerged when it was agreed that he should become a consultant and advisor to the group. The international mediation endeavour soon fell flat on its face, however. In fact, having convened on Wednesday 13 April, just two weeks before the beginning of the election, it collapsed the next evening.

With Kissinger, Carrington and the whole group set to leave the country the next day and predicting Armageddon, Washington Okumu phoned Michael to say he too was planning to leave. The AE leader urged him not to and pressed him to remain and soldier on on his own with the wide linkages he now had, to try and bring some understanding and accord between the government, the ANC and the Inkhata Freedom Party on outstanding issues preventing the IFP coming into the elections. Meanwhile the war atmosphere in KwaZulu-Natal built up fearfully, and extremely serious tensions were also developing amongst Zulus and other groups on the Reef in the Johannesburg area. Everything seemed maximally explosive.

From 15–17 April, Okumu moved like quicksilver in a series of dramatic encounters and conversations, all the time working on a draft document proposal that could meet the demands and concerns of all sides in the political struggle. (For the full story of this, see Michael Cassidy's book *A Witness For Ever*, pp. 141–214.)

That Prayer Meeting

By Sunday 17 April Okumu was ready with a proposal to present to Buthelezi at a giant prayer rally in Kings Park rugby stadium in Durban which AE had called some weeks previously and where they had agreed to meet. AE had no idea in the civil war atmosphere whether 30, 300 or 3,000 would turn out. In the event, between 25,000 and 30,000 people came together for one of the most extraordinary prayer meetings South Africa has ever seen.

Just before the prayer meeting began, Nelson Mandela phoned from Cape Town and called Okumu to go down there by charter plane laid on by some businessmen. Okumu and Buthelezi had been chatting in a Durban hotel prior to the prayer meeting. Once at the VIP lounge at Kings Park stadium, Buthelezi showed Okumu's document, which had just been given him, to Minister Danie Schutte, who was there representing President De Klerk, and to Jacob Zuma, who was representing Mandela. In the VIP lounge, with the prayers and cries (literally) of the prayer meeting down below them, they scrutinised the document and began to feel that the Okumu proposals just might work. From the lounge Buthelezi phoned Ulundi to convene the central committee of the Inkhata Freedom Party late that afternoon while Danie Schutte phoned President De Klerk in Pretoria, the latter calling his cabinet minister back to Pretoria for meetings that evening to discuss Okumu's proposals. As for Okumu, he was doing the same thing in Cape Town face to face with Mandela.

So while the anguished prayer meeting was underway, in the VIP lounge of the stadium, with that great throng unaware, a meeting of minds was in process that was going to provide the way through in the next few days. On Monday 18 April in Pretoria the i's were dotted and the t's crossed of Okumu's document. And on Tuesday 19 April, with the election a week away, Mandela, De Klerk and Buthelezi announced on radio and television that an agreement had been reached. All was set for the elections to take place peacefully with the crucial involvement of the IFP.

It was an incredible moment in the history of South Africa. No one there will ever forget it. Massive conflict had been averted. Maybe civil war.

Miracle

Numbers of journalists reported that there was almost a holy hush in many newsrooms as they reached for the language of faith to describe what had happened. The word "miracle" appeared at the head of editorial after editorial. A big article in the *Natal Daily News* was headlined: "The Day God Stepped In to Save South Africa." The BBC in London the next day said: "It was the Jesus Peace Rally that tipped the scales." In the British House of Commons the next day an MP stated: "If there are miracles in politics, then this is one." *Time* magazine said the following week: "History has thrown up an authentic miracle." The *Wall Street Journal* carried a full-page article entitled: "God in Politics".

And in South Africa, amidst a euphoric mood unprecedented in the country's history, "peace broke out". People who had been ready to kill each other some days previously were now ready to embrace and move forward peacefully. Some 84 million ballot papers were adjusted in a matter of days. Parliament met the day before an election, which was unprecedented, to do business and to clear the way relating to agreements reached around the Okumu Document. On 26, 27 and 28 April, South Africa went to the polls. They were the most peaceful few days in the nation's history, with scarcely a crime anywhere of any sort reported. History had been made.

Commented Michael: "While we honour the astonishing endeavours of all the politicians, political parties, freedom movements, business people, Young Comrades, the churches and so on, nevertheless I believe that in the last analysis we have to acknowledge that God indeed intervened in history and gave South Africa the miracle for which multitudes in South Africa and worldwide had prayed."

Indeed, on 27 April as the peaceful election got underway around the country, the Minister of Home Affairs, Danie Schutte, who had been at Kolobe, and who had been running the election, drove with some of his security people to Michael's home and said to him:

> Everything which money, power politics and the secular world could do to bring forth the South African election was done. But it was all in vain. It took a miracle of God. And for me personally, that miracle began, when I came to your home late that night and was introduced to Washington Okumu. From that moment on something new began happening.

Burundi

With the 1994 elections behind them, and political normality returning to South Africa, AE busied itself elsewhere in terms of reconciliation ministries. Pride of place went to Burundi, still torn and rent by deep civil strife between Hutu and Tutsi. The endeavours were spearheaded by Emmanuel Kopwe, AE's Pan-African Executive Officer for Reconciliation and Peace-Making Ministries.

Ministry in Kigali, Rwanda, in 1994 had deepened a compelling concern for reconciliation and also led to Emmanuel's ever-deepening burden for Burundi, still gripped by awful tribal conflict between Hutu and Tutsi.

In the event the Kigali ministry providentially gave AE many significant contacts with Burundians, who gave a Macedonian call for help. This call was realised when Emmanuel got together the Burundian church leaders both exiled and in the country in Nairobi for a couple of days in January/February 1996. This resulted in a follow-up workshop in Bujumbura in the middle of March 1996. In this workshop, Michael, with his experience in South Africa, and Emmanuel were able to help the church of Burundi, with input from some senior politicians, to generate a well and widely received statement of vision for a new Burundi.

In reality however, political events in Burundi have developed so fast since then, with some help from Nelson Mandela, that specifically Christian reconciliation work has had to trail behind the political activities, leaving much still unresolved. However, suffice it to say that AE's reconciliation work in Burundi has had some influence at least on the developments there at political level. Indeed these labours, spearheaded by Emmanuel Kopwe, continue.

Project Ukuthula

Before the century closed, South Africa was going to make one more call on AE's reconciliation ministries.

In mid-1996, with the country's first provincial elections due in six weeks time, violence had flared once again in KwaZulu-Natal between the two major groupings, the ANC and the IFP. Deaths were again taking place at the rate of 20 a day and nearly 60 every weekend. The prospect of holding the elections became remote.

At a meeting in Ladysmith, President Mandela met Anglican Bishop Matthew Makhaye and asked whether the Natal church leaders and African Enterprise could try to do something about this. A week or so later Bishop Makhaye, Bishop Mmutlanyane Mogoba, Presiding Bishop of the Methodist Church, and Michael Cassidy met President Mandela for an extended lunch at his residence in Durban. "We politicians cannot fix this thing," confessed the president, "maybe you church people can do it."

Thus was launched "Project Ukuthula" (Zulu for "Peace"). The three Christian leaders were daily in contact with Premier Dr Frank Mdlalose and other key players. In the next six weeks, led by the Natal church leaders and AE, the Christians of Natal were activated into the mechanisms of peacemaking. Whether Christians were in the police, the military, the media, schools, industry, business or wherever, they were urged to change the rhetoric of violence and talk peace and pursue it.

In six short weeks Michael and the two bishops addressed meeting after meeting, including the KwaZulu-Natal Parliament, the Natal Press Club, the police headquarters and business groups, teachers' associations, church meetings and clergy groups. Radio, the press and TV were also exploited. School kids by the thousands were given peace brochures to take home to their parents. Senior politicians and the Zulu king were visited privately. Above all thousands and thousands of lay people stood up to be counted and to call off the ways of conflict and violence. Once again, as in 1994, multitudes in the churches committed it all constantly to prayer.

Michael reported on behalf of Mogoba, Makhaye, himself and other church leaders every few days directly to President Mandela as to the progress being made.

Finally a one-day conference was called in Durban with church, business and media leaders present, plus senior politicians from all parties, the premier and King Goodwill Zwelethini.

As Project Ukuthula advanced under the Natal church leaders and AE, with all Christians everywhere seeking "to do their bit", so the death rate in the province dwindled. By the time the elections were due, the daily death rate was down to zero. As the provincial elections went ahead in peace, *Time* magazine again commented on "the three of the most peaceful days in KwaZulu-Natal in several years".

"Project Ukuthula was a wonderful illustration," commented Michael later, "of the political, social and spiritual power of the Christian church when it activates itself with every member involvement towards a given end."

The Ministry of Reconciliation

AE believes it is noteworthy that St Paul can say of the church that "God has given *us* the ministry of reconciliation" (2 Corinthians 5:18). It has not been committed with any primacy to the politicians, or the business community, or the military, or academia. It has, says St Paul, been committed and given "to us".

This is a distinctive and primary ministry. And no one else can do it with the same undergirding power as can Christians. While the primary call is to vertical and personal reconciliation with God, the secondary but equally fundamental call is to horizontal reconciliation with our neighbour. Especially our alienated neighbour.

That dimension of the call, says AE, will inevitably embrace the social and political arenas. To respond to it is demanding, sometimes dangerous, invariably difficult, but always deeply rewarding.

And in a continent of alienations such as Africa, it is also clearly unavoidable.

PART FOUR

Backup: The Special People Who Keep It All Going

Chapter *25*　　　　　　　　　*Every Willing,*
Skilful Person

In the early months and years of the work, the Spirit of God gave Michael Cassidy different scriptures which would be key and crucial for the ministry. One of these was 1 Chronicles 28:21 which comes in the context of David's charge to Solomon, his son, about the building of the temple. The promise was wonderful and it spoke directly and decisively to Michael's heart. "And with you in all the work will be every willing, skilful person for any manner of service."

Michael seized on this with all his heart, as did the other team members. They were not going to do the work alone. There would be many other skilful and qualified people who would help at any number of different points along the way.

There was another scripture which also contained and enshrined a key principle which Michael and the team would always hold dear: 1 Samuel 30:24–25. The context is David's battles against the Amalekites. David recognises that those who have kept the home fort and the home base steady, and provided an assortment of support systems, are just as important as those who have gone out to fight in the front lines of the battle. Says David: "For as his share is who goes down to the battle, so shall his share be who stays by the baggage; they shall share alike." Then a powerful postscript is added: "And from that day forward he made it a statute and an ordinance for Israel to this day." The same key principle is captured a few chapters earlier when, in the more quaint language of the King James version it says: "And there went up after David about 400 men; 200 abode by the stuff" (1 Samuel 25:13).

Yes, those who stay by the stuff and look after the baggage, in other words those who do the backroom work are as important and significant as those who go out to the front lines and into the public eye teaching, preaching, evangelising and running the campaigns.

This means that people in the AE boards and the staff in the various offices are seen to be bringing contributions of equal importance to the evangelists and teachers. Once in a meeting in the old Pasadena office of AE, Michael went round the staff and asked each one what they did. One young woman replied: "I am just a secretary." "You are what?" questioned Michael. "I am just a secretary." Michael kept repeating his insistent question until the young lady rather impatiently said: "I – AM – A – SEC-RETARY." "Ah," said Michael. "You see, no one is 'just a secretary' or 'just this' or 'just that'. So please stand tall, because you as a secretary are a key person to the ministry and without people like you, we could never function." This is the Body of Christ principle the apostle Paul is on about when he says in Ephesians (4:16) that the Body grows and gets built up when "every joint" and "each part is working properly".

Over the years, Michael was often heard telling others that he could never have carried out his ministry and accomplished some of the things achieved without the help and backup support of his long-time secretary Colleen Smith, who served at his desk for over twelve years. And over the years there were many such people serving in various capacities in different sections of the ministry. Elisha Omusula came into AE after PACLA in 1976 and served diligently as a messenger and helper in the Kenya and East African office for over 20 years until his retirement. Likewise the faithful Teoneste Mutsimbanyi, the driver for Uganda and Rwanda teams at different times. The faithfulness and gracious Christian spirit of these brothers have amazed and blessed everyone over the years. And there is Derick Bruce in the South African office, who has worked the ministry's mailing room, stuffed hundreds of thousands of envelopes, worked the printing machines and done a thousand and one things to keep the ministry on track, including getting out the monthly mailings and seeing that everything is ship-shape backstage. All of this has added up to a single contribution as vital as any brought by a senior evangelist.

Or take the East African office and the Kenya context. Their administrative secretary, Ruth Mamboleo, a lovely woman of gracious Christian demeanour, has kept that operation together at so many levels, handled hundreds and hundreds of air bookings and been a wise friend and counsellor to everyone on the Karen property and indeed to senior leaders in the work. Likewise Gloria Julius in the South African office, whose daily calls to the amazing travel agent and Christian friend, Lynn Vogel, about team travel, have made it possible on endless occasions for team members to get away expeditiously, on time and up to speed as they have left on mission assignments. Then in the California office, Barbara Ramos, a dear and special lady seriously challenged with speech and hearing defects, has kept the ministry's donor records there with consummate faithfulness over 22 years.

Gifts of Administration

Michael and the team were always thankful that in the Pauline list of charismatic gifts, given by the Spirit of God for the benefit of the whole Body of Christ, there stands very significantly and importantly the gift of administration. Says the apostle: "And God has appointed in the church first apostles, second prophets, third teachers, then workers of miracles, then healers, helpers, administrators, speakers and various kinds of tongues" (1 Corinthians 12:28).

From the very start this gift was in the work. For example, Don Ehat, who set up the first Mission to Maritzburg in 1962, was a brilliant administrator. When the team returned to Africa at the end of 1964, and Don had decided to stay in the United States, Chris Smith, one of the most multi-gifted people the ministry ever saw, revealed that apart from being able to teach, preach, lead and train choirs, he could also administer. And he did so as he set up the AE missions for the next fourteen or fifteen years. In the early 1970s, Rob Thompson, an able actuary, came to provide leadership on the administrative side. Mike Odell, who for years led AE's media team, also revealed as he progressed in the work great gifts in administration until in due time he rose to the office manager and later, team leader in South Africa. On the accounting side, the work was blessed with the incredible labours of Allan Peckham, a quadriplegic, and Barbara English, a paraplegic, both of whose services Michael adjudged to be "of incalculable value to the ministry". Other offices were similarly blessed. For example East Africa had the talented contribution of Daniel Serwanga, while administrator Ephraim Gensi has kept the Uganda operation on track for many, many years. Kevin Lyne, an Australian, gave wonderful administrative oversight to AE's Secretariat for Aid and Development for a number of years from 1981 onwards. AE's finances in the United States would never have been kept in the good order they were without the financial and administrative gifts of Marylou Herrera, a Filipina-American. Ann Outred has done the same in the Australian office while the irrepressibly cheerful and steady Heather Valentine was the administrative key under the able direction of the Aussie director, Mike Woodall, himself an accountant and former businessman. For ten years or more, Mike has also given administrative oversight to AE's Aid and Development ministries. Nor could the ministry across Africa have progressed without the financial genius of Ken Burns, a man of amazing industry, meticulous thoroughness and blessed with a powerful gift of friendship who has been the pan-African Executive Officer for Finances. Nothing escapes Ken, but nor does the spirit of love and wisdom with which on a volunteer basis he gives oversight to AE's pan-African finances.

Queen Jean

In the UK there is AE's imperturbable International Treasurer, Jean Wilson. A former merchant banker in London and then financial miracle worker for the Billy Graham Association, "Queen Jean", as everyone affectionately calls her, has worked an average of 16 hours a day for as long as anybody can remember. She is the receiver of constant phone calls from Africa: Kenya wants this, Tanzania wants that, South Africa are kicking over the traces here, Zimbabwe wants a loan there, someone is flying through London and needs to be met at the airport, someone else in Africa has a sick child and there is no medical insurance, some team's financial allocation for the month has not arrived, and so on. Can Jean help? "OK sure!" she will reply. If ever there was a case of a heroic few doing too much with too little for too long, it has been Jean and her AE London office. The AE ministry's debt to her is incalculable.

Pride of Place

However, pride of place for the administration of AE over the last 27 or 28 years has to go to Malcolm Graham. As the work built up in the early 1970s, and as the versatile team became too stretched in too many directions, Michael realised the desperate need for a truly professional and top-class administrator. The team endlessly bombarded the Lord in prayer for this. Rev Brian Fennell, a Methodist minister and later one of AE South Africa's board chairmen, came up with a name. Someone who had formerly been superintendent for his Sunday school work in the Methodist Church. He was then an Insurance Director of a very large company in Johannesburg and had some 700 people under him. His name was Malcolm Graham.

By one of God's strange coincidences, Malcolm and Bertha Graham, who were well settled in Johannesburg, with a large house, large income, big car and all the trappings of success, were becoming spiritually restless and searching for a more fulfilling responsibility in life. Malcolm made contact with Michael Cassidy and AE and was invited to go to an inter-team conference, the very first between the Southern and Eastern teams, which was being held in Glion, Switzerland, just before the famous Lausanne Congress on World Evangelisation, to which all the AE team had been invited, with their fares generously covered by the Billy Graham Association. Malcolm shared a room with the Ugandan businessman John Wilson, former director of Caltex in Uganda, who had just joined the team. The incredible fellowship and delight which Malcolm experienced in his newfound friendship with John Wilson made him feel that here in AE he could make a real contribution, in a context which would be not only thoroughly fulfilling, but deeply challenging of his great administrative expertise.

Said Malcolm later:

> I've always had a sense of God's call on my life from the day of my commitment to Christ. So I have always been open and responsive when approached to serve. However, my first response to AE was that I didn't think I was the right person for the post they had in mind. But they were persistent. And who would turn down a free ticket to Switzerland! Little did I realise that God had a plan as he had me mixing with a bunch of fellows from different

nations, tribes, cultures and denominations. At first they were tense and agitated with each other, with some even angry. Then suddenly they were entering reconciliation and beginning truly to love each other. This happening was truly the work of the Holy Spirit. At the same time I had to share my bedroom with a Ugandan. This tall, elegant and handsome man of God, John Wilson, with similar business pursuits to mine had an infectious relationship with Jesus that started the process for me of accepting the offer from AE of full-time Christian service.

When Malcolm and Bertha agreed to join AE, Michael and the team knew that a mighty answer to a mighty prayer had come forth. Malcolm entered the work in that same year (1974) and quickly became the administrative centre and lynchpin of the whole operation, not only in South Africa, but on the whole international front.

Unlike other administrators such as Chris Smith, who wanted to be out there teaching, preaching and leading choirs, or Dan Serwanga who loved to preach, Malcolm wanted only to bring his gift of administration to bear upon the deep and manifest needs of the ministry.

"It is Malcolm Graham," states Michael categorically, "who has really under God kept this whole ministry organisationally together, progressing and on track for over a quarter of a century. AE would have folded up many times along the way but for the administrative skills of Malcolm, and always so ably backed up by his wife Bertha, who worked alongside him first in South Africa and then in the States."

Commenting on his second career as AE's senior administrator, Malcolm says:

> My recollection is that the board asked me simply to "manage and organise the team". I was so naïve... it turned out to be much, much more. For example I had to improve salaries, develop staff benefits, set up a pension scheme and do fundraising, counselling, planning and even scheduling of missions. Church relationships was in the job too and seeing we kept properly in touch and properly appreciative of our donors. First it was just for a small bunch of energetic guys and their staff, then it grew like Jack's beanstalk into Regional Teams, Pan African Teams, International Operations and so on.

I also found that handling 700 people in an insurance company far easier than controlling a few dozen crazy evangelists. But it's been fun, frustrating and fulfilling all at the same time and has given me a deep sense of this being the Lord's purpose for Bertha and me and our lives – and all because of his sustaining grace and love.

His longstanding secretary, Sandra Pillay, later to become AE South Africa's Fundraising Director and Prayer Coordinator, says about her more than ten years of working with Malcolm: "What an honour and privilege it was to work alongside Malcolm all those years – truly a man of the highest integrity, an example of Christian character, a true servant leader, and a person of such compassion and caring. He also has that wonderful ability to bring out the best in one."

Inevitably Malcolm was *de facto* and then the *de jure* Administrative Director, coordinating the entire ministry at an international level. When a major financial crisis developed in the US office in 1995, Michael Cassidy made the critically important but personally costly decision of asking Malcolm and Bertha to go to the United States and, in addition to his other international responsibilities, take on the directorship of the USA office. In next to no time that office turned around and the US board, realising they were on to a good thing, refused to let Malcolm go. He and Bertha serve AE to this day from California, while continuing to give the international administrative coordination to the whole ministry. Malcolm and Michael are in touch by e-mail or on the phone almost daily. Says Michael: "Malcolm has been and is and in a sense will always be my right hand administrative and organisational man, as well as a totally treasured friend. I owe him the world. So does AE."

Boards and Board Members

As significant as these kinds of contributions have been, equally significant have been the astonishing contributions of many Christian brothers and sisters who have served AE through its various boards in North America, Europe, Australasia, and of course Africa. In fact it can safely be said that hundreds of gifted people, from college professors to senior clergy to captains of industry have served on AE boards over the years. Their wisdom, farsightedness, generosity and passion for excellence have steered the little AE boat from the safe port of Pasadena in the early 1960s through some stormy, tumultuous African storms over the years and kept it afloat and still sailing.

Top billing must of course go to the parent board of the ministry in California. First on to the board were the appointees of Dr Charles Fuller after he had called Michael to him and said he wanted to help him get the AE vision up and running. Fuller's appointees were Dr Bruce Bare, a senior insurance agent and director of New England Life Insurance. Then there was James Gorton, a businessman, who was followed after his death by his widow, Marj, who was on the board for decades. The third was Rose Baessler, Fuller's secretary. Soon thereafter came Dr Carlton Booth, the effervescent Professor of Evangelism at Fuller, who spent endless hours in Michael's first few years at the seminary counselling him, guiding him, praying with him and encouraging him as the AE vision developed. Very early in the equation came also Val Hellickson, Director of Haven of Rest Radio, a worldwide Christian programme, then Paul Winter, a civil engineer, Sue McGill, a Christian of note in the Pasadena area, Merlin Call, a distinguished lawyer, and very specially, Dr Ted Engstrom, Executive Vice President of Youth for Christ. Also there was the deeply committed Rev Jim Morrison, Pastor of the Beverly Hills Presbyterian Church, whose son Jamie and daughter-in-law Amy would one day become able and invaluable assistants to Michael.

"If you want to know what commitment is all about," Michael would often say over the years, "then look at that AE USA board." In over 30 years and to this point of writing, Dr Ted Engstrom has scarcely missed more than seven or eight board meetings. His friendship with Michael has remained constant and he has brought an astonishing gift of encouragement. Over the last eight or ten years his regular word to Michael has been: "Mike, you must keep praying 'Lord, help me finish better than I started.'" As recently as April 2002 Ted, in his late 80s, could write to Michael saying: "Mike, it seems this past year or two I've seen more of my special friends called home to glory. Every time I hear of one of them passing on, it of course reminds me of the frailty of life and the importance of making every day count in light of eternity. I trust that in your busy schedule you're finding some time for relaxation and renewal. You keep up a hectic pace and I want you to programme and schedule time away with Carol on frequent vacations. Spoken to you as an elder brother!" "Thus the caring spirit of so many of our Board members," comments Michael.

Carlton Booth served on the US board from the early 1960s to the early 1990s and the time of his death. Looking back to those early beginnings, Carlton Booth once wrote:

> Each time I met with him, the call on Michael's life seemed more demanding and more inescapable. Never can I forget those times of prayer and heart searching which he and I had in my little office at Fuller Seminary because even there and then there was this germ of African Enterprise as Michael was seeking to know that "high calling of God in Christ Jesus" (Philippians 3:14) for his life. Then suddenly it happened and came to fruition: AE was born.

Of course there were others who came and went, and some who have gone to be with the Lord, and others, such as Dr Archie Hart, former Dean of the School of Psychology at Fuller Seminary, who have come on board and taken a lead and brought their own high and distinctive gifts to bear upon the work.

However, in the eyes of most of the team, few contributions can compare with that of Bruce Bare, who came on to the board in 1960 and is still there. Bruce has been to Africa 57 times at his own expense to be with the team, to encourage them, to give counsel to Michael Cassidy and others, to bring his administrative skill and expertise to bear upon the miscellaneous needs of the ministry. Over all these years he and his endlessly supportive wife, Adeline, have prayed for Michael and Carol and their family and the team on a daily basis. Bruce was delighted when Michael and Carol asked him to be godfather to their young son Martin, and "Uncle Bruce" has always remained high on Marty's list of favourite people. Equally special for the Cassidys has been "Aunty Marj" (Marjorie Gorton) who became godmother to Cathy Cassidy (now Scott) when she was born in 1972. Marj says her nearly 30 years on the US board "will always stand as one of the most special and enriching experiences of my life".

Clearly all these relationships as they were woven together over the years became the warp and woof of the AE tapestry which is the ministry today.

Another board which began in the early 1960s was that in Canada, where Dorothy and Robert Birch, parents of Paul, the pianist on the initial team, were the anchor people. On his return from Africa in the late 1960s, Paul and his wife Margaret served AE from their kitchen table, which became AE Canada's office. Paul remains Canada's Chairman Emeritus of AE, another relationship which has stood the test of time over more than 40 years.

Finally a Board in Africa

If what the team used to call "the Pasadena Board" was the parent board, then it soon found itself moving into the role of being fraternal rather than merely paternal as a first African board came into existence in South Africa in the early 1970s, chaired by the legendary parliamentarian, historian and scholar, Dr Edgar Brookes. Brookes had been a senator in the South African Parliament and a famous fighter and champion of black rights in South Africa. Along with Alan Paton, Peter Brown and Patrick Duncan, he had helped get the fledging Liberal Party of South Africa underway. He was a prolific and incisive political writer and commentator, often writing about the challenging theme of bringing Christian faith and politics together. His deep devotion to Christ was accompanied by an irrepressible and wry sense of humour. Once as he came up the stairs to the AE office in the old Barclays Bank building in Longmarket Street, there was a vigorous prayer meeting going on with one of the more Pentecostal African staff appealing in loud tones for the Lord's intervention in something.

As Edgar Brookes came up the stairs he heard these thunderous cries to heaven and quietly said to Michael: "I'm sure God won't be able to miss hearing that one!"

"Yes, Edgar," chuckled Michael, "she always operates on the presupposition that God is stone deaf."

On another occasion Brookes told Michael how he had gone to see Dr Hendrik Verwoerd, the famous if not notorious architect of the apartheid policy and ideology. Verwoerd was not yet prime minister, but at the time had just been appointed the new minister of so-called "Native Affairs".

"So I went to see him in his office," said Edgar to Michael with a wry smile, "and said to him, 'Dr Verwoerd, I want to congratulate you on becoming Minister of Native Affairs. Long may you remain so.'"

"But I am surprised at you, Senator Brookes," said Verwoerd, "what with you being a senior liberal and my political enemy and all that. How can you now congratulate me and wish me long service in this post of Native Affairs?"

"Well," replied Edgar, "I want you long to be the Minister of Native Affairs because every such minister has been worse than the last and we would not want anyone worse than you!"

Even Verwoerd smiled. He knew he had met his match!

Also into Edgar Brooke's board, among others, came Dr Calvin Cook who had been the main formal initiator in getting Michael and the earliest team invited to Pietermaritzburg for the August 1962 citywide mission. At that time Calvin was minister of the Presbyterian Church in Maritzburg, but then went on to be lecturer in Divinity and Religious studies at Wits University in Johannesburg, and finally was appointed to head up the Church History Department at Rhodes University in Grahamstown. It seemed that each place Calvin went, AE followed hot on his heels to do a mission there, thanks to Calvin's initiating endeavours and promptings. Thus came the Wits Mission in '67, then Mission '70 in Johannesburg and the Rhodes University Mission in 1972.

Michael comments:

> What has been totally amazing over all these years is that Calvin has been able to be not only the wisest of counsellors to the board and team, but also the most special of friends and care-givers, along with his wife Pat, to individual members of the team, and most particularly to Carol and me and our family. In fact, I can never head out on mission or a ministry assignment without Calvin wanting to see me, or pray for me over the phone. And certainly he would want me to report back for his interest and evaluation whenever I returned from missions. Amazing and astonishing indeed. Perhaps he and Bruce Bare on two different sides of the Atlantic have been the two most major pillars of the work at board level.

Alphaeus Zulu

Another distinguished member of the early South African Board was Bishop Alphaeus Zulu, the first black bishop appointed by the Anglican Church (CPSA) in South Africa. Although one of the six presidents of the World Council of Churches, Bishop Zulu's gentle, gracious and evangelical heart flowed out to one and all, regardless of where they stood theologically in the church spectrum. Known in South Africa as a man of consummate wisdom and graciousness, Bishop Zulu brought to the AE ministry an astonishing range of connections and relationships. These ranged from the ecclesiastical to the political. In fact, he even encouraged the then chief minister of the KwaZulu homeland, Mangosutho Buthelezi, to identify with the AE ministry and even serve for a while, before the demands of other duties overtook him, on the AE board. The friendship with Buthelezi was to mean much to Michael and the team in subsequent years. Elsie Buthelezi, the cousin of the chief minister, later minister of home affairs in the Mandela and then in the Mbeki government, continues to serve on the AE board with spiritual passion, humour, and above all a great intercessory commitment. Michael often met privately with Bishop Zulu and always wished he had somehow or other found the time to write the biography of such a distinguished son of Africa. When Zulu was dying, he called Michael to Ulundi and asked him if he would preach at his funeral, which Michael did some months later in the presence of Minister Buthelezi and a constellation of stars, ecclesiastical, political and professional, from all over South Africa.

After Bishop Alphaeus had died, the AE South Africa board, in a manner of speaking, seemed to decide to go Methodist! An outstanding succession of Methodist bishops chaired the work, beginning with Presiding Bishop Dr Mmutlanyane Mogoba, now the leader in Parliament of the Pan-African Congress; then came Bishop Brian Fennell, a very longstanding friend of Malcolm Graham and a man with a deep commitment to evangelism. Indeed, it had been Bishop Brian who steered Malcolm Graham towards AE in the early 1970s. Following Fennell came Bishop Mvume Dandala, Presiding Bishop of the Methodist Church and President of the South African Council of Churches. The Methodist chain was broken when a charismatic "newer church" leader, Abraham Sibiya, National President of "the Christ-Centred Church" took over.

East African Beginnings

Somehow or other AE never seemed to be short of bishops or archbishops who seemed willing to come in as chairpersons of the work. Thus it was the saintly and great Archbishop Erica Sabiti who became the first Chairperson of the Uganda board following an initial meeting in Limuru, Kenya, in 1971 when invitees selected by Bishop Festo came together along with him and Michael in Limuru to get the East African work more formally up and running. Of course all sorts of church and other Christian leaders were keen to be involved with anything Bishop Festo was involved in. So there was no lack of volunteers in the coming years as the boards got going in Uganda, Tanzania, Kenya and finally Rwanda. In Tanzania it was the Revival Fellowship leader, prominent Lutheran layman and director of the Bible Society of Tanzania, Mr Emmanuel Kibira, who took the chair. He had been at that first 1971 meeting in Limuru and identified strongly with the activities of the young East African teams. He always laughed and teased Michael that while Michael could not get into Tanzania, being a South African, Kibira could certainly not get into South Africa being a Tanzanian! Finally one day, while Kibira was in transit through Johannesburg airport, Michael got a photograph of him there, and then wrote to him saying: "Now, my brother, I have this incriminating evidence against you of a photograph of you in South Africa, where you are not allowed or meant to be. You need to know that I will show this to your political authorities unless you do me a lot of new favours in the coming years." Kibira always laughed about that, but he laughed louder when for the Harambee '92 ministry tour he was allowed into South Africa proper to minister, preach and do his bit in breaking down political and racial barriers.

In Kenya, when that board came on stream, it was John Mpaayei, director of the Bible Society and translator of the first Bible into Masai, who took the lead. Mpaayei had been the chairman of the Crossroads Mission in 1969 and he always reminded Michael how the two of them had talked in a Nairobi restaurant one day during that mission and how Mpaayei had said: "This ministry must be for all of Africa."

Wider Denominational Linkages

When Mpaayei stepped down from the chairmanship of the Kenya board, another board member, Rev Dr George Wanjau, pastor of St Andrew's Presbyterian Church in Nairobi, took over. George had been a translator at one point during the Crossroads Mission in Nairobi back in 1968/9. He had come out of the fires of the years of Christian witness and struggle during the Mau Mau time and had a great testimony of the love, forgiveness and Calvary Spirit of Christ. While Mpaayei had connected the Kenya work strongly to the Africa Inland Church, and other board members such as Daniel Serwanga had connected it to the Anglican Church, now George Wanjau connected it deeply to the Presbyterians, of which he would in due course become moderator. This consolidated links which had been established in that church through the famous John Gatu, a close friend and advisor to the ministry, and the person through whom the so-called Revival Brethren of Kenya were brought around to view the work with favour. Initially they were suspicious, thinking that Revival Brethren should not be out there in fulltime ministry receiving salaries from overseas agencies such as AE. Their concerns had been directed at Festo and other AE members in Tanzania, Uganda and Kenya. But between John Gatu, Festo and people like George Wanjau, their fears were laid to rest and they became supportive.

Another person who had translated for Festo in the 1968 Crossroads Mission was Dr Don Jacobs, a Mennonite missionary, anthropologist and biblical scholar. Don and his wife Anna Ruth had been missionaries in Tanzania some years previously and had been profoundly touched by the East African Revival and drawn into its deep and spiritually penetrating dynamics of constant repentance from sin, confession and walking in the light. Out of the Crossroads Mission linkages to AE, Don became a firm friend of the work, first in Kenya and East Africa generally, and then later becoming not only a member of the US board, but also a wonderfully pastoral chairperson of the International Partnership Board for a number of years.

"The fellowship is the key thing amongst us," Don would always emphasise. "We are nothing as a ministry if we lose the fellowship. So we must keep short accounts with each other, stay strong in our relationships, keep repenting when we get it wrong, and follow the Lord in a close walk of obedience."

In the United States, Don became one of the directors of the Mennonite Christian Leadership Foundation, but Africa always held a very special place in his heart. Then he would add: "I share deeply AE's vision of African missionaries going into the post-Christian West in the 21st century."

Rwanda

When the Rwanda team came on stream in the 1980s, its board, though interdenominational, was dominated by Anglican bishops. Bishop Onesiphore Rwaje was and is the chairman, along with Archbishop Emmanuel Kolini, who led the African charge at the last Lambeth Conference against the ordination of practising homosexuals. Sharing in that charge was Bishop Alexis Bilindabagabo, also on AE's board, who had had a series of miraculous escapes and experiences of "angelic protection" during the 1994 Rwanda genocide. Antoine Rutayisire and the Rwanda team were thankful that their board had been part of a credible witness before, during and after the genocide, especially as they took into their care some 2,500 orphans and some 900 widows. Bishop Rwaje drove Michael and Malcolm down to one of the refugee camps shortly before the genocide and the two team members from South Africa were thrilled to see the school classrooms, feeding schemes and projects which the AE team and board had undertaken in that camp, as in others. Bishop Rwaje also drove Malcolm and Michael to Gahini, where the East African Revival had begun in the early 1930s. "It is incredible that we could have had revival all these years in this country," said the bishop later, "and then we have a genocide in which nearly 1,000,000 people die. What has gone wrong? Where did we lose the way?"

Michael suspected that the problem was that perhaps in the later phases of the revival movement, as in many other parts of Africa, the preaching had focused more on a salvationist message than a kingdom one. People knew how to be converted and saved and say their sins were forgiven, but not how to live fully under the kingship and kingly rule of Christ in all aspects of life from the personal, private and family through to the political, social and economic.

In Uganda another Anglican bishop served the board as chairman with distinction for 15 or more years. Bishop Yokona Mukasa was one of those saintly men who brought a tremendous testimony through the traumatic years of Idi Amin, followed by further years of rampant slaughter under Milton Obote. His loyalty to Festo Kivengere, his friendship with Edward Muhima and his profound commitment to the overall ministry, always made him a very valuable contributor in the IPB discussions whenever the international board met.

Zimbabwe and Malawi Lay Leaders

Not all AE boards were chaired by clergy, and Zimbabwe was one of the notable exceptions. Here the leadership was given by Mr Harry Mkombe, a giant of a man with a perpetual and uproarious laugh and the ability to keep everyone laughing as well. The spitting image of Idi Amin, Harry would get up in the International Partnership Board (IPB) meetings and have everyone in stitches before he had even said anything!

"He is the only person I have ever known," commented Michael, "who can give a financial report and make it hysterically funny! But then AE's finances are often a bit that way!"

Following the fine chairmanship of Rev Yeremiah Chienda, a Presbyterian minister, in Malawi, the Malawi board was then chaired by Mr Nedson Somanje, another layperson and a prominent banker in Lilongwe, the capital of the country. Following him came Mr Rangford Chokhotho, another prominent banker well connected in the Malawi business and professional communities.

Australia

Preceding Don Jacobs as IPB chairperson, and following Bruce Bare, came Warwick Olson, a tough, no-nonsense Australian who never pulled his punches and never avoided confronting difficult issues. It was Warwick who had first got the Australian board going when Festo Kivengere, then a refugee in exile, was travelling the world raising money for Ugandan refugees in the aftermath of the Idi Amin massacres. Warwick had invited Festo to Australia to share his poignant but powerful message. So great was the response, both spiritual and financial, from all across Australia that it became very clear that a board needed to be established to cope with all of this. Although initially strongly connected to the Ugandan needs and problems, the Australian board quickly took on its heart the whole ministry in all its geographical and methodological diversity.

Jungle Doctor

As director of Pilgrim International, a major Christian communications organisation, Warwick had a skilled eye for bringing in on to the board people deeply concerned to communicate the gospel in new or different ways. These included Graham Wade, a graphic design artist of genius, the legendary Dr Paul White of Jungle Doctor story fame, whose children's books spanned the world and have been translated into dozens of languages, and Canon David Hewetson, an Anglican rector, theologian and writer of note in his own right. In fact Paul White and David Hewetson succeeded each other in turn over the years as chairman of the Aussie board.

Not only was Paul White rightly concerned for the wellbeing of the work and its effective communication of the gospel, but as a doctor, he was concerned for the health and wellbeing of individual AE team members. Thus he could once send a letter to Michael urging him to slow down a bit and take better care of himself. "You don't want to kill yourself before your time. And remember what Ecclesiastes says (9:4): 'Better a living dog than a dead lion!'" On another occasion when Michael was about to go into hospital for surgery on a particularly tender and sensitive portion of his anatomy, Paul White phoned from Australia to tell Michael he would be praying for him very particularly the next day as the surgery took place. Then just before he put the phone down, he added with wicked humour: "By the way, Michael, they say there are two states in the afterlife – purgatory and haemorrhoidectomy!"

Michael will always remember how in his final telephone

conversation with Paul White when everyone knew Paul was in the home straight of his life, the great doctor, rather like a Paul giving final words to a Timothy, said: "Michael, there is something I always want you to remember. It is a word from Revelation 19:6–7: 'Hallelujah! For the Lord our God the Almighty reigns. Let us rejoice and exult and give Him the glory!'" Paul had a great sense of the sovereignty of God and felt it critically important that any leader of a Christian ministry should likewise hold on to this great truth that "God the Almighty reigns" in every situation and over everything.

Study and Multiplication

After Paul White had gone to be with the Lord, David Hewetson took over the Aussie board and was later also to become a distinguished chairperson of the International Partnership Board. He and his wife Ann had been long-serving missionaries in Tanzania and so they knew Africa well and loved its people with all their hearts. David's concern was to see AE's evangelicalism remain gracious and loving and yet totally true to the Word of God. With his keen theological mind he was also always concerned to see the team reading "cutting edge" theological books. Periodically he would select one of these and send it to Michael and the team for study and absorption. He and Mike Woodal, the Aussie office's executive director, were also concerned with communicating the team's writings to a wider audience. They worked on the publication of Michael's "Window on the Word" newspaper articles and his "Theologically Speaking" essays, and edited some of his earlier books for re-publication.

UK

Another contribution from the Aussie board, but most particularly from Warwick Olson in the late 1970s, was collaborating with Jean Wilson, and Richard Bewes, Rector of All Souls, Langham Place, in getting a British board up and running. This too was related to the fundraising endeavours of Bishop Festo at the time of Amin. Richard Bewes, who had been at Cambridge with Michael, had been raised in East Africa and so knew the East African situation intimately and had a great love and regard for Festo and the Revival Brethren, along with a heart for the spiritual and theological emphases of the East African Revival Movement. Warwick had met Jean Wilson through the Billy Graham Ministries, Jean being a close friend of Billy and Ruth Graham. Thus it was that Richard and Jean got the UK board underway along with Lillian Clark, a missionary who had served for decades with Bishop Festo in East Africa.

Others who knew East Africa well were added, and then came some who knew the South African end more intimately, such as Michael's sister Olave Snelling, and Canon David Prior, an Anglican rector and great expository preacher who had served for many years in a Cape Town parish. Being one of the major evangelical preachers, writers and communicators of the UK, and chairperson of the Anglican Evangelical Council, Richard Bewes was connected in every conceivable direction, even in the entertainment world, where he knew Cliff Richard well. Bewes was therefore able along with Jean Wilson to steer the AE UK board into one of the most rock-steady, reliable and effective boards and fundraising operations in the whole of the AE partnership. Richard loved his annual visits to Africa for the IPB meetings and always made a point of issuing major tennis challenges to all and sundry, his wildest and most perilous opponent on the court being evangelist Stephen Lungu, the one-time petrol bomb thrower, and now team leader of Malawi. As Richard ran Stephen around the court he might have been tempted to think that Steve must have been a better petrol bomb thrower than he was at throwing the ball into the sky just before serving it with a miss hit!

If Warwick Olson had had a part in helping get the UK board underway, along with Richard and Jean, then Mike Woodall and that board would also be instrumental in launching a chapter of AE in New Zealand under the direction of the irrepressible Rev Canon Ron Taylor, a retired Anglican minister.

Festo's wide linkages in the early 1980s were also largely responsible for AE boards getting up and running in Germany and Switzerland, plus developing strong linkages to Norway, where Sig Aske and Knud Jørgensen in turn flew the AE flag. Later on, largely through Michael's initiatives, other European boards would begin to develop in Belgium and Ireland.

Saving the Union

Perhaps at no time does a ministry more need the leadership of its boards than when it enters serious crisis. And such a crisis hit the work in the late 1970s and early 1980s. The labours of Warwick Olson, Bruce Bare, Richard Bewes and other board members were never more important than through those years when it seemed that the fragile partnership between the East and Southern African teams could blow apart. As IPB chairman, Warwick's labours through those years were prodigious as he shuttled back and forth between various key players in the ministry trying to bring greater understanding and more effective working relationships.

"Like Lincoln, you saved the Union," Michael would often say to Warwick in the aftermath of that dreadful time. The crisis, which came to a climax in 1983, had been building for some time.

A Fragile Partnership

The partnership of Michael and Festo and the Southern and East African teams was inevitably a tender and fragile one, given the massively polarised politics of Africa through those years, when for almost every African in independent Africa, including all the Christian ones, South Africans, and most especially white South Africans, were anathema and an embarrassment. In fact, when Festo agreed in 1969 to come into AE and then in subsequent years begin travelling the continent and the world with a white South African, it was something which took considerable courage and love on his part.

The reality was that many in East Africa could not but feel he was compromising himself by linking up with white South Africans in this way. But Festo would reply: "Michael is my miracle brother. And because I have come to Jesus and he has come to Jesus, we are stuck with each other!" And indeed the two men held on to this principle and on to each other through thick and thin.

Thankfully the bond and the commitment finally held even when it seemed things could not get any worse. As the teams in both South and East grew and developed and ministry and financial pressures of every sort intensified, relationships became strained. Yet by God's grace things held together as all team members on all sides worked at it in the conviction that difficult though it may be, the testimony of an inter-racial and pan-African team coming out of all relational, ethnic, tribal, denominational, economical and educational backgrounds, was a testimony in itself, however difficult it might be to maintain that testimony. Indeed, Michael and Festo would often affirm together that: "Before AE is a work and a ministry, it is a testimony." No wonder the Devil attacked it.

Stresses and Strains

However, by the end of the 1970s it seemed as if that testimony could shatter. After Festo had had to flee Uganda in 1977 following the assassination of Archbishop Janani Luwum, AE's Chairman at that time, it was not unnatural that AE/Uganda/East Africa should become powerfully and properly preoccupied not just with issues of justice, but with caring for exiles, trying to find educational scholarships for refugees (in the end AE provided hundreds of overseas scholarships for prominent exiles to do tertiary education), and catering to limitless other needs related to orphans, widows, starvation, illness, and 101 other crushing physical, economic and social problems. With Festo's genius for sharing a message and for fundraising, suddenly AE was swamped with money from all corners of the globe to try and meet these Ugandan needs. The organisation jumped almost overnight from being what Michael called "a short-trousers organisation into a long-trousers organisation". Swimming in money, for once in its life, AE's administrative and financial management capabilities began to be stretched, both in the United States but more specifically in East Africa, almost to breaking point. All of this produced new stresses and strains.

Bigger Worry

However, beyond all that there was for Michael and others the bigger worry that the ministry risked changing its nature almost totally by being sidetracked from evangelism and being an evangelistic organisation to one focusing primarily on social care and projects ministering to physical needs. The work was committed to holism and to "Word *and deed*", but so big now were the aid, social care and development projects and with such huge sums of money going to them, that it seemed to Michael and others that AE was almost starting to usurp in places the work and role of World Vision, yet without the organisational gifting and resources of the latter organisation. As the two leaders of AE struggled with the ever-developing problems of balance and allocation of financial resources, Michael challenged Festo as to whether he was leading the work off into another direction, while Festo felt Michael was holding him back from an adequate response to the profound tragedy which had befallen his country. Maybe both were right.

Not surprisingly the financial and administrative difficulties in East Africa could not be concealed from some of the believers in that part of the world, and when Michael visited Kenya, various people, generally from outside the organisation, but also from inside, would descend upon him within hours of his arrival in Nairobi and share concerns, laments or cries for help. But East Africa was Festo's area. When Michael sought to share some of these difficulties with Festo and with the US Office Administrator, Keith Jesson, a man of extraordinary administrative and fundraising capabilities, it was not difficult for them to feel that Michael was interfering in an arena which was not his. One person even said to Festo: "Michael is in a power grab to try and take over your area." Michael for his part knew nothing could be further from the truth, as his own hands were more than full in Southern Africa, what with the expanding ministry plus the political crises in South Africa itself and in Rhodesia/Zimbabwe. But he was worried about what could happen if the organisation did not get its administrative and financial act together and beyond that if it began to deflect from evangelism as its major calling.

It does not take much imagination to understand how these tensions could escalate and begin to infect other team members in the two different geographical regions. Michael and Festo's personal relationship and friendship remained firm and strong, though strained at times, and they did their best to hold on to one another.

Keith Jesson took the view that a separation of East Africa from Southern Africa was in the best interests of the AE partnership, and put it to Festo that this was the way to go. Festo responded sympathetically to the idea and communicated this to the International Chairman, Warwick Olson. Warwick immediately travelled to the USA, where Festo was on a ministry tour and asked AE's East African Co-ordinator Daniel Serwanga to join them. En route Warwick communicated with the support boards in the USA, Australia and the UK. None of them supported the move to separate. Nor did Daniel Serwanga, who took a brave stand against his leader Festo in opposing the idea.

Said Warwick later: "Great credit should go to Daniel for standing firm."

Following lengthy discussions and prayer, Festo agreed that the change should not take place and that the issues which brought this crisis to a head should be discussed by the whole international leadership of African Enterprise.

Crisis

The crisis reached a head in a team conference at De Burght Conference Centre near Amsterdam a week before the Billy Graham Amsterdam '83 Conference for Evangelists. Tensions exploded and all of a sudden the African Enterprise ministry seemed to be in smithereens. Once in Amsterdam the team met again for many hours to share, confront, express anger, confess sin, and seek mutual forgiveness and reconciliation. It was however more verbal than real. There was a long way to go.

As indicated, it was people like Warwick Olson, Bruce Bare and Richard Bewes who throughout these difficult years did everything they could to see the ministry hold together.

"It's worth working at, Mike," said Tom Houston, then International Director of World Vision, after Michael had shared some of AE's problems with him. "It is a unique partnership in the world, you know."

Meeting some while later in the United States, with Warwick Olson having flown over from Australia, and several of the other key players such as Daniel Serwanga having come from Kenya, the ministry struggled for its soul and its future.

Thankfully, everyone, and especially Festo and Michael,

held on desperately to the principles of repentance, walking in the light, the imperatives of reconciliation and the maximally important principle of real gospel fellowship as the matrix out of which any successful and effective ministry had to come.

Not Enough Cross

At a team and board conference in California Michael said:

> I can see that South Africa has become way more embarrassing to Festo and my East African brethren than I had ever grasped. I regret this insensitivity but had been feeling that this was in fact part of the cost and demonstration and miracle of our testimony as an organisation. Seemingly I and my other South African colleagues have failed in terms of the way of the Cross because we have been too naive and have thought we were all further along in our race relations than we were. But I pray that what we have said or done may not be seen as unforgivable so that we are rejected or cast off. Please forgive us our failures. Let's hang on to one another.

As to the notion of the two regions of AE separating Michael said that "AE would then cease to be a sign and symbol of hope to Africa and beyond but would just be another token of despair that heterogeneous groupings of Christians, with different races, denominations and backgrounds could be able to stand together in unity. It would be disillusioning to all who pray for us and support us."

Michael was seeking to heed a word given him by Dorothy Smoker, a former Tanzanian missionary who also worked as a co-author of Festo's books. She had said to Michael: "You are not showing enough Cross. You are not bending low enough."

Festo for his part put it this way:

> We have become strangers in a community of the ill. This is because we have not crossed over to each other through the Cross. But we have to remember that healing comes from Calvary only with perspiration. Our divisions may seem reasonable in human terms, but they are not reasonable at the cross. Michael and I cannot separate spiritually because we find ourselves stuck with each other, not having been brought together by AE, but by Jesus. I con-

fess I have in some way been trying to break some ropes which have made it hard for my feet to keep running with the gospel. That is why we must sit. We have to share and confront. Only then can we run. Michael and I are now freeing each other so that our ministries can be released and we can stop creating little colonies of suspicion and prejudice. Isn't it wonderful to see again that it takes God to "unmess" all the garbage. When garbage heaps up, brethren separate. And they throw stones or verses at each other and think they are communicating but when we speak truth like that to each other we leave people bleeding. That's why when we minister the truth, we have to put it in the envelope of love. This will also mean talking and prayer and sweat. Then as we do that the river of God sweeps through the garbage and carries it away and we are freed not from each other but for each other.

As the two AE leaders repented before the Lord and sought forgiveness from one another, the hearts of brothers and sisters in both teams and boards were melted. The ministry was back together again and could continue with its testimony that at the cross of Jesus reconciliation with God and with one another is possible. This is the good news.

The Longest Week

Leaving California in mid-October 1983 and flying from Los Angeles to Denver to spend time with Chris Smith, Michael wrote in his journal:

Harold Wilson said "A week is a long time in politics." It is in the kingdom of God too. So I record the home straight of probably the longest week of my life. I feel as if I have been caught up with others in hand to hand combat with the Prince of the Power of the Air, plus also the Prince of California, plus the Principalities and Powers of Africa, and then the strongholds of many people's minds, no doubt my own included.

Board members Warwick Olson, Bruce Bare, Jim Morrison and others throughout Africa rejoiced. They too had held on to one another and on to the ministry. Deep reconcilers such as the Ugandan John Wilson had held on tightly to both Michael and Festo throughout. Said Michael: "John Wilson's deep friendship with me always meant the world. But never more so than in those years and months." Other relationships, not only between board members across the partnership, but between many board members and individual team members, had also been tested and prevailed. The working of gospel principles and the operation of plain, old fashioned, deep friendships had carried the day. "The work was together." And as in the book of Acts it could be said again of the AE ministry that "all who believed were together" (Acts 2:44).

And from that new togetherness came once again a testimony renewed in power and love and effectiveness to be spread across the continent and the world.

PART FIVE

And to the Uttermost Parts of the Earth

Chapter 26

All the World Their Stage

When Michael Cassidy was still a student at Fuller Seminary he felt challenged to incorporate into his prayers that astonishing divine invitation in Psalm 2:8: "Ask of me, and I will give you the heathen for your inheritance and the uttermost parts of the earth for your possession."

That prayer became regular for Michael from that day on. As Navigator founder, Dawson Trotman, had prayed systematically for the world and "claimed" ministry all across the globe, so Michael felt inspired to follow suit.

He began, along with the early team, in praying every month around the major 31 cities of Africa, a city a day, for the 31 days of the month, asking the Lord to open each city for ministry of the gospel. This practice continues all across the AE partnership to this day. Then the various states of the USA were "claimed". Then other parts of the world. One prayer yet to be answered was one first prayed in 1962 to preach in Moscow!

Though Africa would always be central and focal, the AE team's concern for the world has always been real and compelling.

Questions

Even so, this did raise questions, not only in the early years, but now as well.

Why go overseas at all? Isn't there enough work in Africa to keep you busy?

When invitations from churches around the world began to pour in to the AE office, this was a question African Enterprise had to think through carefully.

It was important to get the balance right.

To say "no" to everything overseas seemed senseless. First of all, much of the AE family were overseas: Christians from America to Great Britain to continental Europe to Australasia prayed for the team regularly and supported it financially. So of course they'd occasionally want to meet AE team members in person as well, receive report-back, get first-hand prayer requests, latest financial needs, and share the ministry of these evangelists from far away who were learning many rich things from the Lord's workings in their countries.

Secondly, there was real benefit to AE in going overseas. The AE evangelists could learn a lot from seeing how Christians in other cultures were tackling mission and church growth. Such "cross-fertilisation" of ideas would be of great benefit back in Africa.

Certainly overseas ministry calls were not a drain on AE funds as these were financed by the overseas churches and receiving communities.

Thirdly, there was much that the AE teams could themselves offer. They had done missions in incredibly difficult conditions, among people heavily oppressed by the occult, and among fractured communities. They'd learned the hard way how to deal with powerful spiritual forces and deepseated hatreds of every sort.

Michael Cassidy put it this way:

> Christians worldwide were curious to discover what spiritual universals were coming out of our African particulars. People saw that the church in Africa had been forced to learn major lessons that Christians in easier parts of the world had been able to duck. We'd come to realise that, in a paradoxical way, there are certain blessings to be derived from crisis situations!

So, it was good to respond positively to these calls. But how much time should they get?

It would have been fatally easy to say "yes" to too many such invitations, to become not AE teams who work in Africa, but AE teams who travel the world, talking about how they used to work in Africa.

Michael Cassidy's starting point was always: Africa is the absolute priority of African Enterprise evangelists. "But in order to maintain healthy links with our support churches, to update our knowledge periodically, and to share our own insights with others, a strictly limited amount of time should be devoted to international ministry."

Setting such priorities from the start was a wise move, because in view of the number of invitations that soon flowed in, AE evangelists could have spent most of their time abroad.

Yet over the years, in spite of dozens of requests, the major focus of the ministry of the AE teams has always remained firmly in Africa. In fact, it would be true to say that not a day goes by when someone in African Enterprise is not out communicating Christ somewhere in Africa.

Where did all the overseas invitations come from?

USA

The United States was top of the list.

Michael Cassidy had studied there, had formed the first AE board there, and Pasadena was home to the "mother" AE support office. American churches had financed AE for years, and from California to Washington, DC, from Pennsylvania to Arizona, they would always welcome an AE team. Michael also had scores of contacts in leading church circles across the United States. He had met Christian senators, African ambassadors and even State Department officials in Washington DC. He was also by now good friends with many in the Billy Graham Association, and with Dr Graham himself, and was personally acquainted with the heads of most major American Christian organisations.

Bishop Festo had also studied for ordination in the United States, and while there had travelled and preached extensively. He was very well known, especially in Presbyterian circles. His Anglican credentials of course also opened endless doors wherever he went.

So over the years, AE teams undertook a good number of ministry tours right across the United States and Canada. Festo and Michael even once did a week-long "crusade", as they called it, in a big arena in Wichita, Kansas. Michael's suitcase got lost, so the locals, to the amusement of all, especially Festo, dressed him up in jazzy American jackets and fancy pants, some even putting multi-coloured ties in the collection box when the nightly "offering" was taken! It was lots of fun and very fruitful. But usually two or three AE team members would visit a wide selection of churches, including Episcopalian, Presbyterian, Baptist, Methodist, Congregational and independent. They preached in people's homes, churches, church halls, restaurants (at prayer breakfasts), and at high school auditoriums. They addressed ladies' coffee mornings, young wives' groups, business lunches, golf teas, youth rallies, men's breakfast clubs, entire congregations, and every other possible social grouping that American and Canadian Christians could come up with.

Sometimes Thousands

The AE teams shared their faith and experiences of what God was doing in Africa with dozens, with hundreds and even occasionally with thousands of Americans at a time. When Michael preached at the Promise Keepers' rally in Charlotte, North Carolina there were 52,000 present, at Soldier Field in Chicago 70,000, and in Knoxville, Tennessee 43,000. Usually Michael was asked to address the issue of racial reconciliation. Sharing out of Africa's traumas in this regard, its brokenness and its experiences also of God's grace, often moved American audiences deeply. In the Chicago Promise Keepers' rally, when Michael and African-American Raleigh Washington gave an appeal at the end of Michael's message on "Walking in Our Brother's Shoes", some 6,000 men ran to the front of the platform, many of them falling on their faces when they got there and calling on God for his mercy for their racial sins and attitudes.

Said Malcolm Graham, who observed this: "It was extraordinary. I'd say also there were another 14,000 in the blocked aisles all trying to go forward in response to Michael's appeal." Berhanu Deresse, AE Team Leader for Ethiopia, also commented: "It was incredible. And even in the aisles many who couldn't get forward because of the squash got down on their knees with their faces to the ground. I never saw such a thing."

TV and media people, who'd also not seen anything like this before, asked the stunned Michael for his explanation.

> I don't really know. Maybe it was just sharing how amidst Africa's awful failures and sins God's mercy and grace have met us.

Certainly I have given no success story. But we do know that God is greater than all the racial and tribal awfulness we have seen in Africa. Perhaps this has encouraged Americans who are also still deeply struggling with this racial thing.

Michael thinks this was possibly the most extraordinary and awesome ministry experience he ever had.

Taking Time

However, when it came to time-conscious churches, there was one slight hitch. Team members were used to preaching for an hour or more in Africa, where anything less would have been barely decent. Here they were told to keep their addresses to ten or fifteen minutes. They tried hard to do this, but they had so much to share that they were not always successful! "You people here have the watches," said Steve Lungu to one congregation, "but we have the time!"

The riches of Fuller Seminary and other theological colleges were also irresistible when study or occasional scholarship offers came. The incredible generosity of the American Christians would make it possible for many of the AE evangelists, from both South African and East African teams, to get scholarships to pursue further study as well.

The AE evangelists welcomed these chances to step back from the coal face, and to try and put their lives' work in Africa into some kind of wider-world Christian perspective. One example of research undertaken by an AE scholarship student was to "consider in depth the prophetic and social responsibilities of the evangelist with regard to the African independent churches, the Charismatic Movement, and black consciousness".

AE evangelists also added a few footnotes of their own to American church history. John Wilson and Ebenezer Sikakane spoke at the very first Black Congress on Evangelism in New York City. Bishop Festo was the first black African bishop to be interviewed by Pat Robertson on the TV show "The 700 Club". AE Pasadena even managed at one stage to get team members a regular radio slot, for broadcasting devotional talks and "African updates" across six western states.

Britain

England and Australia probably ranked equal as the next most visited foreign countries. Michael Cassidy certainly considered England a second home after his time at Cambridge, and many subsequent visits there. "Having been converted to Christ in England, I always felt a special debt of gratitude to that nation and was always thankful indeed for opportunities to minister there, whether in churches or Spiritual Life Conferences such as Spring Harvest or Filey."

Festo, as a Ugandan, had always also looked to England as the source of his spiritual roots, because the missionaries who had come to Uganda had all been English. What's more, Festo's home town of Kabale even had regular Keswick Conventions!

AE made a small slice of British church history, too: in November 1974 Bishop Festo led an East African AE team to the UK where for the first time ever, black Christians from independent Africa conducted a series of citywide evangelistic meetings in major British cities, including Manchester, London and Belfast. The East African team came at the invitation of the Church Missionary Society (CMS), who had after all been the ones to send out white missionaries to East Africa in the first place. British Christians were delighted at the idea of welcoming back the spiritual "fruits" of those early endeavours, and took the East Africans to their hearts.

Other visits to Britain down the years, especially "From Uganda with Love" in 1981, after the fall of Idi Amin, were equally popular, packing out English cathedrals with thousands of people. That year, the Archbishop of Canterbury, the Most Rev Dr Robert Runcie, decorated Bishop Festo and the Rev John Wilson with the Canterbury Order of the Cross, as a symbol of distinguished service in the Anglican Communion.

All Souls, Langham Place in London was top of the list for English support churches for AE. John Stott had been a friend of Michael's and Festo's for many years, and his successor, the Rev Richard Bewes, was head of the AE English board.

Michael was especially privileged on one occasion to be invited to speak on "A Leadership Led by God" in the Speaker's Lounge in the House of Commons to a sizeable group of members of the House of Commons and House of Lords and their wives.

"It was extraordinary," said Michael, "to see these people in such high places and such social prominence eager to exercise their key leadership according to the principles of Christ."

In the United States, Britain and Australia, African Enterprise teams also discovered they had a "renewing" ministry within many churches. These countries had sent missionaries to Africa in the first place. But in the intervening years, many churches had "cooled" down into frozen middle-class respectability or even apathy. The Africans could bounce in and say "Hey, wake up! Where is your enthusiasm for Jesus? You were good enough to send someone to tell us about him! It changed our lives! Don't lose *your* love for him!" For example, on the East African team alone, Bishop Festo Kivengere, Bishop Gresford Chitemo, Canon James Katarikawe, Stephen Lungu and Abiel Thipanyane were all directly or indirectly the products of foreign missionary work from England or Australia. In several cases, the English or Australian churches the AE teams visited had even *known* the white missionaries in question. It was a powerful, moving link.

The churches responded again and again to the Africans' encouragement. The American, British and Australian Christians were first amused, then intrigued, and then finally touched at the idea of black Africans coming to evangelise *them*. However they took to heart what the Africans said in a way they would not have done with white fellow countrymen.

Australia and New Zealand

Australia was certainly another "home from home" for African Enterprise. Not only had several Tanzanian AE team members become Christians through Australian CMS missionaries, but Australians had also provided some of AE's most outstanding leadership at board level over the years, and many Australian churches supported the work.

It was in Australia, New Zealand and Papua New Guinea, perhaps more than anywhere else, that AE teams found a rich ministry in cross-cultural evangelism. They were an instant hit with both Aborigines and Maoris. There was a deep natural empathy between them. The Africans *knew* what it was like to have been brought up in "traditional" religions that honoured the spirits of ancestors, and which involved the use of charms, etc. They *knew* the initial hesitation new converts felt when they forsook the spirits and began to trust Jesus completely. The Africans also knew what it was like to be judged on the colour of their skin.

So, during various tours of Australia down the years, the AE teams worked extensively with the Aborigines. Matt Nyagwaswa, Team Leader of Tanzania, was a particular favourite among the Aborigines, and, in Papua New Guinea, Festo had been a sensation. When aboriginal witch-doctors renounced all contact with evil spirits, they found AE team members a tower of strength and encouragement. Hundreds and even thousands of Aborigines came to find a trust in this Jesus they had thought was only for white men, but now knew was for black men as well. AE teams spoke to many aboriginal pastors' conferences, where they made a huge impact. The black Africans could certainly say things about forgiveness and reconciliation that the white Australians could not.

In New Zealand, too, the racial reconciliation message was much needed, and when Edward and Vasta Muhima and Michael conducted a Reconciliation Conference in 1999 in Gisborne for Maoris and Pakeha (whites), the response was overwhelming. In the closing service an exuberant spirit of joy and even dance overcame the inter-racial gathering and even the Rev Canon Dr Edward Muhima burst from his Anglican conservatism and, to the astonishment of Vasta, jigged around in a most un-Anglican fashion!

Michael took a photo of this to send Edward's archbishop back in Uganda for blackmail purposes if ever Edward misbehaved!

Aussie Schools

Another fruitful arena of evangelising for AE team members was in Australian schools. The first big challenge was the famous Kings School, Paramatta, where Michael Cassidy, John Wilson, Matt Nyagwaswa and Brian Gibson did a week-long mission. The team always remembers Matt Nyagwaswa's guitar song "There's a Great Hallelujah Meeting Over There – and the white man will be there – and the brown man will be there –

and the yellow man will be there – AND I'LL BE THERE!" At which he beamed a winning smile as wide as Africa. This at first shocked the staid and classically oriented Kings School chapel out of its mind – and then before the final verse was reached brought the house down with an unprecedented eruption of clapping, stomping and a standing ovation. In fact, so euphoric were the boys that after John Wilson had led them in prayer, they again applauded!

Headmaster Stanley Kurrle, still, amazingly after all that, a friend to Michael and the team, raised his semi-horrified eyebrows, smiled weakly and whispered to Michael: "I think you've all got a breakthrough!"

And so the team had. Even Mr Asbo ("Jazzie Azzie", as the boys called him), the school's highly conservative classical music master and organist, who believed nothing worthwhile musically had been written since the 17th century, was won over and three days into the mission was letting down what little hair he had, and bouncing with Brian and Matt and a spontaneously assembled scholars' band through "When the Saints Go Marching In", plus an assortment of old and new gospel songs! The boys were ecstatic. Jazzie Azzie was "into it" and sounds were heard from his grand piano that had never been heard before.

Not surprisingly, by the end of the week, the school had been profoundly impacted. The "African Way" had broken through. "It's been a wonderful experience," wrote Jazzie Azzie to the team later, "and the school is a kinder place."

Other school missions were held in Perth, Sydney, Melbourne and the Gold Coast, as Edward Muhima, Jack Garratt and Songe Chibambo brought their skills, different cultures and vibrant personalities to bear upon the tough but open Aussie youngsters. Edward Muhima's two missions at Melbourne Grammar School are still talked about.

Central America and Middle East

South America, Central America and the Middle East were another story altogether, offering a different set of riches for the Africans. Here, when AE team members met local Christian leaders, things really fizzed. Africans, South Americans and Middle Easterners quickly discovered they had a lot in common.

Their empathy lay in the fact that they were all ministering in countries that were burgeoning and chaotic, torn by political factions and enmities, with other world faiths hovering in the shadows, and the future highly uncertain. AE had learned about reconciliation and united Christian witnesses the hard way: in the crucible of African experience. Suddenly those lessons, so painfully learned, became a rich vein of experience and wisdom which they could tap to help their perplexed Christian colleagues in the cauldron of Middle East politics and South American revolutions. That and "best practice" ideas for grounding new converts in churches kept many an evangelist up late into the night talking to South American and Central American counterparts. Nurturing enthusiastic young Christians when communications, transport and resource materials were hard to come by was what AE specialised in.

In the mid and late 70s Michael and Festo, along with Ebenezer Sikakane, and with preparatory help from Keith Jesson and John Tooke, did missions in Panama, Nicaragua and Costa Rica, involving some hair-raising jungle-hopping in rickety planes.

"How we ever survived some of those flights, I'll never know," said Michael later, "but we did. And in between being terrified out of our minds on some of these journeys, we had some of the most rewarding and fruitful ministry experiences ever, our focus being 'the forgotten places' evangelists don't normally go to." That had been the aim of Dr Orlando Costas, the great theologian and missiologist of San José, Costa Rica, who had engineered and opened up these opportunities. Nicaraguans, unable to pronounce Ebenezer's Zulu name and forgetting he was merely a Baptist evangelist, kept calling him "Bishop Sugar-cane", much to the amusement of AE's real Bishop Festo Kivengere!

Egypt

The churches in Egypt became especially good friends to AE, perhaps because Egypt is tacked on to the north of Africa itself. In 1978 Festo and Michael held one church seminar in Assuit in Upper Egypt expecting 50 clergymen, and several hundred turned up. Nothing like that had ever happened in Egypt before.

There were also wonderful pastors' conferences in both Cairo and Alexandria. Michael wrote to the AE family: "I would say that we haven't done a mission yet where we made as full an impact on the Protestant clergy of a whole country as this one."

Israel

Israel was another country where AE had a useful contribution to make. For example, in April 1982 Bishop Festo and Mera Kivengere and John Wilson of Uganda, Michael and Carol Cassidy and their children, David Peters and Abiel Thipanyane of South Africa, Dr Don Jacobs of the US, and Gershon Mwiti and Stephen Mung'oma of Kenya did a "mission" to Jerusalem, Nazareth, Haifa, Jericho, Bethlehem and Tel Aviv. It was for Michael, now en route back from ministries in England to which Carol and the children had been invited, the only time in the history of the work when his whole family could be in on a mission, thanks to generous sponsors in England.

Between all the evangelists, they took 90 meetings in twelve days, literally moving across "the Land" from "Dan to Beersheba". They'd been invited by the United Christian Council of Israel, because "we are desperately in need of a message of reconciliation". South Africa with its racial tensions and Uganda with its wounds and bitterness had a lot to say to the situation in Israel.

One day David Peters went with Audeh Rantisi, the Christian Mayor of Ramallah on the West Bank, to preach in one of the high schools of Ramallah and share his testimony. The town then, as now, was in violent turmoil. In the streets, Palestinian youths were pelting Israeli army soldiers with stones. Live shots rang in the air and rubber bullets were occasionally fired by Israeli soldiers. The atmosphere was highly charged. In the middle of all of this, Audeh Rantisi and David left the school after the meeting in their car and began driving out of town. When the throng of Palestinian youths saw Rantisi, their Mayor, in the back of the car, they altered the trajectory of their stones and lobbed them in great looping throws high into the air and over the top of the car. Thus did David and Audeh leave Ramallah driving under a great arch of flying stones.

"One of the more interesting drives I have ever been on,"

said David, as he geared up thereafter to head to Nazareth for ministry in Jesus' home town with Bishop Festo and John Wilson.

Then came Peta-Tikva. In the centre of what everyone guardedly called "the Land", the team drew together the largest group of Israeli and Palestinian believers (some 500 strong) which had ever assembled. It took the form of a picnic with people intentionally clustered in groups comprising both Israelis and Palestinians so that dialogue and relatedness could occur. Festo and Michael both preached, and the atmosphere was charged with the love and reconciling power of Christ.

An elderly Jewish believer, surveying the unprecedented gathering said: "I have been a believer in Jesus the Messiah for 32 years, and I can say I have never before been in a meeting like this."

Closing Cameo

One interesting little cameo in the closing days of the mission to "the Land" captured what God was doing.

After the team had ministered one Saturday night in Tel Aviv, a young Israeli Messianic believer (we will call her Helen), who had found Christ while in the Israeli army, came to Michael Cassidy after the meeting. "Michael," she said, "I have truly found Jesus as my Lord and Messiah. I love him very much. But I just cannot get victory over my bitterness and hatred for Arabs and Palestinians. Please pray for me."

Michael counselled her for a while and then said: "You know what, Helen, I believe you would find yourself really healed if you could experience Christian love and acceptance from some Arab and Palestinian believers. Let's pray that the Lord will really make this happen."

The team was taken back to Jerusalem late that same night to their pre-arranged lodgings, prior to their preaching assignments, mainly around Jerusalem, the next day. However, Michael's assignment early next morning was in one of the major churches in Bethlehem. Once again the atmosphere was tense, electric and sullen as Israeli soldiers had the previous day shot and killed two or three Palestinian youths who had been pelting them with stones. The mood in the congregation was one of icy fury. Michael never felt before as he preached that he was talking to such a wall of impenetrable concrete. After the service, Michael was taken to tea with the elders of the church, all of whom spent the next hour or more in a thundering tirade against the Israelis.

"After all," said one, "what more can you expect from such people when they even killed the Son of God?"

From Sadness to Joy

Having just hours before heard the anguished cry and bitter feelings of Helen, the Israeli, and now hearing similar or more intense feelings from these Palestinian believers, Michael found himself tempted to despair of the whole situation in "the Land". The team was due to leave the country the next day and Michael felt himself longing to experience a true gospel happening to rescue him from deep sadness and send him on his way rejoicing.

He, Festo and the team were due to close out the whole ministry of those weeks that night with a service in a big Anglican Cathedral church in Jerusalem. Just before the service Michael was confronted by Rev Yosef Odeh, a leading light in the mission and a Palestinian pastor from Galilee. As they were talking, Yosef testified that he was seeing wonderful things in his congregation, which was made up not just of Palestinians but of Israeli believers as well.

"In fact," he said, "I love Israelis more even than they love themselves." Michael's heart rose in doxology.

During the service Festo preached most movingly, and a brief word from Michael followed. As Michael stood in that high pulpit and looked out over the packed congregation, he was astonished to spot Helen down there in a central pew. She had dashed up from Tel Aviv to be in on the team's final meeting. He then also spotted in the congregation not only the Galilean pastor, Yosef Odeh, but also Audeh Rantisi, the remarkable Christian Mayor of Ramallah.

Healing for Helen

Here in these brethren might perhaps be the beginning of healing for Helen. When the service was over, Michael beckoned across the church to Helen, to Yosef and to Audeh. As they all converged on him, he introduced Helen to the two exuberant Palestinians. Immediately both their faces lit up and they hugged Helen in a great embrace of love and acceptance.

"We have heard all about you, Helen, and know of your testimony in the Israeli army, and we praise God for you and have been praying for you." Their appreciation for her was real and deep. As Helen's eyes lit up and a mighty smile of delight spread across her face, Michael felt he was watching before his very eyes a healing miracle of God's grace, forgiveness and love.

Leaving next day from Tel Aviv airport, his spirits were on a high. He had seen the love of Christ triumphantly at work again, and besides all that his beloved Carol, plus Cathy, Debbie and Marty, were for once on the plane with him. In reality, he hardly needed the plane, for he had wings of his own!

David Peters was likewise on a high because he had had a rich opportunity to minister not only to Israelis and Palestinians, but to some senior South Africans who had been visiting the South African embassy in Tel Aviv and had come to one of his services. Every one of the team members rejoiced in once again having been witnesses to the presence and power of the Lord Jesus at work in the very area where he had carried out his earthly ministry.

Other Ministry Visits

Other ministry visits overseas down the years have been wide-ranging, and included ministry in Bahrain, Jordan, Syria, Lebanon, Turkey, Cyprus, Greece, India, Japan, East Germany, West Germany, Indonesia and the Solomon Islands. Even in China, Festo led several teams and ministered in depth to many people. More recently in the mid-1990s a large AE team conducted a mission to Lausanne, Switzerland and packed out Lausanne Cathedral each night.

Other rich recent opportunities have come for Michael in Ireland, both in the Republic and in Ulster. A special occasion was sharing the platform with the then President Mary Robinson at the United Nations' 50th Anniversary Dinner in Dublin Castle in 1995. The next year came the privilege of addressing the "United Ireland Prayer Breakfast" bringing together leaders from North and South and including not only the Roman Catholic Cardinal from Ulster but the head of the Protestant Orange Order. Michael's message from Jeremiah 29:11 on "A Future and a Hope", and telling of the South African 1994 election experience moved many to tears. Said one politician from the Republic: "I've cried through all my handkerchiefs plus all the serviettes on the table."

Perhaps many were so touched because hope for Ireland, as one of the few places seemingly more of a lost cause than South Africa, had been reborn. If South Africans could move from being prisoners of history to prisoners of hope, maybe there could yet under God be hope for Irish people as well.

That night Michael Cassidy and Paddy Monaghan met privately in Armagh with the Roman Catholic leader, Cardinal Daly, who had been at the breakfast, for a session of sharing and prayer. Driving south late that night Paddy and Michael parked right on the border, with the car's front wheels in the south and the back wheels in the north, and then prayed for the healing of Ireland! The prayer was abruptly terminated by a very suspicious policeman who obviously wondered what these dubious characters were doing. He then trailed them down the road for ten or 15 miles to make sure they were not up to mischief. Little did he know of the nature or power of the prayerful mischief they were really up to!

Other open doors came to Ireland in subsequent years to minister first to Presbyterian and then to Methodist leadership.

As AE develops an Ireland board, the hope and dream is that its evangelists will contribute richly and positively to the healing of the lovely but anguished "Emerald Isle".

In 1998 the doors opened through Rev Nigel Walker and Lynn Badcock in Brussels for Michael, Emmanuel Kopwe of Tanzania and Olave Snelling (Michael's sister) to do a mission to the leadership circles of Brussels in Belgium. Especially challenging were gospel opportunities in the diplomatic community, in the European Commission, the European Parliament, in the business sector, among refugees, and in NATO.

Re-evangelising the West

African Enterprise has ministered now in every corner of the globe save the North and South Poles, and links with believers in Christ across the world will hopefully deepen and develop as the years go by.

When 40 per cent of one entire town turned out for an AE mission in Costa Rica, one newspaper summed up the whole thing pretty well in a single headline: "Will Africa re-evangelise the West?"

To be sure, AE would like to be part of that.

In fact Michael Cassidy's firm belief, and that of many in the AE partnership, is that it is Africa's destiny some time in the 21st century to become the major fulcrum of world mission.

After all, Asia Minor and Greece had their *kairos* moments of missionary responsibility and opportunity in the first few centuries, Rome and Italy in the next few, and Constantinople and Turkey thereafter. Then it was Western Europe's turn in the Middle Ages. In the 19th century Britain assumed the major mantle of gospel outreach across the world. In the 20th century America's glory was to bear and provide the lion's share of both the costs and human resources for world evangelisation. It has been a mighty historical moment of spiritual privilege and matchless performance.

Africa's Moment of Destiny

But now we are in the 21st century. Will this at some point provide Africa with its moment of missionary destiny under God?

Michael and the AE teams believe that this is exactly what is written into the providential plan of God. Not only is the African church growing apace, in places faster than anywhere in the history of Christendom, but its missionary zeal and burden for world evangelisation are slowly being birthed out of the fires of its fragility, fracture and pain, along with its mighty experience of God's amazing grace and precious power.

Prior Task

However, Michael and the AE team believe that an enormous task remains before Africa can fulfil its full destiny in world mission. And this is to deepen in its discipleship.

Phineas Dube of Zimbabwe often says: "Africa's Christianity is a mile wide and an inch deep."

That may or may not be so. But certainly the AE teams do feel that the credibility of the African church is less than compelling when some 380 million people in the continent profess Christianity yet it is going down the tube politically, socially, agriculturally, economically and morally faster than any other continent. Civil wars, tribal conflicts, political corruption, economic declension, undemocratic political behaviour, rampant promiscuity, the worst Aids, violence and crime pandemics in the world – none of this augurs well for a church which is meant to be salt arresting decay, and light dispelling darkness.

Michael comments:

> However, if – if – if – the African church will rise to the occasion and graduate from merely preaching a salvationist message to preaching a truly kingdom one, with all life, whether political, economic, social, moral or marital, being brought under the kingship of Christ, then there is no telling what the God of Heaven may be ready to do both in the African church and through it to the world.
>
> In other words, the African church must do a bit of credible cleaning up of its own back yard before it can help clean up the world's front yard. To be sure there will be no so-called African Renaissance without African Reformation.

Michael and the teams feel therefore that evangelising Africa and discipling its converts and believers must always be AE's first priority, as indeed it was always its first calling. "For the gifts and the calling of God are irrevocable" (Romans 11:29, NKJV).

But if the Lord in addition will continue to bless and privilege AE with the uttermost parts of the earth for (their) possession, then the team's personal praises to their Lord will rise ever higher with each passing day.

Both the African Harvest and the World Harvest are more than ready for reaping.

So, as Michael and all the AE team say, "Let us work the works of him who sent (us) while it is day; for the night is coming when no one can work" (John 9:4).

Epilogue:
AE 40 Years On –
Michael Cassidy Looks
Backwards and
Forwards

I am deeply thankful to Anne Coomes for the years of work and research that have brought forth this volume, a labour of love. She deserves medals of honour and glowing "mentions in despatches". I am also appreciative of the invitation to me to write this Epilogue to her story.

One of the forgotten arts of life, I think, is regular thanksgiving to God and also saying in time the Big Thank You's of Life. I have a good few of these, but first let me affirm my overwhelming "deep-soul" gratitude to the Lord, first for this mysterious opportunity of life and being a human being on Planet Earth and then for finding me, so that I could walk the road together with him and be at the centre of his particular purposes for me.

Never, ever, could I be adequately thankful that he found me when I was still a young man and had my full life ahead of me, and brought me to himself through the witness at Cambridge of Robbie Footner, for whose faithfulness and love I will always stand in eternal debt.

Of all the miracles of life, and I have seen a few, nothing compares with the miracle of new birth in coming to know Christ personally as Lord and Saviour. That has to head the bill and stand forth supreme. No wonder St Paul could exult: "I count everything as loss because of the surpassing worth of knowing Christ Jesus my Lord" (Philippians 3:8). All I can do is to echo that with 10,000 amens.

Then following that comes the rich, riveting and often bumpy ride of following Christ as a disciple and knowing his daily companionship as "a friend who sticks closer than a brother". I thank him too for his mercy and grace and for being the God not only of the Second Chance but the Hundred and Second Chance. I have needed many of those in my time as I have got many things wrong, messed up, sinned and often let the side down. But the Lord has always been there to forgive, restore, put me back on my feet and prompt friends, loved ones and colleagues to forgive me too. That is Amazing Grace.

Of course God comes to one much through those around one and in African Enterprise over the years this is how so often my Lord has come to me – through my brothers and sisters in the work who have shown much patience with me. Thus was I right in a diary entry on 25 January 1981 in Nairobi to write, during a difficult time in our team relationships: "I have also to accept afresh that the people around me are God's providences to me, and that I dare not indulge in too much mote-seeking when the beam in my own eye is so great. Anyway, most blessed Lord, I come to you today justifying you in your judgements and looking to you for cleansing, filling and guiding in the days ahead." Yes, I have found it a key principle in life to accept the sovereignty of God in the people with whom I am ranged.

Calling

In blessing God for his goodness to me I have to say also that receiving a clear calling and life-work mandate when I was still young has been a benediction indeed. Being a stubborn and rebellious sort of fellow, and very self-willed, I needed a strong, clear call if I was to do anything for the Lord. And I got one.

The AE call to give myself to evangelism in Africa and beyond has dominated my life and been its driving passion. Thankfully the Lord alerted me early to the fact that it would be difficult, and involve "the possession of difficulties", because Africa is a difficult place. So many times I wanted to give up, but instead of struggling to hold on to a call, the call held me. I was in its grip. It would not let go. That was fortunate for me as otherwise I might well have been a casualty along the way.

Special Family

In all this I can say I have been much blessed by love and support from a special family starting with my parents. My Mum and Dad were true heroes to me for their integrity of life and example and for the sacrificial way they opened up both school and university opportunities of a fine and formative nature. My sisters, Olave and Judy, were always there for me too with love and loyalty. And they still are. Life's journey without such a family can be a grim affair. But I was blessed beyond measure in this regard.

Capping all that came Carol, beloved wife, partner, encourager and friend for nearly 33 years now. God knew what he was doing when he brought such a one to me, one who would be in the words of Proverbs "far more precious than jewels" (Proverbs 31:10). It was a very miraculous thing, and I was undeserving to say the least, and have remained so. To say that I could not have coped with this work without her would be the understatement of the century. While she might not feature very overtly in this story of the work, in reality her life, presence, counsel and support are on every page, unseen, but gentle, powerful and pervasive. Beyond all that my debt to her is incalculable for keeping such a steady and secure ship going at home for Cathy, Debs and Martin, while her crazy, peripatetic evangelist husband rushed round all over Africa and the world on his work. For Carol this was her special offering and "living sacrifice unto God", to hold the family fort, keep the home-fires burning, and release me for the Lord's work. After travelling excessively for many years, we settled on 100 days' absence per year. More than that got destructive. And we have aimed to establish that target for all travelling evangelists in the work. Yes, in Carol the Lord gave me one of his best, make no mistake. And AE was a major beneficiary too, I assure you. Said Bruce Bare to me once: "Carol is the best thing that ever happened to AE." I wholeheartedly concur.

So it has been a team thing at home, with my kids behind me all the way too. I can never praise God enough for Catherine,

Deborah and Martin and the way they let me be both their father and their close friend and then resolved for their part to follow the Lord their mother and father followed. The blessing now of seeing them all married in the Lord with great spouses in Jonathan, Gary and Sam respectively fills my heart with overflowing doxologies to God. Carol's mum and dad, John and Noenkie Bam, have been the best in-laws possible and her extended family have added deep friendships, richness, joy and stability both for me and our whole family. What a benediction!

Key Influences

Of course there have been many other key influences – Pat Duncan, who politicised me when very young to the notions of social justice, and Michaelhouse, with its opposition posture to apartheid, were seminal influences.

Then I think of Dr Basil Atkinson at Cambridge, who fired me to accept the Bible as the Word of God, and John Stott whose biblical faithfulness and theological balance always gave me a worthy theological goal to strive after. In fact he and Billy Graham are the two who have also influenced me most in terms of preaching, John for content and structure and Billy for spirit, urgency and passion. I have to say it is wonderful that Dr Graham agreed to do the foreword to this book as he has been, albeit mostly at a distance, a foundational influence in my life, in our ministry and I would say in the lives of most of my colleagues. And the Billy Graham Evangelistic Association (BGEA) has been inspirational also.

I once sensed the Lord wanting me to go to Montreat to see Billy Graham and just say "Life's Big Thank You" while I could. Nothing else.

"That's amazing," said Ruth Graham to her husband as we sat over tea on the verandah of their lovely log-cabin home in the Montreat Mountains. "No one's ever come here before just to say 'Thank You!'"

I was glad the Lord had prompted me to do so.

We have spoken elsewhere of our board members, but I must highlight the friendship of Bruce Bare and Ted Engstrom in the USA and Calvin Cook in South Africa. These sorts of supportive friendships of those to whom in effect one is accountable stand like Sequoia redwood pillars giving one's life and work further structure, stability and warmth.

Someone else critically important to this work was Festo Kivengere. But for his courage, faith and I believe obedience in coming into the work in late 1970 and early 1971, this ministry would never have been remotely where it is today. Festo it was who really enabled AE to be "AFRICAN Enterprise", and not just a "SOUTH African Enterprise"! In a sense he gave us and brought to us the wider continent. Also the wider development of boards in Australia, UK, Germany, even Switzerland, really sprang in the first instance from his relationships and from those immense funding endeavours related to the Idi Amin crisis in Uganda in 1977 and onwards.

It was Festo who also brought into the work the Holy Spirit and "Cross" theology of the East African Revival to blend and synthesise with more traditional evangelicalism on the one hand and the Charismatic Renewal on the other. That too has been consequential.

So I praise God for my late brother. We had a few struggles now and then, but no two strong-willed people from such very different backgrounds could work together closely without some of that. But our friendship and partnership in the Lord held firm and that fact has bequeathed to the ministry a dimension of its legacy which should be neither forgotten nor forsaken.

The Team's the Thing

AE has been and is a team ministry, not a one-man band. That has been important. Nor is it just all the up-front people, such as the friends and colleagues who have featured through these pages. My life and work would have been totally impossible but for my backstage team who have helped me so specially over all the years and kept my systems, desk and pretty formidable correspondence operating. Personal assistants such as Brenda Petersen, Lois Stephenson, Nellis du Preez, Peter Kerton-Johnson and David Ryman, and particularly assistants Jamie and Amy Morrison in recent years, have quite literally made the difference between keeping it all together and having it all fly apart. They've also been friends, and one needs those. Likewise wonderful secretaries such as Loraine Evans, Dorothy White, Colleen Smith (with an epic and amazing twelve-year stint) and Brenda Harrison. One can't quantify their contributions. They are integral to an overall work, vital cogs in a machine which would otherwise splutter to a stop. They are also part of the "upbuilding of the Body in love" which St Paul speaks of "when every joint... and part with which it is supplied... is working properly" (Ephesians 4:16).

Prayer Partners and Donors

And what about our prayer partners and donors? This has been a truly extraordinary thing; for me a supernatural thing – that God should have raised up, as he has, people of all ages, races and backgrounds to take on their hearts the prayer and financial support of this work.

Thus I think of Alan Rosenberg, my first room-mate at Fuller, coming to me one day with a one dollar bill.

"Mike, I believe African Enterprise is of the Lord, and I want the privilege of giving the first dollar to this work." Amazing, though I doubt if he ever got a receipt!

And what of the thousands of other donors and supporters since? To be sure, they are "in team" with us. Without them the ministry's life would have been snuffed out in weeks.

Think of the prayer partners, intercessors and prayer-warriors before God. People like my sister Olave, there for me almost from day one as an intercessor, or Mrs Bruce, Indian matriarch and mother-in-law to David Peters, or Elsie Buthelezi, or Sandra Pillay, or Margaret Davis or Cora Vines and Marjorie Cranage, AE's aged but special heavenly twins who spend hours a day in prayer for the work. These and so many others will have front seats in Heaven, while for us evangelists it will be the back row, make no mistake.

Birthing Prayer

And what about Mrs Violet Webb, an old lady in Pietermaritzburg, whom I never met and whose 23 August 1962 letter to us I only recently rediscovered. Perhaps Heaven will reveal that it was she in truth who really birthed in intercession that first and most strategic mission to Maritzburg that was determinative for the whole future of the work.

Writing to us as "Very Dear Friends", she tells of a deep burden over three months (January to April 1961) to pray first for her own dimming sight, then for "our government and nation of South Africa".

She goes on:

> Then I realised that a special prayer must be for the churches in this city. So I prayed for a messenger from another land to be sent to guide us, and teach us, in our city hall; for without that special messenger we could do nothing on our own. I prayed for this at all times, and many times during the 24 hours of day and night. I had no country in mind, and knew not from whence the messenger would come.

She tells also how she learned to pray for her enemies and then received "a sign from God that my prayers had been answered".

"How God has answered my prayer for 'the messenger'! He sent five when I had just asked for one! Then I thought one week (of meetings) and God provided several weeks. I thought the City Hall would be half full, but it has been full to overflowing. God be praised!"

Is that perhaps where AE's South African ministry really began? In the prayers of a little old lady going blind? Who knows?

And it is prayers like that from that day to this that have kept us going. Truly could we say then, as we must still do now, to our friends: "You also must help us by prayer so that many will give thanks on our behalf for the blessing granted us in answer to many prayers" (2 Corinthians 1:11).

Gentle Graph

Looking back, I would say that the AE ministry has not been a spectacular one for newspaper headlines, if one compares it to the ministries of say Billy Graham or Luis Palau. But the graph of the work is one of a gentle incline from day one. The Lord has thankfully allowed us to make progress. A gracious promise I have claimed for years is Deuteronomy 28:13: "You shall tend upwards only and not downward if you obey the command-ments of the Lord your God." It's a lovely word and principle and I think we have seen it at work in this ministry.

The Lord has also enabled us to plough a pretty straight furrow theologically and spiritually. We haven't gyrated madly from side to side, or presented a crazily swinging pendulum. From the beginning we brought together evangelism and social concern and that's still how it is. We didn't suddenly discover one or the other and quickly embrace it like a novelty. We were clear and firm on the Word of God when we started, and that's still how we are. We were concerned way back then for truth and biblical faithfulness in the age of modernism as we still are now in these so-called "Postmodern times".

We were committed at the ministry's inception to the absoluteness of Judaeo-Christian morals, ethics and the sanc-tity of family and home, with the only biblically sanctioned model of marriage being monogamous and heterosexual. And that's how we still see it.

We affirmed very early the person, work, fruit and gifts of the Spirit, and we still do. We sought from our first campaigns to manifest both piety and activism, both prayerfulness and action, both waiting on God and taking initiative. And I believe that's still our style and will continue to be.

My prayer is that the ministry will always hold true to all these commitments.

Pillars on Which the House Stands

In the book of Judges, Chapter 16 and verse 26, the blinded, and weakened Samson, now in the temple of the Philistines, says to the young lad who held him by the hand: "Let me feel the pillars on which the house rests."

If I were to try and outline the pillars on which I feel the AE house has sought to rest, and on which I hope it will always rest, I would want to name the following:

The Pillar of Jesus and our Love for Him
Jesus is what AE is all about, along with our love relationship with him. It is instructive that in John 21:15, the only question he wanted Peter to answer for him was: "Do you love me more than these?" Our love relationship with him has to be primary and we grasp that we are first of all saved to love rather than saved to serve. Service follows and flows from the love relationship.

The Pillar of Family Priorities
Our families and family life in AE have always been very key. Although at times we have run too hard in answer to assorted ministry calls, nevertheless I have often said to others and to my colleagues that I never took a vow about AE and evangelism comparable to the one I took about Carol. Nor dare we ever sacrifice our spouses and families on the altar of our evangelistic zeal.

The Pillar of Team and Inter-Team Fellowship and Sound Relationships
Festo and I quite often preached on Revelation 12:11 which speaks of the Lord's people and says: "They overcame him by the blood of the lamb and the word of *their* testimony." Before AE is a ministry, it is a testimony. The gospel is not just about me and God, but about us and God. And it is this testimony that the Devil has sought to attack at many points along the line. And it is this testimony that has to be kept and preserved at all costs. If in our own relationships we cease to be at one, then we have become part of the bad news and can have no good news for any bad news situations.

The Pillar of Faithfulness to the Bible as the Word of God
At Fuller Seminary, Charlie Fuller always used to say to me: "Mike, stay true to the Word. Mike, preach the Word!" I believe that once any ministry, denomination or congregation detaches from the Bible as the Word of God, as reliable, authoritative and fully inspired, then they are adrift in a sea of relativism and confusion. This we have believed these 40 years.

The Pillar of Obedience to our Calling

At our International Partnership Board meeting in 1982, we said: "It is our vision to obey the calling of God primarily to evangelise, as defined in the Lausanne Covenant, the urban complexes of Africa without ignoring, as God leads, the great opportunities for ministry which come our way in the wider world." At our IPB in 1992, ten years later, the primary focus and mission statement was articulated and settled on as follows: "To Evangelise the cities of Africa through Word and Deed in Partnership with the Church." Although it is not inappropriate to revisit mission statements, and I am sure we will and should do that from time to time, nevertheless that has been our fundamental calling and to that I believe this ministry must be true.

The Pillar of Renewal and Revival in the Holy Spirit

One can never, ever, outgrow or move on from the work of the Spirit. That's why I thank God that the East African Revival, plus other more conventional evangelical models of revival in history (e.g. through Knox, Wesley, Finney, Jonathan Edwards etc.), plus the modern Charismatic Renewal, have all made their way like different rivulets into this stream which is AE. They are there and they are central. Thankfully over these four decades we have never sought, as have some, to graduate from the work of the Spirit into social activism or something of that kind, as if one is a more mature gospel expression than the other. AE holds both together in tension. And certainly no effective work, whether evangelistic, social or activistic or whatever, can ever be carried out without the power and person of the Holy Spirit. "It is not by might or by power but by my Spirit, saith the Lord" (Zechariah 4:6).

The Pillar of Contextual Relevance and Biblical Ethics

The Bible is very clear that our Lord is indeed concerned not only about Heaven, but about Earth. In the so-called Lord's Prayer he taught us to pray: "Thy Kingdom come, Thy will be done ON EARTH, as it is in Heaven." In Jeremiah 9:23 and 24 the Lord tells us we are not to glory in anything other than himself, "but let him who glories glory in this, that he understands and knows me, and that I am the Lord who practises steadfast love, justice and righteousness IN THE EARTH." Our God is concerned for us here on Earth, and on Earth he acts and does things. This requires all believers to have a strong contextual concern for where they are on Earth. While we connect by prayer and faith constantly to the Play Upstairs, we are also called to be players and actors in the Play Downstairs. This is why AE's commitments to evangelise through not only word but also deed are important and pivotal.

The Future When Dreams Become Prayers

But let me now build and elaborate on some of those pillars which have held us in the past and speak of my own "prayer-dreams" for the future.

I need to preface this by recognising that the founder of a ministry needs to have a measure of caution about his own dreams, especially if he is expressing them at the end of one generation, because whatever dreams there are will have to be carried out largely by others in the second generation. And to be sure they should not be bound by the past or anyone else's visionary hopes. Perhaps that's why the dreams of a founder need to convert only into prayers, along with at one level a laying down of these dreams and visions. After all, if our Lord could involve himself in a "self-emptying", as we see in Philippians 2, then certainly all of us have to do some self-emptying of deeply cherished goals and worthy ambitions which may have become for us personally something to be grasped (cf Philippians 2:6). Perhaps that's why Jesus often requires of us even along the way to let go of our ambitions, agendas, visions, dreams, positions we hold or roles we play.

However there's nothing to forbid us taking the dreams and ambitions we have, and having laid them down at the Cross, then letting them transform into prayers about what we want to see happen, though still affirming: "nevertheless, not my will but Thine be done".

So here then are some dreams laid at the cross but which I am busy trying to transform into prayers. I'll call them prayer-dreams, things I am praying for but which I either may not see or which the Lord may not grant.

Prayer-dreams for Us as a People

My first prayer-dream is that we in AE and all believers will always be first and foremost a "Jesus People". That people in this ministry will always make loving, pleasing and obeying Jesus our first and last preoccupation. All the universe, all history, all life and all afterlife is about Jesus and focused on Jesus.

Says Giles Fletcher, a poet of yesteryear,

> He is a path, if any be misled;
> He is robe, if any naked be;
> If any chance to hunger, He is bread;
> If any be a bondman, He is free;
> If any be but weak, how strong is He!
> To dead men, life is He; to sick men, health;
> To blind men, sight;
> And to the needy, wealth;
> A pleasure without loss,
> A Treasure without stealth.

In Ireland they often pray a prayer of their Patron Saint, St Patrick: "Christ be with me, Christ within me, Christ behind me, Christ before me, Christ beside me, Christ to win me, Christ to comfort and restore me, Christ beneath me, Christ above me, Christ in quiet, Christ in danger, Christ in hearts of them that love me, Christ in mouth of friend and stranger."

Yes, Jesus is to be all in all, because as St Paul writes: "For from Him, and through Him, and to Him are all things. And to Him be glory forever, Amen" (Romans 11:36). He is at the heart of history's origins, process and consummation.

Then my next prayer-dream is that we and all believers will be ever more fully Holy Spirit people.

In the late 1970s we moved strongly into embracing Renewal in order to discover afresh the person, work, fruit and gifts of the Holy Spirit. We were seeking deeply to be led by him in our daily walk and ministry. I even wrote a little book about this called *Bursting the Wineskins*. If any book I have written has had any significance or importance, then perhaps this is the one, seeking, as it does, to bridge the evangelical, pentecostal and charismatic communities and draw into synthesis the rich legacies of experience and teaching about the Holy Spirit from each sector. In some ways, I feel I personally have slipped somewhat from that quest, those commitments and that experience. Maybe it is time for all of us in this ministry and for the wider church once again to re-explore and refocus into the Person and work of the Holy Spirit. The fact is that it is only through the Holy Spirit that we can know "the presence of the Lord" whether in minimal, modest or mighty dimensions. Says the pentecostal theologian Gordon Fee, "Nothing else can take the place of the Presence." Moses knew this and said: "If Thy Presence go not with me, carry us not up hence" (Exodus 33:15). Isaiah also could write: "It was no angel or messenger but His Presence which saved them" (Isaiah 63:9).

And so I pray, "Lord, make us evermore a Holy Spirit people because, not only is it 'not by might or by power, but by my Spirit says the Lord' (Zechariah 4:6), but also, and may all evangelists especially hear this, 'No one can say Jesus is Lord except by the Holy Spirit' (1 Corinthians 12:3)."

The fact is that without the Holy Spirit, any person, church or ministry is literally dead in the water.

Related to being a Jesus and a Holy Spirit people is the need for us and all in the church to be a worshipful people.

Over and above all in Christian life and ministry is the primacy of worship. It stands before evangelism, discipling, compassionate acts of kindness or sociopolitical concern. Worship is first. Says the Bible simply and succinctly: "Worship the Lord in the beauty of Holiness" (1 Chronicles 16:29). Said Jesus clearly and plainly when Satan sought to tempt him: "Get thee behind me Satan, for thou shalt *worship* the Lord thy God, and Him only shalt thou serve."

For myself worship took on new meaning, dimensions and delight after my renewal experience in the Spirit at Milner Park in 1977. And I think into AE something fresh came at that time as well. Certainly multiple special moments of spiritual delight came for all of us over the years as we were led in worship in AE devotions by that special and lovely lady Lois Stephenson, along with the tender depth of Songe Chibambo. However, my prayer-dream is that AE will deepen in worship and grow into that vision and definition of worship brought once by Archbishop William Temple in his book *The Hope of a New World*: "To worship is to quicken the conscience by the holiness of God, to feed the mind with the truth of God, to purge the imagination by the beauty of God, to open the heart to the love of God, to devote the will to the purpose of God. All this is gathered up in that emotion which cleanses us from selfishness because it is the most selfless of all emotions – adoration."

Now there's something to aim for.

My next prayer-dream for us as a people, and that we should preach this far and wide in the church, is for deepened *koinonia* and fellowship.

Thankfully we have in the ministry had much incredible fellowship over the years. But I believe it needs to deepen. This means we need more trust, more communication, more unity of purpose, more cross-cultural understanding, and the full elimination of any racial feelings, whether from white to black or black to white. Indeed, I would pray and long to see a time when neither race, nor colour or culture, nor different backgrounds will mean anything whatsoever in this work.

Napoleon once said: "It is my privilege to lead a band of brothers and a group of friends." Along with the sisters also that's how it must ever seek to be.

Another prayer-dream is that we will also ever remain a People of the Word, and urge this on one and all.

The Reformers said that their authority was "sola scriptura" (scripture alone). John Wesley was described as "homo unius libri" (a man of one book). For him, as for us, there were and are other books to be read. But they should all pale into insignificance when compared with this one incomparable book – God's Word in the Bible.

During World War II the German prophetic figure Dietrich Bonhoeffer wrote: "It is not our judgement of the situation which can show us what is wise, but only the truth of the Word of God. Here alone lies the promise of God's faithfulness and help. It will always be true that the wisest course for the disciple is always to abide solely by the Word of God in all simplicity."

That says it all.

My next prayer-dream is that we will always be a growing people.

No ministry can grow satisfactorily unless its people are growing in the Lord.

First, there has to be spiritual growth. One colleague who had left AE a number of years previously came to visit us again and remarked to me on how easy it was in a way to spot "those who have grown spiritually in the last few years and those who have not".

In reality it is very easy, but very perilous, to stand still. This is why I have always loved Livingstone's affirmation, and it's one I often inscribe in gift books for people, when he said: "Anywhere – provided it be forward."

St Paul for his part could resolve: "I press on towards the goal for the prize of the upward call of God in Christ Jesus" (Philippians 3:14).

We also have to grow emotionally and psychologically. I guess we all still have aspects of the child in us. I remember once being profoundly challenged and also saddened when Argentinean Juan Carlos Ortiz, whom we had brought to South Africa, felt it necessary to bring a challenge to South African Christians entitled: "Beware the Eternal Babyhood of the Believer."

To live in spiritual or psychological babyhood or mere adolescence is not enough for those who are in the arduous pressures of a fulltime evangelistic ministry. No wonder the Apostle Paul, in his concern for the Ephesians could say: "We are to *grow up* in every way into Him who is the Head, into Christ" (Ephesians 4:15).

Then we have to grow intellectually and theologically. In these very demanding times preachers and teachers will not relate the gospel meaningfully or reflectively to either outsiders or insiders unless they are constantly seeking to grow intellectually and in theological understanding. In AE and in the church as a whole we all have to work on this.

Then we have to grow in diligence and industry. I would never want Christian workers to be neurotic or compulsive about hard work, and in my life I have probably been a bit too compulsive and hard-working, but I have to say that laziness, slackness or shoddiness in the Lord's work is unforgivable. People who cruise and are basically passengers cannot be afforded in ministries of this nature. I got a letter once from the manager of a Christian publishing house in the UK and he said: "I am surrounded by a team of professionals with a 'can-do' approach."

Now there's a target to aim for. And without wanting to over-commend or over-imitate the past, nevertheless one biographer's word on John Wesley at age 85 is not uninstructive: "That year he preached in almost every county in England and Wales. The next year he admitted he 'could not easily preach more than twice a day' and had been annoyed, a little earlier, to find that he could no longer write for more than 15 hours in the day without hurting his eyes!"

So one prayer-dream from me for AE and for all in Christian ministry is that, while always leaving appropriate time for rest, recreation, family life, holidays and Sabbaths, never would any become strangers to hard work. I know of no one who has succeeded in Christian ministry without being deeply industrious.

Then we all need to grow in Joy. I believe all believers should always be growing in joy. Thus could Jesus pray in John 17:13 "that they may have my joy fulfilled in themselves". In John 15:11 he said he had spoken certain things to his disciples "that My joy may be in you, and that your joy may be full".

I don't believe that AE has lacked joy, but it is something into which we and all the Lord's people need to deepen because it relates to biblical obedience, faithfulness and being at the centre of his will. Just check Jesus' example in Hebrews 12:2. Indeed joy relates to his presence because he is the one "in whose presence is fullness of joy" (Psalm 16:11).

Every ministry has rough patches; we have certainly had many of our own along the way, and they can produce deep sadness, grief, brokenness, remorse and regret. But one always has to come back to the Lord as the one who restores our fortunes and our joy. How wonderful therefore that after the Exile the Lord's people could testify that "when the Lord restored the fortunes of Zion, we were like those who dream. Then our mouth was filled with laughter and our tongue with shouts of joy" (Psalm 126:1).

Comments Eugene Peterson in his book *The Journey* (page 82):

Joy is the authentic Christian note, a sign of those who are on the way of salvation. Joy is characteristic of Christian pilgrimage. It is the second in Paul's list of the fruits of the Spirit (Galatians 5:22).

It is the first of Jesus' signs in the gospel of John when he turns water into wine... Joy is not a requirement of Christian discipleship, it is a consequence. It is not what we have to aquire in order to experience life in Christ; it is what comes to us when we are walking in the way of faith and obedience.

Once many years ago when I was visiting Abraham Vereide and Doug Coe in the so-called "Fellowship" in Washington DC, they said their aim was to manifest "a living, loving, laughing Christianity".

Now that's worth emulating, wouldn't you say?

Now a few prayer-dreams for ministry effectiveness.

Not just a work but one day a movement. One special prayer-dream is that AE might not be just a work but become a movement. There are great historical and instructive precedents. For example, take the difference between the ministries of George Whitefield and John Wesley. Whitefield preached mightily and multiplied thousands came to Christ. But Wesley trained and grounded people in Christ and his endeavours became not just a work but a movement which continues to this day. In a biography by Garth Lean provocatively entitled (for Methodists at least!) *John Wesley Anglican*, the author writes:

> It was John's concern for individuals which made him found societies wherever he went. "Preaching like an apostle, without joining together those that are awakened, and training them in the way of God, is only begetting children for the murderer... How much preaching has there been for these 20 years, for example, in Pembrokeshire! But no regular societies, no discipline, order or connection; and the consequence is that nine out of ten of the once awakened are now faster asleep than ever."

Lean now makes his own comparison between Wesley and Whitefield regarding what happened in America.

> There, tens of thousands of people had been converted by Whitefield's preaching. But Whitefield felt he had not the aptitude for founding and nurturing societies, so most of them faded away. Whitefield himself once described it as "weaving a rope of sand". Wesley on the other hand, grasped what was involved in winning, confirming and setting men and women to work so that

the nation could be "reformed" and he faced the labour of doing the work necessary (*John Wesley Anglican*, page 56).

This kind of historical precedent sets several challenges for AE in the future. The first is to ensure, in spite of all our previous and current strong endeavours, that our follow-up and discipling after missions is more thorough, more intense, more sustained and more effective. This is something at which we can never work too hard. Secondly it requires that the work give itself more fully to training and developing leaders of depth who can truly and effectively lead others also. It's coming back in a sense to Paul's model described in his epistle to Timothy when he says: "What you have heard from me before many witnesses entrust to faithful people who will be able to teach others also" (2 Timothy 2:2). While the first generation AE has indeed sought and often achieved this with reasonable effectiveness, nevertheless I believe that training and discipling have to be much more diligently prosecuted in the second-generation ministry.

New Ministry Excellence

My next prayer-dream for AE missions relates to our pressing on ever more vigorously into the arenas of true excellence in prayer preparation, set-up, execution and follow-up. These efforts need to be not just good but superior. Otherwise we risk being sidelined by the Lord. Dedicated mediocrity of either personnel or product will never suffice for the deep demands of this new century.

Then I have a prayer-dream for us financially. One of the little things I have said to the Lord *à propros* arriving in heaven one day is that I hope he will give me in my heavenly life a corner of the universe where finances are not a constant anxiety and preoccupation! Maybe for us rather faithless ones on Earth this cannot be avoided or evaded. However, if I must be honest, I believe that our struggle in the financial area has been too intense and preoccupying in this first generation. How great it would be if God would give us greater financial blessings and seasons of abundance in this regard so that we could move more consistently into the task of evangelising and discipling itself without endless attention to the struggles of making ends meet. I hope this utterance is not too heretical. If so, the Lord must forgive me!

In our first generation the Lord raised up an astonishing array of donors and prayer partners. My prayer is that he will multiply that number beyond what we can ask or think so that we always have what is required to do the job and focus on it.

Personal Prayer-dreams

The first is that I *should not let the Lord down*, or my family, or my friends, or work colleagues or our ministry supporters, or the kingdom generally in this home-straight of life. One does not want to trip and fall at some of the final hurdles.

So I pray then, as Ted Engstrom has taught me to pray, that "I might finish better than I started". And I covet this for all my senior colleagues who have laboured in this work throughout this first generation whether in teams or on boards. And for all who follow them.

This requires also that I pray that I and my other long-standing colleagues in both teams and boards would have *the spirit and gift of perseverance*. Eugene Peterson in his previously quoted book *The Journey* says this: "The essential thing in heaven and earth is that there should be a long obedience in the same direction. There thereby results, as has always resulted in the long run, something which has made life worth living."

Commenting on Jeremiah's perseverance, Petersen writes: "The mark of a certain kind of genius is the ability and energy to keep returning to the same task relentlessly, imaginatively, curiously, for a lifetime. Never give up and go on to something else; never get distracted and be diverted to something else." Petersen's exhortation is, to be sure, one worth seeking to heed.

John Stott in his landmark book *Issues Facing Christians Today* has a final and splendid chapter on Christian leadership. There he writes: "Perseverance is certainly an indispensable quality of leadership. It is one thing to dream dreams and see visions. It is another to convert a dream into a plan of action. It is yet a third to persevere with it when opposition comes. For opposition is bound to arise." So, for the future leadership of this ministry, I would pray again in the words of Stott that they would have "the resilience to take setbacks in (their) stride, the tenacity to overcome fatigue and discouragement and the wisdom (in a favourite phrase of John R. Mott's) to 'turn stumbling blocks into stepping stones'. For the real leader adds to vision and industry the grace of perseverance."

My prayer is that this would always be in the ministry and in all the Lord's people everywhere in the years to come.

An Overwhelming and Supreme Privilege

Finally I want to say that it has been an overwhelming and supreme privilege in life, and it will always continue to be until my dying breath, to be in the work of evangelism. Somebody once said: "If God has called you to preach, do not stoop to be a king."

For me, I feel that no calling could have been higher, more demanding or more worthwhile, because with every moment of working it out one is not simply affecting time but more especially eternity.

Thus in closing I would want to identify myself with the words of that great doyen of Anglican evangelists, Canon Brian Green, when he wrote near the end of his life in his classic *The Practice of Evangelism* (page 221):

> Finally, however much, on looking back, one wishes that this or that had not been done or said, there is one thing I would never have altered; it is that on a day many years ago the compulsion of Christ came to my heart and mind and I knew that I must share the Christ that I had discovered for myself as Saviour and Lord. In that sharing, most fearfully and self-consciously begun, I started to discover what evangelism meant, and that discovery has been the greatest I have ever made. I would not have done anything else with my life than to seek with every power that I possess to share the gospel of Christ with all who will listen.

Index

Addresses Worldwide

Field Offices

African Enterprise
PO Box 24974
Nairobi
KENYA

African Enterprise
PO Box 30768
Kampala
UGANDA

African Enterprise
PO Box 10055
Dar es Salaam
TANZANIA

African Enterprise
BP 1435
Kigali
RWANDA

African Enterprise
Box 13140
Cascades 3202
SOUTH AFRICA

African Enterprise
PO Box 4300
Harare
ZIMBABWE

African Enterprise
PO Box 30332
Capital City
Lilongwe
MALAWI

African Enterprise
PO Box 8720
Accra North
GHANA

African Enterprise
BP 4502
Kinshasa 2
CONGO

African Enterprise
PO Box 70271
Addis Ababa
ETHIOPIA

Support Offices

African Enterprise
4509 11th Avenue
Vancouver BC
V6R 2M5
CANADA

African Enterprise
PO Box 727
Monrovia
CA 91016
USA

African Enterprise
PO Box 155
St Leonards
NSW 1590
AUSTRALIA

African Enterprise
Victoria House
Victoria Road
BUCKHURST HILL
Essex IG9 5EX
UK

African Enterprise
BP 1
1081 Brussels 8
BELGIUM